A Faustian Foreign Policy from Woodrow Wilson to George W. Bush

A Faustian Foreign Policy from Woodrow Wilson to George W. Bush: Dreams of Perfectibility critiques U.S. foreign policy during this period by showing how moralistic diplomacy has increasingly assumed Faustian overtones, especially during the Cold War and following September 11. The ideological components of American diplomacy, originating in the late eighteenth and nineteenth centuries, evolved through the twentieth century as U.S. economic and political power steadily increased. Seeing myth making as essential in any country's founding and a common determinant of its foreign policy, Professor Joan Hoff reveals how the basic belief in its exceptionalism has driven America's past and present attempts to remake the world in its own image. She expands her original concept of "independent internationalism" as the modus operandi of U.S. diplomacy to reveal the many unethical Faustian deals the United States has entered into since 1920 to obtain its current global supremacy.

Joan Hoff is the former CEO and President of the Center for the Study of the Presidency in New York City, former Executive Secretary of the Organization of American Historians, and former Professor of History and Director of the Contemporary History Institute at Ohio University. She is now Research Professor of History at Montana State University, Bozeman.

D0042570

A Faustian Foreign Policy from Woodrow Wilson to George W. Bush

Dreams of Perfectibility

JOAN HOFF
Montana State University

CAMBRIDGE
UNIVERSITY PRESS

CAMBRIDGE UNIVERSITY PRESS
Cambridge, New York, Melbourne, Madrid, Cape Town, Singapore, São Paulo, Delhi

Cambridge University Press
32 Avenue of the Americas, New York, NY 10013-2473, USA

www.cambridge.org
Information on this title: www.cambridge.org/9780521879057

© Joan Hoff 2008

This publication is in copyright. Subject to statutory exception
and to the provisions of relevant collective licensing agreements,
no reproduction of any part may take place without
the written permission of Cambridge University Press.

First published 2008

Printed in the United States of America

A catalog record for this publication is available from the British Library.

Library of Congress Cataloging in Publication Data

Hoff, Joan, 1939–
A Faustian foreign policy from Woodrow Wilson to George W. Bush : Dreams of
perfectibility / Joan Hoff.
    p.   cm.
Includes bibliographical references and index.
ISBN-13: 978-0-521-87905-7 (hardback)
1. United States – Foreign relations – 20th century.   2. United States – Foreign relations –
2001–   3. United States – Foreign relations – Philosophy.   I. Title.
E744.H6   2008
327.73009′04 – dc22   2007014566

ISBN   978-0-521-87905-7 hardback
ISBN   978-0-521-71404-4 paperback

Cambridge University Press has no responsibility for
the persistence or accuracy of URLs for external or
third-party Internet Web sites referred to in this publication
and does not guarantee that any content on such
Web sites is, or will remain, accurate or appropriate.

Contents

A Faustian Foreign Policy from Woodrow Wilson to
George W. Bush

Introduction

Toward a Faustian Diplomacy

> Forgetfulness and ... even historical falsehoods are an essential factor in the formation of a nation, and so it is that the progress of historical studies is often a danger for the spirit of nationality.
>
> Ernest Renan, *Qu'est-ce qu'une nation?* (1882)

Unkowningly, American colonists took the first step on the path to a Faustian foreign policy the moment they set out on their "errand into the wilderness" in the New World. Despite their constant jeremiads about sinfulness and "incessant and never successful cry for repentance, the Puritans launched themselves upon the process of Americanization." Even though the Puritans initially expressed doubts about territorial expansion because of their fears of encountering the "profane," later explorers, immigrants, homesteaders, and fur traders carried this Americanization process across the continent with largely the same unshakable and shared belief that their endeavor was blessed by God. In effect, they turned the jeremiad "doctrine of [God's] vengeance into a promise of ultimate success, affirming the world, and despite the world, the inviolability of the colonial cause." Americans came to believe that they would achieve their errand – and ultimately their dream of Manifest Destiny – because they represented a sanguine force for good.[1]

The United States is not alone in developing and nurturing the notion that it is a force for good; all nation-states have their self-serving creation myths. Nations (and sometimes even regions within nations) contrive narratives surrounding the conditions of their foundation. In times of extreme crisis, these original myths are elaborated upon or amended to suit new conditions and, occasionally, new origin accounts are generated. It does not matter whether national myths are positive or negative or represent more faith than fact; they are absolutely essential for the body politic in any country to function collectively. When defeats assume more mythological importance for nations than their victories, they often give rise to fantasies about revenge and restoration of past glory.[2]

Elaboration on and reinvention of these national public myths, sometimes called national cultural identity, also occur after countries have reached the height of their powers and hold sway over other nations. Regardless of the reason for the creation of national myths, whether the impetus derives from negative or positive events or from weakness or strength, national origins stories obscure reality. The clouds of myth are especially useful when it comes to justifying foreign policy. Walter L. Hixson has argued that America's national myth ultimately "create[d] a structure of consent that enable[d] the hegemony of a militant and undemocratic foreign policy in an ostensibly democratic society." Thus, "'taming the frontier,' advancing 'civilization,' or leading the 'Free World' all are inextricably linked to foreign policy goals of the United States." The national creation myth was "crucial in fostering consensus or hegemony; it is a mythical discourse that masquerades as truth to justify imperial conduct as well as the ordering of domestic hierarchies."[3]

Once the United States emerged from the First World War powerful enough to begin asserting its foreign policy worldwide instead of just in the Western Hemisphere, there was little, except rhetoric, left of the Puritan harangues against sin or desire for repentance or doubts about unfulfilled "errands into the wilderness." Instead, the country began to cut "deals with the devil" in order to maintain an expanding list of global goals. Like Jonathan Wolfgang von Goethe's Faust, who gloried in the youth, unlimited knowledge, and fortune temporarily bestowed upon him by Mephistopheles, the United States gloried in its rapid rise in prosperity and power during the American Century. Just as Faust ignored the sordidness and violence of his liaison with Margarete, American presidents from Woodrow Wilson to George W. Bush failed to acknowledge the often-dirty diplomatic deals they made because to do so would undermine their own and the country's belief in American virtue and exceptionalism.

The comparison to Faust is especially apt in terms of the U.S. foreign policy after the end of the Cold War. Faust, at the zenith of his happiness and potency, broke his pact with the devil by wishing that things would never change. Carrying the metaphor forward, it could be argued that the United States, at the height of its power upon winning the Cold War, made a similar mistake by trying to stop time and impose its hegemony indefinitely on the rest of world. Philosophically, one could retreat to Oswald Spengler's much-maligned theory about the decline of the West and see the United States as the ultimate example of his "Faustian civilization" where the populace constantly strives for the unattainable and goes into protracted, inevitable, and tragic decline, knowing that its goals cannot be achieved but refusing to settle for less. In either metaphor, Faust's relationship to Mephistopheles is emblematic of the ways the United States has conducted its foreign policy from 1920 through 2007.

American Exceptionalism

From its inception religious and political leaders have nourished and perpetuated a mythical view of America as an exceptional nation with God always on its side. John Winthrop preached that the crucial purpose of the Puritan venture into the New World in 1630 was to establish a "city set on the hill" with the "eies of all people uppon us." In a variety of religious and secularized versions this Puritan vision of America as "uniquely pleasing to God" and as "the new Jerusalem" or "the New Israel" became one of the enduring features of U.S. foreign policy down to the present. Perpetuation of this mythical view has been enormously successful: a Pew Center poll taken in 2003 indicated that 71 percent of evangelical Christians believed that the United States had "special protection of God"; 40 percent of mainline Christians did, and 39 percent of all Catholics did. Given the fact that a little over three-quarters of Americans are Christian and only 10 percent of the remainder consider themselves neither religious nor spiritual, it is difficult to overestimate how deeply this God-endowed exceptionalism permeates contemporary society. This permeation makes it next to impossible for average citizens to recognize limits to national power by viewing the "American way of life [as] no more than one variation among many to which humanity adheres."[4]

Cultural and literary scholars have elaborated on this foundation of American exceptionalism and its secularization. They point out that the use of morality, pseudo-religious concepts, and linguistic gymnastics has consistently been present and behind the "divinely sanctioned national greatness" at the heart of American cultural identity as a nation. From the early colonial period, the Puritans (and their southern counterparts) began to impose "civilization" on "savages" and on the environment in order to create a New World that they believed was foreordained by God. This constituted a "cultural approach to understanding national identity" that Sacvan Bercovitch called the "myth of America," meaning the pursuit of an unattainable "errand into the wilderness... through the technique of the Biblical jeremiad, a ritualized denunciation of sin with an attendant call for redemption." This American myth is rooted in Puritan Massachusetts and its convictions about "inherent virtue, providential destiny, and mission." According to Bercovitch, "the ritual of the jeremiad" provided "a frame for understanding the emergence of a [capitalist middle-class] hegemonic national identity... [which] 'bespeaks an ideological consensus... unmatched in any other modern culture' [and is] unsurpassed by any other modern nation."[5] While the mythical foundation of American national cultural identity is not unprecedented in the history of the world, it is the dominant one at the moment.

The New World's physical isolation from other continents augmented this myth of moral and geographic exceptionalism and ultimately led to the idea that the United States had sovereignty over the entire Western Hemisphere and could always protect itself from the rest of world if it had to. President Woodrow Wilson would later refer to the sanctity and physical separation and superiority of the United States as its "self-possession," meaning he believed that whatever America touched – that is embraced, whether it be justice, democracy, or self-government – it "made holy" because it operated out of a sense of disinterest and universal service to the world. Such beneficent selflessness arose from the fact that the United States, according to Wilson, had no "reason to fear that from any quarter our independence or the integrity of our territory" could be threatened and because as a Christian nation the country "exemplif[ied] that devotion to the elements of righteousness . . . derived from the revelations of Holy Scripture."[6]

This exceptionalist belief in the county's "rightness" and military capability led to the corollary that it should at the same time protect itself from the evils of the world whenever American principles were perceived to be rejected or ignored or under attack. While September 11 temporarily shattered "the ethos of American invulnerability," as not even Pearl Harbor or the Cuban missile crisis had, it quickly became unpatriotic to question the myth about the exceptional ability of the United States to protect itself. Exceptionalism is also at the core of the singular American belief in its foreordained prosperity and at the core of the victim mentality and loss of innocence expressed by its politicians and pundits every time America experiences a major domestic or foreign policy setback or disaster.[7]

Without too much exaggeration one could say that upon entering the new millennium the United States was at the height of its myth-affirming powers. Unfortunately, instead of triggering new domestic perspectives and a reassessment of its Cold War foreign policies, the tragic events of September 11 simply reinforced the country's view of its moral and physical uniqueness among nations as it tried to compensate for its most severe encounter with vulnerability.

What is often forgotten about this conflation of exceptionalism, invulnerability, endless prosperity, and periodic loss of innocence is that, to preserve these myths, presidents beginning with Wilson have revealed themselves willing to enter into "pacts with the devil" in foreign policy matters. As subsequent chapters will illustrate, Wilson entered into a series of mini-Faustian bargains both before and after World War I, as have most presidents since, particularly in time of war. The cumulative effect of these greater and lesser "deals with the devil" to impose American values and win foreign policy conflicts at any cost reached such an apex during the Cold War that even critics of U.S. diplomacy did not think the Cold War Faustian bargains could be surpassed following the fall of Communism. Yet they were confounded and often silenced by government propaganda in the wake of September 11 as the United States embraced any unsavory government that promised to fight terrorism.

Consequently, since the end of the Cold War there has been little public reevaluation of how the United States obtained the unprecedented position of power in the world that it now occupies. This means that even after the terrorist attacks, most Americans continue to perceive themselves as blessed and deserving, never questioning the domestic or foreign price of the victory in the Cold War. There is little recognition that hubris about the country's ability to maintain its current unrivaled position in the world may not be the best basis on which the United States should continue to conduct itself. Thus, although September 11 exposed U.S. vulnerability, most of the country's leaders still cling to certain Cold War foreign policies that are no longer germane in an age of random terrorism, including the idea that the United States is always an innocent victim on the world stage.

The need to reassess past and present assumptions about U.S. foreign policy is the underlying theme of this book. This need arises from the way in which the original creation myth of exceptionalism fostered several foreign policy concepts such as self-determination. Beginning with Wilson during the First World War, self-determination came to be associated with the ahistorical notion that democracy and capitalism are inextricably intertwined and can be imposed on all parts of the world. Another questionable aspect of U.S. foreign policy is the conviction that the unfettered pursuit of free trade is a prerequisite for world peace. Still another is the idea that the United States can create a lasting New World Order in which it is the sole, unchallenged hegemonic force. Finally, there is the refusal of most Americans and their leaders to admit that by the end of the twentieth century their country had, for reasons other than jealousy, become an unloved empire in many parts of the world.[8] Unless the United States critically reexamines all these foreign policy assumptions, it will not be able to formulate a new diplomacy for promoting a more peaceful and humanitarian twenty-first century.

The Problems with Democracy and Capitalism

The end of the Cold War gave the United States the opportunity not only to take stock of its domestic political and economic problems, but also to shoulder responsibility and rethink the coercive aspects of its successes abroad as well as some of the less-than-savory and unsuccessful endeavors in the last fifty years of American foreign policy – not the least of which is the fact that "war seldom creates democracy." According to a 2003 Carnegie Endowment survey in *The Christian Science Monitor*, "of the eighteen regime changes forced by the United States in the 20th century, only 5 resulted in democracy, and in the case of wars fought unilaterally, the number goes down to one – Panama." Yet throughout the Cold War groups on both the left and the right argued that democracy could or should be imposed from above. Theoretically at least, the original meaning of democracy was "the rule of everyone by everyone." It rises from below, not from the top, and is, therefore, conditioned more by cultural and economic conditions than by military might. So it should not have come as any surprise that at the end of the twentieth century one could read many variations on the following theme: "[D]emocracy does not result from either military intervention and regime change or from the various current models of 'transition to democracy,' which are generally based on some form of Latin American *caudillismo* and have proved better at creating new oligarchies than a democratic system."[9]

Specifically, a 2004 UN report indicated that a majority of Latin Americans in eighteen nations would support the return of authoritarian governments, rather than the current democratic ones, because the latter had not resulted in enough economic benefits, social equality, effective legal systems, or social services. If this trend continues, it could mean that economic progress might become more important than the support of democracy. The Mexican ambassador to the United States pessimistically concluded in 2004: "This shows that democracy is not something that has taken hold of peoples' minds as strongly as we had thought it would." His statement reflected the economic harm that Mexico had suffered after Congress passed the North American Free Trade Agreement (NAFTA) in 1993. Despite exaggerated claims by the Clinton administration, NAFTA failed to produce jobs in either the United States or Mexico. Moreover, it contributed to speculative foreign investment and the subsequent peso deval-uation crisis in Mexico. The contestable results of NAFTA logically delayed the approval of the Central American Free Trade Agreement (CAFTA) until 2006 because it is based on the same "Washington Consensus" economic principles, also known as neo-liberal economics, liberal capitalist internationalism, or by the more modern term "economism." By the 1990s, these terms, when applied globally, referred to privatization of state-owned businesses, free trade, open-ness to foreign investments, balanced budgets (based on cutting social welfare programs), and deregulation (which had the backing of Wall Street and conser-vative think tanks, as well as the centrist wing of the Democratic Party). But instead of "lead[ing] to economic takeoff," the "Washington Consensus" has often produced sluggish growth, increased economic inequality, and a series of economic crises.[10]

Attempts by the United States to force its economic views on other areas of the world have also been problematic. Even the advent in the 1980s, of mod-ern global capitalism, based on free trade, open markets, unregulated interna-tional investments, and dramatic improvements in communication technology, has "yet to produce anything like universal prosperity." (Globalism is simply a hyper version of the "Washington Consensus," or neo-liberal economics.) Because capitalism is the product of Western values, some societies are simply less culturally adaptable to its development. Major reasons why capitalism has largely failed outside of the West are the absence of property rights, the existence of underground, nontaxable economies, and corrupt or collapsing legal and political institutions in most poor countries – all of which provide a breeding ground for terrorism. There also is evidence that unregulated global capitalism actually hinders the development of democracy because it fosters anarchical economic forces that undermine national cultural and political institutions that might otherwise foster democratic governments.[11]

Historically, moreover, there is no more connection between democracy and free-market capitalism than there is between social justice and the bottom line. "Neither history nor philosophy link free markets and free men," according to John Ralston Saul. "They have nothing more to do with each than the acci-dents of time and place." One need only look at both England and the United States in the different centuries when these countries industrialized to realize that it happened before universal suffrage, child labor laws, and health regula-tions existed. Likewise, capitalism thrived in the undemocratic times of Louis Philippe, again under Emperor Napoleon III, and under Kaiser Wilhelm II and

Nicholas II. In the last fifty years, "market economies have shown a remarkable adaptability and have flourished in many tyrannical states from Chile to South Korea, from Panama to Singapore.... On the level of the individual, capitalism seeks consumers susceptible to the shaping of their needs and the manipulation of their wants while democracy needs citizens autonomous in their thoughts and independent in their deliberative judgments.... but capitalism wishes to tame anarchic democracy and appears to have little problem tolerating tyranny as long as it secures stability."[12]

Honest recognition of these jarring hypotheses about democracy, war, and capitalism should have produced a self-critical, rather than triumphal, exceptionalist, or defensive mind-set at the end of the Cold War. Yet such a reevaluation has not taken place, in part because U.S. diplomacy for most of the twentieth century has been characterized by a mercurial assortment of unilateral and collective actions that I first described in the 1970s as the practice of "independent internationalism" and that now can perhaps more accurately be described as "unilateral internationalism."

Independent or Unilateral Internationalism

Both terms refer, not to the ideology that had imbued U.S. diplomacy by 1900, but to the modus operandi characterizing the country's foreign affairs. Most simply, it means that when the United States cannot, or does not, want to solve a particular diplomatic problem through unilateral action, it seeks cooperative methods for pursuing its goals. The country's first inclination for most of the last century was to act unilaterally whenever possible and to cooperate with other nations only when absolutely necessary. A presidential commission first noticed this trend in 1933, reporting to the outgoing and discredited Depression president, Herbert Hoover, that the postwar diplomacy of the United States in the 1920s had alternated

> between isolation and independence, between sharply marked economic nationalism and notable international initiatives in cooperation moving in a highly unstable zigzag course.... Some signs point in the direction of independence and imperialism of a new Roman type, reaching aggressively for more land or wider markets under political auspices; others toward amiable cooperation in the most highly developed forms of world order. It is not unreasonable to anticipate that these opposing trends will continue to alternate sharply in their control over American policy. In any case there can be little doubt that the trend will be in the future as in recent years in the direction of more intimate relations through developing modes of intercommunication and through economic interchange and on the whole toward an increasing number of international contacts; and this, whether the future pattern of action [by the United States] is predominantly imperialistic or cooperative in form and spirit.[13]

This summary of American foreign policy in the 1920s fairly well describes the diplomacy of the United States for the next seventy years. The only thing this commission report logically could not have anticipated in the early 1930s was the impact the practice of independent or unilateral internationalism would have on the powers of the modern presidency. The premier modern president, Franklin Delano Roosevelt, set in motion increased executive powers – first over domestic policy and later over foreign policy. The Cold War greatly enhanced these "semi-constitutional" powers of successive presidents. They are still in place and remain unquestioned even though that bipolar conflict is over. The evolutionary relationship between the power of the United States and the power of the president is another of the themes of this book – from the premodern, mercurial presidency, to the modern, imperial presidency, to the postmodern, imponderable presidency.

The United States began to follow this "highly unstable [and] zigzag course" of independent internationalism in the 1920s and 1930s, again after the Second World War, and still again in the post–Cold War era. All modern and post-modern presidents have engaged in independent or unilateral internationalistic behavior. American exceptionalism encouraged their conduct as they also believed in the country's invulnerability because of its continental isolation, its abundant natural resources, its ability to protect itself, regardless of world events, and its stable, balance-of-power political system.

Most significantly, the practice of independent internationalism since 1920 has perverted in practice any sustained commitment to collective diplomacy on the part of the United States – except, temporarily, in times of crises. Because the 1990s was not perceived as a crisis decade,[14] the United States did not develop any consistent cooperative foreign policy for the post–Cold War era. It remains to be seen whether it will in the first decade of the twenty-first century. So far, it has not, even though the war on terrorism has thrown U.S. diplomacy back into crisis mode.

Using this definition of independent or unilateral internationalism as an analytical tool also helps to explain the exaggerated moralistic fervor with which the United States has pursued its foreign policy since the American Revolution – particularly after winning both world wars, at the end of Cold War, and now, again, since September 11 – because it exposes the exceptionalism that prevails whether the United States is acting cooperatively or unilaterally. Arrogant sanctimoniousness is natural following any unexpected military and economic victory such as the United States enjoyed with the collapse of the Soviet Union. Unlike the First and Second World Wars, the Cold War wrapped up with a whimper. Europe and Asia were physically undamaged. The two previous global conflicts had been fought with real bullets, real bombs, real deaths, and real devastation of entire countries in real time. In each case the United States had emerged stronger than ever – uninjured except for wartime casualties. At the end of the Cold War, by contrast, Europe (and most of Asia) were actually better off than ever before, and so was the United States, except that it faced regional trade and technological competition for the first time. What was there for American leaders to think about? Victors, untouched by crises of confidence or identity, usually view history as their intellectual property, especially when there are no discernible enemies of any size or danger left.

As long as the ideological outcome of the Cold War remained in doubt, there was little reason for American presidents or government decision makers to question the Faustian results of independent internationalism. Once the United States emerged victorious from that conflict, it should have been possible for American foreign affairs experts and scholars to reassess established strategies for controlling Hobbesian nation-state conflict between (and sometimes inside) countries and to devise a less erratic and arbitrary way of implementing them in the best interests of the world. In order to do so realistically, however, a critical mass of such diplomatic authorities inside and outside government would have had to admit past American diplomatic mistakes and Faustian deals. They would also have had to factor in the "irreversible effects" of economic globalization based on modern technology, and to look hard at the impact of the information revolution, not only on conventional capitalism, but also on the traditional nation-state system and, perhaps equally important, on classical Western civilization.[15]

Something less obvious than smug triumphalism has also contributed to the lazy intellectual vacuum or lack of imagination demonstrated by American post–Cold War diplomacy during the 1990s and by the country's open embrace of the seductive age-old idea of hegemonic dominance after September 11. This something has so benumbed U.S. foreign policy experts that they have retreated to, and seem only capable of perfecting, actions that prevailed during the height of the Cold War with a hubris typical of conquerors. Why hasn't there been more creative, cooperative conceptual thinking now that the United States is the preeminent power on the globe? The answer lies in the way the United States fought and ultimately won the Cold War, and it can be found symbolically in the use of the term "Wilsonian" before September 11, to mean anything and everything from unilateralism to international cooperation.

"Good" and "Bad" Wilsonianism

After September 11 the idea that "virtually every American concerned with international issues is, or at least claims to be, a Wilsonian" has become increasingly problematic. In contrast to the post–Cold War Wilsonians of the 1990s, who, according to Ronald Steel, "favor[ed] open market economies, self-determination for restive ethnic or nationality groups, collective security, and democratic governments," twenty-first-century Republican neo-conservatives have misappropriated the idealistic aspects of the foreign policy of the twentieth-eighth president of the United States to endorse American domination of the world by any means. They have done this using various euphemisms to refer to U.S. imperialism and empire, invoking "Wilson's name . . . to sanctify virtually every military action that an American president has chosen to pursue, including the current war in Iraq." Wilson's rhetoric about freedom, democracy, free trade, and the rule of law has been easily co-opted over the years to justify the United States "act[ing] as the chief of the constabulatory" to impose its values on the world, particularly in those areas deemed unenlightened.[16]

When placed in historical context, Wilson's foreign policy legacy appears, at best, to have been "richly hypocritical." This is because two types of Wilsonianism existed by the end of the First World War, and the United States pursued both as it began to practice independent internationalism for the rest of the twentieth century. The major American political and economic component of what I am calling the "good" Wilsonian diplomacy consisted of the president's belief in spreading self-determination and free trade capitalism to the world through collective security arrangements. The positive Wilsonian legacy was not simply one of liberal capitalist internationalism but also one of anticolonialism, ethnic national sovereignty, and multilateral cooperation. As early as May 1915, he informed the League to Enforce Peace that "every people has a right to choose the sovereignty under which they shall live," and Wilson later came to believe that his beloved League of Nations would be able to make peaceful territorial adjustments "pursuant to the principle of self-determination." At the end of his presidency Wilson fervently asserted that U.S. foreign policy would be used only "toward the greater good of mankind, not toward aggrandizement and oppression."[17]

However, even this positive view of Wilsonianism is based on a very selective analysis of his diplomatic record from 1913 to 1921. It is a view that mainly focuses on the three years from the spring of 1917 to the fall of 1920, and it ignores Wilson's less-than-altruistic diplomacy from 1913 through 1916. During these years he moralistically justified unilateral U.S. military and economic action against sovereign nations in the Western Hemisphere that were not threatening the United States. Similarly, he demanded that American neutrality rights be honored by the warring powers in the First World War even though his economic dealings with them were not neutral, and neither was his belated sending of American troops in 1919 and 1920 to interfere with the Russian civil war on the side of the anti-Bolshevik forces.

Naturally, materialism played a role in U.S. foreign policy during the twentieth century, but Wilson thought that the League of Nations had the ability to restrain capitalist greed for the benefit of all nations. As the United States grew more powerful after 1920, based on an evolving sense of its economic self-interest, little restrained its expansionism following the Great Depression as the country emerged ever more prosperous from the Second World War and then from the Cold War. Yet since 1945 the United States has seldom acknowledged that its "foreign policy in a given instance may be driven by economic and financial interests." While economic considerations (and even imperial interests) are logically an essential part of any major country's foreign policy, American leaders hid these crasser aspects of U.S. diplomacy from the public with self-serving legitimating claims about the moral superiority and defensive nature of the country's diplomacy.[18]

This misleading rhetoric combined with the negative, or what I am calling the "bad," unilateral interventionist aspects of the Wilsonian legacy led the United States to commit excesses during the Cold War, specifically with respect to access to such natural resources as oil deemed necessary to shore up its economic well-being. In effect, successive Cold War presidents ended up indicating to the rest of the world that they would "not permit a foreign people to take control of their own resources ... if the United States had come to depend on getting those resources under terms of our choosing, and if we [had] reason to fear that [a] new regime [in any country might] change those terms or, worse, shut off the supply."[19]

This truly remarkable interventionist assumption on the part of the United States in defense of its own brand of capitalism became an accepted, but unacknowledged, fact of the Cold War – accepted by politicians, the public, the press, and most pundits–because it became indistinguishable from military containment of Communism all over the world. Yet Washington's use of unprovoked covert or overt unilateral interventions to protect or enhance American economic and ideological interests often violated customary and formal international law. Moreover, such actions had little in common with Wilson's concept of cooperative internationalism, although they did reflect his initial commitment to, and legacy of, unilateralism.

Both versions of Wilsonianism have the same philosophical core based on "the doctrine of American exceptionalism." The ingrained presumptuousness about America as the "city on the hill" to be emulated and admired was all well and good until the country became a major power as of 1920. Both "good" and "bad" Wilsonians, whether they call themselves idealists or realists, shared this common creation myth about the country's exceptionalist origins and intentions. They took for granted that the uniqueness of the United States among the nations of the world guaranteed that it would use its newly acquired economic and military power after 1920 in a disinterested, even-handed way.[20]

Wilson's assumption that the American model of politics and economics would prevail against the forces of darkness is back in vogue with a vengeance since September 11. The Wilsonian idea that the United States should serve as a universal example for the rest of the world and, if need be, set the world right contains a contrary side that became an increasingly important feature of American foreign policy after 1920. Because Wilsonian idealists and Wilsonian realists alike have implicitly and explicitly assumed that America's diplomatic actions are always untainted by base motives, there has been a tendency for the country to preach its own concept of "universal morality" rather than listen to other nations – to act impetuously rather than patiently. This has meant in practice that when the United States believed it wasn't being listened to, it would either turn inward and refuse to cooperate on the international scene or lash out on a vainglorious, unilateral course.[21]

Since 1920 American leaders have repeatedly incorporated buzzwords like liberty, democracy, freedom, and self-determination into their diplomatic rhetoric – words that masked or disguised the fact that the country had any material or ideological self-interests other than moral purity as it contemplated intervention in world affairs on a grand scale. As a result, U.S. foreign policy during the Cold War increasingly exhibited a "pathological dualism ... creating a confusing symbiotic link between self-righteous protective claims based on confusing admixtures of defensive necessity, idealistic endorsements of democracy and freedom, and a greedy geopolitics that [sought] to sustain military, economic, and culture dominance into the indefinite future."[22]

Adopting the Tactics of the Enemy during the Cold War

Despite this myth-driven Wilsonian rhetoric about American's perennial innocence, good intentions, commitment to just causes, and general law-abiding uniqueness among nations, it would appear in retrospect that the United States not only adopted the enemy's methods during the Cold War, but also compromised its values (to say nothing of its constitutional principles) on such issues as torture, race, self-determination, free trade, and decolonization at home and abroad. At the same time, the country also probably exceeded the enemy in carrying out successful overt and covert measures to ensure the existence of anticommunist regimes, regardless of their antidemocratic objectives and dictatorial oppression of their own people. Indeed, it even practiced state terrorism from time to time, beginning with "the most extreme and permanently traumatizing instance... perhaps in the history warfare" – the atomic bombing of Hiroshima and Nagasaki. Coming out of World War II all sides "downplay[ed] the degree to which state terror had been relied upon by both the victors and the vanquished," and this disposition of the United States to sublimate its use of state terror in the name of saving the world from Communism continued during such wars in the Pacific as Korea and Vietnam. Both conflicts "exhibited in different ways a reliance on state terrorism," largely through the use of air power. Moreover, as more nations acquired nuclear weapons during the Cold War, some began to test and produce hydrogen bombs. In order to accommodate this heightened "nuclearism," the United States "incorporat[ed] 'state terrorism' into... [its] strategic doctrine... at the highest level, and with acceptance of its potentially catastrophic results for the entire planet." Politicians sold nuclear state terrorism to the American people through euphemisms and fear propaganda.[23]

Such deception about nuclear state terrorism remained the best-kept secret of the Cold War. However, this elephant in the room quickly became painfully evident when the USSR collapsed, no longer posing an ideological threat, and the United States along with other nuclear powers did not immediately enter into phased disarmament agreements. Also, unlike the situation after both world wars, Congress did not consider decreasing U.S. military spending this time. As of 2004 the annual Pentagon budget stood at $400 billion, exceeding the defense budgets of the next twenty-four countries combined. The 2008 budget included a defense request for $624 billion. With this unprecedented military might and ever-growing demand for oil, it was not by coincidence that the United States resorted to war after the end of the Cold War against the country in the Middle East with the second-largest oil reserves. The much-reduced Russian state needed Western aid and so did not offer any opposition to these wars through the United Nations. Its silence was notable with the Persian Gulf

War in 1991 after Iraq invaded Kuwait. Then, after the national humiliation of September 11, the United States again implicitly asserted its right to the world's most precious resource under the pretense of fighting a war on terrorism, eliminating weapons of mass destruction, and regime change by launching a second invasion of Iraq in 2003.[24]

The extreme economic and military spin-offs of unilateral Wilsonianism during the Cold War were undergirded by several ideological premises in addition to self-determination, namely, an ingrained racism and, after the Bolshevik Revolution, adamant anti-Communism – both of which the United States rationalized in the name of national security in order to justify its military and economic interventions. Often the tactics employed in these interventions emulated those of the enemy. Additionally, Wilson bequeathed a heightened sense of secrecy and moral self-righteousness to American diplomacy. While secrecy is a given in the formulation and execution of any country's foreign policy, for all of his talk about "open covenants openly arrived at" and his "declarations against secret diplomacy," Wilson's "penchant for secrecy" became more evident in his second term as events in Europe seemed to spin out of his control and Communism reared its head in Russia. This set a strong precedent for later presidents to devise even more secretive ways to keep the public and Congress uninformed or misinformed when formulating and carrying out U.S. foreign policy. While a moralistic approach to foreign policy did not originate with Wilson, in the course of the twentieth century he came to personify the idea that power in the hands of the United States automatically translated into virtue. He also came to symbolize a propensity for taking unilateral action because Washington knows best what is right for the world. For example, Wilson asserted in 1917 that "American principles, American policies . . . are the principles and policies of forward looking men and women everywhere, of every modern nation, of every enlightened community. They are the principles of mankind and must prevail."[25]

This same combination of secrecy and moral self-righteousness led to an assortment of unilateral or pseudo-collective activities during and after the Cold War that primarily reflected the negative or Faustian aspects of Wilsonianism. Many were undertaken without the knowledge of the American people and usually without approval from Congress. Questionable covert and overt military and intelligence actions ordered by presidents from Eisenhower through Clinton often resulted in unintended negative consequences, or what the CIA now calls "blowback." Little wonder that once George W. Bush turned the war in Iraq into his own personal moralistic crusade he was dubbed "the most Wilsonian president since Wilson himself." Fighting the war on terrorism has produced its own profound "blowback, including the use of torture techniques adopted during the Cold War based on presumptions about how the USSR and its allies treated prisoners."[26]

Since the end of the Cold War, Wilsonianism has been used to rationalize overthrowing "rogue states" because, like the self-righteous twenty-eighth president of the United States "who gave to the American nation the blasphemous conviction that it, like himself, had been created by God 'to show the way to the nations of the world how they shall walk in the path of liberty,'" the United States has once again assumed the role of savior of the world and preacher of universal morality under the second President Bush, but with a difference of kind, rather than simply of degree, as will be noted.[27]

This is not to say that the United States failed to achieve some constructive global results from 1945 to 1989, regardless of its less-than-Simon-pure motivations. It did reconstruct Europe; it did ensure democratic governments in Germany, Italy, and Japan; it did on occasion support self-determination and national independence in nations emerging from colonization; it did help create a partial global free trade system, sometimes at the expense of its own industries; and it did allow, if not always enthusiastically, the United Nations to function for five decades. But the constructive aspects of the Cold War are not by any means the whole story of that forty-plus-year conflict. Moreover, it could be argued that some of these positive outcomes were the products of Faustian means that were taken in pursuit of less salutary goals.

That other story is the concern of this book. It will argue that in fighting the Cold War the United States entered into a number of Faustian bargains and deceived the American public about them because ideological victory and/or control of resources became more important than either ethical or humanitarian principles. In the long run, Faustian behavior, especially the adoption of enemy tactics, would come back to haunt the United States in the post–Cold War world even though it had contributed to the country's becoming the preeminent power in the world. Deceitful historical acts can only be hidden or denied for so long before they begin to wear away even the beneficial results they may also have produced. Democracy demands accountability.

The United States as a Virtuous Empire

This failure to address the Faustian aspects of Wilsonianism during the last fifty years of U.S. foreign policy makes it difficult for Americans to understand why "the miserable of the earth should resent the richest and most powerful country."[28] This hatred is not caused by some abstract clash of civilizations or fear of freedom and democracy but by actual U.S. foreign policies around the world, most notably in the Middle East and Latin America. In fact, in Central America the United States had honed the model for preemptive economic or military action to achieve regime change and to try to impose democracy by force long before Bush decided to invade Iraq and do the same. There has never been an empire that has been loved. Most Americans do not even want to admit that the United States is an empire whose actions have enraged many abroad as much they have been praised at home.

Because the United States is in a state of denial about being an empire, it refuses to recognize how disliked it is in many parts of the world. Consequently, there was much talk after September 11 about how those terrorist actions represented another blow to American innocence. The evocation of this mantra about the country's loss of innocence occurs so often in so many different crises that it has become almost meaningless. The reason the country can "lose" its innocence so many times is that it has never matured as a nation and so refuses to recognize that innocence, like virginity, can be lost only once – whether you are Miss America or the United States of America.

Even those Americans who are willing to accept the myth of the United States as a benign or liberal empire (or those pundits and politicians who advocate that the United States should consolidate its empire with vigor and force) do so based on the concept of American exceptionalism and the country's fictional image of its national cultural identity as the embodiment of everything good and desirable – an innocent in an evil world. The flip side of this view of American innocence can be found in Graham Greene's novel *The Quiet American* when he describes an idealistic CIA man who blows up women and children to bring democracy to Vietnam: "Innocence is like a dumb leper who has lost his bell, wandering the world, meaning no harm."

However, there is the school of American political scientists who argue that empires can be essentially benign and bring public goods to the world by providing collective security and economic prosperity. Known as the "hegemonic stability theory," it is based on assumptions such as: mutually beneficially economic collective action, political morality (as opposed to personal morality) that justifies the existence of asymmetrical hierarchies in international relations, and the superiority and uniqueness of American liberalism compared to most other nation-state domestic political economies.[29]

Indeed, the American empire is unique, but not simply because of the country's belief in its own exceptionalism or innocence or virtue. According to Niall Ferguson, the uniqueness of the American empire begins with the fact that it is so often unspoken and denied, and its major characteristic is that it is a debtor empire based on conspicuous domestic consumption and foreign investors (lenders). Foreign countries now own approximately 46 percent of the federal U.S. debt. Moreover, with the exception of the occupations of Germany and Japan after World War II, the United States suffers from a "chronic attention deficit disorder" when it comes to sustaining occupations or suppressing insurgencies.[30]

As a result, the American empire does not consist of large colonial land holdings or direct control of foreign populations, as Great Britain's did. The United States currently occupies only one-half of 1 percent of the planet. Even with its few noncontiguous dependencies, the country accounts for scarcely 5 percent of the world's population. Viewed in its most favorable light, it is a "new kind of empire, divorced from national interest, economic exploitation, racism or colonialism, and that exists only to promote freedom and human rights." Critics refer to this new so-called virtuous empire as economic imperialism without colonies or the imperialism of free trade. Most succinctly, it can be described an informal empire – a "burden" that the United States claims has fallen fortuitously on its shoulders.[31]

The informal and unspoken empire of the United States is made up primarily of military outposts and free trade assumptions. Taking the narrowest definition of what the Defense Department says constitutes a "major" military installation, there are sixty-one base complexes operating in nineteen countries. But there are at least 750 reported installations housing the U.S. military worldwide in 159 countries and territories, and new ones have opened up since the end of the Cold War in some countries with the most autocratic governments or military dictatorships, in keeping with previous Faustian practice. This does not include secret spy intelligence bases, or the fourteen "enduring (permanent)" bases scattered around existing airfields, oil fields, and pipelines in Iraq. The plan is to consolidate the fourteen into four mega-bases. However, the Pentagon has begun to abandon the term "military base" in favor of two new types of installations: "forward operating sites" (or "forward operating locations") and "cooperative security locations." Both are designed "to avoid the impression that the United States is seeking a permanent, colonial-like presence in the counties it views as possible hosts for such installations," to "protect the global production and transport of oil," and to control other vital trade routes. In addition to its unchallenged military might, the United States is also the most powerful economic and cultural entity the world has ever known.[32] So the "burden" of this virtuous informal empire is scarcely an accidental or unpremeditated phenomenon, despite its recent origins.

The United States become an empire in a little over fifty years and so remains an immature giant. No other empire or hegemonic power in history has ever emerged as rapidly as has the United States. After all, Rome wasn't built in a day, and neither was the Roman Empire or the British Empire or any other imperial power of the past. But for all intents and purposes, in terms of the history of the world, the United States was built in a day. It didn't learn to crawl before it walked as a hegemon, suddenly finding itself alone astride the globe as the sixty-eighth empire the world has known.[33] What does this portend about the psyche of the nation? Are Americans forever trapped within their youth and callowness, as Faust was? Will their leaders ever anticipate probable unintended negative consequences of their Faustian diplomatic actions or admit that they helped bring them about? Will they ever understand that their "claim for incommensurable uniqueness will not help to locate the United States in the world of nations," no matter how powerful it is or will become? Will they ever stop telling Americans that the country is hated for such abstract values as freedom and universal morality rather than for the destabilizing results of its independent internationalist foreign policy?[34]

I ask these questions because the rise of the United States to the status of a hegemonic power occurred in such an incredibly short period of time; that is, in a little over a half-century the country has become the most prosperous, powerful nation in history, a rise that corresponds almost exactly with the years of the Cold War, the "longest of all [undeclared] America wars." This poses the nagging possibility that elite diplomatic formulators have successfully employed the myth-ridden national cultural consensus about the nation's exceptionalism to secure generations of popular support for what is basically a "militant and undemocratic foreign policy" by "resort[ing] to war on a consistent basis." James Woolsey, a former CIA director, has proudly referred to the Cold War as

World War III and predicted that the U.S. battle against terrorism marked the beginning of World War IV. In this case, it is to be an endless global war with no exit strategy because there is no definition of what will constitute victory.[35]

It is almost as though September 11 gave the United States carte blanche to rule the world and control its resources with unbridled arrogance in order to compensate for having its own vulnerability exposed. Once a superpower believes it has been violated or victimized in some way, a common reaction is to demonstrate how powerful it really is with excessively aggressive unilateral action. Now, in the first decade of the twenty-first century, there is an implicit tinge of revanche rather than virtue to U.S. foreign policy arising out of the still-lingering subliminal sting of defeat in Vietnam and the current chagrin over the loss of the iconic twin towers.[36]

It may, however, be asking too much – not only of the United States but of all previous empires – to call upon them to rise above the myths of their self-importance and their ever-expanding urgency about national security to cooperate with the rest of the world, to continue to honor national sovereignty (unless humanitarian intervention is absolutely necessary to save innocent lives), and to abide by international law. It is conceivable that an ethical hegemon is an oxymoron – in other words, a myth. Because the United States predominates at the moment, it may prove impossible for it to reassess the founding myth about its universal morality in order to create a more modest, rather than a more arrogant, new ethical self-image that will better serve its own long-term self-interest and that of the world.

To date, the country appears to have responded by simply beefing up its belief in its own exceptional moral superiority. Some argue that its world dominance gives the United States a mandate to impose freedom, democracy, and capitalism on the world, "throwing off traditional restraints on the will to power and . . . exercising American power on the largest possible scale." Others think that it would be much more honest and practical for the United States to admit that the "world needs an effective liberal empire and that [it] is the best candidate for the job. . . . and [it] should try to do a better rather than a worse job of policing an unruly world than their British predecessors." This latter point of view creates a new myth of America – not of an ethical hegemon, but of a virtuous empire with no limits on its ability to act in the world. However, "creating a better world [in its own image] is an endless task" that could lead to endless war in the name of peace reminiscent of George Orwell's Newspeak.[37]

Moralism and Ethics

Gradually since 1920, but especially during the Cold War, the United States may have lost, as a nation and as a people, any sense of ethics or knowledge of what constitutes ethical behavior, the moralistic rhetoric of Woodrow Wilson and George W. Bush notwithstanding. A messianic vision of a virtuous empire does not make any nation less imperialistic or paternalistic or ethnocentric. Nor does it prevent abandonment of traditional values and taboos while proclaiming virtuous global leadership. Unregulated goodness is no excuse for forsaking ethical traditions, especially when the "doing good for the world . . . is fundamentally motivated by a will to dominate."[38]

Ethics, after all, consists of public, rather than private, rules and cultural standards governing the conduct of countries and is usually embodied in custom, law, and national policy. At the global level, ethics now consists of customary and formal international law as propounded by UN resolutions and covenants, the World Court, and various war crimes tribunals. Most recently, ethics has been embodied in the International Criminal Court, which the United State has refused to join. At the domestic level in the United States and many other Western nations, it consists of common law jurisprudence based on habeus corpus, which Blackstone called "the principal and most perfect branch of ethics." For nations that purport to honor the rule of law and classical Enlightenment definitions of civilization, this means that there are recognized fair and equitable ways for countries to conduct themselves at home and abroad that can be enforced absent a hegemonic power. Such ethical behavior is more humane and less ethnocentric than the concept of political morality adhered to by advocates of the "hegemonic stability theory."

I am not making a moral argument in asking whether the United States sold its soul as it perfected the practice of independent or unilateral internationalism in the course of the twentieth century. Morality is largely a personal guide for private behavior, and it often involves self-sacrifice. Hence, the term has almost always been misused when applied to any country's foreign policy, despite numerous books and speeches on the subject promoting U.S. diplomacy in excessively moralistic terms. Ideally, even personal moral choice should not involve blind adherence to values considered absolute as this represents simple compliance or conformity. Instead, personal morality represents a conscious individual choice to believe in values that are relative and to act on them anyway because they are freely chosen.[39]

The reason that individual or personal moralistic absolutism is both dangerous and inappropriate when applied to the country's foreign relations is that it "exempts America from self-criticism or from addressing the grievances others have with respect to [U.S.] policies, [and] such [moralistic] sentiments imply a repudiation of dialogue and negotiation." Moralistic absolutism also leads to non-negotiable demands – the anathema of diplomacy, which, even more than domestic politics, is the art of compromise. Wilson gave new life to this rhetorical device during the First World War, and it flourished exponentially during the Cold War. Now it has reached a crescendo level because of the war on terrorism. From the president on down, most segments of American society, including government officials, religious groups, and mainstream media, have egregiously misused the words "moral" and "morality" since September 11. Regardless of the time period in which it is used, such careless public rhetoric does not recognize that if "there can be no compromise with the forces of evil, there can be no reasonable restraint on the forces of good."[40]

The careless yet incessant infusion of moralism into discussions about U.S. foreign policy also disguises the distinct possibility that in the course of carrying out covert and overt Cold War interventions based on an ever-widening perception of threats to its ubiquitous security interests, the United States began to lose its ethical and democratic compass. As a result, the country began defending its diplomacy using a rationale similar to that expressed in the 1963 novel *The Spy Who Came In from the Cold* when author John le Carré has Control [the head of British intelligence] say to agent Alec Leamas:

Thus we do disagreeable things, but we are *defensive*. That, I think, is still fair. We do disagreeable things so that ordinary people here and elsewhere can sleep safely in their beds at night. Is that too romantic? Of course, we occasionally do very wicked things.... And in weighing up the moralities, we rather go in for dishonest comparisons; after all, you can't compare the ideals of one side with the methods of the other, can you now?...I mean, you've got to compare method with method, and ideal with ideal. I would say that since the [Second World] war, our methods – ours and those of the opposition – have become much the same. I mean you can't be less ruthless than the opposition simply because your government's *policy* is benevolent, can you now? That would *never* do....I mean in our world we pass so quickly out of the register of hate or love – like certain sounds a dog can't hear. All that's left in the end is a kind of nausea.[41]

I don't believe that a nation can adopt over time the tactics of the enemy in public or private and walk away ethically unscathed. To pretend that such tactics were not repeatedly and successfully implemented during the Cold War only compounds the conundrum in which the country finds itself now that it has declared a never-ending war against terrorism and tyranny beginning with the invasions of Afghanistan and Iraq. Because the United States has all too often assumed the methods of its enemies while professing to uphold Wilsonian democratic and humanitarian principles, it no longer seems to recognize any limits on its power. Some pundits and politicians now glory in the hitherto taboo topic of empire building, all the while insisting that the United States is being forced to take up this imperial burden.[42] This represents the worst use of Wilsonian rhetoric to mask naked imperialism.

Nations cannot adhere to the moral standards expected of individuals for the reasons I have already noted. But this doesn't mean that countries have license to systematically adopt unethical methods, particularly those nations that profess to believe in and practice democracy, freedom, and liberty. They must also examine themselves and try to alleviate national character flaws such as hubris, self-indulgence, arrogance, inflexibility, intolerance, and belligerence. It is true that sometimes countries have to fight dirty if good is to prevail. But after being "driven to barbarism," there must be a recognition, an acknowledgment of such behavior – a searching of national consciousness.[43] Otherwise, barbarous acts become a normal part of national defense whether they are warranted or not.

The only modern president to admit in public that the United States may have been subverting its own ethics in fighting the Cold War was, not surprisingly, the first born-again evangelical occupant of the White House in the twentieth century, namely, Jimmy Carter. At the very beginning of his administration he gave a commencement address at Notre Dame in which he said: "For too many years, we've been willing to adopt the flawed and erroneous principles and tactics of our adversaries, sometimes abandoning our values for theirs. We've fought fire with fire, never thinking fire was better quenched with water." Critics characterized Carter's attempts to make human rights a factor in his administration's foreign policy decisions as weak and naive. This critique stemmed largely from his refusal to intervene to stop Sandinista attacks on the dictatorial regime of Anastasio Somoza in Nicaragua, allowing the Communists to come into power under Daniel Ortega, and from his perceived and real mishandling of the Iranian hostage crisis. In retrospect, however, his administration set the stage for "a post-Cold War foreign policy for the United States that rejected the bipolar world view of the containment doctrine and sought to introduce American ideals into the making of the nation's foreign policy."[44]

If the United States, in emblematic Faustian fashion, did lose a sense of ethics during the course of the Cold War, it may have lost the basis for evaluating past foreign policy in order to formulate a coherent one in the dramatically changed world of the last decade of the twentieth century and the first decade of the twenty-first. There can be no new ideas about self-determination, peace keeping and nation building, the relationship between capitalism and democracy, national security in an age of terrorism, humanitarian interventions, or what constitutes state sovereignty until American foreign policy experts and politicians explain to the American people, among other things, the questionable ethics behind U.S. refusal to ratify four major UN human rights conventions, including the latest one on the rights of the child. The only other country not acceding to this convention is Somalia. Also, the United States "heavily qualified its acceptance of the International Covenant on Civil and Political Rights (ICCPR) and the 2005 Supreme Court decision continued to defy that treaty's prohibition against the execution of juvenile offenders (along with Iran, Nigeria, Pakistan, and Saudi Arabia)."[45]

Until a future president and a future Senate commit the country to such humanitarian international regimes as these UN conventions and the International Criminal Court, and begin consistently to cooperate with humane interventions in areas of the world where there are no clear U.S. strategic or national security concerns, American leaders will be increasingly unable to make a convincing case for ethical leadership that will ring true internationally. Assertions about federalism preventing the United States from unconditionally adopting international human rights conventions and other multinational treaties have assumed mythical proportions in the United States Senate. Yet this intractability is bound to become more and more problematic in a twenty-first century characterized by economic globalism at the expense of national power. Unreflective adherence to federalism will not help the United States preserve the traditional ethical, cultural, and political functions of democratic nation-states from the inherently undemocratic and chaotic tentacles of unregulated global capitalism.[46]

The United States cannot continue to practice both brands of Wilsonianism through independent internationalism by spasmodically promoting free trade globalism and cooperation when it is convenient and profitable for its economic interests. Nor can it revert to willful unilateral interventionism and refuse to cooperate with other nations when more and more situations in the twenty-first century cry out for collective, humanitarian, and ethical actions. This refusal to honor international ethical norms is not a result of September 11. For most of the twentieth century America unilaterally defied various global norms with impunity and flaunted its exceptionalism as it practiced independent internationalism.[47] It cut Faustian deal after Faustian deal without acknowledging the damage to its soul and ethics as a nation. The youth of the United States as an empire is no longer (if it ever was) an excuse for acting just as ancient empires did before their demise, even if America does consider itself more virtuous and exceptional than any other empire in history.

I

The United States Forms and Refines Its Diplomacy

> America, in the assembly of nations, since her admission among them, . . . has uniformly spoken . . . though often to heedless and often to disdainful ears, the language of equal liberty, of equal justice, and of equal rights. . . . [But] she has abstained from interference in the concerns of others, even when the conflict has been for principles to which she clings.
>
> John Adams, July 4, 1821

Of all the diplomatic concepts associated with American exceptionalism and Wilsonianism, self-determination emerged as the most important and long-lasting. It can be said that the United States was born in an absent-minded fit of self-determination during the American Revolution, because British colonists in the New World did not start out demanding independence, let alone democracy. Rather, they claimed "for themselves the rights and liberties of Englishmen."[1] However, once push came to shove and independence based on self-determination became the driving force behind the American Revolution, the country quietly nourished and groomed this autonomous brand of nationhood for itself and, for most of the nineteenth century, touted it to other emerging nations that found themselves in civil turmoil.[2]

Self-determined, but not necessarily democratic, self-government became the symbolic and mythological hallmark of the origins of the United States and lay at the heart of its perception of itself as exceptional and its drive to become the example for how the rest of world should operate. This was true, therefore, long before Woodrow Wilson revived the term "self-determination" and made it an international code word for national sovereignty during the First World War.

Following the American Revolution, however, there were more explicit theories devised and practical attempts made on behalf of national self-determination in Europe than in the Western Hemisphere. The fate of both Corsica and Poland gave rise to issues of national identity from the 1760s to the 1790s as the first was swallowed up by the French and the latter partitioned by

Russia, Prussia, and Austria. Edmund Burke and Jean-Jacques Rousseau commented quite pointedly on the violation of national self-determination in the case of Corsica, comparing the transfer of a nation without its consent to moving "trees on an estate" or "herds of cattle, without consulting [the people's] interests or their wishes." These and other theorists outside the United States came to define national self-determination as the right of people to be consulted about how and by whom they should be governed. What was meant by "people" (or nation or nationality, for that matter) remained very ambiguous, except for the fact that until the twentieth century "women have never been viewed as a 'people' for the purposes of right to self-determination,"[3] and this remains true in many parts of the world today.

Whether self-determination could be possible without national identity also remained unclear. In other words, initially nationalism and self-determination were not necessarily synonymous because a "sense of national identity can exist without the attendant requirement of an expression of will by the people." Nationalism is such a modern development that it cannot be considered to fulfill some universal need; it is primarily a cultural phenomenon, that is, a social construct. In its purest form, nationalism can spawn democracy if it is rooted in the sovereignty of the people, but as nationalist and self-determination concepts spread in the nineteenth century, nationhood became associated with the uniqueness or ethnicity of the people and thus more removed from democratic principles. Democracy, according to Liah Greenfeld, "may be an inherent predisposition in certain nations (inherent in their very definition as nationals – that is, the original national concept), yet entirely alien to others, and the ability to adopt and develop it [democracy] in the latter may require a change of [national] identity." This suggests the very sobering possibility that because of its inherently Western cultural overtones, democracy may not be as exportable by economic or military means to emerging or historically tyrannical nations as American leaders have insisted for most of the twentieth century and now again in the twenty-first.[4]

To the degree that nations come to think of themselves as superior and exceptional, they make value judgments about other nations, usually without recognizing the closed system in which their own nationalist uniqueness operates. And most countries down to the present do think of themselves as superior to other nations, ignoring the fact that they are subscribing to a set of patriotic values that are relative to specific historical time periods. Little wonder, then, that since the proliferation of nation-states beginning in the nineteenth century, warfare has been on the rise. This does not mean that "murderous nationalism" is ethically equal to "benevolent nationalism." *Nonetheless, both are legitimate when placed in a sociological and historical context.* Since nationalism (and its variations of politics and economics) is a product of a definite set of historical circumstances, it could eventually disappear; but that is not likely to happen soon. So conflict among nations – all claiming to be superior – is a fact of foreign policy for the foreseeable future, as Hobbes so correctly predicted. The moral relativism of this argument is, of course, rejected by those, such as Charles P. Kindleberger and Robert Gilpin, who believe in the myth of American exceptionalism and the country's duty to provide hegemonic stability to the world.[5]

From 1776 until 1900, however, American foreign policy adhered to realistic principles based largely on its position as a relatively powerless developing nation in a world dominated by Spain, France, and England. For example, in 1793 George Washington's Proclamation of Neutrality announced that America would "pursue a conduct friendly and impartial toward the belligerent Powers" of Europe. Then, three years later, the nation's first president described America's political, *but not economic,* isolationism in his 1796 Farewell Address, warning the nation against permanent alliances and involvement in the diplomatic affairs of other nations, but not against "temporary alliances for extraordinary emergencies" or "extending our commercial relations." In 1821, Secretary of State John Quincy Adams warned that despite the fact that America was the "well-wisher to the freedom and independence of all," it should not go "abroad, in search of monsters to destroy," because if the country's foreign policy "insensibly changed from *liberty* to *force* . . . [s]he might become the dictatress of the world." Adams underscored this idea by noting that "[America's] glory is not *dominion,* but *liberty.*"[6] For most of the nineteenth century the United States followed his advice because as a young, emerging nation its economic and military weakness did not allow it to play an important role in international affairs.

Several other foreign policy principles also emerged from the American Revolution and likewise found practical application following the War for Independence. Sometimes these have been referred to as components of Thomas Paine's New World Order. They included political isolationism, neutrality, freedom of the seas, the vague idea that somehow free trade led to peace,[7] continental expansion, better known by the term Manifest Destiny, coined in 1845, and, finally, international cooperation, largely limited to arbitration of boundary and fishing disputes.

The Monroe Doctrine

Although from the late eighteenth century until World War I the United States defined neutrality and freedom of the seas in absolute terms, it did not yet have sufficient economic or military power to enforce these or any of its other early diplomatic principles. The same was true of the presidential declaration known as the Monroe Doctrine. Proclaimed by President James Monroe in 1823, but written largely by his secretary of state, John Quincy Adams, the document included a sentence with the two prescience words "manifestation" and "destiny." The doctrine contained four unenforceable provisions at the time it was issued: (1) no more colonization of either North or South America by European powers would be permitted; (2) no more interference or extension of their systems by European powers would be tolerated anywhere in the Western Hemisphere (this was a veiled reference to Russian claims to the Pacific coast north of the fifty-first parallel within what was then known as the Oregon Territory); (3) no attempts should be made by these same powers to tamper with what was an essentially different political system in the New World (this was an indirect encouragement of revolutions against French and Spanish colonial rule as symbols of self-determination in Columbia, Mexico, Brazil, Chile, Argentina, Peru, and the Federation of Central American States); and finally, in a fourth provision, the United States very graciously promised not to interfere with the existing European colonies in the New World or with the internal affairs of European nations, or to take part in "European wars of solely foreign interest."[8] This became known as the nonintervention or nonentanglement provision.

The only new ingredient of the Monroe Doctrine was the noncolonization principle; the other three had been anticipated by or actually closely associated with the earlier American foreign policy concepts of neutrality and political isolationism. Noncolonization, however, was an oblique way to claim the right of self-determination for all of the Western Hemisphere, not simply the United States. At the same time, however, it should be noted that the noncolonization principle did not apply to the United States. Instead, it targeted only the European commercial and territorial competitors of America. As such, the doctrine appealed not only to domestic economic interests, but also to the antimonarchial, xenophobic (especially anti-European), isolationist, nationalistic, and chauvinistic sentiments in the United States – all of which were stimulated by the War of 1812 and the Depression of 1819.

However self-righteous and confident-sounding, Monroe's Doctrine was largely a reflection of Adams's imperious personality and his belief that, in any case, Britain would use its military might to keep other European nations from gaining much more power in North and South America. In essence, he was implicitly counting on England to enforce some the doctrine's provisions that were beyond the capabilities of the weak United States. Adams also turned down an offer from England to make a joint declaration opposing the supposed dastardly intentions of the five nations of the Holy Alliance (Russia, Austria, Germany, France, and Spain) toward the newly established Central and Latin American nations because he did not want to place any limitations on the future ability of the United States to annex such additional territory as Texas and Cuba.[9] So he convinced President Monroe to make a bold, if unenforceable, unilateral declaration.

The unilateralism of the Monroe Doctrine, however, doomed any overt English support for it at the time. In fact, the Monroe Doctrine went virtually unnoticed abroad for most of the nineteenth century and was randomly violated by the very nations against which it was directed. One could not have predicted from this inauspicious beginning that the doctrine would achieve both mythical heights in the American imagination and very real authority in the first two decades of the twentieth century as first Theodore Roosevelt and then the Senate announced corollaries to the Monroe Doctrine that expanded the powers of the United States to enforce it.

The administration that originated the Monroe Doctrine did not intend it to become a permanent feature of American foreign policy; and yet it did. A series of corollaries to the Monroe Doctrine from the 1870s through 1912[10] reinforced or expanded the original 1823 document, giving it a life of its own that has extended to the present day, notwithstanding the fact that President Monroe (or rather John Quincy Adams) had naively intended it as a "temporary expedient – a stopgap measure intended to hold the line against the designs of Europe." This is the inherent, unintended danger of all presidential doctrines. Thus, by 1901 the General Board, a federal military advisory body, matter-of-factly asserted: "the Monroe Doctrine, so far as it is the policy of the Government, covers all South America, including Patagonia and the Argentine."[11]

The possibility that diplomatic doctrines designed for another era will live on after they have outlived their original purpose simply because growth in national power makes them enforceable underscores the peril embodied in such proclamations. This "life after obsolescence" is distinctly true of presidential doctrines that become official without congressional approval (a practice going back to Washington's Proclamation of Neutrality with its insistence on political isolationism). Such doctrines became more common with the onset of the Cold War.

Nationalism, Self-Determination, and Democracy

Theoretical understanding of the relation of nationalism to self-determination and the little-understood prerequisites for democracy did not transpire until the late eighteenth and early nineteenth centuries. Although the first modern nation had begun emerging in early sixteenth-century England, not until the middle of the seventeenth century had England been transformed from a country into the first nation-state. This meant, among many other profound socioeconomic and political developments, that the meaning of the word "nation" changed so that it no longer referred to an elite form of councilor government and came to be applied "to the population of the country and made synonymous with the word 'people.'" Before this radical semantic and political nationalization of the word "people," the term had specifically been used to connate the lower classes as "rabble" or "plebs." Nationalism in essence gave elite status and dignity to the masses and presaged the emergence of democracy. National identity is, therefore, one of many socially conditioned forms of identity, and, like sexual identity, it is one of the most powerful and basic components of any individual's makeup and is not easily, if ever, relinquished.[12]

Nationalism and national identity were born in the modern sense in England, with American nationalism being initially a variant of English nationalism. This first kind of nationalism (and the type that has remained the rarest type in the world down to the present) had basically an individualistic and civic connotation, meaning that "national identity – nationality – was, in effect, identical with citizenship." Such nationalism is usually referred to as liberal because it gave rise to democratic governments in contrast to collectivist nationalisms (the most common type of nationalism in existence today) that tend to lead to "various forms and degrees of authoritarianism." Collectivist nationalism usually grounds citizenship in the ethnic rather than the civic; that is, citizenship is not voluntary and cannot be acquired – it is inherent. Theoretically, it is easier (or used to be before the existence of mass media propaganda) to mobilize for war in countries with collectivist nationalisms because less diversity of opinion exists than in those honoring the primacy of the individual. From a psychological and empirical point of view, "ethnic nationalism serves its function better than individualistic and civic nationalism," according to Greenfeld, "and its appeal is, for this reason stronger."[13]

However, there are two types of the collectivist nationalism. French nationalism developed after that in England and the United States. Although collectivistic, it was also civic, unlike the third type of collectivistic nationalism that developed in Russia and then in Germany in the twentieth century, in which the freedom and civic rights of the individual were denied and submerged in the interests of the nation-state. The French Revolution, rather than the American one, set in motion the temporary establishment of free republics based primarily on the concept of the collective individual in Europe and Latin America, raising questions about the complex results when people come together as a nation and whether their practice of popular sovereignty will result in democratic or authoritarianism nationalism. These questions have yet to be fully answered.[14]

After all, on the four occasions, in the nineteenth and twentieth centuries when attempts were made to supplant tyrannical regimes with more representative governments, the results were less than impressive when it came to producing democracy. This was true in the nineteenth century after the American and French Revolutions encouraged myriad attempts at establishing free republics in Europe and Latin America. Most of them resulted in the restoration of traditional monarchies or military rule. A similar phenomenon occurred after the First World War. Out of all the new nations emerging from the Russian, German, Austro-Hungarian, and Ottoman-Turkish empires, only Poland and Czechoslovakia established democratic governments, and they lasted for a brief half-dozen years in the 1920s. The Second World War saw successful democratic regime change in such already-industrialized countries as Japan, West Germany, and Italy, but only after years of multilateral effort. However, democracy did not generally take hold in most former colonial countries. Following the end of the Cold War, results are still mixed, but the United States' track record in imposing democratic rule in less-developed nations is largely one of failure throughout the twentieth century, having been unsuccessful, as noted in the Introduction, seventeen of the eighteen times it has attempted to do so by itself. These results strongly suggest that democracy cannot be ordained or forced from above.[15] Following September 11, the George W. Bush administration set in motion a grandiose fifth attempt at unilateral democratic nation building in Iraq, stating that its overall goal is to democratize the entire Middle East.

Another often-misinterpreted feature of early U.S. foreign policy was the degree to which its insistence on the right of peoples in the name of self-determination to decide their own national destinies had anything to do with the evolution of democracy at home or abroad later in the nineteenth century. Once independence had been militarily achieved and constitutionally institutionalized, rhetoric about self-determination on the part of early American leaders seemed primarily aimed at setting a foreign example rather than a domestic one. So, regardless of where one comes down in the endless debate among neo-republicans and neo-liberals about the origins and intentions of the American Revolution,[16] figurative commitment to self-determination (with its implicit emphasis on popular will, if not actual democracy) initially provided the country's leaders with a domestic and foreign policy self-image conducive to myth making long before democracy became a political reality in the United States and a bona fide guiding diplomatic principle in the second decade of the twentieth century.

Denials of Self-Determination

Male plebiscites became one method for determining popular national will from the 1820s through the 1860s as Serbs, Greeks, Romanians, Czechs, Croats, and Italians all tried to unite, with varying degrees of failure.[17] None of their nationalizing efforts received anything but superficial support from the United States, which remained more involved in domestic matters having to do with internal improvements, continental expansion, and finally the irresolvable issue of slavery. Pursuing these domestic goals actually meant denying self-determination – that is, self-government – to Native Americans and, ultimately, to the South when it tried to secede.

While early U.S. presidents and members of Congress made public statements supporting foreign struggles for self-determination off and on during the nineteenth century, the country never took committed military or other diplomatic action to back such rhetoric. For example, President Monroe, under Adams's influence, ostensibly supported Greek and Latin American revolutionaries in his celebrated 1823 doctrine. However, Adams had no faith that either the new Latin American republics or Greek independence would survive, and he successfully fought off efforts by Congress to intervene on behalf of their fights for independence.[18] In fact, up to the Civil War most U.S. presidents tended to ignore the proclamation. President Polk tried unsuccessfully to revive Monroe's message in December 1845, when he criticized French and British "interference" in Texas, and again in April 1848 when trouble in the Mexican province of Yucatan raised the question of whether territory in the New World could be voluntarily transferred to a foreign power. Polk firmly told Congress on April 29 that no such transfer – in this case, to the British – could take place "even *with the consent of the inhabitants.*" Likewise, the much more mild-mannered President Millard Fillmore criticized popular support for the failed Hungarian revolution in a December 2, 1850, congressional address, and his secretary of state, Daniel Webster, assured the Austrian government that the United States remained committed to noninterference in the internal affairs of other countries. Congress, for its part, continued from time to time before 1860 to pass sympathetic resolutions supporting foreign peoples seeking freedom, but it took no practical action. Little wonder that Congress did not belatedly bestow upon Monroe's proclamation the official title of "doctrine" until the 1850s; and from that point forward it was referred to as such by the press and in diplomatic notes.[19]

The Civil War temporarily and abruptly ended what little presidential and congressional support existed for implementation of the idea of self-determination inherent in the American Revolution, in the Monroe Doctrine, and even (circumspectly) in Manifest Destiny. As a result, Abraham Lincoln and his secretary of state, William H. Seward, found it necessary to disavow groups continuing to support the perennially popular Hungarian and Polish revolutions of 1863. And, of course, the Union took precedent over southern demands for self-determination. Thus, federal policy during and immediately following the Civil War contradicted the previous, albeit largely rhetorical, U.S. commitment to self-determination for other nations, although Secretary Seward briefly reasserted the Monroe Doctrine against both Austria and France in Mexico in 1866 during the Andrew Johnson administration. In doing so, he served notice that "the temporary suspension of the Monroe Doctrine occasioned by the Civil War had come to an end." While Seward's expansionist unilateral actions were often thwarted by Congress, he is best remembered for his bold negotiation of a treaty with Russia in 1867 to purchase Alaska.[20]

The United States appeared to give greater real support for self-determination when the country fought to free Cuba from Spanish rule in 1898, especially after Congress approved the Teller Amendment, which disclaimed any intention by the United States "to exercise sovereignty, jurisdiction or control over Cuba." However, the 1901 Platt Amendment voided the Teller Amendment, leaving Cuba with "little or no independence," according to a private letter that General Leonard Wood, the American-appointed governor of the island, wrote to President Roosevelt.[21] Clearly, the Spanish-American War violated Cuba's self-determination and set in motion a nascent Faustian pattern of violations on the part of Congress and future U.S. presidents. This pattern would continue, beginning with a series of economic and military forays in the early decades of the twentieth century, including support for the military dictatorship of Fulgencio Batista beginning in the 1930s because he favored U.S. business interests. Then, despite the abrogation of the Platt Amendment in 1934, John F. Kennedy authorized the failed Bay of Pigs invasion in 1961 and pursued reckless and secret attempts to assassinate Fidel Castro, which "helped precipitate the showdown over Soviet missiles in Cuba." From the 1960s through the 1990s economic sanctions encroached on Cuba's sovereignty, climaxing with the Helms-Burton Act, referred to as the second Platt Amendment. Although the "economic embargo against Cuba has been an abject failure," even tougher U.S. sanctions against trade and travel with Cuba were issued in 2003.[22] All such violations of Cuban self-determination and sovereignty since the beginning of the twentieth century have been in keeping with the interventionist features implicit in the original Monroe Doctrine and the Platt Amendment.

Economic Sea Changes

Obviously erratic assertions of the Monroe Doctrine in the course of the nineteenth century, both for and against self-determination, gradually undermined the Founders' support for American political isolationism. Initially, such selective isolationism was dictated as much by the country's inferior economic and military position in the world as by its geographical separation from Europe and Asia. While moving from a colonial mercantilist economy to a commercial agricultural one in the first half of the nineteenth century, the United States concentrated on improving internal transportation systems, establishing a national currency, and expanding across the continent. The progress of its nascent manufacturing industry and railway development, which reached a "take-off" point as early as 1843, with another surge in the 1850s, was retarded by the Civil War and did not begin to flourish again until the 1870s, with the help of protective tariffs and monopolistic capitalist practices. Unfettered by government regulation or consideration for the working conditions of laborers, the U.S. manufacturing sector expanded exponentially. In the course of the 1890s it outstripped the industrial output of Britain, with a phenomenal average GDP growth of almost 4 percent for four decades beginning in the 1870s, despite a lingering agricultural depression for three of those same decades.[23] Yet, at the same time, America in the decade of the 1890s experienced social and economic upheaval, especially after the onset of the depression of 1893, that made its industrial progress less noticeable to the average American. The 1890s is, therefore, considered a watershed economic decade that resulted in an identity crisis producing a cacophony of dissenting views and a sense of national crisis that, in turn, produced a change in U.S. diplomacy.

The most obvious and interesting foreign policy aspect of the unprecedented industrial and commercial growth of the United States by 1900 can be seen in its desire to rely on economic power, rather than on its relatively puny army and navy – the "splendid little war" against Spain notwithstanding. In fact, President William McKinley's belated decision to go war in April 1898 and his subsequent annexation of Hawaii and the Philippines were largely supported (if not actually dictated) by a whole host of business interests, in addition to Protestant missionaries and the U.S. military. The economic issues surrounding this war were legion and fraught with political overtones that historians only slowly unraveled much later in the twentieth century. In summary, despite its rapid economic development in the last quarter of the nineteenth century, its insignificant position in world affairs for most of the nineteenth century meant that the United States had the power and volition to pursue consistently only two of the diplomatic principles coming out of the American Revolution: continental expansionism and international arbitration of minor disputes. Thus, the country added contiguous territory – except for Alaska, the Philippines, Puerto Rico, Guam, and Hawaii – through treaties or wars with Native American Indians and foreign countries, starting with the Louisiana Purchase in 1803, reaching new heights at the end of the Spanish-American War in 1898, and dwindling to such isolated acquisitions as the Panama Canal Zone in 1904, the Virgin Islands in 1916, and several small islands after each world war.

This propensity for territorial expansionism in the nineteenth and early twentieth centuries would have been unthinkable without American economic expansionism. There have been four historic sea changes in American economic history. As just noted, the first occurred in the U.S. economy gradually up to the 1890s as the nation industrialized. The second took place dramatically after World War I as it became a creditor nation for the first time. The third came after World War II as the United States reconstructed the economies of Europe and Japan. Finally, at the end of the Cold War the country became the wealthiest nation in world history. These economic sea changes have typically been accompanied by periods of national identity crisis and changes in the domestic culture and political economy (the 1890s, 1920s, 1950s, and 1990s). America's last identity crisis began in the early 1990s, temporarily receded with the return of prosperity in 1996, was resurrected by the September 11 terrorist attacks, seemed to disappear with the patriotism prompted by those events, only to return when Iraq did not turn out to be another "splendid little" Gulf War.

Most of these dramatic changes in the political economy of the United States corresponded to enormous global capital movements beginning in the late nineteenth century that constituted primitive forms of globalization that antedate the first formal use of the word in 1983. All previous rapid capital transfers have been associated with revolutions in technology and transportation such as railroads, telegraph and telephone, and air travel. All these early technological innovations changed the speed of commerce at least as dramatically as faxes, satellite communications, and computers have today. These first waves of globalization (that is, massive capital movements) arose when mature economies (for their time periods) found that their domestic enterprises were yielding lower profits and that there weren't enough investments at home for all their surplus venture capital. The unending capitalist problem remains how to produce higher returns with accumulating funds. Beginning in the 1980s, the answer was unregulated and careening global capital flows, deregulation, and privatization that sometimes produced disastrous results.[24]

Each wave of technological change and subsequent increase in the speed of capital movements was also accompanied by official statements that such rapid transfers of capital would benefit everybody and peacefully unify the world. And, indeed, each wave did make people around the world more aware of and dependent upon one another. But each wave also ebbed after it peaked, and the international economy sometimes contracted painfully, as with the Great Depression and the collapse of the Pacific Rim "tiger" economies in the 1990s.[25]

In retrospect it can be seen that the four sea changes in the American economy were related to these periods of increasingly rapid global capital transfers and contributed to domestic identity crises. It is also possible to understand how different stages in the economic development of the United States have affected the implementation of its nineteenth-century-based foreign policy principles in the twentieth century. Beginning as a small, indebted, commercial and agricultural nation following the American Revolution, the country became a major industrial nation by the late nineteenth century with the aid of considerable foreign investment, and finally a major international creditor nation following the First World War. In the last two centuries the United States continuously adapted its foreign policy goals and doctrines as its economic, political, and military power evolved. The Cold War marked the third major adaptation of American diplomacy when in late 1940s the USSR and the United States squared off in a bipolar conflict. This occurred when America was at the height of its economic power in the world because World War II had devastated the economies of England, Europe, Japan, and the Soviet Union. The United States is now in the process of adapting its foreign policy to meet the economic and military demands of a drastically altered post–Cold War world in which terrorism has replaced the demons of Nazism, Fascism, and Communism.

Presidential Leadership and Power

These changes in the economic position of the United States had an impact not only on U.S. foreign policy, but also on U.S. presidents as they conducted American diplomacy and initiated or inherited or interpreted early foreign policy principles and exercised various kinds of executive leadership. There have been three major types of presidencies since George Washington's: the premodern presidents (from Washington through Calvin Coolidge), the modern presidents (including the transitional administration of Herbert Hoover) through Ronald Reagan, and the transition to postmodern or imponderable presidents beginning with the George H. W. Bush, which came into full bloom under Bill Clinton and is being continued by George W. Bush. Most simply put, traditional or premodern presidents were – with a few notable exceptions – more subject to the will of Congress in both foreign and domestic policies than either modern or postmodern presidents. However, those few exceptions to this rule of the weak executive envisioned by the Founders have given the premodern presidency a mercurial – one might say even a whimsical – reputation.

For every two or three passive or ineffectual presidents of the late eighteenth, nineteenth, and early twentieth centuries there were those who took dramatic actions, beginning with George Washington, who, as the first president, set a precedent with practically everything he did. With the simple words of his 1793 Proclamation of Neutrality, Washington bequeathed to U.S. foreign policy an over-a-century-long doctrine of neutrality. This would be the first of many presidential doctrines, most of which were proclaimed in the twentieth century, and all of which assumed lives of their own. This meant that they usually outlived the purpose for which they had originally been issued. This has proven particularly true of Cold War doctrines, discussed later.

Then three years later, in his 1796 Farewell Address, Washington not only denounced political parties but also told the country "to steer clear of permanent Alliances." Scholars have long since discounted his antiparty views; yet they have given mythological status to his anti–political alliance advice. With respect to this point, however, he went to great lengths in this address to distinguish "political connection[s]" with European nations from "extending our commercial relations" with them. Washington's promotion of commercial intercourse abroad is often forgotten or confounded with his warning against permanent political alliances. Also forgotten is Washington's admonition to the nation to "avoid the necessity of those overgrown military establishments which, under any form of government, are inauspicious to liberty."

Washington's notable statements in 1793 and 1796 perfectly reflected the vulnerable position that the newly created United States occupied in the world. For most of the nineteenth century it was an emerging developing nation whose economic and military weakness did not allow it to play an important role in international affairs. So it was not surprising that Thomas Jefferson underscored Washington's Farewell Address at his own inauguration in 1801 when he said he wanted "peace, commerce, and honest friendship with all nations, [but] "entangling alliances with none." The political isolationism combined with economic expansionism recommended by both Washington and Jefferson was pragmatic advice of the highest order and served the country well until its economic strength finally turned it into a major nation in the early twentieth century and undermined its commitment to political isolationism.

Presidents following Washington from time to time also exercised unilateral executive authority in the realm of foreign policy, as can be seen with Jefferson's purchase of Louisiana and his decision to take action against the Barbary pirates. Strong presidential leadership or, in the case of the 1823 Monroe Doctrine, an aggressive secretary of state was also evident in Jackson's killing of the Bank of the United States and forced dispossession of the Cherokees; in Polk's manipulating the country into a war against Mexico; in Lincoln's forcefully independent and suspiciously extra-constitutional actions on behalf of preserving the Union; in McKinley's decision to retain some of the former Spanish colonies for the United States after the Spanish-American War; in Theodore Roosevelt's "taking of the Panama [isthmus]" from Columbia; and finally, of course, in Wilson's unprecedented personal efforts to bring the United States into the League of Nations.

Looking back at these dramatic individual assertions of unilateral executive power on the part of premodern presidents from the 1790s through the 1920s, it can be argued that they amount to an idiosyncratic assortment of actions even though most of them are associated with territorial or economic expansionism. I use the term "mercurial" to describe the premodern presidency as far as the country's diplomacy is concerned because these examples of dramatic, forceful presidential behavior, whether in domestic or foreign matters, were the exception rather than the rule. By and large, therefore, "Congress remained the main engine of national policy-making" throughout the nineteenth century, even though several presidents began to manipulate the commander-in-chief clause of Article II, section 2 of the U.S. Constitution to claim more power for themselves.[26] Consequently, many of the nineteenth-century principles of U.S. foreign policy that came to characterize American diplomacy in the twentieth century came out of Congress or from political parties in the nineteenth century – not out of the office of the president or the executive branch of government.

Nonetheless, the executive branch diplomatic assertiveness in the name of economic, racial, ethnic, and cultural superiority that characterized the presidencies of James K. Polk, William McKinley, Theodore Roosevelt, William Howard Taft, and Woodrow Wilson cannot be ignored. For purposes of this book, the roles of Roosevelt and Wilson are singularly important. For example, in gendered, macho language, TR confirmed this denial of self-determination to the Western Hemisphere when he proclaimed in his famous 1904 Corollary to the Monroe Doctrine:

Chronic wrongdoing, or an impotence which results in a general loosening of the ties of civilized society, may in America, as elsewhere, ultimately require intervention by some civilized nation, and in the Western Hemisphere the adherence of the United States to the Monroe Doctrine may force the United States, however reluctantly, in flagrant cases of such wrong doing or impotence, to the exercise of an international police power.

Although Roosevelt denied any aggrandizing intent on the part of the United States, for the bulk of twentieth century his corollary became the basis for arbitrary American intervention in Latin America. Roosevelt's Corollary ultimately transformed the Monroe Doctrine from one of nonintervention by European powers to one of aggressive intervention by the United States in the Caribbean and Central America. Despite a few attempts in the 1920s and 1930s to distance U.S. policy from this corollary, Roosevelt, according to Walter LaFeber, "inverted" the Monroe Doctrine and in so doing initiated one of the first significant increases in presidential power in the twentieth century. "In 1823 it [the Monroe Doctrine] had been created to protect Latin American revolutionaries against foreign intervention; in 1905, he redefined it to protect U.S. interventionism against Latin American revolutionaries." The "inversion" created by the Roosevelt Corollary to the Monroe Doctrine gave the green light to a century of U.S. intervention in the affairs of the Southern Hemisphere, and it anticipated the assertion of American muscle in other parts of the world as well.[27]

In fact, until the Cold War, the first two decades of the twentieth century marked the most willful exercise of U.S. power outside its own boundaries. For example, U.S. Marines raided Caribbean nations twenty times between 1898 and 1920. Under several different presidents America ruthlessly subdued Filipinos, mercilessly put down the nationalist, black pride *Noirisme* movement in Haiti, intervened repeatedly in Cuba, and tried to bluff its way into the Far Eastern spheres of influence of major world powers with Secretary of State John

Hay's "Open Door Notes." At the same time, the country simultaneously began to practice a Closed Door policy whenever it could in the Western Hemisphere.

Given the weakness of the United States as an international power in 1823 it could not enforce any of the principles of the Monroe Doctrine, but, by making a unilateral statement, American leaders reserved for themselves the sole right to determine which principles would be implemented in accordance with perceived national interests. In this sense, the doctrine can be seen to have been a realistically limited unilateral assertion of U.S. power as the country gradually emerged as a major force in world affairs, *until* the presidency of Theodore Roosevelt. He not only conspired to aid Panama in seceding from Columbia but then encouraged the Panamanian junta to overthrow the government that resisted granting American rule over a strip of land for the Panama canal. In this sense Roosevelt did later rightfully boast in 1911 that he "took the Canal Zone." However, he usually acted with a show or threat of U.S. force, and, in general, he took less direct military ground action against Caribbean and Central American nations than his predecessor, preferring, even in the Philippines, to negotiate assertions of U.S. power and domination, although his language remained excessively racist, referring to Columbians as "Dagos," bandits, and jackrabbits, and to Filipinos, especially the darker-skinned ones, as "Tagal" or "Malay" bandits or "Chinese half-breed." He also negatively compared Filipinos to the Sioux, Comanche, and Apache Indians. Outside of his rhetorical and threatened military action in the Caribbean and Central America, he thought the rest of Latin America could be controlled through a combination of Open and Closed Door economic pursuits. His successor, William Howard Taft, systematically added an enterprising dollar diplomacy component to all of U.S. foreign policy, including the Monroe Doctrine.[28]

Taft probably had a more sophisticated awareness of the global implications of American economic power before 1920 than either Roosevelt or Wilson. In fact, he could be considered ahead of his time in terms of crafting U.S. economic foreign policy. He not only used military force in the Caribbean, Mexico, and Asia but also fostered American corporate and commercial expansion abroad as no other president had. In anticipation of a North American continental market, he negotiated a reciprocity treaty with Canada and envisioned an even greater share of the market for the United States. Finally, he shocked many when he said that "matters of national honor" should be arbitrated as should property matters and proceeded to negotiate treaties to settle disputes through arbitration rather than the use of force.[29] In this manner, Taft bolstered international cooperation as one of the basic principles of U.S. foreign policy established by 1900. Enter Woodrow Wilson.

Wilson and Intervention into Latin America

Despite initially implying that his would be a kinder, gentler Latin American foreign policy, Wilson implemented the enhanced Monroe Doctrine with primarily a moralistic military vengeance once he assumed office in 1913. While seemingly rejecting the most blatant aspects of Taft's government support for big business abroad, Wilson resorted instead to more military interventions in foreign countries without declarations of war, often for economic reasons, than any president in the twentieth century until William Jefferson Clinton. Long before intervening in the Russian civil war following the Bolshevik Revolution during World War I, he employed the marines and/or warships against Mexico, Haiti, the Dominican Republic, and Nicaragua. All of these Central American incursions clearly placed Wilson in line with the Roosevelt Corollary. He even compared his military action against Haiti in 1915, albeit in a not-altogether-approving tone, to that of TR in Panama in 1904, saying: "we are in danger of going a course not unlike that which Roosevelt followed on the isthmus." Of all these Wilsonian interventions, perhaps the one in Haiti is most iconic, although Nicaragua is a close second because of the overt guerrilla war U.S. Marines conducted against the Sandinistas in the late 1920s and early 1930s and the covert U.S. aid to the contras against the Sandinistas during the Iran/Contra affair under President Ronald Reagan in the 1980s.[30]

Not only was Haiti brutally occupied by U.S. forces from 1915 to 1934, the United States also supported military dictators there until the election of Jean-Bertrand Aristide in 1990. Subsequently, as discussed later, the United States used force to restore Aristide to power in 1994 and then summarily removed him from office in 2004, leaving the nation in probably the worst shape in its entire history – suffering from AIDS, flooding, general governmental incompetence, and gang killings. Of all the American interventions into the Caribbean, those in Haiti remain singular, if for no other reason than that Haiti was not listed in 1823 with other countries coming under the jurisdiction of the Monroe Doctrine. Yet that exclusion has not prevented the United States from treating it as an unruly stepchild deserving periodic paternalistic discipline throughout the twentieth century and into the twenty-first.[31]

Despite the fact that Wilson ultimately supported both dollar diplomacy and military intervention in Central America, he started his presidency thinking that his foreign policy would be a departure from Taft's concessions to big business and Roosevelt's big stick. Apparently oblivious of the fact that by 1913 Latin America consumed $135 million in U.S. manufactured goods and was the recipient of almost half of all U.S. foreign investments, Wilson announced that his policy in that area of the world would not be economic in nature. Instead, it would be the harbinger of an era of "human liberty and national opportunity" because the "real relationship [of the United States] with the rest of America is ... of a family of mankind devoted to the development of true constitutional liberty."[32]

In actuality, Wilson's moral and egalitarian approach to Central and South America was always tinged with authoritarian paternalism (or what he once supported in his scholarly writings, "paternalistic imperialism"), often disguised with metaphors about the universalism of democracy, capitalism, and constitutionalism. Within a week of occupying the Oval Office, for example, in a press announcement he specifically gave Latin American nations notice that he would cooperate with them "only when [they] supported at every turn [the] orderly processes of just government based on law, not upon arbitrary or irregular force." He stated that he would not tolerate "agitators in certain countries [who] wanted revolutions." In a word, he would do everything he could to prevent revolutions – a sentiment he harbored long before the Bolsheviks presented him with a real one. So when he insisted that Americans were compelled by an "obligation of honour . . . to constitute ourselves the champions of constitutional government and of the integrity and independence of free states throughout America, North and South," he nonetheless meant that the people of northern Latin America needed benevolent, fatherly guidance and discipline because, unlike Americans, they lacked the "fine lineage" of Anglo-Saxons and, therefore, were in a state of political and economic infancy. As such, they, like African Americans, were "wards" who needed the tutelage of the U.S. government to progress and prove they had mastered the finer points of democracy and capitalism. Wilson's words marked the beginning of over a century of America's paradoxical and sporadic attempts at "dictating democracy, of enforcing freedom, [and] of extorting emancipation" in the name of world peace and free trade.[33]

The Roots of Wilson's Views

It is often said that Wilson's views on race and the rights of minorities came from his southern background. However, he actually came from a Midwestern, Presbyterian family, portions of which migrated between Pennsylvania and Ohio after arriving in America in 1807. His minister father, Joseph Ruggles Wilson, received his seminary training in Allegheny, Pennsylvania, and Princeton, New Jersey. He taught for a few years in Steubenville, Pennsylvania, until finally being called to his first pastorate in Staunton, Virginia, in 1855, where Wilson was born the next year on December 28. As president, he always identified himself as a Virginian, even though from the age of two to fourteen he lived in Georgia because his family had moved to Augusta early in 1858. Then in 1870 they moved to Columbia, South Carolina, staying there until 1874, when they moved Wilmington, Virginia. A year before, at the age of seventeen, Wilson had left home to attend Davidson College in North Carolina. Although the family accommodated itself to the Confederacy, his father, in particular, appears to have remained an unreconstructed and fairly liberal Midwestern minister who did not hold strict Calvinist beliefs about predestination, but rather adhered to the strain of Presbyterianism stemming from the Scotch Enlightenment and based on the humanism of Adam Smith and David Hume, which stressed that even the Presbyterian elect had to "show signs of that saved state in this world." In all probability this meant that Wilson's father never assumed the parochial values of the slave-owning, landed aristocracy. Nonetheless, in

1861 Joseph Ruggles Wilson called for the meeting of southern presbyteries that resulted in the establishment of the North and South branches of the church. Yet after the Civil War he likely would have agreed with his son when, as a law student at the University of Virginia, Wilson stated in a public lecture in 1880 that "because I love the South I rejoice in the failure of the Confederacy." By this he meant that independence would have relegated the Confederacy to an inferior relationship with the industrial, resource-rich Union. At the same time he thought blacks too inferior a race for political leadership, and told his parents that he supported the Democrat Samuel V. Tilden, who had opposed radical reconstruction of the South by Republicans in the contested 1876 presidential election.[34]

While there is little evidence that Wilson and his father ever embraced southern romanticism about its slave past or that they were typical orthodox southerners, it is significant that both father and son seem to have believed that the Bible sanctioned slavery.[35] This belief more than anything else may have undergirded Wilson's later manifestations of racism and his related disregard for minority rights before the First World War. It should be remembered that at this time most people made racist assumptions based on nationality and ethnicity, in addition to color. So minority rights and racial rights were often equated and rejected.

Born in 1855 in Virginia, Wilson remembered little of the Civil War during which the family lived in Augusta, Georgia. His formative years in the 1860s and 1870s look unimpressive if one were searching for a future southern president of the United States. Diffident and seemingly lazy as a young boy, by his own admission Wilson was a dreamer. He later recalled to a friend in 1911: "I lived a dream life (almost too exclusively, perhaps) when I was a lad and even now my thought goes back for refreshment to those days when all the world seemed to me to be a place of heroic adventure, in which one's heart must keep its own counsel." More to the point, he apparently suffered from dyslexia, not reading until he was nine and not writing until he was eleven. This "neurological handicap," more than anything else, explains the dream world into which he lapsed for much of his young adulthood and the fact that his mother and sisters became overly protective of him, especially with regard to his demanding father's demonstrable disappointment over his first son's slow educational progress. Dyslexia would not be the last of Wilson's neurological problems. He suffered from cerebral vascular disease starting in 1896, when his first stroke left him with a weak right hand. In 1906, another stroke weakened his right arm and almost blinded his right eye. Continuing carotid artery disease resulted in a final massive stroke in 1919 that incapacitated him as president and until his death in 1924. From childhood he suffered from debilitating headaches, stomach problems, and bouts of depression, particularly when under stress. Generally speaking, it seems fair to say that Wilson was a sickly, bespectacled child and a less-than-healthy young man and later mature adult – a fact that would ultimately affect his ability to obtain U.S. entrance into the League of Nations.[36]

Wilson's Views before World War I

Wilson's paternalistically condescending attitude toward non-Anglo-Saxon peoples did not originate with his presidency. It can also be found in his textbooks and in other writings going back before the turn of the century. Before becoming president, Wilson wrote political science and American history works that also contained racist and anti-immigrant observations. For example, in essays in the 1880s and 1890s and in his five-volume *History of the American People* he referred to the "partial corruption of foreign blood" by a "miscellaneous immigration" that contributed to "social chaos," and to blacks as "children" and "ignorant negroes" who did not deserve the franchise. He thought that the Ku Klux Klan was a group whose purpose it was "to protect the southern country from some of the ugliest hazards of a time of revolution."[37]

In his very first 1885 book, *Constitutional Government*, Wilson also indicated that not all peoples were ready for self-government until they had demonstrated "the long discipline which gives a people self-possession, self-mastery, the habit of order and peace and common counsel, and a reverence for law which will not fail when they themselves become the makers of the law: the steadiness and self-control of political maturity." And in 1908 he declared that self-government could not be "'given' to any people because it is a form of character and not a form of constitution."[38]

There is much in Wilson's upbringing and pre–World War I views that explains his paternalistic and racist diplomacy. As the first southern president since the Civil War, Wilson was also the first to initiate and enforce segregation in the federal government. However, he did not do this without being challenged in a petition signed by 20,000 "Afro-Americans in thirty-eight states." Twice, in 1913 and 1914, William Monroe Trotter, who had voted for Wilson in the 1912 election, led a delegation to protest this discriminatory treatment of blacks by the president. And twice Wilson replied in condescending racist language. First he maintained that he had ordered the segregation of African American employees in order to prevent "any kind of friction" and to avoid making "them" feel "uncomfortable." When Trotter insisted that segregation implied inequality and that blacks should not be treated as "wards," Wilson agreed with the implication of inequality (ignoring the question of whether blacks were wards) but then tried to rationalize his position with paternalistic religiosity: "It is not a question of intrinsic equality because we all have human souls. We are absolutely equal in that respect. It is just at the present a question of economic equality – whether the Negro can do the same things with equal efficiency. Now I think they are proving that they can. After they have proved it, a lot of things are going to solve themselves." Throughout these two encounters, Wilson distinguished between "the American people" and the "Negro race" and made it clear that despite the "advancement of the Negro race in America," blacks still fell far behind Anglo-Saxon standards in terms of political and economic development. Therefore, they were not yet deserving of self-determination within the United States. Hence, segregation was "the best way to help the Negro...[because it would begin] to relieve him of his dependence upon the white element of our population."[39]

Wilson's paternalism on race extended to matters of gender and even to economics. The first was rooted in white superiority, the second in white male superiority, and the third in white capitalism. All three could be (and were) defended in the first two decades of the twentieth century in the name of the rule of law. Assertions about the rule of law in domestic, but especially in foreign, affairs always carry with them an aura of nationalistic superiority whereby lawbreakers are made to feel inferior for not recognizing the putative universality of the dominant set of rules and regulations. This type of superiority is often tinged with both racism and sexism and always couched in moralistic terms. At the same time, it should be noted that wherever the United States has sent troops – for example, in Haiti and Philippines – it also has made many material improvements by building hospitals, road, barracks, bridges, and government buildings, and by upgrading communication systems, not only out of a humanitarian sense of its superiority, but also to increase the efficiency of its occupation. This is a lesson that TR and Taft had learned in the Philippines because military repression had proven so costly in terms of money and American and Filipino lives. In the end, until the United States granted it independence after World War II the Philippines "had to accept American sovereignty [as]...another name for [its] liberty." As historian David Healy has noted, since at least 1898 the United States had acted like a thinly veiled racist, "imperialist thug" as it pursued self-interested hegemony – all the while hiding behind the rhetoric of disinterested, fatherly benevolence.[40]

As president, Wilson vacillated over whether to impose capitalism through the paternalistic rule of law and/or military intervention. Thus, he asserted right after his inauguration in 1913 that the U.S. government would follow "orderly processes of just government, based on law, not upon arbitrary or irregular force" on behalf of economic interests. This would appear to contradict what he said while campaigning for the presidency in 1912: "If prosperity is not to be checked in this country we must broaden our borders and make conquest of the markets of the world." Furthermore, as the result of one of Wilson's first pieces of reform legislation, the 1913 Federal Reserve Act, U.S. banks could establish foreign branches, and most went into Latin America. Little wonder, therefore, that once the situation in Haiti deteriorated to the point where Wilson came to believe that France and Germany, especially the latter, were colluding with the revolutionaries and threatening American control of the National Bank of Haiti and other American business interests, he decided that the "United States cannot consent to stand by and permit revolutionary conditions to exist there." In this manner, the rule of law succumbed to economic expediency as the president admitted to his secretary of state, Robert Lansing, before authorizing sending Marines to Haiti in August 1915: "I fear we have not the legal authority to do what we apparently ought to do.... I suppose there is nothing for it but to take the bull by the horns and restore order." Like other American presidents between 1900 and 1917, Wilson brooked no other economic model, particularly in less-developed countries of color, than the superior white capitalist one.[41] It did not take the Russian revolution to convince the United States of the universal superiority of its economic system and, as it would turn out, of its political system as well.

Most importantly, to this already-volatile mix of the white man's paternalistic racism and capitalism Wilson added a virtuous insistence on democracy as another worldwide goal of American foreign policy. Democracy had not been one of the original principles of U.S. diplomacy as of 1900. It was Wilson who, before the United States entered the First World War, sent American troops into Mexico in order to "teach the South American republics to elect good men," and who, of course, coined the renowned description of that war as one that would make the world "safe for democracy." While Cold War presidents often took a similar stand with respect to Third World nations after World War II, George W. Bush best exemplified Wilson's arrogance and moral self-righteousness in June 2002 when he told the Palestinians they needed to hold new elections but had better not return Yassir Arafat to power, and when he insisted in 2003 that the invasions of Afghanistan and Iraq would produce democracy not only in these countries, but throughout the Middle East.[42]

Wilson Does an About-Face

There is little, therefore, in Woodrow Wilson's family background, upbringing, or education that would have foreshadowed his about-face on foreign policy in the course of the First World War. What, then, prompted his conversion to, and revitalization of, the foreign policy concept of self-determination after the outbreak of war in Europe in 1914? As noted, Wilson had not previously honored this concept at home or in the Caribbean and Central America. The reasons for his diplomatic turnaround, discussed later, were primarily rooted in his simplistic, moralistic response to the unprecedented devastation of World War I and a "theology of politics in which the individual, the church, society and the nations of the world were all properly placed in a progressive global order." This is not surprising given the fact that Wilson also practiced a reformed brand of Presbyterianism imbued with the Social Gospel of the late nineteenth century. This meant that he had previously "used the language of traditional morality to advance progressive political reform...[and] he trust[ed] in the promise of redemption in politics, especially foreign policy...based on modern social science."[43]

Having taken such strong actions based on racism and an enhanced version of the Monroe Doctrine to impose democracy and capitalism by force in Mexico and Central America, with the outbreak of war in Europe in 1914 Wilson suddenly realized that if the United States entered that conflict it would violate the nonentanglement provision of the Monroe Doctrine. So, under the influence of his confidant Colonel Edward M. House, the president began to try to turn the unilateral Monroe Doctrine into a multilateral Pan-American Pact, even though his unilateral actions in Central America and Mexico had already clashed with House's grandiose plan to bring Argentina, Brazil, and Chile into a treaty that would join them and the United States in a "common and mutual guaranty of territorial integrity and of political independence under republican forms of government." House's views in 1914 may not have been Wilson's, but the president permitted his friend to pursue the idea of a Pan-American Pact that represented "a true regional security system." House's idea also alienated Wilson's first secretary of state, William Jennings Bryan, because he apparently thought that his "cooling-off" treaties had already provided ways to avoid conflict with the ABC nations. Blithely contradicting the military and economic interventions he had already undertaken or was contemplating in the region, Wilson made a point of idealistically asserting in his 1915 annual address to Congress that "the moral is that the states of America are not hostile rivals, but cooperating friends, and that their growing sense of community of interest, alike in matters political and alike in matters economic, is likely to give them a new significance as factors in international affairs and in the political history of the world."[44]

House's ambitious pan-American plan and Wilson's tenuous offer of a multilateral treaty fell by the wayside as he and the president became more and more involved in the relations of the United States with the warring powers in Europe. Chile had not been very enthusiastic about the treaty in any case, but, according to House, "in its general intent the Pan-American Pact [was] the immediate prototype of the Covenant of the League of Nations." And, indeed, Wilson announced in an unexpected speech to the Senate in January 1917 that he wanted to extend the Monroe Doctrine to the entire world by having "the nations with one accord adopt the doctrine of President Monroe as the doctrine of the world" by agreeing that they would not "seek to extend its polity over any other nation or people," and that "every people should be left free to determine its own polity . . . the little along with the great and powerful." Since secret treaties had led to World War I, Wilson belatedly (and in words reminiscent of Thomas Jefferson) urged "all nations henceforth [to] avoid entangling alliances which would draw them into competitions of power."[45]

In this speech Wilson apparently was trying to modify the unilateral nature and unpopularity of the Monroe Doctrine abroad by "purg[ing] all taint of an exclusive United States sphere of influence from the doctrine by transforming it into a universal sphere of influence for democracy and self-determination." Gaddis Smith has called this attempt "an interesting piece of intellectual gymnastics bound to cause confusion," concluding that Wilson succeeded in compromising the limited regional purpose of the original 1823 doctrine by trying to "universalize" it. Of course, he had already contradicted himself by deploying American forces in Mexico and the Caribbean between 1914 and 1917. The resulting confusion about whether the president had actually abandoned his previous interventionist policies was exacerbated when he entered into Faustian bargains with the Allies at the Versailles Peace Conference. He did this to make sure that Article XXI of the Covenant of the League of Nations specifically upheld the validity of the original Monroe Doctrine (and presumably its interventionist corollaries) against international interference. Smith goes so far as to suggest that Article XXI meant that the "authority of the League covered only half the world, the 'Eastern half'"; that is, the League would have no authority over the Western Hemisphere.[46]

Woodrow Wilson thus muddied the regional realism of the Monroe Doctrine by first ruthlessly employing it, then seemingly denying that it had well served American material interests in Latin America, then trying to universalize it, and finally by codifying its interventionist intent in the League Covenant. This confusion and denial about the relationship between self-determination and spheres of influence and the zigzag employment of independent internationalist diplomacy is one of Wilson's major diplomatic legacies. Although he reintroduced self-determination as the basis for national sovereignty during World War I, he ultimately acceded when the Allies took exception to and/or took advantage of this principle in order to satisfy the territorial promises they had made each other in secret pre-war alliances. Their conduct was more in keeping with the president's own earlier violations of self-determination in the Dominican Republic, Haiti, Nicaragua, and Mexico. Wilson even tried to insert into the 1916 treaty with Nicaragua a clause similar to the Platt Amendment denying the independence of Cuba, and his statements about self-government for the Philippines made it clear that it could not be granted until "our work there is done and they are ready." And for the most part, while Congress, the press, and the public on occasion questioned Wilson's tactics, they generally agreed with his goal of establishing peace, stability, and prosperity, especially in the Caribbean region, at the expense of self-determination, national sovereignty, and democracy.[47]

Wilson did not simply conflate realism and idealism with respect to his own application and interpretation of the Monroe Doctrine while president, he bequeathed this conundrum to his successors in the Oval Office. Ultimately, most U.S. presidents after Wilson would sporadically exert "hard" influence over Central American nations in the first half of the twentieth century and both "hard" and "soft" influence over most of South America during the Cold War – all in the name of democratic self-determination. In fact, they were simply shoring up an American Closed Door sphere of influence in the Western Hemisphere[48] – something the country's unselfconscious ideology did not allow it to admit to itself or to the world.

For example, Franklin Roosevelt temporarily moved away from applying the Monroe Doctrine until the outbreak of World War II, and then Eisenhower covertly revived it in Guatemala. Next, the Bay of Pigs fiasco under John Kennedy represented one of the unsuccessful examples of American use of force in keeping with the Monroe Doctrine. Later, Richard Nixon reverted to covert implementation of the doctrine in Chile, and Jimmy Carter declared it dead. Both Ronald Reagan and George H. W. Bush invoked it when employing covert and overt force to interfere in the politics of El Salvador, Guatemala,

Nicaragua, Honduras, Grenada, and Panama. This pattern continued in the post–Cold War era as Bill Clinton relied on the Monroe Doctrine when he tried to restore democracy in Haiti. Finally, George W. Bush appears to have returned to Wilson's attempt to universalize the doctrine – not through multilateral cooperation, but through preemptive unilateral U.S. action.

2

The Faustian Impact of World War I on U.S. Diplomacy

> There can be no question of our ceasing to be a major power. The only question
> is whether we can refuse the moral leadership that is offered us, whether we shall
> accept or reject the confidence of the world.... The stage is set, the destiny is
> disclosed. It has come about by no plan of our conceiving, but by the hand of
> God who led us into this way.... It was of this that we dreamed at our birth.
> America shall in truth show the way.
>
> Woodrow Wilson, presenting the Versailles Peace Treaty
> to the U.S. Senate, July 10, 1919

Although Woodrow Wilson initially urged the country to be "impartial in
thought as well as in action" in 1914, by the time the United States finally
entered the First World War in 1917 he had failed to steer the country on a
neutral course. The country accepted the president's idea that the United States
should remain neutral when war broke out in Europe in 1914. Yet Wilson contradicted himself about what it meant for the United States to practice neutrality.
In doing so, he led the country into that conflict on the highest moral, if unrealistic, grounds and reinforced the Faustian substructure of American diplomacy
that would remain in place for the remainder of the twentieth century and into
the twenty-first.

As early as February 1915 Wilson had embarked on a slanted moralistic
diplomacy by sending a mild note of protest when England declared a war
zone in the North Sea and a "strict accountability" warning to Germany when
it declared a war zone around the British Isles. This political favoritism was
soon followed by economic partiality in the form of loans and arms trade with
the Allied (Entente) powers. It was not surprising that the United States would
side with England because of a similar cultural heritage, because the British
propaganda effort in America was much superior to that of Germany, and
because his closest advisers, Colonel House and Robert Lansing, were strong
Anglophiles. By the time America entered the war in April 1917, it had lent
over $2.5 billion to the Allies and only $27 million to the Central powers. It

can be argued that this reflected the economic self-interest of the United States, which, at the beginning of the war in 1914, was in the midst of a twenty-month depression, but it did not reflect the "impartial neutrality" urged by Wilson's secretary of state, William Jennings Bryan.

By the summer of 1915 Wilson had drastically limited the country's diplomatic options by making American honor and prestige inviolate with a series of notes over the sinking of the British luxury liner the *Lusitania*. He did this by insisting that German submarine warfare violated the questionable right of American citizens to travel on any passenger ship of belligerent nations and therefore was more immoral, and thus less tolerable, than English violations of American commercial rights. "The Government of the United States is contending for something much greater than mere right of property or privileges of commerce," he proclaimed in the second *Lusitania* note, "it is contending for nothing less high and sacred than the rights of humanity." Then in the third note he went further, saying: "The rights of neutrals in time of war are based upon principle, not upon expediency, *and the principles are immutable.*"

With these words Wilson forever transgressed the "impartial neutrality" that Bryan had been advocating, prompting the secretary of state to resign. Once again, as with self-determination, the president reverted to a universal concept that was far from accepted by other nations – especially the warring powers in World War I. But in this case, Wilson backed himself into a non-negotiable position and made U.S. entrance into the war inevitable once Germany announced a return to unrestricted submarine warfare in violation of his "strict accountability" doctrine as elaborated in the three *Lusitania* notes. It would have been one thing for him to accept the maritime system of England and to finance the Allied cause, and still leave himself the option of reverting to armed neutrality against Germany in 1917, but Wilson stubbornly refused to retreat from the myth of universal principles involving American honor and prestige entirely of his own making. World War I simply allowed him to repossess the jeremiad of exceptionalism in order to denounce sin and call for redemption of the world through American leadership. Perhaps the most arrogant and yet poignant justification he gave for his flawed foreign policy when dealing with the war in Europe came in a February 24, 1916, letter to Senator William J. Stone (D-MO):

For my own part, I cannot consent to any abridgement of the rights of American citizens in any respect. The honour and self-respect of the nation is involved. We covet peace, and shall preserve it at any cost but the loss of honour. To forbid our people to exercise their rights for fear we might be called upon to vindicate them would be a deep humiliation indeed. . . . an implicit, all but explicit, acquiescence in the violation of the rights of mankind everywhere. . . . It would be a deliberate abdication of our hitherto proud position as spokesmen even amidst the turmoil of war for the law and the right. . . . Once [we] accept a single abatement of right . . . many other humiliations would certainly follow, and the whole fine fabric of international law might crumble under our hands piece by piece. What we are contending for in this matter is of the very essence of the things that have made America a sovereign nation. She cannot yield them without conceding her own impotency as a nation, and making virtual surrender of her independent position among the nations of the world.[1]

With these words and similar ones that followed, Wilson crossed the line from negotiation to ultimatum – the anathema of diplomacy, except to this most self-righteous of presidents.

While Secretary Lansing clearly supported the dubious universal principles upon which Wilson's unneutral policy was based between 1914 and 1917, it is well known that he never encouraged the president's equally expansive statements on the subject of self-determination. "The more I think about the President's declaration as to the right of 'self-determination,'" he wrote in a confidential memorandum on December 30, 1918, "the more convinced I am of the danger of putting such ideas into the minds of certain races. It is bound to be the basis of impossible demands on the Peace Congress, and create trouble in many lands.... In the end it is bound to be called the dream of an idealist who failed to realize the danger until too late to check those who attempted to put the principle into force." In his postwar memoir Lansing continued to question what the term meant and to fear its implications. "Does he [Wilson] mean a race, a territorial area, or a community? Without a definite unit which is practical, application of this principle is dangerous to peace and stability [because]... fixity of national boundaries and of national alliance, and political stability would disappear if this principle was uniformly applied." Lansing then perspicaciously quoted from his earlier memorandum: "Will it not breed discontent, disorder and rebellion?... The phrase [self-determination] is simply loaded with dynamite. It will raise hopes which can never be realized. It will, I fear, cost thousands of lives.... What a calamity that the phrase was ever uttered! What misery it will cause!"[2]

Wilson's Fourteen Points and Self-Determination

So after violating self-determination for blacks inside the United States and for peoples of color in Mexico and in Caribbean and Central American countries up to 1917, and then intervening in Siberia in 1918, and after refusing to support independence for Ireland, Ukraine, Byelorussia [Belarus], Georgia, Finland, and the Baltic and Caucasia countries, by 1920 Woodrow Wilson had somehow miraculously managed to give the concept of national self-determination international status, first through his Fourteen Points in 1918, and their subsequent elaboration in an additional thirteen points, and then with the League of Nations Covenant.[3] Although his Fourteen Points address did not contain the term "self-determination," points five through thirteen dealt with territorial, sovereignty, and nationality questions. However, in an attempt to keep Russia in the war, point six called for the "evacuation of all Russian territory" and assured the Bolsheviks of the "intelligent and unselfish sympathy" of "her sister nations." Only Poland was specifically given the right to secede from Russia, despite the problems that created for its large German minority population. The special treatment that Poland received in Wilson's Fourteen Points can be traced in large measure to the failed American relief effort for that country – an effort that the president exploited for political purposes among Polish immigrant groups during his reelection campaign in 1916. This is not to underplay the horrible destitution suffered by the Poles during the First World War. It was unusually severe, largely because of the German invasion and English blockade. Consequently, both sides in the war approved of some form of independence for Poland by the end of 1916.[4]

Ironically, Wilson's Fourteen Points violated his principle of self-determination as far as ethnic and national groups within Poland and Russia were concerned. According to Derek Heater, the document was "anything but a wholehearted exposition of the principle of national self-determination." Lenin, Trotsky, and even British Prime Minister Lloyd George had made more definitive pronouncements about self-determination before Wilson did. But it was the president's Fourteen Points that temporarily captured the imagination of Americans and the peacemakers at Versailles, in part because Russia was excluded for having opted out of the war with the Brest-Litovsk Treaty in March 1918 and in part because by the time of the Paris Peace Conference Wilson had resolved not to deal with the Bolsheviks. He thought that they could not possibly succeed in uniting the country because it had already broken up into "at least five parts – Finland, the Baltic provinces, European Russia, Siberia and the Ukraine." Thus, Wilson contradicted the sixth of his original Fourteen Points when he announced during the peace talks that his principle of self-determination should also be applied to Russia to determine "under what sovereignty these various states desire to come."[5]

According to George Kennan, by the end of the war the Soviets were considered nothing more than German puppets who would have used the peace conference for propaganda purposes. Yet Lenin's and Trotsky's strict socialist-driven notions about self-determination might well have produced fewer nationality and ethnic compromises at the peace conference than Wilson's more ambiguous ones had either man been permitted to attend and represent his country at Versailles. After all, in December 1917 Trotsky had taunted France, Italy, Britain, and America by asking when they would apply "the right to the determination of their own destinies" to their colonial holdings as the "Russian Revolution . . . [had] given to the peoples of Finland, Ukrainia, [and] White Russia." This statement must be taken with a grain of salt, since Lenin, at least, viewed national self-determination through the myopic lens of proletarian revolutions. Where these were imminent, self-determination would work in favor of Communism; where they were not, bourgeois self-determination could not be trusted to foster the cause of the a worldwide overthrow of capitalism.[6]

While the Bolsheviks supported self-determination in anticipation of Communist proletariat revolutions in newly emerging nations, Wilson conflated democracy and capitalism (as his successors in the White House would continue to do down to the present), folding them into his concept of self-determination and then embedding that in his Fourteen Points and League of Nations Covenant. Both Communist and capitalist brands of self-determination proved wanting in practical terms when it came to protecting the rights of minorities within national boundaries determined by majority will. Indeed, the Soviet Union quickly violated the principle of self-determination within its own borders, and Wilson's version was corrupted around the world through the League's mandate system, which represented "the principle of national self-determination deferred."[7] Just as Wilson's (and previous presidents') protectorates in the Caribbean had violated the national sovereignty of those nations, so did the mandate system, which, during the interwar years, looked more and more like annexation and old-fashioned colonialism, especially in Africa and Asia.

Obviously, Wilson could not have been expected to understand the potentially ferocious and discriminatory ramifications of self-determination when combined with rampant ethnic nationalism. What is disturbing is that he does not seem to have seriously contemplated any of the theoretical or practical problems his redefinition and reassessment of self-determination entailed, nor did he ever acknowledge the obvious revolutionary implications of self-determination, as Lenin and Trotsky did. To the contrary, he favored achieving self-determination only "slowly through legal processes." One of the few comments he made indicating that his concept of self-determination might have gotten out of hand came toward the end of 1919 in a written statement he sent to Congress: "When I gave utterance to those words [that all nations had a right to self-determination], I said them without the knowledge that nationalities existed, which are coming to us day after day." By that time Wilson's mind was so stroke-disabled there was little he could do to remedy the out-of-control postwar minority claims to nationhood. The genie was out of the bottle, and there was no stopping the ethnic chauvinism of the interwar years. Wilson had not created the "over-exciting feeling of nationality" that World War I set in motion, but as the Italian foreign minister summed it up: "Perhaps America fostered it by putting the principles so clearly."[8]

It must be remembered that there are few events in recorded history that actually have caused ruptures in the much-touted seamless chronological web of humankind. The First World War is usually cited as one of these singular historical events. It has been referred to as the "irredeemably stupid fatality that governed so much of the twentieth [century]," and as "nothing less than the greatest error in modern history." That catastrophe, which began in August 1914, marked the end of the "Concert of Europe" alliance system and the downfall of four empires: the Habsburg, Hohenzollern, Romanov, and Ottoman. The outbreak and outcome of this first global war set in motion "mass violence on a scale that dwarfs all previous centuries."[9]

Another aspect of the historical fissure represented by World War I was the "seismic shift in the definition of self-determination," which, ironically, contributed to the most murderous aspects of the rest of the twentieth century

by encouraging ethnic, religious, tribal, and refugee strife. As the century pro-
gressed, improvements in mass communications disseminated barbaric scenes
to the world at an increasingly rapid pace until they are now available twenty-
four hours a day, further undermining ethical standards by inuring people to
violence.[10] Wilson could not have anticipated the barbarism set in motion by
World War I as he took the United States into it with great optimism and
naivete to "make the world safe for democracy," placing undue confidence in
the positive nature of self-determination and American exceptionalism.

Wilson at Versailles

For a variety of reasons, therefore, Wilson set a precedent at the Paris Peace
Conference for how *not* to end a war – an unfortunate one that would be
followed by FDR (at Yalta) and Eisenhower (Korea) and Nixon (Vietnam)
and Bush, Sr. (the first Gulf War), Clinton (Bosnia and Kosovo), and Bush, Jr.
(Iraq).[11] In Wilson's case, he simply proved not as interested in the details of
terminating the First World War as he was in those that pertained to abstract
principles about how the peace should be structured to prevent future wars.

For example, in January 1918, in a private conversation with his close
friend and adviser Colonel Edward M. House, he said he had decided that
general terms of the peace should take precedence over specific territorial
adjustments. Despite his numerous moralistic public pronouncements about
self-determination and the fact that his famous Fourteen Points, which House
had helped him draft, addressed some very specific territorial issues, at Versailles
Wilson relegated them to secondary status. Instead, he subordinated the idea
of honoring new nations based on self-determination to global peace because
he believed that the world was on "the eve of a great consummation" and that
he, as one of the Presbyterian elect, was uniquely positioned to bring it about
through the Covenant of the League of Nations. (He had written about a world
federation as early as 1887.) While "only the elect could be saved for eternity,
he thought it his Christian duty to save the world temporally."[12] Ironically, this
theological version of international politics led him to slip into Faustian bargains at Versailles that belied his much-publicized conversion to, and conviction
about, peoples' right to choose how and where they should be governed.

At no point at the Paris Peace Conference did Wilson focus on the specific
national conflicts of interests represented by the secret pre-war treaties and how
the break-up of the Ottoman, Russian, and Austro-Hungarian empires could
be practically resolved without sowing more seeds of minority and majority
discord within newly created or reshaped nations. It is worth noting that there
were three waves of state fragmentation in the twentieth century: the first after
World War I, the second after World War II, and the third at the end of the
Cold War. All involved the thorny question of minority rights.

Not only were national minority questions beyond solution when put in the
hands of experts in 1919 because of the ethnic heterogeneity of Central and

Eastern Europe, the adoption of Wilson's vague principle of self-determination into the Versailles peace settlement proved its Achilles heel because it was never applied to Germany even though thousands of Germans did not live within the Reich at the end of the war. Had self-determination actually been applied evenhandedly, Germany would have gained territory after being defeated instead of losing 13 percent of its territory and 10 percent of its population. Thus, the large numbers of Germans living in Austria and Poland, in particular, were denied the self-determination granted to other national groups, and hundreds of thousands of Turks, Greeks, and Germans were involuntarily "repatriated" in the first half of the 1920s.[13]

To compound matters, the most disputed clause in the Treaty of Versailles, requiring that Germany pay not only indemnity for damages but also reparations, was rationalized in the name of Wilson's Fourteen Points. The president assigned John Foster Dulles to draft what became Article 231, which placed responsibility for the war on Germany and which the Germans immediately dubbed the "war guilt clause." At the time Dulles thought he had come up with a compromise satisfying British and French demands for reparations, while protecting Germany from unlimited payments with Article 232. The treaties with Austria and Hungary contained similar clauses, but only in Germany did they exacerbate postwar German nationalism and that country's sense of being mistreated by the international community in the 1920s and 1930s. Germans came to believe that they had been betrayed by Wilson, in whom they had placed hope for terms less severe than those in the 1919 armistice agreement.[14]

Wilson as Armenia's Only Hope

Wilson's most personal and detailed participation in the Versailles territorial adjustment process came with his agreement to determine the boundaries of the newly established and vulnerable state of Armenia. Armenians had not figured in international diplomacy until the 1878 Treaty of Berlin ending the Russian-Turkish War. As a result, Serbia, Rumania, and Montenegro became independent of Turkey and Bulgaria became autonomous, but the previous Russian guarantee of reforms in Armenian areas was withdrawn when this territory was returned to Turkish control, ostensibly under British supervision. This set the stage for the Turks to take out their imperial frustrations against the Armenians, whose nationalism had grown by this time and who assumed they would be protected by the Treaty of Berlin.[15]

The result was the 1894–96 Armenian massacre, in which 300,000 perished even though the Armenian revolutionaries asked Europe to honor the Treaty of Berlin and intervene. Then, in 1908, after the Young Turks (Ittihadists) overthrew Sultan Abdul Hamit[d] and reintroduced the 1876 Constitution, things momentarily looked hopeful for the Armenian nationalists, who temporarily supported the Young Turks – not realizing that their two nationalisms were incompatible. The Young Turk government degenerated into dictatorship and killed another 30,000 Armenians. By 1914 there had been no European intervention, but because of repeated protests the Young Turks agreed to a reform plan under which the European inspector generals and a European police force would supervise six semiautonomous Armenian provinces. The outbreak of World War I voided this scheme, and by the end of that conflict the Young Turks had put to death 1.5 million Armenians (one in three of this ethnic group) through executions, forced deportation marches, torture, and starvation.[16]

Although in a May 24, 1915, joint declaration the Allies condemned the Armenian genocide as it began, they sadly repeated the past and refused to intervene either to prevent the killings or even to prosecute and punish the Turkish leaders responsible for them. Ironically, the 1915 joint declaration remains historically important because it originated the phrase "crimes... against humanity and civilization." As a result of previous Armenian massacres and out of guilt for not intervening during the genocide of 1915–18, the Allies proclaimed the creation of the Armenian Republic on May 28, 1918. The state existed for two years before it was absorbed by both Turkey and Russia.

As early as December 1917 several of the president's informal advisers recommended that Armenia become autonomous not simply because of Turkish "oppression and misrule," but also to prevent Germany from obtaining a direct economic route from Constantinople to China after the war. There is no indication that Wilson read the American policy paper until the beginning of 1918. However, after Lord Robert Cecil supported this economic argument in a December 1917 confidential memorandum to Wilson, the president approvingly passed it on to Secretary of State Robert Lansing. In 1919, a famine broke out among Armenians who had survived the genocide of 1915–18, and this highlighted the need to take action that was both humanitarian and anti-Bolshevik. Wilson apparently became convinced that "force cannot stop it [communism] but food can!" Documents from this period make it clear that, among certain American advisers and the British, economic and ideological considerations ranked as high as humanitarian ones for establishing an anticommunist Armenian nation.[17] Wilson, however, did not appear to place economics as high as human rights when thinking about the creation of an independent Armenian state, although by 1919 the fear of Bolshevism gave the president an additional reason to favor it.

The president first expressed personal concern over the plight of the Armenians when the British in August 1919 proposed withdrawing their troops near the borders of the new state for which they had acted as protectors. Writing on August 12 to Senator John Sharp Williams (D-MS), a strong Armenian supporter, Wilson said that the outrages against them were

more terrible, I believe, than history ever before witnessed, so heartbreaking indeed that I have found it impossible to hold my spirits steady enough to read accounts of them. I wish with all my heart that Congress and the county could assent to our assuming the trusteeship for Armenia and going to the help of those suffering people in an effective way.

Yet a few days later he wrote in another private letter that

it is manifestly impossible for us, at any rate in the present temper of the Congress, to send American troops there, much as I should like to do so, and I am making every effort, both at London and at Paris, to induce the British to change their military plans in that quarter [Batum], but I must say the outlook is not hopeful, and we are at our wits' ends what to do.[18]

Since the United States had not, as an "Associated Power" in World War I, declared war against Turkey, it had no standing in the postwar discussions about the disposal of Arab lands. Granted, the twelfth of Wilson's Fourteen Points had promised that "the Turkish portions of the present Ottoman Empire should be assured secure sovereignty, but the other nationalities which are now under Turkish rule should be assured an undoubted security of like and an absolutely unmolested opportunity of autonomous development." Not until years later did it become known that all of the Middle East had been the subject of a secret U.S. government document created as a result of a stalemate among members of the Council of Four at Paris over how to divide portions of the former Ottoman Empire. Once France, Britain, and Italy accepted Wilson's proposal for a neutral inter-Allied commission to talk with local inhabitants in Syria, Palestine, and Turkey, he promptly appointed two Americans – Henry King and Charles Crane. The other three countries did not appoint any delegates, so it became Wilson's Commission of Inquiry into the Middle East, and only King and Crane with nine American technical advisers visited the disputed areas. Wilson also thought that by having King and Crane speak with Palestinians they could mollify Arab hostility toward Zionist plans for a Jewish state. There was much need for mollification because the establishment of a Jewish state where few Jews actually lived violated the normal application of Wilson's "numerical self-determination."[19]

The King–Crane Commission returned a surprisingly even-handed report on August 28, 1919, saying that Palestinian Arabs were "emphatically against the entire Zionist program," and concluding that the Council of Four should recommend that Jewish immigration be limited and that the Jews should give up the idea of a homeland in Palestine. It also recommended mandate rule for all regions in Turkey; a unified Armenian state, with the United States to assume a mandate over the new nation; an international protectorate for Constantinople under the authority of the League of Nations; autonomy for the Smyrna Greeks; and the unification of Mesopotamia under an English mandate. With recommendations such as these, it is not surprising that the King–Crane Commission's report went unheeded at the Paris Peace Conference as France and England proceeded to honor their pre-war agreements on the Middle East. Moreover, the United States kept the King–Crane report a secret until 1922.

In all likelihood, Wilson never read the secret report because he had already returned to the United States, and it officially arrived at the White House in September after his stroke.[20]

After the Senate finally defeated U.S. entrance into the League of Nations on March 19, 1920, Wilson's aides indicated that he would rely on the recommendations of the committee of experts in mediating the boundaries of the new republic. In May, at the urging of then Senator Warren Harding, the Senate unanimously passed an innocuous resolution supporting Armenian independence that referred to the "deplorable conditions of insecurity, starvation, and misery" of that people. Congress also authorized sending a battleship to protect American lives and property at Batum, which by then was a port of Georgia and where the Armenians needed help against Turkish forces.[21]

In response, the White House unexpectedly sent a message asking Congress to follow up this legislation by permitting a U.S. mandate over Armenia. Republican Senators dismissed the president's request out of hand in June, along with several other Democratic mandate resolutions. Still, the Armenian situation remained in limbo until November 20, 1920, when the president of the League Council informed Wilson that it had passed a resolution, not requesting that the United States reconsider accepting a mandate, but rather suggesting that the United States offer its good offices to try to settle the hostilities in Armenia as soon as possible. In light of congressional action back in May and June, Secretary of State Bainbridge Colby nonetheless advised Wilson in no uncertain terms that "unless you exercise your moral authority it would almost seem that there is no way to avert the fate that hangs over Armenia." On November 30, Wilson sent a reply to the League of Nations written by Colby saying in part, "I am without authorization to offer or employ military forces of the United States in any project for the relief of Armenia.... I am willing... to use my good offices and to proffer my personal mediation through a representative whom I may designate to end the hostilities now being waged against the Armenian people." In December, Wilson pleaded in vain with Congress to make a loan to "the struggling Government of Armenia... as was made to several of the Allied Governments during the war." However, he wanted the money supervised by a U.S. commissioner so that it would not further "revolutionary tendencies," reflecting his lingering fear of Communism taking hold in the area. Later that same month, Wilson appointed the former ambassador to Turkey (1914–16), Henry Morgenthau, to discuss the situation with the various parties involved. As ambassador, Morgenthau had been outspokenly pro-Armenian and later pessimistically wrote in his memoirs in 1919 that "I am confident that the whole history of the human race contains no such horrible episode as this. The great massacres and persecutions of the past seem almost insignificant when compared with the sufferings of the Armenian race.... [it is the planned] destruction of a race."[22]

Typically, the president vacillated about whether the United States should send U.S. troops to protect the Armenian Republic and/or assume guardianship over the new nation. The very first action item proposed at the Versailles Peace

Conference was for the United States to assume a mandate for Armenia. While campaigning for the League in the fall of 1919 before his paralyzing stroke, Wilson mentioned the Armenian situation only twice, and in neither statement did he advocate accepting either an American mandate for Armenia or the sending of American troops to protect the new state. In August 1920 Armenia signed the Treaty of Sèvres, which recognized its independence. However, the Turkish nationalists never accepted this treaty because it had been signed by the beleaguered sultan, and so it was never officially ratified. The terms from their point of view were draconian because the treaty stripped Turkey of all its Arab lands, and in keeping with secret arrangements among the Allies it assigned Palestine, Transjordan, and Mesopotamia to Britain and Syria and Lebanon to France. At the first meeting of the League of Nations in the fall of 1920, the Assembly discussed admitting Armenia to membership. Later that same year when Wilson pressed the Senate to support both Armenian independence and a U.S. mandate over the country, it was too little, too late in the face of increased domestic partisan opposition that developed in the protracted national debate over the League of Nations.[23]

Wilson's poor health probably explains most of his ambivalence over Armenia, while political rivalry explains the change in Republican sympathy for the Armenian cause that had originally been led by Theodore Roosevelt and Henry Cabot Lodge. Even had his health held up, it is unlikely that the United States would have shouldered either responsibility for Armenia that the president had suggested. By the time he (or rather his aides) accepted an invitation from the Supreme Council of the League of Nations to arbitrate its boundaries, he had been stricken and could not follow the details the experts ultimately sent him. It is John Milton Cooper's opinion that Wilson should have stepped down as president because he was incapable of carrying out the functions of his office at one of the most crucial times in the history of U.S. foreign policy.[24] In retrospect, Armenia represented one of many, and possibly the most iconic, of the casualties of Wilson's incapacity because its ramifications continue to echo into the twenty-first century.

When the League held its first official meeting in Geneva on November 15, 1920, the disabled president was bitter toward the major powers he had worked with to create the international organization because he now accused them of wanting to use it to guarantee unjust colonial and other settlements and renewed militarism. On November 17 he relayed through his wife, Edith Bolling Galt, that he was not ready to consider the Treaty of Sèvres with Turkey recognizing the independence of Armenia until he was stronger. But within weeks the nationalist Turkish leader Mustafa Kemal (Ataturk) rejected the treaty that the sultan had signed and the Kemalists, and Bolsheviks began dividing up the new nation. When, on November 22, Wilson finally indicated what he thought the boundaries of the new state should be, the Republic of Armenia was only a few weeks away from being partitioned by Turkey and Russia in violation of the Treaty of Sèvres, even though the second and third Assemblies of the League had discussed a national homeland for the Armenians and passed a resolution recommending that this be considered in the negotiations taking place at Lausanne. None of the Great Powers would guarantee with force even the reduced borders for the Armenian state recommended by Wilson.[25]

On July 24, 1923, the Treaty of Lausanne officially replaced the defunct Treaty of Sèvres. It recognized the new nationalist Republic of Turkey without mentioning that there had ever been an Armenian genocide and without establishing rights or a homeland for the Armenians, who, according to the new nationalist Turkish leader Mustafa Kemal (Ataturk), had already been "liquidated;" that is, they had been killed or expelled. In fact, by that time there were fewer than 100,000 Armenians living in Turkey, and there was no clause in the treaty protecting minorities. This treaty only guaranteed protection, not privileges, let alone equality, to three non-Muslim communities – Jewish, Greek Orthodox, and Armenian – who were called "indigenous foreigners." From that point forward, the official position of the Turkish government has been to deny that any genocide took place through the manipulation of documents and the claim that Armenians were killed as traitors during wartime as a military necessity. And for the most part, from that time to the present Western nations have allowed Turkey to make this denial with impunity and to discriminate against other minority groups such as the Alewites and Kurds.[26]

Woodrow Wilson died the following February, and for all intents and purposes official recognition of the first genocide of the twentieth century died with him, only to be revived just before Hitler invaded Poland in 1939 when he told his military commanders: "Who after all, speaks today of the annihilation of the Armenians? ... The world believes in success alone." Although Presidents Theodore Roosevelt, William Howard Taft, Wilson, Warren G. Harding, Herbert Hoover, Jimmy Carter, and even Ronald Reagan all acknowledged the Armenian genocide and said it deserved official public recognition by the United States, none has taken place.[27]

Wilson and Intervention into Russia

While the postwar Armenian situation cried out for humanitarian intervention on behalf of minority rights that did not materialize, the Allied powers did intervene in Russia. In this case Wilson's position on minority rights combined with his fear of Communism abroad because he thought the latter might infect African-Americans and other hyphenate-Americans at home. So his domestic racism and ethnocentrism fed his anti-Communism.[28] For example, in a speech on May 21, 1919, he implied that support of guarantees for national minorities could fragment Europe into nonviolable, discontented ethnic groups, which would at best threaten peace and at worst foment tiny multiple mini-Bolshevik revolutions in Europe. Yet by September 1919, on his western tour to garner support for ratification of the Treaty of Versailles, he told a group in Montana that only the League of Nations could provide an "alternative to Bolshevism that was threatening to spread from Russia across western Europe to the United States." He continued to view Bolshevism as an "infectious poison," and to assert that even the United States was "not immune" to this disease. Additionally, his anti-Bolshevik rhetoric fanned the flames of what was emerging as the first "Red Scare" in the United States. By that time, however, American troops had been deployed in northern Russia and Siberia for over a year and would not be withdrawn until early 1920, in a military action that Wilson pretended was neither anti-Bolshevik nor in violation of the principles of self-determination.[29]

Wilson and his defenders have touted the commitment of American troops to the port cities of Archangel, Murmansk, and Valdivostok as primarily a humanitarian intervention on behalf of the stranded Czech Legion, who just happened to be fighting local Soviet factions in Siberia. In casting about for why he had authorized this invasion he at one point toyed with the idea of explaining it to Congress in terms of preserving an Open Door to the Siberian and Chinese Eastern Railway. However, he never publicly endorsed this argument, even though the British and French pressured him to intervene to counter the threat of Japanese expansion in Siberia. While there is no denying that all foreign troops ended up supporting anti-Bolshevik forces in the Russian civil war, Wilson rationalized his cooperation with the Allied Expeditionary Force in Russia (a military action he had originally opposed) as furthering the moral purposes of both democracy and self-determination. Again, the president's good intentions were outweighed by the actual results and contradicted his original insistence that he did not want to see the former Russian empire dismembered. Why not, since this would have been in keeping with democratic self-determination?[30]

The answer is complicated by the fact that Wilson first excluded Russia from the self-determination clauses of his Fourteen Points address because he wanted to keep the country in the war on the side of the Allies. He also feared that the Allies, particularly France and England, intended to divide Russia into their respective spheres of influence and that Germany had similar designs on Russia's western border. He also hoped that keeping the former Russian empire together would neutralize Japan's expansionist designs in Siberia and Sakhalin. Unfortunately, the Wilson administration's aid to the provisional government in the spring and summer of 1917 was "too little and too late," and in general his policy toward Russia was characteristically unfocused, indecisive, and never clearly articulated or implemented. Finally, as indicated, he had become so fearful of Communism that by the time the Allies convened in Paris he had decided that the Bolsheviks could not (or should not) unite the country.[31]

While historians have long debated the complex reasons for America's reluctant intervention into Siberia and whether it produced positive or negative results, the latest research leaves no doubt about the secret ways in which Wilson implemented earlier actions (many of them economic) against the Bolsheviks by proxy. Granted, Wilson's second and third secretaries of state were probably more aggressively anti-Bolshevik than he was. Nonetheless, he accepted Lansing's unofficial nonrecognition of the Russian Soviet Federated Socialist Republics (the USSR's name until 1922) in a December 4, 1917, memorandum. Later he approved Secretary Bainbridge Colby's August 10, 1920, statement to the Italian ambassador that officially established the nonrecognition policy of the United States.[32]

The "Colby Note" insisted that the American refusal to recognize the revolutionary government "had nothing to do with any political or social structure" that the Russians might adopt in the future. Instead, it reflected the belief that "the existing regime in Russia is based upon the negation of every principle of honor and good faith and every usage and convention underlying the whole structure of international law – the negation, in short, of every principle upon which it is possible to base harmonious and trustful relations." Most significantly, Colby's statement specifically opposed the dismemberment of Russia by reiterating that the United States would not recognize the independence of the "so-called Republics of Georgia and Azerbaijan" because this violated the "territorial integrity and true boundaries . . . of the former Russian empire." So once again the Wilson administration backed away from the president's proclamations on behalf of self-determination. In this instance ideology prevailed over principle, and for the next thirteen years the United States would stand firm against recognizing the Soviet Union. Noteworthy, however, is that the "Colby Note" did not cite economic issues such as nationalization of property in the USSR as a reason for nonrecognition, leaving the "door open for future trade relations without formal recognition" – an opening that some American businessmen would pursue in the 1920s.[33]

With hindsight it is possible to speculate that had the United States strictly applied self-determination during the Russian civil war – that is, recognized the small European portion of Russia then controlled by the Bolsheviks in 1920 – that non-Communist countries might have developed on its shrunken boarders, ultimately depriving the revolutionary leaders of essential valuable resources so important to the development and power of the Soviet Union. But in the end Wilson vacillated on applying self-determination to Russia and instead ideologically held out for the country's ancient boundaries without the Bolsheviks, and so the "United States pursued a policy that resulted in the loss of the entire nation to Western political and economic traditions." Similarly, according to Norman E. Saul, Wilson really wanted Russia to become a clone of the United States, even though this was a delusional expectation at the time, and consequently "failure to solve the Russian problem damaged severely any hopes to realize the American Wilsonian goal of a democratic world protected by a powerful League of Nations. The legacy of this failure would shape much of the international history of the twentieth century."[34]

Wilson and the Rights of Other Minorities

While guarantees for minorities stemmed logically from Wilson's endorsement of self-determination, Russia was not the only country in which his stubborn diplomatic idealism failed. Belatedly realizing that not all national minorities could be independent without creating chaos in Europe, he settled for less than minority groups at home or abroad were happy with. Although he initially proposed that protection of minority rights be included in the Covenant of the League, both his original Articles VI and XIX, dealing with national minorities and "prohibiting or interfering with the free exercise of religion," were dropped. Wilson quickly forsook the one on national minorities once the Japanese representative, Baron Makino, proposed that equality of treatment should extend to both race and religion. In the end, the World War I victors relegated the protection of national, religious, and racial minorities to a package of treaties that were not part of Treaty of Versailles peace settlement. Eight minority treaties were signed between June 1919 and July 1923 – all with slightly different and contradictory provisions and all proving unenforceable during the interwar years.[35]

Thus, despite the fact that self-determination became embodied in Wilson's Fourteen Points and League of Nations Covenant, the principle largely miscarried in practical terms when it came to protecting the rights of minorities from majority discrimination within newly created national boundaries or through bilateral treaties coming out of the Versailles or the League's mandate system. Most of these territorial and treaty agreements ultimately came to represent "the principle of national self-determination deferred," in part due to German manipulation of the League's Committee on New States and the inherently racist and anti-Communist views of the major Western nations, including the United States, following World War I.[36] The most prominent and important of these minority treaties was the Polish one, and it became the model for the others. After it faltered and failed in the 1920s and 1930s, the world community abandoned this entire bilateral treaty approach to protecting minorities following the Second World War.

After Wilson failed to give minority rights (in terms of both race and religion) universal stature in the Covenant of the League of Nations, the British view prevailed. This meant that the question of national and racial minorities would be settled with multi- and bilateral treaties signed with the Allied Associated Powers. As a result, the fate of 25 to 30 million minorities in Central and Eastern Europe was left outside of the Versailles peace settlement and represented only a minor part of the procedures set up under the League – largely through the Committee on Minorities. The League did not guarantee any of these treaties – unlike the mandate system. Nonetheless, the creation of the Committee on Minorities temporarily created a "new international minorities system."[37]

The minority rights and border dispute in which President Wilson became most publicly entangled involved Italy. Again, he can be seen to manipulate his stated principle of self-determination when it came to Italian demands for territory along the Adriatic. He initially and very publicly opposed Italy's acquiring a boundary in the South Tyrol as far north as the Brenner Pass because the population there was 85 percent German-speaking. His position seemed inviolable, since the ninth of his Fourteen Points stated that Italy's frontier should be adjusted "along clearly recognizable lines of nationality." Yet despite several reports by his own experts in Paris indicating that both Germans and Yugoslavs would suffer if the Brenner Pass became Italy's northern boundary, Wilson conceded to the Italians "before the Conference formally opened" in order to secure their support for the League of Nations. By the end of the war, Italy had switched to the Allied side and thus was considered a victorious power. So it did not have to sign a minority rights treaty as did the defeated powers. Although Italy promised to honor limited cultural and linguistic rights for the German and Slavic peoples it had acquired, after Benito Mussolini came into power in 1922 he voided these guaranteed rights and established a "de-nationalization" program designed to "Italianize" the South Tyrol.[38]

The Nazis reached an agreement with Italy in 1939 allowing for the South Tyrolese to return to Germany if they were willing to give up their homeland, but the Second World War interrupted this resettlement movement and South Tyrol, despite Austrian protests, remained in Italy's hands at the end of that conflict. Their disagreement did not end with the signing of the Agreement of 1946 detailing the rights of the German-speaking population, which Italy only minimally tried to implement with the Autonomy Statute of 1948. As a result, Austria complained to the UN. This prompted Italy to adopt in 1970 another Autonomy Statute amending the 1948 one. Even then, it took the United Nations until 1992 to finally conclude that Italy was at last in compliance with the 1946 document and for Austria to withdraw its complaints. Since then, other bilateral agreements protecting minority rights have been signed with nations emerging from the former Soviet Union based on the success of the Italian-Australian one, which took over fifty years to settle.[39]

The original United Nations Charter did not include any clauses addressing the group rights of minorities. Instead, the minority question was "de-internationalized" after 1945 and replaced by a system based on the universal recognition of human rights rather than the rights of specific minorities. This meant the substitution of individual for collective or group rights. Victorious powers after the Second World War did not want minorities as a group to become an international question again and threaten peace and security as it had after the First World War. So twelve million Germans were transferred from Poland, Czechoslovakia, and Hungary, and seven million Poles, Czechs, Slovaks, and Ukrainians were returned to their native lands, leaving Europe with national minorities representing "less than 3 percent of its total population." Such demographic dislocation raised the ethical question, largely unaddressed by the international community, of the humanity of "forced repatriation." The United Nations buried the model represented by the Polish treaty during the Cold War, but its record on protecting minority rights has not been that much better than the League's.[40] However, bilateral treaties protecting minority rights have come back into vogue since the end of the Cold War.

Ubiquitous Wilsonianism

Because of Wilson's inability or stubborn refusal to separate his own exceptionalist and idealist views from the Faustian aspects of his foreign policy at Versailles, a plethora of definitions for Wilsonianism have materialized since 1920. What is "normal" Wilsonianism remains contested today. For some, it is "inspiring liberal internationalism" based on adherence to self-determination and nonintervention; for others, Wilsonianism is "the exemplar of humanitarian intervention around the world," making U.S. foreign policy a paragon of carefully defined and restricted use of force. Accordingly, Amos Perlmutter says that Wilsonianism consists of "liberal internationalism, self-determination, nonintervention, humanitarian intervention... [yet it is at one and the same time] anti-revolutionary, capitalist, pacifist in nature, and exceptionalist... [supporting] free, open borders, open diplomacy, and collective security."[41]

Yet Frank Ninkovich, who has written an entire book called *The Wilsonian Century*, does not define the term in this manner. While he underscores the interventionist nature of Wilsonianism, he denies that it had much, if any, applicability in the interwar years (or, it should be noted, in the post–Cold War period before September 11) because his version of Wilsonian interventionism states that it works only in crisis situations, such as the First World War or the Cold War, not during times of relative peace such as the 1920s or 1930s or in the 1990s. Ninkovich's definition of Wilsonianism is based on the idea that however traditional Wilson's foreign policy views may have been before World War I, that global conflict changed his ideas dramatically. So Ninkovich believes that Wilson came to the following conclusions about modern war before most other international leaders did. He realized that total, modern war (1) could not be used as a reliable, contained instrument of diplomacy; (2) created a danger beyond mere physical conflict because it could lead nations to be hostile toward liberal democracy; and (3) had made traditional balance-of-power arrangements obsolete. (Interestingly, Ninkovich does not include self-determination in his definition of Wilsonianism.)[42] While all this sounds well and good, Ninkovich and most other scholars who defend Wilson's perspicaciousness have ignored the less desirable features of his legacy.

In other words, as discussed in the Introduction, there was a good or positive brand of Wilsonianism and a bad or less desirable one. The good one (and the one most mythologized) concentrates on liberal capitalistic internationalism based on free trade, self-determination, international organization, and collective security. Negative Wilsonianism, which simultaneously fostered the most extreme aspects of the foreign policy ideology of the United States, consisted of an ingrained racism, suspicion of nationalist revolutions, unilateral interventionism, and blind anti-Communism, and, in the cases of the Russian revolution and the Middle East, foreshadowed a good deal of diplomatic secrecy. Wilson also set a presidential precedent for deceiving the American public by manipulating the media with aphoristic slogans. For example, he refused to admit that his policy between 1914 and 1917 was not neutral toward the warring powers in Europe and that he had covertly opposed the Bolsheviks before formally deciding to intervene in Siberia. Even after committing American troops there and earlier in Mexico, the Caribbean, and Central America, the president somehow convinced himself (and most of his successors in the Oval Office would do likewise) that these kinds of interventions were really so well-intentioned that they could not be questioned and that they did not contradict his proclaimed support for the self-determination and national sovereignty of such nations. In fact, Wilson gave credence to the illogical diplomatic idea that when the United States intervenes in foreign countries, it somehow is not interfering with their sovereignty because the action is for their own good. The Byzantine relationship between promoting democracy at home and abroad and economic or military interventions into the affairs of other nations remains the most lasting of the conundrums Wilson bequeathed to future presidents – one that remains unresolved and more unbridled than ever since September 11.

This negative legacy of Wilsonianism skewed the most humane intentions of U.S. foreign policy following both the First and Second World Wars as demonstrated by this review of the most important original component of Wilsonianism: the concept of self-determination. Wilson's manipulation of this concept probably remains the best example of ideology turning a reasonable nineteenth-century principle into a formidable myth about U.S. foreign policy – a myth that gained momentum during the rest of twentieth century. Until his presidency, this concept had not been acted upon to any significant degree by premodern presidents. After he left office, it became a mantra and justification for action on the part of all modern presidents during the Cold War and remains one today.

But both self-determination and the traditional idea of sovereignty upon which it rests cry out to be redefined following the end of the Cold War–a task the country has yet to undertake, in part because Wilson's legacy of liberal capitalist internationalism, however flawed in theory and practice, became the basis of post–World War II foreign policy. For almost fifty years American policy formulators paid little attention to promoting democracy or recognizing legitimate anticolonial and nationalist claims of newly emerging nations unless they sided with the United States in the Cold War against the Soviet Union. The Cold War also contributed to the creation of the imperial presidency as Congress gradually conceded diplomatic power to the executive branch. Thus, with the help of Cold War ideological propaganda, successive administrations reinforced the public's mythical belief about the American commitment to the nineteenth-century foreign policy concepts of self-determination, free trade as a means for promoting peace, and global cooperation.[43]

Wilson's liberal-capitalist internationalism has been both praised as creating "world views that shaped American foreign policy for the remainder of the century" and condemned for creating a "confusion of purpose . . . made worse by loose phraseology . . . [with] phrases such as . . . 'self-determination' . . . freely bandied about without clear definition of their meaning."[44] While neither extreme view of Wilsonianism is absolutely correct, each contains a strong element of truth that continues to drive historians crazy when they analyze its short- and long-term influence on U.S. foreign policy. In particular, his ambiguous definition of self-determination left many questions for future generations to resolve, among them: How much secret foreign policy and hyperbolic diplomatic rhetoric in the form of misleading slogans can (or should) a democracy support? When governments created through popular sovereignty later decide to deny freedom and basic civil and political rights to all or some of their minority citizens, should other nations undertake humanitarian interventions?

Another aspect of Wilson's legacy has to do with economics. It is often overlooked that at the beginning of the First World War, despite an existing recession, the United States already had a larger economy than any other nation. At that time Germany and England were the major trading partners of the United States, and these two nations were also each others' best customers. So much for the pre-1914 theory that nations trading with each other would not fight one another. Nevertheless, this primitive type of pre-war globalization based on the economic interdependence of major nations led many businessman and politicians before World War I to believe that international disputes in the future would be mediated peacefully. In fact, the U.S. business community played a prominent role in the American peace movement before the First World War. The outbreak of war in 1914 temporarily discredited the notion that commercial relations insured international peace. Instead, interlocking political and military alliances among Western nations kicked in and "disrupted the first international economy [the world had known] and set back the globalization process for two generations."[45]

Just as Wilson promoted self-determination at Versailles without completely understanding its potential to create postwar conflict, he also could not have known that even though the League of Nations contained the institutions necessary for promoting global commercial and financial interdependence, it would never fulfill his dream of economic internationalism based on free trade and freedom of the seas. This was particularly true after the onset of the Great Depression. But before that global economic collapse, leading post-war American businessmen and politicians such as Herbert Hoover agreed with Wilson that the League provided the means "for eliminating [the most economically] ... objectionable features of the treaty" and, therefore, could be used to promote world peace and democracy through commerce.[46]

While Wilson and certain U.S. business interests may have believed that economic "interdependence compelled international [political] cooperation" and advocated removing "all economic barriers," the other victorious powers at Versailles did not. They acceded to the overall structure of the League of Nations for international political cooperation but protected their national economic interests with colonies, restraints on trade, and insistence on excessive reparations through specific clauses in the peace treaty. Thus, when the United States refused to ratify the Treaty of Versailles, it appeared to turn its back on both Wilson's vision of collective security and his hope that the League would return the world to pre-war economic interdependence by overcoming the nationalistic propensities of the former European Allies. In reality, the defeat of the treaty did not mean that the United States retreated to either economic or political isolationism in the 1920s; it simply began to practice independent internationalism as a way to foster its own world power primarily through economic means.[47]

Given its economic importance going into, and coming out of, World War I, it should not come as a surprise that the United States found that some of its nineteenth-century foreign policy principles were in conflict with its new-found position in the world. In fact, only three or the original seven foreign policy principles survived the reassessment to which they had been subjected: commitment to self-determination, however compromised; international coop-eration, which in the previous century had been largely confined to contiguous boundary and fishing disputes; and free trade, although the country's high-tariff policy belied its rhetoric on this subject throughout the nineteenth century and well into the first third of the twentieth. Until World War I none of the three had ever been associated with spreading democracy until they were internationally revived as a result of President Wilson's complex redefinition of, and erratic adherence to, these concepts during that conflict, at the Versailles peace negoti-ations, and during his unsuccessful attempt to bring the United States into the League of Nations in 1919.

Four other concepts gradually became extinct as postwar American leaders in the course of the 1920s and 1930s forsook neutrality (the violation of which had led Wilson to declare war on Germay), freedom of the seas, and, to a degree, political isolationism, and very definitely continental expansion, because these foreign policy principles no longer served the economic or political interests of the United States as it became a powerful force on the world scene. As significant as these four original diplomatic concepts had been in the nineteenth century, only political isolation reemerged in the middle of the 1930s and then died (in all but political rhetoric) once the United States entered the Second World War.

Of the three major remaining foreign policy concepts – commitment to self-determination, international cooperation, and free trade – U.S. promotion of self-determination following World War I tugged most fervently at politicians' heartstrings because it could much more easily be packaged in the mystique of the American Revolution than collective security through the League of Nations.

Wilson's Legacy of Self-Determination

Try as it might, the United States logically could not preserve or adhere to all of the foreign policy principles it started out with in 1900, especially in the face of the first and second sea changes in its economy. But one of these goals – self-determination – became a symbolic rallying cry of American diplomacy into the twenty-first century. Yet, in reality, the country has traditionally exhibited at best a haphazard commitment to this nineteenth-century concept of self-determination as it practiced independent or unilateral internationalism, and then only when it was in its economic and national security self-interest to do so.

Self-determination as a component of U.S. foreign policy staggered into the twentieth century badly wounded. Both the Civil War and the vicious sup-pression of Filipinos in the aftermath of the Spanish-American War dealt body blows to the concept, and it almost died in the first two decades of the twentieth century as the United States began to violate the self-determination of nations in the Western hemisphere from 1900 to 1920. Thus, the McKinley, Roosevelt, and Taft administrations suppressed Filipino rebels and Cuban nationalists; TR arrogantly appropriated territory from Columbia to build the Panama Canal; and Wilson waged war against successive Mexican rebels and militarily intervened in the Carribean, Central America, and Siberia.

The Monroe Doctrine justified most of these undertakings. They were also encouraged when Secretary of State John Hay proclaimed the Open Door policy in a series of diplomatic notes at the end of the nineteenth century. These notes consisted of a "dramatic public gesture" meant "to inspire business confidence that Washington was more committed than ever before to preserving American economic opportunity" in Asia.[48] While the Open Door policy (the advocacy of equal economic opportunity where the United States faced serious economic competition abroad) failed to limit the economic and territorial expansion of foreign powers in China, the term became the slogan under which the United States pursued economic (and military) expansionism for most of the twentieth century, except in those areas of the world where it dominated. In those cases it almost always tried to impose a Closed Door policy. By the time the United States entered the First World War, it had successfully pursued both the Monroe Doctrine and a Closed Door policy in the Caribbean and Central America by establishing economic protectorates through force or negotiation, thus blocking most meaningful foreign competition.

By 1920, for example, the United States had acquired protectorates through financial supervision and militarily interventions in eight Caribbean and Central American countries, and had annexed Puerto Rico and purchased the Virgin Islands from Denmark – all in the name of establishing stability to protect U.S. property and citizens and at the expense of the self-determination of these peoples. These actions, combined with the results of the Spanish-American War, produced more diplomatically bold presidents. As a consequence, the United States began to "impose its will [more] bluntly" in Central America than in any other part of the world.[49]

These first systematic attempts of the United States to become a hegemonic power in the Western Hemisphere mirrored the way it had turned its back on self-determination for Native Americans and southern secessionists in the nineteenth century.Perhaps this was to be expected when it is remembered that although the Monroe Doctrine endorsed the concept of self-determination, it also implicitly sustained both "soft" and "hard" U.S. approaches to diplomacy with Latin America, to use John Vloyantes's terms. "Soft" power, as opposed to "hard" power, is based on noncoercive diplomacy that relies on economic and cultural influence, credibility, and reputation, and is implemented by example and co-optation rather than by force.[50]

Wilson bequeathed to his successors in the White House the theory that self-determination depended upon the amalgamation of nationalism and self-government rooted in some form of democracy. Nationality, as Wilson defined it, consisted of a vague state of consciousness, a "community of thought," rather than rigid geographical or ethno-religious characteristics as it is more commonly thought of now. He thus blurred the fact that manifestations of nationalism have no intrinsic relationship to democratic government by insisting that the "peace should rest upon the right of peoples, not the rights of Government – the rights of people great or small, weak or powerful – their equal rights to freedom and security and self-government."[51]

These words were reminiscent of what he had said when trying to universalize the Monroe Doctrine and were in essence at the heart of Wilson's concept of self-determination, but in neither instance did he clarify what he meant by "people," let alone "community" or "self-government." He also never indicated what he meant by such phrases and statements as "well-defined" nationalism, or "autonomous development," or "the right of those who submit to authority to have a voice in their own governments." Did this mean that nationhood should be determined by plebiscites? Should any people who said they were a nation be granted their own state? While he asserted that it was "the American principle" that "people have the right to live their own lives under governments which they themselves choose to set up," and that "every People should be left free to determine its own polity," Wilson did not think that the Irish nationalists deserved their own state, and initially he did not favor dividing up the multinational Austro-Hungarian Empire or Russia. Even his second secretary of state, Robert Lansing, no friend of self-determination, noted the glaring contradiction in Wilson's thinking about Irish independence, saying that the United States "would be, I think, embarrassed in no small degree at the peace table by having admitted beforehand the claims of the subject races of the Central Powers and Turkey, and by having ignored the claims of the Irish and others under the sovereignty of the Entente [Allied] powers."[52]

As an Anglophile and Presbyterian, Wilson's anti-Irish sentiments might have been understandable at the time. Despite the pressure he faced domestically from Irish-Americans to free Ireland from British occupation, he realized that his relationship with England during the peace process was more important than keeping a domestic hyphenate-American group happy – especially one that had supported Germany – although he would rue this decision later in the 1918 midterm elections and in the battle over the treaty in 1919.[53] However, the president's initial reluctance to recognize the national aspirations of the Finns, Poles, Czechs, Slovaks, Serbs, Croats, Yugoslavs, Rumanians, Lithuanians, and Ukrainians is not really a mystery and perhaps presaged his later compromises on minority rights at Versailles.

In all likelihood these compromises stemmed from the ethnic insensitivity and racism Wilson had so clearly evidenced at home against immigrants and blacks and against colored peoples in the Philippines, the Caribbean, Mexico, and Central America. This nationalistic, anti-self-determination stance was in keeping with Wilson's strong initial indifference, if not outright hostility, to minority and ethnic rights as a young man, professor, university president, and politician. Until World War I he had exhibited a generally rigid, self-righteous attitude toward peoples of color inside and outside the United States and suspicions about the politics of American immigrants, especially those from southern and eastern Europe who began pouring into the United States in the late nineteenth century. While he publicly moderated his anti-ethnic views when he ran for governor of immigrant-populated New Jersey in 1910, he showed little interest in the rights of ethnic or racial minorities before assuming the presidency, and, if anything, his views, especially about hyphenate-Americans, became more hostile after war broke out in Europe in 1914. During his campaign for reelection as president in 1916, for example, he openly attacked the Poles, Italians, and Hungarians for infusing "the poison of disloyalty into the very arteries of our national life," promising to overcome "such creatures of passion, disloyalty, and anarchy."[54]

Despite his domestic anti-ethnic views, Wilson's idealization of self-determination during World War I resonated with the struggles of the new postwar nations in the interwar years. Wilson moralistically believed that the war had turned the international political tide in the direction of an ethnically pluralistic world of democratically elected, self-determined nations. Because the 1920s and 1930s proved a disaster for self-determination and minority rights, these unresolved issues returned to haunt the world in the 1990s after the end of the Cold War and continued into the first decade of the twenty-first century. Once again, the legacy of Wilson's moralism took on exceptionalist and Faustian overtones.

3

The Faustian Aspects of Prosperity, Depression, and War

> The business groups are the most intelligently class conscious elements in American Society.... Wealth and talent are at their command. They are inspired by an irrepressible enthusiasm and a dogmatic self-righteousness. Can anyone doubt but that as the decades of the twentieth century pass by, their influence in the molding of policies will continue to be powerfully exerted?... But such influences should be given weight only in so far as they are in line with the dictates of wise statesmanship, taking into consideration the interests of the whole nation.
>
> Benjamin H. Williams, *Economic Foreign Policy of the United States* (1929)

Acting on its unprecedented economic position in the world after World War I, the United States expanded internationally in ways that ultimately altered its former commitment to some of its nineteenth-century diplomatic principles. For example, instead of supporting traditional neutrality (as it had at the outbreak of war in Europe in 1914), American leaders no longer defended the rights of neutral nations or honored their claims to freedom of the seas as their predecessors had before the nation became a major naval and economic power. In a word, the United States began to act as England had when it ruled the oceans and world finance. The Republicans in charge of the White House in the 1920s also began to modify the country's original concept of political isolationism. Because the United States became a leading industrial and creditor nation for the first time during that decade, politicians and businessmen cooperated in limiting the country's practice of traditional isolationism as the country's political and economic interests expanded. The United States also took a strong interest in a variety of international problems such as disarmament, the scaling down of Allied war debts and German reparations, the outlawing of war, membership in the World Court, indirect cooperation with the League of Nations, and the quite different postwar anxieties of both Germany and France.[1]

Contrary to conventional wisdom, therefore, Republican administrations did not retreat to an isolationist stance. Even though the United States did not become a member of either the League of Nations or the World Court in the

1920s and 1930s, it began to participate in a greater number of international conferences on disarmament, peace, and international economic matters than ever before and, of course, became a major force behind the creation of the United Nations in 1945. So the country's nineteenth-century commitment to international arbitration (which had been particularly noticeable in the late nineteenth and early twentieth centuries with its participation in the Hague Peace Conferences of 1899 and 1907) continued unabated until the outbreak of the Cold War.

The Kellogg-Briand Pact stands as the most idealistic (and impractical) collective attempt to ensure peace during those years. But it should not be forgotten that its supporters also realistically urged greater cooperation between the United States and the League of Nations and generally encouraged Wilson's idea of collective security to solve specific international problems. The single most important application of the 1928 Kellogg-Briand Pact occurred when it became the legal basis for the Nuremberg Trials following World War II, although the United States also invoked it during the Manchurian crisis discussed later. At the same time, however, Congress passed xenophobic immigration and protectionist tariff legislation, and refused to cancel Allied debts or to recognize the Soviet Union until 1933. These examples of ingrained American unilateralism (and nineteenth-century isolationism) even carried over to the Kellogg-Briand Pact. Although the Senate approved the pact in 1928, it added this caveat: "the [Senate Foreign Relations] committee reports the above treaty with the understanding that the right of self-defense is in no way curtailed or impaired. . . . The United States regards the Monroe Doctrine as part of its national security and defense."[2]

Wild fluctuations in domestic and international economics in the 1920s and 1930s primarily drove this mercurial, zigzag combination of unilateralism and internationalism. Unfortunately, in the interwar years Washington did not develop any systematic coordination of economic and political foreign policy. Instead, it initiated an erratic independent internationalist course for the first time, assuming that unregulated Yankee capitalism was the key to carrying out Wilson's promise of making the world safe for democracy. Therefore, the Faustian foreign policy of the United States in the 1920s and 1930s consisted not so much of dirty political deals as it did of selfishly short-sighted commercial and financial transactions that reflected its inexperience as the world's leading economic power.

The Struggle over Economic Foreign Policy

In the 1920s the United States leaped into the material and financial void created by World War I, taking advantage of the disarray in postwar England and Europe to shore up its predominant economic position. In other words, the United States, as the leading creditor, exporter, financier, and maritime power in the world, set out to assume Britain's historical position as the leader in reestablishing global economic interdependence. By 1928, it looked as though it had at least consolidated its own international ascendancy, producing 46 percent of the world's industrial output, and accounting for 70 percent of the world's petroleum and 40 percent of its coal production.

However, there was little betterment of the overall world economy because the expansion of U.S. commerce and investments abroad was in the hands of private financiers and businessmen whose activities were never coordinated with any comprehensive U.S. government recovery program for Europe. Thus, American trade doubled from 1913 to 1929, but it rose only 13 percent for all other countries. Japan and Canada replaced Europe as the major consumers of American products and also as the two countries from which the United States imported most of its goods. U.S. exports to Asia rose from a mere 5.7 percent before the First World War to 12.3 percent. Moreover, 37 percent of all American exports went to Western Hemisphere countries by the end of the 1920s, up from 31 percent before the war. This increase occurred at the expense of European trade.[3]

What was wrong with this picture? As the leading creditor nation, the United States should not have continued to act as a though it were still a debtor by continuing to export more than it imported. To reduce the imbalance between exports and imports would have required the country to abandon the Open Door policy, whose goal was unlimited American economic expansion. U.S. exports abroad grew fivefold in the 1920s, largely because of unsupervised loans and investments abroad by American bankers and financiers as the country accumulated its largest merchandise export balance for any decade before World War II. Direct U.S. foreign investments increased from $3.8 billion to $7.5 billion. When these ceased because of the Great Depression, it became clear that the favorable balance of trade the United States enjoyed in the 1920s increased the severity of that worldwide economic crisis. To remedy this trade imbalance, the United States government would have had to greatly inflate its domestic credit structure to allow Americans to consume more, shift labor and capital away from industries competing with foreign imports, lower its protectionist tariffs, and in general bring down the economic expectations of the business community.[4] In order to do any of these things, the United States would have had to act like a mature economic power when it remained a juvenile, lacking the necessary experience to conduct itself in less selfish ways.

As secretary of commerce, Herbert Hoover fought for some nontraditional and ameliorative economic measures, particularly government supervision of all foreign loans. However, Secretary of State Charles Evans Hughes, supported by prominent bankers and financiers, defeated him on this issue. Hoover understood that when payment problems arose the business community looked to the government to intervene. "[T]here is no method by which failure in payment of such [foreign] loans can be prosecuted," he wrote Hughes in April 1922, "except by diplomatic intervention of our government." Therefore, he logically pointed out "that the security and form of these loans should, at the outset, involve the fair hope that Federal Government will not be required to enter upon intervention." But Hoover failed to convince the secretary of state and powerful banking and financial interests of this. He also could not convince them that supervision of loans would ensure that they were "repro-ductive," meaning that they should contain clauses requiring the purchase of American products or spare parts, not be used to compete with businesses in the United States, or to balance spendthrift budgets, or to bolster inflationary currencies, or for military expenditures. In the end Secretary Hughes refused to allow individual loans or investments to be subjected to government merit reviews.[5]

Partially as a result of Hoover's failure to win acceptance for greater gov-ernmental oversight of American loans and for more coordination of economic and political foreign policy, an orgy of private lending and investment ensued, especially in Central America, the Caribbean, and South America. From 1919 to 1930, the annual amount of capital exported from the United States averaged $1 billion. In the course of the 1920s, U.S. direct investments expanded from the pre-war concentration in Mexico and Cuba to include Haiti, the Domini-can Republic, Honduras, Nicaragua, Venezuela, Brazil, Argentina, Columbia, Peru, Bolivia, and Chile. In fact, direct investments in twenty republics in Latin America outranked those in Europe and Canada by 1930, having increased a whopping 1,200 percent since 1900 – from $320 million to $5.2 billion.[6]

The best indication of the irresponsible way in which these unregulated foreign loans were increasingly "forced" on countries that should have been considered bad credit risks is the fact that 50 percent of all bond issue loans made by American bankers between 1925 and 1928 defaulted in the 1930s, compared to only 18 percent of those made between 1920 and 1924. By 1935, Latin America had defaulted on 85 percent of American dollar bonds, compared with a 52 percent default rate for Europe and a 3 percent rate for Canada.[7] So it can be argued that the United States became a good neighbor of Latin America under FDR in order to extricate its business community from these defaults and to work out equitable treatment for future trade and investments to make up for the losses due to the Great Depression.

German Reparations and Allied Debts

Another major defect in U.S. economic foreign policy in the 1920s was the refusal of the United States to recognize the obvious connection between Ger-man reparations and Allied debts. The economic health of the postwar world depended, in the last analysis, upon how America dealt with these two unprece-dented and intertwined financial variables. In retrospect, had the United States combined the reparations and debts into a single package, it is conceivable that it could have obtained a dramatic reduction in the reparations program from the Allied powers in return for significant reductions in the money owed it. The United States might have been able to bargain for changes in mandated terri-tory and other economic privileges that the Allies had reserved for themselves at Versailles in order to substitute its Open Door policy for existing preferential trading systems. Instead, American business and political leaders stubbornly refused in public to link reparations with debts, even though in private many of them admitted the connection.[8]

Alternatively, the United States appointed businessmen and bankers to reduce the exorbitant German indemnity of $33 billion informally set at the Paris Peace Conference. As a result, the government encouraged and unofficially endorsed two large international loans to Germany based on a long-term reduction of the indemnity it had to pay: the 1924 Dawes Plan and the 1929 Young Plan. Named after two U.S. bankers, Norman H. Dawes and Owen D. Young, these two plans set up a graduated schedule of payments accompanied by massive loans to the German government through American banks and also by private loans to German municipalities and industries. The Young Plan actually reduced the original $33 billion to $8 billion payable over $58\frac{1}{2}$ years at 5.5 percent interest. Had Germany continued to make payments after 1932, it would have paid a total of $28 billion – hardly a long-term bargain. On the other hand, it has been argued by Niall Ferguson that the "Weimar economy was not wrecked by reparations; it wrecked itself." Regardless, the perception that reparations were an undue burden on Germany prevailed in part because it was promoted by noted economists of the day such as John Maynard Keynes and Max Warburg.[9]

Determined to keep German reparations separate from Allied debts, Washington promoted major debt-funding agreements in the 1920s. The war debts represented the money the United States had lent the Allied powers during and immediately following the First World War. As early as December 1918, England proposed to Woodrow Wilson that it would cancel the Allied debts owed it (approximately $10 billion) if the United States would cancel the $4 billion that the UK had borrowed from America. France also argued for debt cancellation, but Wilson refused to consider these suggestions, as did Presidents Warren Harding and Calvin Coolidge, although no historian has ever been able to prove that the latter actually said, "They hired the money, didn't they?" In February 1922, Congress created the World War Foreign Debt Commission, which negotiated specific agreements ostensibly based on each former ally's capacity to pay. Congress originally instructed the commission to set a 4.5 percent interest rate to be paid over a twenty-five-year period. However, debtor nations initially accepted only obligations to the United States of over $11.5 billion, payable over a sixty-two-year period at an average interest rate of 2.135 percent. Under these agreements, principle and interest would have amounted to $22 billion.[10]

Owing to deteriorating financial conditions in Europe by the end of the 1920s, and despite congressional opposition, the United States through its World War Foreign Debt Commission reduced the combined outstanding indebtedness of fifteen nations by 43 percent, or almost half, with the average interest rate on the remaining refunded debts falling to 2.1 percent. The onset of the Great Depression made even these reduced payments impossible. Hoover announced a one-year moratorium on all such payments in June 1931, but this did not prevent the former Allied countries from defaulting on their war debts beginning in 1933 – with the exception of Cuba, Liberia, and Finland, which paid off their loans, and Nicaragua, whose debt was cancelled by agreement in 1938.[11]

These debt reductions were not as generous as they appeared on the surface because the original loans to the Allies were not strictly business transactions. They did not meet normal banking standards between 1914 and 1918 because the credit of the warring nations was not good. The Allies became virtually bankrupt during the war, and so the purposes for which the borrowed money was used could not be justified in business terms – at least according to peacetime lending rules and regulations. In fact, these American wartime loans were political in character, as government-to-government loans typically are. Moreover, these loans could not be paid off in gold because the United States already held a disproportionate amount of the world's gold by the end of the First World War. They also could not be offset by direct exports to the United States because of the 1922 Fordney-McCumber and 1930 Smoot-Hawley tariffs, which impeded European goods from coming into the country. Finally, the former Allied powers faced prices in the 1920s that were only two-thirds what they had been during the war, and so they found themselves paying off their debts in currency whose value was higher than it had been when the debts were incurred.[12]

To honor these loans European nations would have had to export to the United States 50 percent more goods than they received, and this did not happen before the Great Depression. Although the Smoot-Hawley tariff was modified by New Dealers with the 1934 Reciprocal Trade Agreements in order to give the president more power to negotiate and reduce import duties, this legislation should not be confused with the adoption of the Wilsonian idea of free trade. Despite its unconditional most-favored-nation provision and the fact that this legislation "was a less nationalistic program than those pursued by other countries in the thirties," the purpose of the 1934 act was to expand the foreign markets of the United States, not to increase imports.[13] This meant that commitment to unilateral Open Door expansionism prevailed in Washington even during the Great Depression.

These less-than-astute economic dealings affecting the related issues of postwar debts and reparations led to the following not-so-coincidental figures by the beginning of the 1930s. The former Allies had paid the United States a total of $2.6 billion; Germany had paid the Allies $2.5 billion; and American loans to Germany (including those of the Dawes and Young Plans) amounted to $2.5 billion. In essence, the United States paid itself back what it was owed through largely unregulated private loans abroad. These figures clearly indicate that the United States had become the "main engine of the global economy" after the First World War, "accounting for two-fifths of global industrial production and 16 percent of its commerce." Once the American stock market collapsed, the world economy followed. The Republican administrations during the 1920s supported a basically private business approach to the postwar economic problems of Europe, and this policy failed with the onset of the Great

Depression, which ended the precarious system of international payments based on American loans.[14]

The Monroe Doctrine versus the Good Neighbor Policy

The Western Hemisphere rather than Europe proved the area of the world where U.S. economic foreign policy during the interwar years remained most in tune with Wilson's earlier "effort to detoxify the [Monroe] doctrine in the eyes of Latin American governments." During these two decades, the United States appeared to honor some semblance of self-government for those nations. In August 1921, as ex-president, Wilson also confided to his former secretary of state, Bainbridge Colby: "I wish that we might be given another opportunity to set the country right in the view of Latin America."[15]

The Republican government official probably most in tune with Wilson's view was Hoover. Both saw the Americas rather than Europe as a "crucible for peace" through economic growth. Additionally, both never lost their "faith in American exceptionalism," because it embodied the "inherent . . . civilizing mission of the nation." Hoover thought that Latin America would prove the American economic system superior to all others and compensate for the problems the nation had encountered during the reconstruction of Europe after World War I. As soon as he became secretary of commerce he said in a press statement: "That the United States is fundamentally interested in Latin-America requires no reiteration. . . . there is nothing more important than our common interest in trade . . . [and] to increase the standard of living of all our peoples. . . . [The] more we can amplify this interchange of goods, the more we can contribute to our joint advance in civilization . . . [and] the more certain is the development of our long established friendships." The Great Depression tainted his effort to "fashion a pacific community within the Americas to serve as a model for other regions of the world," but his attempt remains more in keeping with the best of Wilsonianism than is usually recognized. As noted earlier, it was also one of the reasons that he wanted government supervision of loans in order to ensure safe loans and investments in Latin America.[16]

So, in the 1920s, as secretary of commerce, Hoover (and even his enemy when it came to supervision of U.S. foreign loans, Secretary of State Hughes) edged toward supporting the Wilsonian principle of self-determination by proposing a less aggressive political use of the Monroe Doctrine against Central and South American nations, although they continued to bring economic pressure against them to protect "legally vested American rights." While they initially succeeded only in withdrawing U.S. troops from the Dominican Republic in 1924, the 1920s saw the revival of the idea of self-determination through the concept present in Wilson's Pan-American plan, stillborn in 1914, that stressed Western hemispheric cooperation based on the principles of equality and self-determined independence for all nations.[17]

Latin Americans rightly perceived these modest changes in policy as confounding because the Monroe Doctrine and its corollaries clearly implied the unilateral right of the United States to protect its citizens and investments by intervening. Yet, once he became president, Hoover tried to reassure them by making public in 1928 the Clark Memorandum. This document stated, albeit quite belatedly and not necessarily truthfully, that the original Monroe Doctrine had never been intended to justify American intervention. Nonetheless, the Clark Memorandum palpably represented a renewed commitment to self-determination on the part of Washington. While this memorandum also specifically separated the Roosevelt Corollary from the Monroe Doctrine, the United States, as it turned out in practice, never abandoned its claim to the unilateral right to intervene in Latin American affairs; it simply temporarily divorced that right from the Monroe Doctrine.[18]

Hoover did encourage negotiations over boundary disputes in Latin America that would have positive results after he left the presidency. He also ended the U.S. policy of not recognizing revolutionary governments in the region, though he failed to obtain arms embargo legislation from Congress as sixty revolutions broke out in Latin America between 1929 and 1933. Even so, by 1930 the United States still had troops in Nicaragua and Haiti and exercised some form of American financial supervision in El Salvador, Bolivia, the Dominican Republic, Haiti, Nicaragua, Cuba, and Panama.[19]

However, the Clark Memorandum and Hoover's commitment to it and to pan-Americanism did lay the groundwork for the removal of the remaining U.S. troops from Nicaragua in 1933 before he left office and from Haiti in 1934 under the Good Neighbor policy of Franklin Roosevelt. According to FDR, the purpose of the Good Neighbor policy was to establish a "kind of hemisphere partnership" by eliminating the threat of military and financial aggression toward South American nations on the part of the United States. In this sense, the Good Neighbor policy was also meant to be a substitute for the Monroe Doctrine and pan-Americanism. Accordingly, in May 1934 the Roosevelt administration negotiated a treaty with Cuba abrogating the Platt Amendment with its right of intervention, and at pan-American conferences in 1933 and 1936 the United States officially renounced the right to armed intervention and nonmilitary interference in the financial and political affairs of Latin American nations.[20]

This did not mean that Washington stopped trying to influence conditions in Central and South America through "customary methods of diplomacy," nor did it mean that U.S. political leaders and businessmen had ceased to look upon the area as "the most accessible ideological proving ground for the exportation of capitalism and democracy." In other words, "the Good Neighbor policy signified business as usual with less muscle and more public relations," that is, as a means for consolidating the "soft" American sphere of influence in Latin America by presenting an ethical rather than a military face. Less positively, in Europe and Asia the Good Neighbor policy seemed to indicate either U.S. withdrawal from "unwanted foreign burdens" or part of a unilateral and "systematic American retreat from the world."[21]

Throughout the 1930s, in return for its Good Neighbor policy Washington expected "Latin Americans to establish stable governments, honor political as well as economic obligations, and extend equitable treatment to American citizens and their property according to standards of due process which existed in the United States." Naturally, Mexico and other countries resented such a unilateral assertion of what was equitable, especially when in the course of the 1930s the United States began to put national security considerations above private property rights as Europe fell further into war. Thus, the Roosevelt administration accepted the right of expropriation as a negotiable issue in return for the right to intervene in Latin America if American national security was threatened, abandoning "all the self-denying components which had gone into the Good Neighbor policy."[22]

This demise of the Good Neighbor policy could have been predicted once economic and political conditions in Europe worsened in the 1930s, and the Roosevelt administration made it clear that the 1933 and 1936 Good Neighbor nonintervention pledges did not deny the right of the United States to interfere in Latin American affairs when its national security interests were threatened. It had already done this when accepting the Kellogg-Briand Pact.

Consequently, the various collective nonintervention pledges that the United States made at Latin American conferences in the 1930s – even the abrogation of the Platt Amendment – were quickly reinterpreted just before and after the Second World War as Washington reasserted its unilateral interventionist rights in Latin America that had always been implicit in the original Monroe Doctrine and its various corollaries. Events leading to World War II clearly voided the intent of the Clark Memorandum. For example, despite such words as those in the 1936 Buenos Aires protocol that "the High Contracting Parties declare inadmissable the intervention of any one of them, directly or indirectly, and for whatever reason, in the internal or external affairs of any other of the Parties," Roosevelt firmly informed the new revolutionary Mexican government in 1938 that the United States would intervene if it thought its national security was threatened by the war in Europe. While this reversed his administration's earlier drift toward cooperative internationalism south of the U.S. border, it was quickly followed by the 1939 Panama Declaration and the 1940 Act of Havana – both of which gave wartime multilateral approval to an extension of the Monroe Doctrine to the entire Southern Hemisphere. So the potential for unilateral use of the Monroe Doctrine by the United States remained intact, and its reassertion during the Cold War simply delivered the coup de grâce to an already weakened Good Neighbor policy.[23]

This unilateral side of New Deal political foreign policy did not initially manifest itself because the Roosevelt administration started out trying to reduce tariffs and to build on the positive, cooperative Latin American policy initiated by Republicans at the end of the previous decade. However, an early example of the unilateral side of independent internationalism at work can be seen when the Great Depression prompted FDR to back out of any more economic cooperation over debts and reparations or currency stabilization at the London Economic Conference in 1933. He arbitrarily devalued the dollar by taking the United States off the gold standard and forbade the shipment of gold overseas. These actions created even greater currency instability and imbalance in world gold holdings. They also further stimulated a retreat from worldwide to regional trade. By the beginning of World War II, two-thirds of the world's gold supply was held in the United States, and most of this massive transfer had occurred after 1935.[24]

Additionally, through domestic price-fixing programs, the Roosevelt administration retreated to a nationalistic domestic economy that was designed to restore domestic public confidence but that did little to improve the worst aspects of the national or international depression. Other nations followed similarly short-sighted nationalistic economic policies as the global economic crisis cast doubt on the ability of Wilsonian liberal capitalist internationalism to promote peace, democracy, and free markets.[25] In this manner, cutthroat economic practices hastened the coming of the Second World War as democratic and fascist nations put their material well-being ahead of meaningful negotiation and peace making.

Political Foreign Policy

As New Deal diplomats took over U.S. foreign policy in 1933, they were no less imbued with a sense of entitlement and mission based on American exceptionalism and independent internationalism, which usually tipped in the direction of unilateral action, than their Republican predecessors. First the FDR administration dealt with unresolved economic problems, but ultimately they had to face deteriorating international political problems. While Republicans had committed errors by allowing private enterprise to prevail in economic foreign policy during the 1920s, Democrats in the 1930s committed errors by allowing domestic partisanship to determine political foreign policy. Republican economic foreign policy had caused a worldwide economic imbalance that contributed to the onset and severity of the Great Depression. Democratic political foreign policy in the 1930s contributed to a worldwide political imbalance with the rise of Nazi and fascist movements that triggered the Second World War. Accompanied by a short-sighted economic sanctions against Japan, New Deal diplomacy, like Wilson's, made it inevitable by the fall of 1941 that the United States would end up fighting in a global war, but this time on two fronts rather than one.

As devastating as the Great Depression was for the political economies of most nations – except for the Soviet Union, which had remained outside of the reemerging economically interdependent system of the 1920s – the international political developments of the 1930s dealt a further blow to Wilsonian internationalism not only with the growth of dictatorships abroad, but also with the growth of isolationist sentiment in the United States. Most symbolic of this trend was the passage of the Neutrality Acts, as a result of which American diplomacy assumed a more isolationist posture in the 1930s than it ever had in the 1920s.

The Great Depression and events leading to World War II thus produced bona fide political isolationism in the United States by the mid-1930s. Manifested primarily in highly charged congressional debates about so-called new neutrality, this hyper-nationalism came to be embodied in the Neutrality Acts of 1935, 1936, and 1937 – acts belatedly repealed in piecemeal fashion between 1939 and 1941. The new neutrality legislation was based on the theory that trade in arms had caused America to enter the First World War, but it did nothing to address the conditions leading the country into the Second World War. These Neutrality Acts represented the highly selective memory of congressmen who thought that bankers and munitions makers had been primarily responsible for U.S. entrance into World War I. However, they correctly exposed the fact that Wilson had not practiced economic neutrality before the United States entered the First World War.

There is little documentary proof that Roosevelt understood or anticipated the tragic results of the Neutrality Acts. Before President Hoover left office, his secretary of state, Henry Stimson, introduced FDR to the idea of supporting arms embargo legislation in order to allow the executive branch to cooperate with other peaceful nations against violators of the Kellogg-Briand Pact (and Stimson's own doctrine opposing the "fruits of aggression"). This type of "discriminatory" legislation would have allowed the president to decide when to apply any embargo against warring nations and represented a collective internationalist use of arms embargoes that Hoover and Stimson had considered during the Manchurian crisis of 1931–32. However, strong congressional nationalists and progressives such as Hiram Johnson (R-CA), William Borah (R-ID), and Gerald Nye (R-ND) had become out-and-out isolationists by the mid-1930s, and they began amending this internationalist bill in 1933. They turned it into a "nondiscriminatory" piece of unilateral legislation by stating that any embargo would have to be applied impartially to all belligerents and hence in a nondiscriminatory manner. Without consulting his secretary of state, Cordell Hull, FDR initially supported the Johnson amendment and continued to vacillate on various versions of the neutrality legislation until the first Neutrality Act was passed in 1935.[26]

To this day no one quite knows whether the president actually realized at the time the significant difference between a discriminatory arms embargo, which gave him the power to decide against which nation it would be used, and a nondiscriminatory one, which removed such power from him. By the time he did understand this in the late 1930s and bit by bit succeeded in repealing the Neutrality Acts, the damage had been done. The nondiscriminatory neutrality legislation placed the United States on the wrong side in both the Italo-Ethiopian crisis in 1935 and later in 1938 during the beginning of the Spanish Civil War. In each instance, U.S. "neutrality" ended up favoring fascist forces and underscored the degree to which the country had abandoned Wilson's pre–World War I commitment to the traditional rights of neutral nations and internationalism. The Faustian results of this misguided nationalistic legislation cannot be overestimated. It did not help that Roosevelt's cavalier leadership style made him as vulnerable as Wilson's moralistic one when it came to appreciating that the devil is always in the details of diplomacy.

FDR and Far Eastern Policy

By far the most short-sighted aspect of New Deal independent internationalism, however, took place in the Far East. Granted, Roosevelt inherited a less-than-astute settlement of the 1931–32 Manchurian crisis with the so-called Stimson Doctrine. After much scrimmaging between President Hoover and his secretary of state over how to respond to the Japanese invasion of Manchuria and the creation of the puppet state of Manchukuo in the southern portion of that Chinese province, Stimson proclaimed on January 7, 1932, the "nonrecognition of the fruits of aggression." Since Hoover and Stimson never agreed about whether to enforce this doctrine through cooperation with the League of Nation or unilateral economic sanctions, they never implemented the Stimson Doctrine.[27]

In truth, the Hoover–Stimson policy was aimed as much at not alienating Japan as it was at preventing more aggression against China. The impossibility of achieving both goals reflected a common defect of American policy toward China throughout the interwar years. Logically, the United States should have either enforced its Open Door policy in China with sufficient military and/or economic aid or protected China by playing Japan and Russia off against one another in the Far East (which in the 1920s would have required the recognition of the Soviet Union). Alternatively, since most American trade was with Japan and not China, the United States could have sided with the Japanese at the expense of both China and the USSR.[28]

Most businessmen trading in the Far East tacitly sided with Japan after its invasion of Manchuria because they generally conceded that Japan had special interests there. After all, by 1929 only 7 percent of all American trade with China took place in Manchuria. Few American businessmen would have gone so far as to agree with what seemed obvious to Japan: that it had the right to a Monroe Doctrine in the region, as first suggested by Theodore Roosevelt. Instead, Manchuria remained a symbolic testing ground for the Open Door policy rather than a practical area for American investment or trade. Within the American business community, oil companies in the Far East were not so sanguine about Japan's expansionism because they correctly interpreted it as a desire to become less dependent on U.S. petroleum products.[29]

Between 1899 and 1930 American investments, trade, and shipping with China trailed far behind those with Japan. In contrast to China's minuscule share of American foreign economy, the Chinese played an increasingly important role in the economic life of Japan. American exports to China averaged only 3 percent of all U.S. exports from 1923 to 1931, while 22 percent of all Japanese exports went to China. On average, U.S. exports to Japan in the 1920s were double those to China. By 1932, Japan was the fourth-largest purchaser of American goods. This meant that the United States supplied a little less than one-third of all Japanese imports and purchased a little more than one-third of Japanese exports. Clearly, significant commercial interdependence existed among the three countries, but in reality the triangular relationship was not one that should have favored political support for China on the part of Washington.

That is, the United States and Japan were each other's best customers, while Japan, not America, was China's best customer by the time of the Manchurian crisis. And the same imbalance existed in the field of investments: the United States invested more in Japan than in China, and Japan dominated investments in China. For example, by the end of the 1930s America had invested twice as much in Japan as in China and enjoyed a favorable trade balance with Japan that was three times as great as its trade with China. Little wonder that by 1941, only 21 percent of businesses in the United States supported economic sanctions against Japan.[30]

Throughout the 1930s, the Roosevelt administration pursued an essentially ineffectual political and economic foreign policy in the Far East: protesting Japanese expansion as a violation of the Open Door policy and the Nine-Power Treaty of 1922, but not imposing any severe economic or political sanctions. By the end of 1939, Japan acknowledged 144 bombings and 73 cases of destruction of American property. The U.S. government protested all of these incidents, and the Japanese responded by accepting responsibility and usually paying damages. At no point did the United States indicate that it would fight to prevent Japan from establishing what that nation logically considered to be its natural sphere of influence in Manchuria. Japanese leaders coveted the province because it could provide a secure source of food and other raw materials, an outlet for excess population, a base from which to expand its industrial output, and a buffer zone that would protect its control over Korea and the Japanese islands.[31]

Needless to say, when Japan began to extend its sphere of influence to other sections of China, such actions became increasingly unpopular in the United States, especially after Japan and Germany signed the 1936 Anti-Comintern Pact. When Japan joined Germany and the Soviet Union by signing the Tripartite Pact in September 1940, the identification of Japan with Germany in American popular opinion and in government circles was completely confirmed. Although this pact quickly became a dead letter, the Roosevelt administration used it to demonize all Japanese leaders through propaganda that associated them indiscriminately with Hitler. By November 1941, on the eve of Pearl Harbor, public opinions polls showed that many Americans (a little over 70 percent) were willing to risk going to war with Japan. The opposite was true for Germany.[32]

This was Roosevelt's dilemma. By the late 1930s, he wanted to support England and the other Allied powers against the Nazis and Fascists, but up to that point, he had been unable, unlike previous American presidents on the brink of war, to find an effective lie with which to lead the country into combat – in this case, into the European theater of World War II. After all, since 1812 presidents had successfully lied to the American people when going to war.[33]

Consequently, because there was so much popular opposition to the United States becoming involved in the European war, during 1940 and 1941 FDR, in Wilsonian fashion, resorted to misleading statements and clever slogans, if not outright lies, and a series of actions without congressional approval. He began with the executive agreement known as the "destroyer-base deal," then obtained lend lease legislation, made the United States the "arsenal of democracy" by doubling military appropriations for arms and other supplies leased to England, reached a private arrangement with the French to train their military pilots, established a temporary protectorate over Greenland, and extended the patrolled neutrality or security zone in the Atlantic Ocean from three hundred miles off the American coast to twenty-five degrees west longitude. He also practiced what has been called "diplomacy or propaganda of the deed" that is, taking advantage of events in war to initiate American defense measures. One example stands out. In September 1941 he used the attack on the USS *Greer*, which had been relaying information to the British about the location of German submarines, to issue "shoot-on-sight" orders to American navy patrols. In November he obtained repeal of all remaining provisions of the Neutrality Act of 1939, thus allowing the arming of American merchant ships. As a result, the United States was in an undeclared naval war with Germany in the Atlantic.[34]

Despite all his cagey maneuvering, FDR knew he did not yet have public support for a declaration of war against Hitler. By the summer and fall of 1941 he simply had failed to concoct a popular deception for going to war with Germany. Racist-driven public opinion polls favored going to war with Japan, with only a little over 30 percent of Americans indicating they would vote in a national referendum to go to war with Germany, and only a little over 20 percent thinking the United States should enter the war at all.[35]

A contradiction in U.S. diplomacy had arisen, as noted, from the fact that Japan had been the best American customer and investment opportunity in the Far East throughout the interwar years despite U.S. efforts to build up better economic and political relations with China. FDR exacerbated this foreign policy flaw with his determination to turn China under Chiang Kai-shek into a major and dependable ally, especially after Germany invaded its ally the Soviet Union in the summer of 1941. This unrealistic view of a united and powerful China had existed, however, since Secretary of State John M. Hay coined the Open Door doctrine at the turn of the twentieth century. At no time in the 1930s did Chiang Kai-shek's Nationalist government ever consolidate its authority over any major portion of China.[36] Thus, the United States not only pursued the myth of the China market beginning in 1900, but increasingly pursued the myth of China under Chiang as a strong political entity and ally when all economic and national indices pointed to Japan as the de facto Asian power. Ironically, Japan was also adamantly anti-Communist, while Chiang flirted with emerging communist leaders during that decade as he tried to fend off other Nationalist leaders.

Perhaps remembering that Theodore Roosevelt and even Woodrow Wilson had seemingly favored a Monroe Doctrine for Japan, in 1934 Japan proposed to the United States in a memorandum from Ambassador Hirosi Saito that together they should "establish a reign of law and order in the regions [of the Pacific] geographically adjacent to their respective countries." That same year Japan also declared in the Amau Doctrine that it had the right to act unilaterally "to preserve peace and order in East Asia." Clearly, this was Japan's most explicit assertion of its own Monroe Doctrine. Unlike either TR or Wilson, Secretary Hull never tolerated any suggestion of a Japanese Monroe Doctrine. In his memoir, Hull later noted that this 1934 proposal indicated that Japan wanted nothing less than a "Monroe Doctrine in the Far East pretendedly such as our Monroe Doctrine for the Western Hemisphere." He then self-righteously rejected this suggestion because it did not recognize what he disingenuously insisted was the defensive nature of the American doctrine – a questionable view also held by other respected State Department officials.[37]

When in November 1938 Japan announced its intention to create a Greater East Asia Co-Prosperity Sphere, it implicitly meant to turn a weak and chaotic China into a semi-vassal state, but American oil interests perceived the move as a potential threat to their control over oil fields in the Netherlands East Indies. After all, Japan already occupied the richest and most populous sections of that nation, including its major cities, great areas in northern and central China, and strategic ports and cities on the southeast coast. Once again in 1938 Hull responded sharply to another Japanese Monroe Doctrine proposal in the form of the Greater East Asian Co-Prosperity Sphere. Probably reacting as well to the pan-German foreign policy of the 1930s promoting the idea of a European New Order, on December 31 he said in a note to the Japanese that "there was no need or warrant for any one Power to take upon itself to prescribe what shall be the terms and conditions of a 'new order' in areas not under its sovereignty and to constitute itself the repository of authority and the agent of destiny in regard thereto." In April 1940, Hull reiterated to the Japanese ambassador that "there is no more resemblance between our Monroe Doctrine and the so-called Monroe Doctrine of Japan than there is between black and white."[38] But at no time in the 1930s did the Roosevelt administration ever take other than rhetorical steps to counter Japanese expansionism or to demand compensation when American property was destroyed.

So as of the summer of 1940 the United States had done little except to try "to attain two limited objectives in the Far East, those of splitting the Axis and of stopping Japan's advance southward" through mild economic pressure and even milder political protest. Both were more or less reasonable and possibly obtainable goals. At least they held out the hope that some kind of modus vivendi could be achieved between the United States and Japan, allowing FDR to concentrate on deploying American forces in Europe. In a word, war with Japan was not inevitable by the end of 1940.[39] Then, six months later, in July 1941, the Roosevelt administration added a third and completely unobtainable component to its Far Eastern policy: the liberation of China.[40] In turn, this shift in political emphasis was accompanied by a hardening of economic policy toward Japan. The result would be an unnecessary two-front war, in part because having inherited exceptionalism and independent internationalism as the twin bases for American diplomacy, FDR proved incapable, despite (or because of) his charisma, of exercising leadership that produced truly innovative solutions to the foreign problems he faced, especially in the Far East.

Once again, it is not clear that the president understood the serious implications of adopting the unrealistic goal of liberating China. Apparently the impetus for the change in policy came from Secretary Hull's personal and uncompromising commitment to moralistic principles where China was concerned. Hull's rigid approach to Far Eastern diplomacy, however, was not wholly responsible for bungled relations with Japan. Economic pressure played the final, determining role in the attack on Pearl Harbor as business and government bureaucratic groupings took over U.S. economic foreign policy in the Far East.

When the United States unilaterally terminated its 1911 commercial treaty with Japan on July, 26, 1939, this meant that restrictive actions could be undertaken after January 26, 1940. The list of items subject to embargo included crude oil (and a variety of petroleum products), scrap iron, steel, and aviation gas. However, Washington did not enforce most of the these restrictions immediately, except on certain grades of high-octane aviation gas and some premium grades of iron and steel. Hull, in particular, opposed any strict embargo for fear it would produce an attack on the American East Indies oil fields, and he convinced the president of this. Nonetheless, a debate ensued in the executive branch over what else to embargo, with the ambassador to Japan, Joseph Grew, having long intimated to Roosevelt that a complete embargo could very likely lead to war. Other presidential advisers insisted that Japan would back down in the face of an all-out sanction on its oil lifeline. Then in September, after the signing of the Tripartite Pact on September 27, 1940, a full scrap iron and steel embargo went into effect. The next month Roosevelt indicated that he still opposed completely shutting off oil supplies to Japan, and as late as August 1941 he apparently still believed that "oil quotas allowed Japan" under previous agreements should continue.[41]

Not until July 1941, when the political metamorphosis in U.S. Far Eastern foreign policy took place, did the sanctions on other items become stricter, but even then the oil embargo remained only partial. That same month the American government froze Japanese assets. While this action in and of itself had the potential to shut off Japan's ability to buy oil from the United States, Roosevelt apparently did not intend for it to be applied rigidly. But he left in August for the meeting with Churchill that produced the Atlantic Charter, and in his absence anti-Japanese officials within the government refused to allow Japan to use any of its assets for purchases. The result was that by September a full embargo on crude oil, and thus on all petroleum products to Japan, had taken place.[42]

Bureaucratic Influence on Japanese Foreign Policy

The question is why? The answer lies in the influence of such American oil companies as Shell and Standard-Vacuum Oil Company (Stanvac) on certain members of the State Department bureaucracy such as Stanley Hornbeck, chief of the Far Eastern Division. Another individual most strongly in favor of a total embargo on oil to Japan was Henry Stimson, who had favored a similar sanction back in the early 1930s as secretary of state under Hoover. Both Roosevelt and Hull harbored reservations when informed of the total embargo in September, but unfortunately did not countermand it, in part because both were still operating under the illusion that China under Chiang could be made into a major power in the Far East. Hull's moralist, anti-Japanese views also help account for his passive response. As usual, no one knows exactly why Roosevelt did not overrule the drastic economic move taken by subordinates in September 1941. It has been suggested that both men, in all likelihood, concluded after the fact that rescinding the full embargo would have been "interpreted by Japan, Britain, and the American public as a sign of weakness." Since the public had no detailed information about economic policy toward Japan, the last part of this suggestion could not be true. Regardless, the fact remains that the total embargo on crude oil and all other petroleum products was not what the president or his secretary of state had ordered or intended. The Japanese were never formally advised of the total embargo, but as they watched dwindling oil tanker movements it became clear that they if they wanted energy independence they would have to seize the Netherlands East Indies.[43]

The influence of oil interests over the State Department is a well known, if usually overlooked, reason for the war with Japan. By 1939, eighty percent of Japanese imported fuel supplies came from the United States and the rest from the Netherlands East Indies, where Shell and Stanvac controlled the oil fields. George S. Walden, chair of the Stanvac board, and his expert on China and Japan, Philo W. Parker, had been in constant contact with Royal Dutch-Shell, the London Foreign Office, and the U.S. State Department since the company's foundation in 1933. The main problem facing Stanvac, Royal Dutch-Shell, and the Anglo-American diplomatic corps consisted of protecting the Indies oil field from Japanese expansion and restraining oil shipments to Japan without both harming commercial trade with that nation and unnecessarily antagonizing its civilian and military leaders. This proved an impossible balancing act because once the idea of embargoing crude oil to Japan emerged in the early 1930s over the Manchurian incident, it slowly assumed a bureaucratic life of its own until by 1941 it outflanked support for retaining trade relations and avoiding war.[44]

This bureaucratic coup did not take place by accident. After Henry Stimson reentered the government as secretary of war in July 1940, he "campaigned for economic warfare in general and sanctions against Japan in particular." By December 1940 he had created a study group within the Army Industrial College, and by May 1941 it had produced no fewer than eighteen economic contingency plans for crippling Japan without regard for whether implementing one or more of them would lead to war. In the meantime, Stimson's sanction campaign had been joined by Secretary of the Treasury Henry Morgenthau, Jr., who succeeded in obtaining Roosevelt's approval for an Economic Defense Board. With broad authority over economic foreign policy, this board was headed by Vice President Henry Wallace, another advocate of shutting off exports to Japan. Additionally, Morgenthau created a three-man State-Treasury-Justice committee to advise the Economic Defense Board, and Assistant Secretary of State Dean Acheson, who agreed with Stimson and Morgenthau on get-tough policies against Japan in Asia, became one of its three members.[45]

Thus, the stage was set for a bureaucratic takeover of Japanese policy by economic hawks. Only Hull and Roosevelt, who did not want to provoke a Japanese attack on the Indies, stood between the United States and war in the Pacific. In the end they were simply outmaneuvered by their own bureaucracy between July and September 1941 because they lost administrative control over segments of the executive branch of government. Of the eight cabinet-level members of the new Economic Defense Board, four – Wallace, Morgenthau, Stimson, and Secretary of the Navy Frank Knox – endorsed a strong, and probably racist, anti-Japanese policy. Little wonder that a de facto embargo against Japan came into existence by mid-September without the initial approval or knowledge of either the president or his secretary of state. Yet neither of them revoked it, even though they knew that in all likelihood Japan would regard the total embargo as an incitement to war.[46]

Moreover, public opinion (always foremost in Roosevelt's mind) posed no problem for this evolution in policy because by the middle of 1939 polls indicated that 66 percent of Americans approved of boycotting Japanese goods and that almost 75 percent saw nothing wrong with an embargo of arms and ammunition to Japan. Obviously, the average American did not know about the connection between a total oil embargo and war with Japan, but by November 1941 a little over 70 percent were willing to risk war with Japan rather than let the country continue its aggressions. Even more impressive and worrisome to the president, 80 percent of Americans and their congressmen opposed a unilateral declaration of war by the United States unless the country was attacked.[47] Having unwittingly permitted the economic action that might provoke war with Japan, Roosevelt, knowing that he had public opinion on his side, then allowed his secretary of state to compound the situation in private negotiations with Japanese representatives in Washington.

Much has been made of Hull's meetings with Japanese Ambassador Kichisaburo Nomura in November 1941. Hull already knew what terms Nomura would present because the United States had broken the Japanese diplomatic code known as Magic. This knowledge did not prevent the secretary of state from taking advantage of Nomura's poor English (the latter stubbornly refused to use a translator) to reject the two proposals from Tokyo that the ambassador presented. The first, Plan A, represented an attempt to reach a comprehensive settlement with the United States, which American officials rejected out of hand by November 15. The second, Plan B, called for a Japanese withdrawal from Indochina and a pledge not to advance in Southeast Asia if the United States would stop aiding and supporting China and lift the trade sanctions. Recent scholarship has now shown that Nomura was not as "hapless" as he is usually portrayed. He submitted on November 19 a modus vivendi he had devised on his own in a last-ditch effort to prevent a war that he perspicaciously knew Japan would lose. It simply called on the United States and Japan to state their postwar economic goals based on the model of the Atlantic Charter and for a rescinding of the July order freezing Japanese assets in return for Japan's withdrawal from southern French Indochina. When Hull and Tokyo both rejected this more conciliatory offer, Nomura was ordered to submit Plan B, which he did on November 20. Washington knew from a deciphered message that Tokyo had set November 29 as a deadline for a response.[48]

Roosevelt seemed inclined to accept a six-month modus vivendi and even proposed that the United States not insist on Japanese withdrawal from China. Members of his cabinet such as Morgenthau, Stimson, and Harold Ickes strongly opposed this idea, as did Chiang and Churchill. Their views directly contradicted a report of the American Joint Board of the Army and Navy, which on November 5 had concluded that "[war] between the United States and Japan should be avoided" because the United States had to concentrate on defeating Germany. These military leaders did not think that war with Japan was warranted even if that country made further incursions into China. Unknown to them, as of November 1941 FDR had in private all but promised Churchill that the United States would protect British and Dutch possessions in the South Pacific, realizing that the Japanese could consider this a casus belli.[49]

Nonetheless, Hull still had the option of proposing a modus vivendi of his own, especially in light of the opinion of the military, but other advisers to Roosevelt and both China and Britain continued to object to any accommodation of Japan. Instead, on November 26 he submitted to Japan a ten-point program drafted by Morgenthau that demanded its withdrawal not only from China, but also from Indochina. Both sides claimed the other had issued an ultimatum, although the American offer was by far the harsher of the two proposals. On December 6, Roosevelt whimsically tried to revive the idea of some kind of modus vivendi by making a personal effort to contact the emperor, but that same day a detailed Magic decoded message revealed that Japan had rejected Hull's ten-point ultimatum and contained an ominous addendum telling Ambassador Nomura to reply "at 1P.M. on the 7th your time." This prompted General George C. Marshall to send a hasty radio dispatch to the Philippines, Panama, and San Francisco and a telegram to Hawaii (because of heavy static preventing wireless communication) saying in part: "Just what the significance of the hour set [1p.m.] may have we do not know be on the alert accordingly. Inform naval authorities of this communication." This message failed to reach the commanders at Hawaii before the attack on Pearl Harbor.[50]

Soon Roosevelt would have an enormously popular reason for going to war against Hitler – the attack on Pearl Harbor. Even so, he waited until Germany, Italy, and Japan had declared war on the United States before asking Congress for a declaration of war against Hitler. Even then, he went out of his way to indicate that Germany had collaborated with Japan in the attack on Pearl Harbor, claiming that the Japanese were Hitler's "chessman." Clearly, FDR still feared that isolationists in Congress would oppose a two-front war because they had not accepted the undeclared naval war the United States was already waging on Germany. Roosevelt was also not personally convinced that Americans would accept an invasion of other-than-U.S. property as grounds for entering the war. Without hesitation and without having to fabricate a reason, therefore, he used the attack on Pearl Harbor to rationalize sending American troops to the European battlefront.[51]

Secret Summit Diplomacy

With the U.S. entrance into the Second World War, the stage was set for Roosevelt to begin to enter into a series of questionable unilateral and multilateral bargains at summit meetings from 1941 to 1945. It should be noted that the first occurred before Pearl Harbor with the secret meeting between FDR and Winston Churchill in Placentia Bay of Argentia, off the coast of Newfoundland. They met for six days beginning August 8, 1941. It proved an impressive initial formal face-to-face encounter, to say the least, since it produced the Atlantic Charter on August 14. As a wartime propaganda tool, the success of the Atlantic Charter cannot be doubted. Although no Allied government ever officially approved the charter, this bilateral joint statement conflated both Wilson's Fourteen Points and Roosevelt's Four Freedoms, containing eight points that were later used to justify the unconditional surrender of the Axis powers and the establishment of the United Nations.[52]

"It is a statement of basic principles and fundamental ideas and policies," Hull later wrote, sounding exactly like Woodrow Wilson, "that are universal in their practical application." Their universality (and practicality), as usual, existed primarily in the eyes of their ethnocentric creators – namely, Roosevelt and Churchill – and they were perfectly in keeping with the American exceptionalist belief that the United States was a model for the rest of world. A more practical and immediate reason for the Atlantic Charter could have been that FDR, already so embattled at home over certain war measures like the draft, wanted to reassure his critics of his commitment to the highest democratic and capitalist ideals should the country enter the war–now that communist Russia was an Allied power. Churchill probably would rather have obtained a greater commitment of military aid from the United States and sterner warnings to Japan in the wake of America's freezing of that nation's assets, but the president refused to do either, and so they settled for a declaration of Wilsonian truisms.[53]

What were these universal ideals that each of the Allied nations used as it saw fit in the course of the Second World War? The Atlantic Charter began with a preamble about the "dangers to world civilization arising from the policies of military domination by conquest" of Hitler and all nations associated with him. It then stated that the United States and Great Britain renounced territorial and other types of aggrandizement; opposed territorial changes contrary to the wishes of those immediately affected; supported the right of all peoples to self-government; condoned, whenever possible, equal access for all nations to trade and raw materials (except for the "existing obligations" of the United States and England); desired the material improvement of the world's population;

supported freedom from fear and want; supported the right of "all men to traverse the high seas and oceans without hindrances" (even though the United States and England, as the two most powerful naval nations, did not support freedom of the seas); and sought total disarmament of the aggressor nations, "pending the establishment of a wider and permanent system of general security."

To say the least, the Atlantic Charter proved a problematic document. At best, it symbolized the personal friendship between two very important world leaders; at worst, it consisted of an informal bilateral alliance whose universalistic (read Western) goals had little chance of being realized during or after the war. It could be asked: What was the president of a "neutral" nation doing conferring secretly on the high seas with the prime minister of a beleaguered Allied nation? After all, the United States was not at war, and England was. To make matters worse, neither he nor Churchill signed it, and no original copy of the document exists. Nonetheless, the Atlantic Charter marked the beginning of what would become ten personal meetings between Roosevelt and Churchill, concluding at Yalta in the spring of 1945.

After their meeting at Argentia, the next important one took place in January 1943 in Casablanca, where Churchill and the president continued to disagree over a second European front so desperately requested by Stalin (and which Roosevelt had prematurely promised Soviet Foreign Minister Vaycheslave Molotov three times back in May 1942, even though the U.S. army at that time was not large enough or organized to undertake such an invasion). At the Casablanca summit FDR also independently and, in a most offhand manner at a press conference, committed the allies to fight for unconditional surrender. Evidently meant to reassure the Russians that there would be no separate Anglo-American negotiated peace with Germany, the unconditional surrender statement reflected more bravado than American military might or Roosevelt's political power to deliver.[54]

FDR and the British prime minister met next at the first Quebec conference in August 1943. There they confidentially pledged their countries not to reveal information about the atomic bomb, should one be developed, and not to use it against another nation without mutual consent. Neither of these private, secret promises were kept. Both of them constituted executive agreements that bypassed Congress (and U.S. military leaders) in the foreign policy and military decision-making process and marked the beginning of the presidential use (and misuse) of such private and often Faustian understandings and commitments that have prevailed since that time.

At a meeting among Anthony Eden, Molotov, and Secretary Hull in Moscow in October 1943, in return for another promise of a second front, the USSR also gave assurance once again that it would enter the war against Japan once Germany was defeated. These foreign secretaries also issued a four-power statement about establishing an international organization for peace and security. The fourth power was China, in keeping with the president's determination to give Chiang Kai-shek putative recognition as an international leader even though his corruption and ineffective leadership was well known among FDR's aides. Moreover, Churchill made no secret of his disdain for the president's efforts to turn China into a great power and postwar anticolonial force in the Far East that might threaten English and other European powers' holdings there. Despite the fact that Lieutenant General Joseph W. Stilwell, Roosevelt's private military representative to Chiang and designated commander of U.S. forces in China, Burma, and India, came to disparagingly refer to the shaven-headed Chinese leader as "the peanut," the president clung to visions of China as a countervailing force in the region against both Japan and the USSR as those two nations recovered from the devastation of war.[55]

Following this successful meeting of subordinates, Roosevelt finally met with Stalin in Tehran after stopping in Cairo from November 22 to 26 for a summit meeting with Churchill and Chiang to discuss the military and political goals of the Allies in the Far East. Russia was not represented at Cairo because it had not yet declared war against Japan. Roosevelt admitted to being singularly unimpressed upon meeting Chiang, finding "him grasping, weak, and indecisive." Nonetheless, he and a reluctant Churchill propped up the Nationalist leader by deciding that Japan must return "all territory [it] had stolen from the Chinese, such as Manchuria, Formosa, and the Pescadores." This joint Cairo declaration also asserted the independence of Korea, stripped Japan of all the islands in the Pacific that it had seized or occupied since 1914, and officially agreed that unconditional surrender now applied to Japan as well as Germany.[56] So much for FDR's bizarre flirtation with Monroe Doctrines for Europe and Asia back in the summer of 1940.

At the Tehran conference from November 27 to December 1, Roosevelt and Churchill finally put aside their strategic military differences and approved a Channel invasion for May 1, 1944. They also made major political concessions to Stalin in return for still another reiteration of his intention to enter the war against Japan, first agreeing to support Marshal Tito's domination of Yugoslavia and then giving him Polish property in violation of the much-touted Atlantic Charter. To make matters worse, Roosevelt agreed to grant a Soviet sphere of influence in Poland and the Balkans, but was ambiguous about Poland's postwar boundaries, which Churchill and Stalin had already talked about. Nonetheless, despite FDR's fears about committing himself to Russian spheres of influence in the Balkans and Poland because it could alienate Americans from those countries in the fall presidential election, he did not overtly discourage Stalin's plans. Moreover, the joint chiefs of staff, with whom Roosevelt had consulted en route to Tehran, opposed any diversion of English or American troops into the Eastern Mediterranean and the Balkans because it would "prolong the War in Europe and delay the end of the war in the Pacific."[57]

Thus, by the end of 1943 a series of secret summits had set the stage for the much-contested last one at Yalta, and most of them basically created misunderstandings and exorbitant expectations on all sides. These meetings also foreshadowed the decline of the Grand Alliance and the beginning of the Cold

War. The Faustian nature of most of these summit agreements climaxed at Yalta in February 1945.

In retrospect, Roosevelt's ill health did not cause the resulting controversy, confusion, and conflict over Yalta that occurred in the United States. That controversy was inevitable because the labyrinthine agreements reached there over peace terms for Germany, Polish borders, governmental policies for Poland and other liberated countries of Eastern Europe, and details about organizing the United Nations would ultimately be interpreted differently by all parties involved, but especially by the president's domestic opponents, who charged that he had handed Eastern Europe over to the Soviets. It was not Roosevelt's to hand over: the Soviet army already occupied all of Poland and most of the rest of Eastern Europe because General Dwight Eisenhower had been only too happy to have the USSR fight its way into Berlin in the last months of the war. Nonetheless, from the end of World War II to the present conservative critics have railed against Yalta, charging that it marked the beginning of Soviet expansionism. That George W. Bush repeated this myth in May 2005 when visiting the Baltic nations makes it no truer than it was in 1945.[58]

Once back in the United States, however, FDR's advanced cardiovascular condition for the first time became painfully evident when in a befuddled manner he tried to explain to a joint session of Congress the problematic last summit meeting of the Big Three. FDR muddied the waters further by dissembling about what went on, neglecting to mention the Far Eastern concessions he had made to Russia, especially in Manchuria (theoretically at Chiang's expense, since the Nationalist leader was not really in control of Manchuria), in return, once again, for Stalin's long-standing secret pledge to fight Japan. He also did not indicate to Congress or the American people that he had agreed to give "Uncle Joe" two extra votes in the General Assembly of the future United Nations for the Soviet Republics of Ukraine and Belarus. Instead, he praised the idea of free elections for Poland and the first meeting of the UN, to take place in San Francisco on April 25. He would not live to experience either.[59]

Despite his deteriorating health, however, after the Yalta Conference the ailing FDR found the time and energy to meet on February 14 aboard the USS *Quincy* with Farouk I of Egypt, Haile Selassie of Ethiopia and, last but most importantly, the Saudi King Ibn Sa'ud. At this secret meeting the president and the king agreed on a number of things – including American access to Saudi ports, temporary construction of military air bases, and involvement of U.S. oil companies in the building of the trans-Arabian pipeline – that would lay the foundation for all future relations between the two countries. The groundwork for this postwar oil diplomacy began with the appointment of Max Thornburg, a California and Texas oilman, to be the State Department's petroleum adviser. He commissioned a study predicated on dwindling domestic oil reserves that prompted Secretary of State Cordell Hull to appoint the Committee on International Petroleum Policy which in turn recommended the creation of a Petroleum Reserves Corporation to be controlled by the State Department. Although this corporation failed to buy any foreign oil options during the war, it presaged the conclusion reached in a 1953 position paper prepared for the National Security Council: "American oil operations are, for all practical purposes, instruments of our foreign policy."[60]

In August 1943 Roosevelt arranged for Iran to receive lend-lease aid and in February 1945 for Saudi Arabia to receive $100 million in lend-lease money – money clearly not needed to end the war in that theater. He did this to counter British and Dutch domination of Middle East oil, because by 1943 American geologists and oil companies had convinced experts within the State Department that the Persian Gulf region should replace Mexico, Venezuela, and other Caribbean nations as the country's major postwar oil-supplying area. In this way the United States might preserve its resources in the Western Hemisphere for future domestic demands. Hull noted that year: "It is to our interest that no great power be established on the Persian Gulf opposite the important American petroleum development in Saudi Arabia."[61] Unlike some of FDR's other diplomatic legacies, this one about the necessity for the United States to guarantee its access to Middle Eastern oil was unequivocal and would be followed by all Cold War presidents.

However, Franklin Delano Roosevelt's death left many foreign policy voids. His insistence on personal, ambiguous, often devious executive orders and secret agreements both before and during the Second World War, while creating the illusion of genius, had actually resulted in an incubus of enormous proportions at home and abroad. No successor or foreign leader could have successfully picked up the loose ends that FDR – always confident of his ability to handle foreign affairs in a freewheeling, supercilious fashion – had strewn in his three-plus terms in office. And Truman certainly was not prepared for the diplomatic mess he inherited, despite (or because of) the fact that the war ended in both theaters shortly after he assumed office. At the same time, the end of the conflict left the American people with confusing expectations about what peace would bring. At best, they had quixotic memories about why and how the war had been fought, and at worst, they anticipated few domestic or diplomatic problems. Most importantly, peace left the United States free to practice independent internationalism at will during the Cold War.

4

Faustian Aspects of U.S. Cold War Foreign Policy

> When we Americans speak seriously about politics, we mean that our principles
> of freedom and equality and the rights based on them are rational and everywhere
> applicable. World War II was really an educational project undertaken to force
> those who did not accept these principles to do so.
>
> Allan Bloom, *The Closing of the American Mind* (1987)

During the various half-century commemorations of the Second World War
in the 1990s, much was heard about the unity and triumph it represented
rather than the viciousness with which the war was fought on both sides or
the domestic problems that followed in its wake. This posthumous positive
consensus about the outcome of the "last good war" confirmed that the twentieth century would be remembered as an "American Century," as Henry Luce,
the publisher of *Time*, *Life*, and *Fortune*, insisted in a little book he wrote in
1941. In this treatise Luce rhapsodized about an American century in which
finance-capitalism and material growth would dominate because, as he said:
"We are the inheritors of all the great principles of Western civilization – above
all Justice, the love of Truth, and the ideal of Charity . . . [and] God has founded
America as a global beacon of freedom." These bombastic words seemed to
reflect the preternatural American past while predicting the postwar mission
and exceptional virtues of the United States.[1]

Thus, the Second World War is remembered primarily as a most glorious
and unifying experience whose victorious outcome confirmed the confluence
of capitalist abundance and democracy at home and the traditional messianic
view of themselves as exceptional that white Americans had held since the
nation's beginning. Yet a multitude of mistakes, contradictions, and Faustian
deals mixed with genuine humanitarian intentions on the part of the United
States and came to characterize the postwar era known by the name Cold War.
The "American Century" ostentatiously proclaimed by Luce became a reality
in the last half of the twentieth century as the United States fought to win the
Cold War. The official Cold War line was that because of its exceptionalism the

country could do no wrong as the most selfless, magnanimous nation on earth. But when one thinks of the horrors of the twentieth century, it is conceivable that in retrospect one would not want to remember it as American.

Faulty Memories

In 1945, postwar moralism and triumphalism dulled the memories of many Americans about the reasons the United States had entered the Second World War. Fifty years later, some thought quite rightly that the war had been fought because of military dictatorships trying to expand their control in Europe and the Far East; others recalled the war as one of justifiable vengeance after the Japanese attack on Pearl Harbor. This is convenient because it allows most Americans not to think about the ethical implications of the United States becoming the first and only nation to drop atomic bombs. In particular, it allows some aging Americans to rage against those who question Truman's decision to deploy the first modern weapon of mass destruction against a defeated Japan or to think of its use only in terms of the average soldier grateful not to be sent to the mainland of Japan to fight. As stories about the Holocaust leaked out and were confirmed at the war's end, genocide, or what today is called ethnic cleansing, became in popular memory another reason why the United States fought World War II. By the time of the millennium, these three reasons for U.S. entrance into the Second World war – dictatorships, Pearl Harbor, the death camps – were remembered imperfectly at best by some and not at all by many younger Americans.

Americans also have long since forgotten that there was another postwar vision, first articulated in 1941, that countered the "American Century." It called for the internationalization of the New Deal in order to create a "People's Century," in the words of Henry Wallace, then FDR's vice president. This would be a world unlike the one forecast by Luce. Instead, it called for the elimination of economic cartels, colonialism, social injustice, and poverty. Eleanor Roosevelt supported this worldview when she wrote that the war would produce a "revolution of people all over the world...who must control their governments in order to have a chance to build a better life throughout the world." This meant, according to her biographer Blanche Wiesen Cook, that she believed there would be a "range of government-to-government aid programs, full employment, international trade free of tariffs [and free of exploitative profits], a world marketplace of goods and ideas, a global TVA and WPA supported by an international lending authority." Eleanor Roosevelt called her version of the "People's Century" an example of "world thinking."[2]

Supporters of Henry Luce's "American Century" were horrified by the "People's Century" concept of government-run aid agencies and state banks that placed worldwide economic cooperation ahead of immediate personal or nationalistic gain. Instead, they "wanted private capital, supported by state agencies, to go international for private profit" (much like what had happened in the 1920s). Luce's wife, Clare Boothe, referred to this Wallace/Eleanor

Roosevelt New Deal version of postwar reconstruction as "globaloney."[3] More important, statements by Winston Churchill and Walter Lippman helped ensure the supremacy of the "American Century" in popular culture. They confirmed for the average person that the country was about to fulfill its economic and exceptionalist vision as a special world "insulated from the sins and failures and travails that affected other nations, standing somehow outside of history, protected by its own strength and virtue." For example, Churchill told the House of Commons at the end of the war: "America stands at this moment at the summit of the world." The American journalist Walter Lippman said in even more grandiose terms: "What Rome was to the ancient world, what Great Britain had been to the modern world, America is to be to the world of tomorrow."[4]

Little wonder that those New Deal Wilsonians in favor of a "People's Century" lost the rhetorical battle over American's role in the postwar world. Their opposition to an aggressive "American Century" was noticeably absent during the fiftieth anniversary celebrations of the Second World War. The emergence of the Cold War sealed the fate of the "People's Century." Wallace clearly saw what was happening, saying in May 1947: "Today, in blind fear of Communism, we are turning aside from the United Nations. We are approaching a century of fear." But by 1948, most average citizens, politicians, pundits, and even Eleanor Roosevelt had abandoned Wallace and his dream of a kinder, gentler, more humane world in which average people would govern in their own best interests rather than be governed by nation-states caught up in geopolitical and corporate games. She became a bona fide Cold Warrior along with most U.S. leaders and citizens, no longer on the cutting edge of human and civil rights at home as she had been in the 1930s, despite her fame as the head of the commission that produced the UN Declaration of Human Rights.[5]

In one sense, the most important legacy of the Second World War *was* the Cold War as the Grand Alliance of the United States, Britain, and the Soviet Union proved unable to sustain itself in the immediate postwar years. This fact has led some to say that the Cold War occurred in large measure because the United States would not accept the geographical, ideological, and economic domination of such communist nations as the Soviet Union and China in certain parts of the postwar world.

This does not mean that the Cold War, as we know it, was inevitable. At least the swiftness with which the United States began to rearm and fight Communism was not inevitable. If Henry Wallace had been vice president in 1945 instead of Harry Truman, the United States probably would not have so hurriedly accepted the worst features of superpower competition, with all of its negative implications for American democracy at home. Wallace did not ignore what he called the "security dilemma," but he and many lawmakers such as Senator Robert Taft asked hard questions of those convinced about Stalin's expansionism. The "tougher we get," Wallace predicted, "the tougher the Russians will get." Under a Wallace presidency, the propensity for U.S. military interventionism abroad would, in all likelihood, also not have materialized as quickly and as unthinkingly as it did. Instead, Truman renounced diplomacy and opted for military containment of the "threat" of a "bloated Red Army sweeping over Western Europe," despite evidence that Stalin had been forced to demobilize drastically in order to rebuild his war-devastated country.[6]

What is clear is that beginning with Truman American presidents tended not to engage in diplomatic compromise with the USSR; that is, they did not think that they could or should negotiate until the Kremlin abandoned its ideology. In part, Truman's failure of leadership at the beginning of the Cold War stems from his rigid application of the concept of containment. For most of the Cold War, containment meant "cooperation with the Soviet Union was impossible ... [because] its leaders possessed an omnivorous and insatiable appetite for power." Not until 1963, with the Limited Test Ban Treaty, and then in 1969, when Nixon became the first president to try to roll back containment, did U.S. foreign policy accommodate any serious dealings with the Soviet Union (or China).[7]

Atomic Bomb Rationalizations

So the Second World War ended in 1945 (if it ended at all) on a more ambiguous note than Americans today usually remember. This is most evident with respect to memories about the dropping of the atomic bomb. That its deployment raised more ethical questions over fifty years ago than it does today references the decline in ethical standards that characterizes contemporary U.S. foreign policy, despite official exhortatory claims to the contrary.

The result has been that many average Americans old enough to remember World War II are now intolerant of any discussion of the atomic bomb issue unless it is based on myth rather than fact, while ethicists around the world and a number of younger Americans, scholars, writers, and activists are questioning conventional wisdom on the subject. According to Jean-Christophe Agnew, a cultural historian at Yale University, "there was a lot more openness and a lot more doubt" expressed about the atomic bomb between 1945 and 1947 than there is today. In fact, though a good deal of apprehensiveness was provoked by what had happened to Hiroshima and Nagasaki, for the most part it remained a subtext to victory even while those viewing the bomb as a "good thing" declined from 69 percent in 1945 to 55 percent in 1947.[8]

Many of the myths regarding the bomb in the popular mind relate to the ad hoc reasons Truman gave for its use. Standard arguments that the bomb was dropped to save 500,000 to a million lives have not stood up to historical scrutiny. In reality, initial military estimates available to Truman by June 1945 projected American losses ranging from forty to fifty thousand – not the 250,000 General George C. Marshall may have given Truman at Potsdam (although there is no record of his having done so), and certainly not the "over a million casualties" figure later concocted by Stimson for a February 1947 article in *Harper's*. McGeorge Bundy, at the insistence of James B. Conant, president of Harvard and a former member of the president's advisory Interim Committee on the atomic bomb, ghostwrote this article for Stimson (who was then eighty) with input from General Leslie Groves. Later, in his memoirs, Truman used a less exaggerated figure, but still said that an invasion of Japan "might cost a half-million American lives," but there is no military evidence for either figure.[9]

Truman and his aides later emphasized this single explanation in order to rationalize the action in an attempt to defuse public criticism about the ethical, racist, and military implications of the largest democracy on earth punishing a defeated enemy – criticism that arose as soon as the unprecedented destructive force of the atomic bomb became public.[10] Among those who considered the bombing so "morally indefensible" that it required some "expression of guilt" was Reinhold Niebuhr. His opposition caused consternation among those who had used Niebuhr's writings defending immoral means to attain moral results in the war against Germany (and later against the Soviet Union). Niebuhr's "Christian realism" had served the cause of war ably until the United States bombed Hiroshima and Nagasaki. Niebuhr never, however, became the strong antiwar, antinuclear advocate that A. J. Muste represented. In fact, Niebuhr became a leading liberal anti-Soviet, while from 1945 forward Muste condemned the argument that "nuclear war was a lesser evil than Communism and that an arms race could prevent war." Not until the 1960s, during the Vietnam War, did Niebuhr come to the realization that "the evils of a general war with modern means of mass destruction are so terrible and so incalculable that it is immoral to prefer them to [Communist domination]."[11]

Nonetheless, because of Niebuhr's prominence as a theologian in 1945, the Truman administration felt obliged to respond to his unexpected criticism of the atomic bomb. This task fell to Conant, who said that the use of atomic bombs was no more immoral than the strategic firebombing of Japanese cities that had already taken place. (By the spring of 1945, 67 Japanese cities had been firebombed by B-29s and 350,000 thousand civilians incinerated – with the approval, among many others, of the then young Air Force colonel Robert S. McNamara. This was the equivalent of 58 percent of the population of Cleveland and 35 percent of Chicago.) Truman, in all likelihood, agreed with Conant that the ethics of such previous incendiary bombings was not that different from the ethics of using nuclear power. However, it should be noted that even he felt obliged to refer to God to rationalize using the atomic bomb, whereas he had not previously invoked Providence to justify traditional use of air power.[12]

Following the April 25, 1945, meeting in which Stimson gave the details of the Manhattan Project to Truman, the most significant meeting took place on June 18 among Truman and his military and civilian advisers.[13] The atomic bomb was not the major purpose or topic of conversation at the special June 18 meeting: the invasion of Japan was. From the existing transcripts, it is clear that no one seriously considered ways to avoid using the bomb, despite Assistant Secretary of War John J. McCloy's 1953 claim to the contrary that he did. Truman and his top advisers did not ask any probing questions about its use then or at any other time that can be documented. There was no decision made about whether to use the atomic bomb, only when and where to drop it after it was successfully tested. The determination occurred in an offhand way on

July 25 while Truman was at Potsdam. There was no special meeting with his military or civilian advisers there; he simply gave Stimson the go-ahead as the secretary of war was about to return to Washington. At that point, according to the historian Alonzo Hamby, "militarily, the [Manhattan] project was on automatic pilot," and, hence, Truman made an independent unilateral nondecision.[14]

To continue to support the original unsophisticated defense of an indefensible weapon based on saving American lives and, as Truman said, "to shorten the agony of war" leaves many of those without adult memories of the Second World War with a vague, uneasy feeling, especially now that the Cold War is over. Younger generations, who do not have firsthand memories of the Second World War, need more than the outdated conventional rationale for dropping the atomic bomb based on the common perception of veterans serving at the time in the Pacific who believed with utmost conviction that their lives were saved by the atomic bomb. This point of view is of little value over fifty years later for understanding why U.S. policy makers came to the conclusion they did about the atomic bomb in the summer of 1945. In essence, it came down to the idea that "Americans could do anything at all to win." Yet, if the Japanese had done something similar to "shorten the agony of war," Truman would have considered it a crime against humanity.[15]

Yet there was something ethically amiss about dropping the atomic bomb that trumped all the other presidential decisions for the rest of the Cold War. It was not only "the most controversial act of Truman's presidency," as Robert Ferrell has noted, it also tainted U.S. foreign policy from that time to the present. According to Jonathan Glover: "The use of weapons of mass destruction is a crime against God and man and remains a crime even if they are used in retaliation or for what is regarded as a morally justified end. It is forbidden to do evil that good may come of it."[16] By this criterion, Truman remains ethically culpable for his decision. Yet his failure of leadership on this issue can be in part blamed on the loose ends he inherited from Franklin Roosevelt's arrogant exceptionalist foreign policy. Only a president more confident of his own abilities could have questioned what his more charismatic predecessor had set in motion.

Nonetheless, mainstream historians continue to portray the use of the atomic bomb as another of Truman's brave and intelligent decisions made in the heat of the moment that brought about the Japanese surrender. A 2005 book by Tsuyoshi Hasegawa reopened this debate among diplomatic historians because he argued that the atomic bomb did not produce the knockout punch causing Japan to surrender; rather, the Soviet entrance into the Pacific war did.[17]

Truman and the Origins of the Cold War

In general, most of Truman's other important early foreign policy decisions, such as the Truman Doctrine in 1947, the creation of NATO in 1949, and his acceptance in September 1950 of National Security Council Paper Number 68

(NSC-68), which argued that the only way the United States could contain the Soviet Union was through a massive military buildup, are usually praised or glossed over in the most recent biographies of the thirty-third president of the United States.[18] Why is this the case?

One answer is that most biographers adhere to what is known as the rational actor theory of history, meaning that events do not make the person, but that the person, acting logically, controls events. Americans, in particular, like to think that their presidents are in control and operating rationally, but many historians and political scientists no longer adhere to this simplistic interpretation. Analysis of the influence of presidential advisers, congressional committees, and federal agencies, as well as economic influences, on decision making have long since made many scholars question the rational actor model. As with economic policy toward Japan before Pearl Harbor, a faceless bureaucracy often triumphs over the best-laid plans and intent of any given president.

Policy toward Japan in 1941 and again in 1945 represents first one, then the other scenario at work. Just as ideology overrode realism when Wilson took the United States into World War I, so did among those who insisted on a complete embargo of Japan in 1941, and among those who insisted that the bomb be used in 1945. The same bureaucratic outmaneuvering of a willing president can be found in Paul H. Nitze's manipulation of the system in drafting NSC-68 and his use of the Korean War to obtain both presidential and congressional approval of it. In his role as head of the State Department's Policy Planning Staff, through this document Nitze laid the foundation for the "universalistic, moralistic theory of anti-communist containment," establishing a "negotiating posture that required Soviet capitulation." Section IV of this document contained the fear propaganda language that would become standard during the Cold War.[19] Once again, as happened in 1917, 1941, and 1945, this founding document of the Cold War should be viewed as setting the ideological course based on American exceptionalism that often overpowered common sense in the formulation of U.S. foreign policy after the Second World War.

Still another factor contributed to Truman's setting in motion the Cold War so quickly. As with all presidents, it is necessary to look for their worst rather than their best characteristics, especially before they are elected, in order to anticipate how they will perform in office. In Truman's case, his predilection for rash judgements and hasty decision making rushed the United States not only into an ideological Cold War, but also into the unnecessarily rapid militarization of that bipolar conflict between the United States and the USSR.[20] Truman's brand of rushed decisiveness based on inadequate information served him fairly well until he became president. After that, it combined with his feelings of inadequacy and inferiority in the Oval Office, as FDR's less-than-impressive successor, and resulted in reckless decisions that did not always serve the country well.[21]

A final way to explain Truman's diplomatic decisions can be summed up in the phrase: Cold War mentality or mind-set. From the perspective of the end of the Cold War, it is possible to see a series of Faustian actions or bargains, beginning with the dropping of the atomic bomb, that ate away at the American soul. As the victor in that conflict, the United States has chosen not to face this troubling ethical dilemma or the erratic pattern of independent internationalism it followed from 1945 to 1989. In the growing anticommunist hysteria of the late 1940s and early 1950s, the specious idea of the Soviet Union as powerful, expansionist, and ideologically unstoppable became imbedded in the American psyche before it was anywhere near true. It still lingers in standard writings about the early Cold War period. And so a forty-plus-year conflict began in which Americans and Russians did not recognize each other as legitimate enemies—as *justi hostes*. Instead, the Cold War became one that could only be won by any means necessary.

Faulty Fears

While Truman precipitously set in motion the unethical, ideological and militaristic aspects of the Cold War, there is no denying that the United States faced three major problems coming out of the Second World War. The first problem cannot be separated from the second: how to compete with Communism and socialism as economic systems and also as political models, especially in war-torn Europe. According to U.S. military estimates, the Soviet Union posed no immediate postwar threat, but civilian leaders determined that its economic system did. Even though the Military Intelligence Division concluded in July 1947 that the USSR could not attack in Europe, let alone the United States, civilian and military planners ultimately disregarded all indications of "Soviet weakness, moderation, and circumspection," such as its reduction of troops in Eastern Europe, its devastating human and infrastructure losses during the war, and its domestic demobilization. Instead, American leaders concentrated on potential Russian military capabilities and the apparent attraction of communist statism in Europe. Therefore, they decided out of fear, based on their perception of a future Soviet threat, to take advantage of the window of opportunity provided by the obvious postwar weakness of the Soviet Union. Rather than trying to perceive the threat that the Soviets sensed in light of U.S. postwar power, they chose to act only on their own "heightened threat perception" and to exaggerate the menace posed by the USSR. Melvyn Leffler has argued that the fears on both sides were not completely irrational. Both were driven by the very real confrontation of two opposing ideologies. This led to precipitous military actions by the United States, such as establishing extensive overseas bases, military air transit and landing bases, and multi- and bilateral military treaties – all of which initiated the early Faustian stages of the Cold War.[22]

So it was not U.S. civilian and military leaders' fear of the armed might of the USSR that caused them to rush into militarizing the Cold War, it was their ideological fear that the American political and economic lifestyle could not prevail at home unless it prevailed abroad. For example, Undersecretary of State Dean Acheson on February 10, 1947, under aggressive questioning by Senator Kenneth McKellar from Tennessee about presumed Russian intentions to take over not only "the remainder of Europe but perhaps the remainder of the world" if the Soviet Union acquired an atomic bomb, admitted that "Russian foreign policy is an aggressive and expanding one." This set the stage for President Truman's famous speech at Baylor University on March 6 in which he proclaimed that freedom was dependent on the freedom of enterprise and that state control of trade and planned economies were "not the American way." Therefore, he both arrogantly and defensively asserted that "the whole world should adopt the American system" and that "the American system could survive in America only if it became a world system."[23]

The first offshoot of Truman's assertion, of course, was the Truman Doctrine. Ostensibly meant only to provide economic and military aid to Greece and Turkey, the president's language on March 12, 1947, implied much more. Among other things, he directly challenged the Soviet Union without mentioning it by name when he announced the willingness of the United States "to help free people maintain their free institutions and national integrity against aggressive movements that seek to impose upon them totalitarian regimes." Then he added that the United States would "support free peoples who are resisting attempted subjugation by armed minorities or outside pressure" and asked America and the world to choose between "two ways of life." General Marshall, then secretary of state, Marshall's Soviet adviser Charles Bohlen, and George Kennan all expressed doubts about the expansive and fear-inducing words that Acheson had composed for Truman.[24]

This unilateral proclamation laid the groundwork for American opposition to legitimate nationalist anticolonial movements for the remainder of the Cold War because of the mistaken assumption that most "armed minorities" would be fostered by "outside pressure" from the Soviet Union. At the same time, it implicitly undercut the newly established United Nations. The next day Henry Wallace correctly predicted that Truman's words

marked a turning point in American history. For it is not a Greek crisis that we face: it is an American crisis. Yesterday President Truman proposed, in effect, that America police Russia's every border. There is no regime too reactionary for us [referring to the oppressive and corrupt regimes in both Greece and Turkey], provided that it stand in Russia's expansionist path. There is no country too remote to serve as a scene of contest which may widen until it becomes a world war.

Almost thirty years later, Senator J. William Fulbright confirmed what Wallace had perceived at the time, saying: "More by far than any other factor the anti-Communism of the Truman Doctrine has been the guiding spirit of American policy since World War II."[25] And thus the Cold War began.

The Marshall Plan

The Marshall Plan, officially known as the European Recovery Program (ERP), became the most positive offshoot of Truman's Baylor address. It was designed to deal with the second postwar problem facing the United States, namely, the restoration of confidence in the Wilsonian idea of liberal capitalist internation-alism that had appeared to collapse with the Great Depression. Hence, the country undertook the Marshall Plan and other economic measures to rebuild both the former allied and enemy powers. But this economic reconstruction came with political strings attached because the United States lacked confi-dence in the ability of democracy and capitalism to prevail in the immediate post–World War II years.

Specifically, the administrative arm of the ERP was the Economic Cooper-ation Administration (ECA). Organized as a separate agency out of the State Department, its head reported only to the president, and it had an ideological mission in addition to rebuilding Europe: to spread the American dream and the American way. Although slated to end officially on December 31, 1951, the onset of the Korean War prompted the Marshall Plan's demise in October of that year with the passage of the Mutual Security Act. This transformed the ECA into the Mutual Security Agency (MSA), and from that time forward money for military buildup abroad replaced economic assistance – under a variety of differ-ent names down to the present Agency for International Development (AID) – as the major emphasis of U.S. foreign aid.

The Marshall Plan was not simply a response to the specific ideological-economic threat of Communism, it also was the beginning of a general attempt by the United States to "restructure the world economy along lines similar to the corporative order that was emerging in the United States." In Europe, this meant replacing what the United States considered traditional and inefficient national economic systems based on labor-intensive production protected by high tariffs with a large-market economy, efficient technological production, and free trade. This attempt to make sure that such a massive recovery program would serve the interests of private business and financial leaders made it the target of such disparate critics as Wallace, Robert Taft, and Herbert Hoover, all of whom wrongly predicted that it would continue Europe's "semicolonial dependence on the United States" and require economic restrictions, scarcity and high prices, and an increase in taxes at home. In fact, the United States industrial and agricultural sectors profited from the $13 billion in foreign aid distributed under the Marshall Plan. Their exports boomed because of the stipulation that the money had to be spent on American products. While the Marshall Plan may have not been the only reason for the industrial "take-off" of postwar Europe, it contributed significantly to it.[26]

Because the Marshall Plan was part of "America's twentieth-century search for a new economic order at home and abroad," it had strategic and political, as well as economic, goals for shaping the Cold War world. It should come as no surprise, therefore, that the first assignment of a new covert agency within the CIA called the Office of Policy Coordination (OPC) was to provide secret non-military political and psychological assistance to the Marshall Plan, especially in France and Italy, in order to subvert elections that might favor communist or socialist politicians. In Germany and Austria the Marshall Plan, with CIA help, supported huge information programs to counter anti-American sentiment, to control the press, and to limit the number of "acceptable" parties in elections. In this manner, the Truman administration "added a Cold War corollary to the [Wilsonian] principle of self-determination: massive foreign aid and nonmilitary covert operations to reshape war-torn Europe in the image of the United States."[27]

Nowhere was U.S. fear of failure in the struggle against Communism more evident or more counterproductive than in postwar Czechoslovakia. Distrust of the West over Munich and opposition to the economic revitalization of West Germany under the Marshall Plan temporarily united communist and noncommunist parties in the Czech National Front, which tried unsuccessfully to carve out greater social and economic democracy for the country through its own brand of state socialism. Unfortunately, many noncommunist Czech intellectuals allowed the Czechoslovak Communist Party (KSC) to set the terms of the political debate between 1945 and 1948 instead of constructing a viable alternative to the communist program. As a result, they contributed to "creat[ing] a context in which the Communist party could and did obtain widespread support, substantially easing its path to total power."[28]

The conventional Cold War version argued that a brave Czech majority opposed to Communism was simply overwhelmed by the unpopular but Soviet-financed KSC after the mysterious death in February 1948 of Czechoslovakia's Foreign Minister Jan Masaryk. This interpretation has now been questioned as the basic reason for the communist takeover of that country later in the year. While some Czechs initially responded positively to the general idea of economic aid from the United States, the Truman administration insisted on its international economic plans based on a strong West German economy and expanding markets, thus compromising the position of the noncommunist Czechs and thereby contributing to the success of the communist coup in 1948. Washington did not understand that except for Catholics, most Czechs actually preferred some form of socialism after the war. Because U.S.-imposed financial and economic controls excluded Soviet participation, the Marshall Plan not only prompted the USSR "to clamp down on Czechoslovakia and Eastern Europe," but also set in motion the division of the world into two camps, of which East and West Germany became the first symbol.[29]

In retrospect, however, as unilateral and rigid as the Marshall Plan appeared on paper, most European nations welcomed, even "invited such American aid and in the process exercise[d] a considerable degree of autonomy with the framework of the ERP." Try as American leaders might, they never succeeded in "recasting Europe in the image of American neocapitalism" because France and Italy used the threat of communist victories to avoid making economic and social reforms. The West Germans did likewise, using the threat of rising nationalism, and even the English "negotiated a special position for themselves in the ERP." In the end, the Marshall Plan became "one of the most successful peacetime foreign polices launched by the United States" in the twentieth century because it wasn't based on crude military interventionism. Instead, it was applied to countries that had a history of industrial development, functioning political systems, and commitment to rehabilitating their war-torn economies. Washington administered the plan in Europe in a much more mild-mannered and sometimes cooperative way than the subsequent unilateral actions it took in Greece, Central America, Southeast Asia, and Africa to protect its self-proclaimed economic and strategic interests.[30] In the rest of the world America would insist in a more heavy-handed way on imposing its version of democracy and capitalism abroad during the Cold War, with the former usually taking a backseat to the latter.

Unfortunately, the best of American materialist postwar fear and drive, as represented by the Marshall Plan, officially ended in 1951. After that, raw economic power combined with two less positive aspects of the ideological premises of U.S. foreign policy in the twentieth century – namely, its deep-seated racism and, since the Bolshevik Revolution, its improvident anti-Communism. All three played important roles as the United States conducted diplomacy during the Cold War in the name of national security.

Minority Rights Redux

The third and least publicized problem confronting the United States after 1945 came straight out of the 1920s and 1930s. What to do with minority groups? In general, the former allied powers and America agreed that never again should minority rights be allowed to disrupt international relations, as they had in the interwar years.

As noted previously, after World War I ethnic or religious minorities had often found themselves isolated within new national boundaries. Since the mandate system and bilateral minority treaties had failed to protect such vulnerable groups in the 1920s, 1930s, and early 1940s, a study issued by the UN secretary general in 1947 deemed the entire League of Nations' protection of minorities system generally null and void, based on the doctrine of changed circumstances. Consequently, the international community decided after World War II to enforce mass migrations in order to avoid creating more minority groups because of the negative attitude toward minorities created in the interwar years, which was based on the belief that German minorities had fostered Hitler's aggressive militarism against other European countries. In this sense, the "issue of minorities was deliberately 'de-internationalized'" after the Second World War.[31]

Instead of group rights, all people would be protected by the institutionalization of individual human rights through the United Nations. Individuals could petition the UN against forced repatriation if they so chose, but in general massive repatriation was the rule of the day because it was thought it would be easier to protect human rights if fewer minorities were left unprotected from hostile majorities within post–World War II nation-states. In fact, a rule of thumb developed that any European country made up of less than 80 percent of one ethnic majority could not be stable. The Cold War period did not favor establishing norms for protecting minorities as groups. Instead, it was thought that having the United Nations proclaim itself in favor of general and universal protection of individual human rights would "automatically take care of the problems of persons belonging to minorities and hence of minority rights as groups."[32]

This assumption did not prove correct after 1945 because – despite the Chapter VII provisions of the UN Charter calling for force to maintain "international peace and security," the 1948 Universal Declaration of Human Rights, and two 1966 International Covenants – "the normal response of states to humanitarian outrages during the cold war was non-intervention." Tragic examples of such nonintervention include the mass murder in the 1960s and 1970s of Tutsis in Burundi, of Ibos when Biafra tried to secede from Nigeria, and of East Timorese when Indonesia invaded and annexed that country. Even when armed interventions took place during the Cold War – ostensibly to save lives – the motives of the invading nations were questioned by the international community and such actions were judged to be exceptions to the prevailing consensus within the UN that sovereignty and nonintervention had to be respected. As a result, India's 1971 intervention in East Pakistan, Vietnam's 1978 intervention in Cambodia, and Tanzania's 1978 intervention in Uganda were all viewed with suspicion, even though each of them resulted in stopping existing human rights violations. In the case of the first, intervention created the state of Bangladesh; the second contributed to the elimination of the vicious Pol Pot regime; and the third ended the reign of Idi Amin.[33]

Throughout the Cold War the international community did not embrace either humanitarian interventions or the right of minorities to self-determination within established nation-states. Little wonder that critics have argued that Wilson's altruistic idealism not only failed during the interwar years, but that during the Cold War years it devolved into a "fundamentally sentimental, megalomaniacal, and ahistorical vision of world democracy organized on the American example...[that] has led to disastrous consequences for the past 80 years...[which] seem to have left no trace on the minds of Wilson's modern followers." Yet advocates of Wilsonianism continued to assert that it has always represented the fusion of "national interest and moral conviction... [representing American foreign policy] at its best," refusing to recognize the harm that Wilson's vision of an economic interdependent and pluralistic world did to both group and individual human rights.[34]

While dealing with the three major post–World War II problems just discussed, the United States repeatedly compromised and contradicted its own rhetoric on these specific issues: (1) the highly charged racial aspects of decolonization; (2) support for nationalist, democratic movements; and (3) free trade.

With respect to the first and second of these issues, *The United States and Decolonization*, edited by David Ryan and Victor Pungong, documents how and why the United States turned a blind eye to many legitimate nationalist demands for self-determination and democracy on the part of peoples of color. American racism at home and abroad, a fear that European allies – France and England, in particular – might withdraw from NATO, and an insistence on preventing the United Nations from focusing on the worldwide racism of former colonial powers in their decolonization processes all played a role.[35] At the beginning of the Cold War the United States supported old colonial domination by cooperating with and supporting white rule, particularly in Africa.

Angola as a Case Study in Decolonization

This policy was given its most explicit certification in the 1970 National Security Study Memorandum (NSSM) 39 of the Nixon administration – one of the few to be completely declassified during his presidency. It resulted from Nixon's review of the remaining white regimes in Africa – those in Angola, Rhodesia, and South Africa. It recommended that Washington "maintain public opposition to racial oppression, but relax political isolation and economic restrictions on white states." In a word, the "tar baby" approach allowed the United States to engage in "selective relaxation of [its] stance toward white regimes" while at the same time publicly opposing "racial oppression." In keeping with NSSM 39, Nixon accepted the Byrd Amendment, which weakened U.S. economic sanctions against the white Rhodesian government by allowing other countries to purchase its chrome and other minerals. Under Nixon, the United States also relaxed the long-standing arms embargo against South Africa.[36] The "tar baby" policy continued, with one or two exceptions, until 1975. Even after that, the United States supported black factions in Africa only if they were anticommunist.

Angola is a prime example of the "tar baby" policy and remains in a state of turmoil as a result of Cold War policies of the United States and the Soviet Union. Civil war began in Angola in 1961 with three tribal groups – each with the backing of superpowers or their surrogates – vying to bring independence to their nation. The Soviet Union supported the Popular Front for the Liberation of Angola (MPLA), ultimately led by José Eduardo dos Santos; China and Zaire subsidized the National Front for the Liberation of Angola (FNLA), led by Holden Roberto; and the United States backed the National Union for the Total Independence of Angola (UNITA), headed by Jonas Savimbi. However, the United States had also been giving covert aid to Roberto off and on since 1961. Such aid undermined a tripartite transitional government that had been set up by the three liberation movements meeting in Alvor, Portugal, in January 1975, and violated federal legislation barring further covert aid to those contending for power in Angola.[37]

Neither Congress nor the public knew about this payment of $300,000 to Roberto, who used it to set off a full-scale civil war by attacking the MPLA. The Soviets and Cubans responded and saved the MPLA from annihilation and appeared to have won the day over the United States. So the CIA requested more secret funding for both the FNLA and the UNITA from the NSC 40 Committee, which oversaw covert operations. Although African specialists within the State Department opposed this request, Henry Kissinger did not, so the

NSC 40 Committee, which he chaired and which oversaw all CIA covert activity, approved $14 million in June and expanded the amount to $32 million by September. Nonetheless, the MPLA prevailed, and when Congress found out in November about this covert activity, it passed the Clark Amendment to the Defense appropriations bill in December 1975, terminating the Angola operation . At the same time, the U.S. Senate officially barred further covert American support to the ongoing civil war. This was the first (and last) time Congress suspended a CIA operation. While both President Gerald Ford and Kissinger tried to blame Congress for the American defeat in Angola, Dick Clark (D-Iowa) and other members of Congress concluded that the administration had mishandled the situation and had even provoked Soviet and Cuban intervention.[38]

Civil war continued in Angola for another twenty-seven years, with UNITA and the MPLA killing with each other at a cost of at least 500,000 lives. A peace agreement in 1990 led to elections in 1992, but when Savimbi lost to dos Santos, he renewed the fighting. By the end of 1993, Savimbi controlled 65 percent of Angola, and approximately a third of the population and more than 30,000 on both sides had died. In that year the United States recognized the MPLA government because dos Santos had abandoned Communism. Even though another peace agreement was signed in 1994, internecine strife continued because Savimbi did not demilitarize the UNITA and began retaking towns he had given up.[39]

Although Angola is awash in oil (only six countries produce more petroleum), two-thirds of its citizens live in abject poverty, dependent on the World Food Program and unaided by Chevron Texaco, which pumps 60 percent of Angola's oil. The United States buys more than half of this oil (more than it buys from Kuwait). Oil companies refuse to make public the large sums they are paying to the MPLA government for their oil rights – extortion money that is feeding corruption and making the Angolan army the most powerful in Africa. Savimbi was killed in 2002, but the suffering of the people of this oil-rich country continues as a testament to the foolery of the Cold War. After George W. Bush welcomed dos Santos to the White House in 2002, a U.S. embassy official in the $40-million-dollar fortified embassy in Luanda proclaimed in language reminiscent of Cold War rhetoric: "Angola can be a force for democracy, stability, and economic development."[40]

Whether the United States pursued democracy in former colonial areas during the Cold War to the degree that it has claimed and whether, even if it had, democracy would "have taken" in newly emerging nations are legitimate questions. With respect to the first, the degree to which the United States actually implemented rather than simply talked about advancing democracy abroad in the twentieth century can certainly be questioned. According to Larry Diamond, "American diplomacy did not make promoting democracy a major goal" in the last century, either in terms of money spent to aid democratic institutions or as a result of covert and overt military interventions. Instead, it inconsistently concentrated on "exporting" the American model of democracy, which was "ill-suited to poor, unstable, and divided countries," or pretended that democracies existed where they didn't.[41]

Middle Eastern Oil

The Middle East constituted an area of the world where the United States pursued oil and not democracy during the Cold War. Even before the Cold War began, as previously noted, Franklin Roosevelt set the stage to counter British and Dutch domination of Middle Eastern oil by arranging for both Iran and Saudi Arabia to receive lend-lease aid and cash. The United States had been interested in Middle Eastern oil reserves since the 1920s, but the area did not become a primary object of diplomacy until during and after the Second World War. Truman faced two postwar oil problems. First, there was the indigenous threat of rising Arab nationalism and Muslim fundamentalism, about which he showed little concern. Second, although Great Britain, the United States, and the USSR had occupied Iran during the war, Stalin did not completely withdraw his troops when the UK and America did. The Soviet Union did not need Iranian oil but, according to George Kennan, feared "potential foreign penetration" in northern Iran. Consequently, Stalin meddled in Iranian politics on behalf of the Autonomous People's Republic of Azerbaijan and the Kurdish People's Republic, keeping the Iranians from controlling these separatist uprisings. Stalin also obtained a northern oil concession and convinced the Iranian prime minister, Qavam as-Saltaneh, to appoint three Communists to his cabinet. To say the least, this irritated Truman, and so he exaggerated and publicized a Soviet threat to the area. Then he encouraged Mohammed Reza Shah Pahlavi, who had succeeded his father to the throne in 1941, to dismantle the separatist regimes and to refuse to ratify the Soviet oil deal.[42]

Eisenhower and John Foster Dulles continued Truman's policy of countering so-called Soviet penetration by boycotting Iranian oil once the new prime minister, Mohammed Mossadegh, began to nationalize his country's oil reserves. The shah left the country for a long "vacation" after Mossadegh was elected head of the government in 1953, but not until he (the shah) had been assured that England and the United States had set in motion a covert operation to overthrow this highly nationalist leader and restore private ownership of the oil fields. "The American intervention of August 1953 was a momentous event in the history of Iranian-American relations," according to James A. Bill. It "left a running wound that bled for twenty-five years and contaminated relations with the Islamic Republic of Iran following the revolution of 1978–79." The fact that Mossadegh "was neither a Communist nor a communist sympathizer" was beside the point. Operation Ajax, headed by the CIA's Middle East chief, Kermit Roosevelt, aided by General H. Norman Schwarzkopf (whose son commanded U.S. forces in the 1991 Persian Gulf War), restored the shah to the Peacock Throne, and he promptly agreed to sell oil through an international consortium, 40 percent of which was owned by American oil companies. This

Faustian operation also signified that the United States had replaced England as the dominant oil power of the Middle East and marked the beginning of a relationship with the shah that exacerbated relations with Arab nationalists and Muslim fundamentalists and finally exploded in the late 1970s.[43]

Securing oil instead of securing democracy dominated American diplomacy in the Middle East during the Cold War. In particular, the United States aimed at promoting exaggerated notions about Soviet encroachment in the area, keeping oil prices low, and, after 1948, first protecting and then arming the state of Israel, particularly after the impressive Israeli defeat of Egypt and Syria (then aligned with Russia) in 1967. U.S. influence in the area increased geometrically after Britain withdrew from the Gulf in 1971, and America began to curry favor with the newly independent states of Bahrain, Qatar, the United Arab Emirates, and Oman without ever suggesting that these sheikhdoms democratize. Throughout the Cold War the United States "flaunt[ed] the banner of democracy in the Middle East only when that advanc[ed] its economic, military or strategic interests."[44]

The deference and favoritism shown Iran and especially Saudi Arabia began with FDR and increased as the United States became more and more dependent on Middle Eastern oil reserves. From Eisenhower through Reagan, the United States massively reinforced the military strength of Saudi Arabia and Iran (until the shah was overthrown in 1979). In 1962, Kennedy even sent in troops when Saudi power was threatened by the civil war in Yeman.[45]

Except for Richard Nixon, no modern American president has significantly deviated from the policy initiated by FDR aimed at guaranteeing a continuous supply of cheap oil. Although Nixon had built his early political career partially off the largesse of California oil interests, by the early 1970s he ignored warnings from American oil executives that the bargaining power over oil prices had shifted from them in favor of the Organization of Petroleum Exporting Countries (OPEC). Instead, Nixon, according to one account, "personally gave the Shah [of Iran] permission to buy any conventional weapon in the American arsenal" in order to build another "trusted local power" (in addition to Israel) in the Middle East. However, the shah could pay for these weapons only by increasing oil prices through OPEC, which was then under his "moderate leadership." That moderation ceased, however, with the onset of the 1973 October [Yom Kippur] War. When the United States began an arms airlift to Israel in October, OPEC quadrupled oil prices and then instituted a five-month embargo on oil to the United States, during which time Kissinger "talked publicly about the possibility of seizing Persian Gulf facilities should the embargo escalate into a strangulation of American industrial capacity." The bitter memory of this embargo prompted the Congressional Research Service (CRS) military feasibility study discussed below.[46]

Nixon's choice of Iran and Israel over U.S. oil interests and his free market policy for arms exports to a series of favored Middle Eastern countries meant higher oil prices for the United States. Regardless, this policy continued under Ford, Carter, Reagan, and Bush Sr., until the first Gulf War produced much deserved criticism of it and of the erratic restriction of production by OPEC that the Nixon administration had set in motion. This war also transformed the role of American presidents from one of privately negotiating U.S. access to oil reserves to publicly waging war for those resources.

In 1975, the Congressional Research Service presented to the Special Sub-committee on Investigations of the House Committee on International Relations a feasibility study detailing what would be required for the United States to take over Persian Gulf oil facilities through force. It was based in part on an early neo-conservative article by Robert W. Tucker in the January 1975 issue of *Commentary*, entitled "Oil: The Issue of American Intervention." Increasingly, during and after the Cold War, the much-touted free flow of oil was (and is) guaranteed not by OPEC or the "world market," but by American armed forces or American sale of arms to select groups of oil-producing nations in the Middle East. To date, Middle Eastern oil supplies have still not been guaranteed by democracy.

The Myth of Free Trade

The final Cold War issue over which the United States contravened itself is that of free trade – an essential component of neo-liberal economics. In this instance, the country entered into domestic Faustian agreements as well as international ones. The United States strayed from free trade principles right after the Second World War. Although many American leaders in the 1940s and 1950s believed that economic nationalism had contributed to that conflict, their professed public faith in multilateral trade liberalization soon succumbed to maintaining Cold War alliances. Technically speaking, the argument in favor of free trade has always been a unilateral one because it assumes that "a country serves its own interests by pursuing free trade regardless of what other countries may do." But the United States did not follow such a policy following the Second World War. Instead, it revived the postwar economies of Europe, Japan, Korea, Taiwan, Mexico, and Brazil, not by insisting on its proclaimed free trade principles, but by privately accepting the protectionist policies of those nations and making "some big tariff cuts" without insisting on reciprocity, often at the expense of domestic industries – steel being the most obvious example. Privately, the Bureau of the Budget admitted that domestic "economic objectives . . . must be subordinated to our politico-security objectives," and President Truman's assistant secretary of state for economic affairs said that "the great question is whether the country is willing to decide in the broader national self-interest to reduce tariffs and increase United States imports even though some domestic industry may suffer serious injury." When the security interests of the Cold War conflicted with the best interests of American workers, cities, and certain industries, American leaders turned a blind eye or laconically recalled, as former Federal Reserve chairman Paul A. Volcker did, that "the strength and prosperity of the American economy was too evident to engender concern about the cost."[47]

It fell to economic historians to document that the result of weaning political allies from the postwar temptation of state socialism or even state capitalism marked the "deindustrialization [of] the United States" because decision makers were "prepared to allow discrimination against [American] exports to alleviate the strain of involvement in international trade for its allies." According to Stephen Krasner, the "United States used its power . . . to promote general political goals rather than specific [domestic] economic interests." This was the major reason why the United States administered the economic aspects of the Marshall Plan in such a mild-mannered fashion in order to create an "empire by invitation," or what Charles S. Maier has called "consensual American hegemony."[48]

For all Washington's talk about postwar trade liberalization, the United States did not always benefit from free trade because of the lack of reciprocity following World War II. Through the 1960s, America's so-called free trade policy advantaged its trading partners more than it did certain domestic industries such as steel because it accepted European subsidies and tariffs without always imposing its own or demanding some form of reciprocity. Yet as long as U.S. trade expanded worldwide, demands for protection from scattered segments of domestic industry did not receive serious governmental attention. Beginning in the 1970s, however, the nation's excessive consumerism produced a trade deficit that has continued unabated ever since. So by the end of the Cold War the "the pattern of foreign trade that resulted from the failure of the United States to have a trade policy that protected its national interests," according to the economic historian John M. Culbertson, "was the central and decisive cause in the economic decline of the United States" in terms of its chronic trade and account deficits, wage stagnation, and weak productivity.[49]

For example, between 1947 and 1967 six multilateral rounds of the General Agreement on Tariffs and Trade (GATT) did not appear to have a negative effect on the U.S. economy. There was reasonable economic growth (averaging 3.5 percent annually), and both median family income and the weekly earnings of workers in factories rose (80 and 55 percent, respectively). But after the 1967 Kennedy Round concessions were extended and then ended in 1972, greater import competition forced factory closings; economic growth fell; median family income stagnated; and real weekly earnings fell 13 percent from 1973 to 1995. These developments occurred because corporate America responded to greater global competition by cutting costs, moving plants abroad, and downsizing – all in the name of jump-starting the economy, regardless of worker pain. This has meant increased profits for the CEOs of the top 3 percent of American companies, but little substantial recovery for the overall domestic or world economy. In fact, profits and wage redistribution began to be more and more skewed by the end of the Cold War. In order to avoid necessary regulation, multinational corporations – some of which "are as big and powerful as nations" – have promoted a failed unilateral free trade policy or, at most, a "strategic trade policy" rather than a reciprocal one. Sometimes referred to as "managed trade," strategic trade policy permits a "limited government industrial policy consisting of carefully targeted subsidies" for certain domestic producers. Which sectors of the U.S. economy are truly strategic and whether a strategic trade policy would benefit the country as much as free trade based on reciprocity remains to be determined. There is a lack of convincing evidence for gains to the United States if it adopted an aggressive managed economy approach–to say nothing of the political debate it would generate.[50]

At the beginning of the twenty-first century even orthodox economists began to question the rhetorical promotion of free trade on the part of multinational corporations and by both Democratic and Republican administrations. They found that free trade had always been oversold and at least since the 1980s had not served the postindustrial trade needs of the United States. Yet free trade remains the mantra of unregulated globalization in the post–Cold War era even though the United States continues not to adhere to free trade principles. The idea that American private enterprise could maintain wages and employment at home in order to continue to fuel domestic consumption while at the same time transferring production to cheap labor abroad as it faced more regional economic competition and as its global markets declined proved fallacious. Polls indicate that the American public has lost faith in the putative positive impact of "free trade vis-à-vis the negative impact on jobs, wages, and the environment," but corporate America and most politicians, regardless of party, continue to claim otherwise, despite disturbing economic statistics since the 1970s.[51]

So the Cold War ended with a number of American twentieth-century foreign policy myths well ensconced and with serious economic and diplomatic problems unresolved. The major ones consisted of the country's well-intentioned desire to spread its economic, political, and cultural values globally based on the three nineteenth-century foreign policy concepts that had survived the First World War: democracy based on self-determination, free trade as a means for promoting peace and prosperity, and international cooperation. Unfortunately, these goals became snarled with the all-consuming drive to triumph over Communism at any cost, including adopting the tactics of the enemy and fear mongering, leading the United States to become the world's largest military security state. In the process, Faustian bargains and rampant independent internationalism often prevailed over both common sense and democratic, humanitarian considerations. Perhaps as important, the Cold War transformed the executive branch into the dominant branch of government, profoundly changing the nature of the American presidency and threatening the constitutional principle of separation of powers.

5

Cold War Transformation of the American Presidency

> The power of modern American presidents manifests itself in its purest form in the global arena, where their actions as commander in chief can determine the fate of the human race.... However, the president's latitude for independent action is even greater in the unstructured post–cold war world than it was during the cold war when the threat of mutual destruction concentrated minds and constrained actions.
>
> Fred I. Greenstein, *The Presidential Difference* (2000)

To talk of the Cold War only in terms of the impact it had on U.S. foreign policy overlooks how it affected the American presidency. Of the forty-three presidents the United States has had, only twelve of them have held office since 1933: FDR, Truman, Eisenhower, JFK, LBJ, Nixon, Ford, Carter, Reagan, Bush Sr., Clinton, and Bush Jr. Of these, nine have served since 1960, and, except for Eisenhower, they all had previous political experience, including five ex-governors and five vice presidents (three of whom had been senators). Only one, JFK, went directly from being a senator to president, and all twelve are known as modern presidents.

Compared to traditional or premodern presidencies (from George Washington through Calvin Coolidge), in which "Congress was the main engine of national policy-making,"[1] modern presidents are modern because they, rather than Congress, have become the major force driving U.S. diplomacy. Granted, there were a few notable exceptions: the temporary assertions of legislative power in the mid-1930s, and at the end of the Vietnam War and Watergate. How did this transfer of power from Congress to the executive branch occur so quickly when the reverse had been true for the previous 150 years of U.S. history? In particular, why did Congress in the course of the Cold War give up its constitutional responsibility for declaring war?

The answer in one sense is very simple. Since the onset of the Cold War over fifty years ago, American presidents have assumed "semi-constitutional" powers for conducting U.S. foreign policy in the name of national security.

These increased "semi-constitutional" powers accruing to the Oval Office in the course of the Cold war remain solidly in place in the post–Cold War era, waiting to be exercised on the whim or wisdom of any current or future president. The imperial presidency is, therefore, in the eye of the beholder because only some presidents are accused of being imperial when the power they are capable of exercising is the same.

The Cold War created these enhanced powers when the term "national security" came to mean "the need for open-ended commitments and the capability of anticipating and responding to political and military changes anywhere in the world." For example, the Cold War gave U.S. presidents aggrandized authority to enter into secret executive agreements without accountability even if they violate human rights or international law, to impound funds, to attach signing statements to legislation voiding sections deemed objectionable by the White House, to conduct covert and overt military interventions abroad without congressional approval, and to engage in "unrestricted nuclear crisis management."[2]

From 1932 to 1983, Congress tried to "exert a measure of control over executive lawmaking with the legislative veto," which allowed either house of Congress to disapprove executive orders within sixty or ninety days. In 1983, the Supreme Court specifically denied this right of legislative veto to Congress. Prior to this decision, however, with very few exceptions, the Court usually upheld the "inherent" presidential authority represented by most executive agreements (or what have been referred to since Clinton as "presidential memoranda") issued on domestic or diplomatic matters. The number of executive agreements increased so rapidly after 1945 that they actually vitiated the traditional treaty process requiring congressional approval. The ratio of executive agreements to treaties from the end of the Second World War to the early 1990s was seven to one. Between 1985 and 1989, Reagan alone approved 1,271 international agreements, but of those he sent only 47 actual treaties to the Senate.[3]

The War Powers Resolution passed by Congress in 1973 during the controversy over Watergate, along with other statutes that provided for some form of legislative veto, proved useless in preventing presidents from unilaterally committing U.S. troops abroad. To a large degree, "the modern presidency is by far a creature of war, war against the wider outside world, and real and metaphorical wars against the American people themselves." As Walter LaFeber has correctly observed: "In reality [the War Powers Resolution] gives the President the power to wage war for sixty days without congressional approval, a power that the founders wisely did not give the chief executive in 1787." In light of the weapons of mass destruction now available to presidents as a result of the Cold War, "sixty days can be a lifetime."[4]

In all likelihood, the exponential expansion of media coverage since the 1940s would also have increased the powers of the executive office, making modern presidents "engines" of diplomacy, but these powers probably would have materialized less quickly and less undemocratically without the Cold War. A more abstract reason for the emergence of the imperial characteristics of the modern presidency is that the public has accepted the media-promoted notion that the president embodies the myth about the exceptional role that the United States was destined to play during the Cold War. As a result, Americans seldom question the country's good intentions or the naive assumption about the ease with which liberty (i.e., American democracy and capitalism) can be transferred anywhere in the world. To paraphrase Tom Dooley, the famous medical missionary who worked with the CIA in Southeast Asia in the "struggle for freedom" against the fear of a communist takeover, the United States is just trying "to do what we can for people who ain't got it so good."[5]

Congruently, successive occupants of the Oval Office seem to have come close to believing that the foreign powers of the president should be beyond congressional, judicial, or public control. Woodrow Wilson anticipated this development even before he occupied the Oval Office when he said that "the initiative in foreign affairs, which the President possesses without restriction whatever, is virtually the power to control them absolutely." At the same time, there is also greater "potential for backlash in response to the president's actions creat[ing] the danger that a president's use of command power will weaken rather than enhance his leadership," especially if an individual policy is in fact, or is misperceived by the media to be, a personal or public failure.[6] Examples of events that redounded to the discredit of presidents include JFK's Bay of Pigs fiasco; LBJ's injudicious commitment of U.S. troops in Vietnam; Nixon's abuse of power in covering up the secret bombing of Cambodia and Laos and the Watergate break-in; Ford's overreaction (on Kissinger's advice) in using force in the 1975 *Mayaguez* incident, which resulted in the unnecessary deaths of forty-one Marines; Carter's mishandling of the U.S. hostage situation in Iran; and Reagan's hostages-for-arms scandal – except that Reagan, unlike his predecessors, walked away unscathed from this unprecedented violation of congressional and constitutional standards. It remains to be seen whether George W. Bush can rebound in the same way as Reagan from his mismanagement of the war in Iraq.

The Imponderable Presidency

Even if the man who occupies it temporarily taints the office, as Richard Nixon and Bill Clinton did, the power and prestige of the office remains. Its dignity is almost immediately restored when a new president enters the Oval Office. Gerry Ford returned respect to the White House, as did George W. Bush, even though his delayed victory in 2000 initially made him less surefooted and imposing than most incoming presidents in recent memory. The power, prestige, and dignity of the office of the presidency and its imperial potential exists, regardless of the misconduct or successes or failures of any individual president. The only limits on presidential power are the degree to which the president is in control of himself, his ability to manipulate the press, and, most recently, his ability to take advantage of gridlock or divided government under certain circumstances.

With the onset of the postmodern presidency in the 1990s, the office assumed imponderable overtones. This means that by the beginning of the twenty-first century it had become next to impossible to discern with any accuracy the true personality, character, or future policies of those running for the highest office in the land because the American presidency had become imponderable as well as imperial. Candidates now hide themselves behind manufactured personas designed by public relations experts to sell their putative best characteristics to the public. So "imponderable" means that it has become more difficult for average citizens, and even for pundits, to recognize the true nature of the person who is a presidential candidate or how he will perform in office. This is why voters must look for the worst characteristics in presidential candidates hiding beneath their surface pre-packaged best ones.[7]

In part, the imponderable presidency is also the result of the conscious dumbing down of presidential candidates to the point that in 2000 the public was subjected to the ridiculous spectacle of George W. Bush and Al Gore competing to claim they had lower college grades than other. Americans, since the Second World War at least, have not wanted "smarties" to occupy the Oval Office – think about the perceived "smartness" of defeated candidates such as Dewey, Stevenson, Mondale, and Dukakis, Gore, and Kerry compared to those who won – Truman, Eisenhower, Reagan, and the two Bushes. (The exception occurred in 1992 – both Clinton and Dole could claim the title of intellectual.) Anti-intellectualism seems to be "one of the more venerable traits of American voters" – at least, "they do not always respect politicians who *act* smart. Instead, voters trust those who seem more like themselves, even if those politicians are masking their intelligence to better appeal to common folk [i.e., the lowest common denominator]." Indeed, "there is a sense even among some scholars . . . that smarties make lousy presidents." Americans seem to be looking for the "ideal blend of brains and Bubba" in presidents, as a *New York Times* article put in back in June of 2000, and in 2004 most Americans agreed that they would rather have a beer and pretzels with Bush than wine and brie with Kerry.[8]

The presidency has also become imponderable because of the appearance of less-than-qualified candidates based on male-model good looks, or financial backing for garnering votes in front-loaded primaries, instead of their ability to govern. Its takes two very different talents to be a successful president. The first is the ability to raise money and get elected; the second is the ability to lead the most powerful nation in the world. Another reason that the presidency has become imponderable is that more recent presidents (and candidates for the presidency) have increasingly relied on polls and focus groups for determining policy rather than on principle or vision. This means of governing was all but perfected by Bill Clinton, and it has not disappeared as a rule of thumb under the George W. Bush, despite his aides' statements to the contrary. For all of these reasons, the modern American presidency has become imponderable because money- and media-dominated domestic politics – largely in the form of packaged personas and negative campaign advertisements – does not inform the body politic but plays to its fears and prejudices.

Cold War Impunity

Despite occasional missteps, modern Cold War presidents, more often than not, took Faustian actions with impunity in order to win the undeclared conflict with the Soviet Union, using their enhanced war powers and fear propaganda. For example, while the Korean War received accidental sanction from the UN Security Council, Harry Truman never bothered to obtain congressional approval for this first "limited" conflict of the Cold War. Eisenhower initiated the use of secret foreign policy activities when he allowed the CIA to help overthrow the nationalist Iranian government of Mossadegh in 1953, sent Marines into Lebanon in 1958, and approved the secret organizing of indigenous military units to invade both Guatemala and Cuba. The 1954 overthrow by the CIA of the democratically elected president Jacobo Arbenz in Guatemala set in motion a brutal civil war and a succession of U.S.-supported military regimes that did not end until 1996. Because documents about covert operations are always highly classified, it took until the 1980s for revisionist historians to begin to question the wisdom of Ike's cloak-and-dagger diplomacy, especially in the Third World.[9]

Likewise, John Kennedy's reputation has seldom been impugned despite a series of bizarre CIA attempts to assassinate Castro and the introduction of American forces in Vietnam, including the use of "stress and duress" torture methods by the Green Berets – the favorite special forces unit of the president. As noted in the Introduction, torture was not invented by Republicans after September 11 to fight terrorism. It represented a Cold War tactic that emulated the presumed methods of the U.S. enemies after 1948, and became an integral part of American foreign policy during the Vietnam War. Moreover, torture had always been present in the colonial wars of other countries. Even the Cuban missile crisis, which Kennedy is usually given much credit for settling, probably could have been avoided had he privately contacted Nikita Khrushchev at the end of August 1962 when a U-2 reconnaissance plane first reported Soviet S-2 missile sites in Cuba. Instead, he waited, hoping to use the information in the November midterm election. Because he has not been held responsible for helping to the create this crisis, JFK has, for the most part, received uncritical credit for resolving it without engaging in a missile trade with the Soviets when this is not what happened. The macho mythology associated with the Cuban missile crisis had an unfortunate impact on all successive presidents who have tried to emulate his tough stand in October 1962.[10]

After dictator Rafael Trujillo was assassinated in a 1961 CIA-backed coup, JFK also tried unsuccessfully to make the Dominican Republic a "showcase for democracy" through economic and military aid under the ten-year program known as the Alliance for Progress. Kennedy's program failed because it was "poorly conceived and overly ambitious" and so "did not create the democratic, economically vibrant, socially just Latin America that the president promised." Again, mainstream scholars have generally praised this unsuccessful policy. Then Lyndon Johnson sent 25,000 U.S. and Organization of American States (OAS) troops into the Dominican Republic to establish order and a reactionary regime. LBJ also endorsed the continued teaching of "stress and duress" torture techniques to client armies throughout the world, especially those of Latin America, at the U.S. Army School of the Americas (SOA) located in Fort Benning, Georgia. (Many of the torture tactics at Abu Ghraib and Guantanamo were perfected at the SOA.) Relying on Kennedy's advisers, especially Secretary of Defense Robert McNamara, and by deliberately issuing misleading information about the Gulf of Tonkin incident, LBJ increased the number of U.S. soldiers in Vietnam until they reached a peak level of 542,000 in 1969 without any congressional declaration of war. The impunity Johnson and McNamara enjoyed after lying about what happened in the Tonkin Gulf allowed those later charged with misinforming Congress about what they knew during the Iran-Contra scandal to cite this in their defense.[11]

Richard Nixon used the CIA and business interests to contribute to the downfall of the democratically elected socialist government of Salvador Allende Gossens in Chile. Declassified CIA documents now clearly indicate that Henry Kissinger and President Gerald Ford turned a blind eye to the military dictator Augusto Pinochet's human rights violations in Chile, involving the deaths of 3,000. Kissinger, in particular, assumed a protective attitude toward him after he set up Operation Condor, a Chilean-led consortium of secret policy agencies, which from 1975 to 1977 constituted a state-sponsored terror network throughout the Western Hemisphere and Europe. Condor practices included the "rendition" of prisoners and torture techniques such as the use of the "submarine" (now called "waterboarding"), which simulates drowning. Pinochet died under house arrest in December 2006 before going on trial, denying his victims their posthumous day in court.[12]

Carter initially tried to formulate a foreign policy based on human rights, and for a time he succeeded in encouraging democracy in Latin America. He also built on Ford's signing of the Helsinki Accords in 1976 by devoting considerable attention to appointing a strong staff to represent the U.S. at Helsinki review conferences that dealt with human rights, including Non-Governmental Organizations (NGOs) monitoring of human rights efforts, especially in the Soviet Union and Eastern Europe. Additionally, he provided financing to American NGOs to allow them to travel and participate in Helsinki human rights review conferences. These ties lasted even after the Reagan's retreat from a human-rights-oriented foreign policy.[13]

However, his human rights initiative soon became muddied when Carter abandoned Nixon's détente (as Ford had begun to do in 1976) for a more aggressive policy toward the Soviet Union. On July 3, 1979, he signed a presidential directive that permitted his national security adviser, Zbigniew Brzezinski, to secretly funnel aid to the *mujahadin*, later the Taliban, in Afghanistan. The object was to entice the Soviets to intervene. Once they did invade in

December, the president self-righteously promulgated his Carter Doctrine in January 1980 opposing "an attempt by any outside force to gain control of the Persian Gulf region."[14] While Carter came to be unfairly blamed for the domestic economic "malaise" during his four years in office, for not successfully settling the Iranian hostage crisis, and for not adequately educating the public about his complicated human rights policies, he should have been pilloried for following Brzezinski's Faustian anti-Soviet advice about secretly funding an arms pipeline beginning in August 1979 that contributed to the start of the 1979–89 war in Afghanistan.

President Ronald Reagan picked up where Carter had left off by aiding the radical Muslim holy warriors in Afghanistan. In the course of the 1980s, the CIA completely took over this assistance with backing from Congress, despite the "virtually unaccountable manner" with which the spy agency operated. This not only prolonged that war for a decade, it also delayed Gorbachev's domestic reforms and extended the Cold War by preventing an earlier implosion of the Soviet Union. Reagan's policies in Afghanistan thus contributed to the formation of the Taliban, al Qaeda and, of course, the early training and career of Osama bin Laden. At the height of this assistance, the CIA funneled 60,000 tons of arms and communications equipment per year into the Afghan-Soviet war, spending $30 million in 1980 and $450–500 million by 1989. Unlike the Iranian Islamic revolution, which had clear nation-state aims, military aid to the Afghan *mujahadin* during the Reagan administration marked the beginning of a largely privatized and ideological stateless resistance in the Middle East based on Islamic fundamentalism that ultimately turned bin Laden and other Arabs extremists against the "infidel" foreign policy of the United States.[15]

To make matters worse, the United States started to approve military aid packages to Pakistan, suspending the previous arms sales ban imposed on the dictator Mohammad Zia ul-Haq because of his negative human rights and drug trafficking record, to say nothing of his nuclear weapon ambitions. In this fashion, Pakistan secretly began to play a major conduit role in American military support for the *mujahadin* in Afghanistan. Despite the fact that this Pakistani pipeline proved hopelessly corrupt and inefficient (it is estimated that anywhere from 20 to 25 percent of the aid "leaked"), it constituted the largest covert CIA military aid program authorized by the Reagan Doctrine in the 1980s. While the pipeline improved U.S. relations with Pakistan, it also delayed the end of the Afghan-Soviet war, and guaranteed direct U.S. military aid to all the Pakistani dictators of that decade. Cold War impunity protected Reagan from being held responsible for the negative results of this Faustian policy. The United States continued to provide arms to Pakistan until 1990, when the Pressler Amendment required the president to discontinue selling arms if he determined that Pakistan possessed nuclear weapons. Clinton did not consistently enforce this legislation, and it became void after September 11.[16]

Compounding its Faustian activity in the Afghan-Soviet war that spawned *jihad* terrorists all over the Middle East, the Reagan administration adopted a schizophrenic policy toward the Iran-Iraq war, which started in September 1980 and lasted until 1989. Initially it aided one side and then unsuccessfully tried to aid the other. It was not the first time during the Cold War that the United States militarily assisted opponents in ongoing conflicts.

Iran-Contra: Cold War Impunity par Excellence

The United States did not have diplomatic relations with either country when the Iran-Iraq War began and initially hoped for a stalemate. But by the summer of 1982, when it looked as though Iran might win, Washington decided to get involved because of the threat of such a victory to Saudi Arabia and the Persian Gulf region in general. Even though intelligence reports as of November 1, 1983, showed the "almost daily use of CW [chemical weapons]" by Saddam Hussein, on November 26 the Reagan administration issued National Security Decision Directive 114, stating the United States had to do "whatever was necessary and legal" to ensure that Iraq did not lose the war with Iran "because any major reversal of Iraq's fortunes [would constitute] a strategic defeat for the West." So the president sent Donald Rumsfeld, then his special envoy to the Middle East, to Baghdad twice in the 1980s. During his December 1983 meeting with Iraq's leader Rumsfeld apparently indicated that the United States wanted to resume full diplomatic relations, and both times he implicitly assured Saddam Hussein that the United States would not protest his use of chemical weapons against Iranian troops. The American government also tried to cover up Hussein's genocidal gassing of Kurds by blaming it on Iran. As early as February 1982 the State Department had removed Iraq from its terrorism list and bullied the Export-Import Bank to provide Iraq financing. This permitted U.S. companies to export pesticides to Iraq that could be used for chemical warfare, and the United States began providing military intelligence, arms, and biological agents to Iraq throughout the 1980s, using largely the same people who would later become involved in the Iran-Contra scandal, including Vice President George H. W. Bush.[17]

The Iran-Contra affair can best be summarized as a feckless operation that began in 1984 when a group within the White House concocted a Byzantine scheme by which arms would be sold to Khomeini in Iran and the money funneled back to the right-wing Contra guerrillas in Central America. Even though Congress had passed legislation forbidding the funding of these death squads – especially the Contras fighting the Sandinista populists in Nicaragua – a criminal shadow government within the National Security Council carried this policy out until it was finally exposed in 1986.

This complicated and inept scheme involved selling U.S. arms to Iran in return for improved relations with that country and the release of American hostages held in Lebanon. The proceeds were diverted through Israeli intermediaries to the Nicaraguan Contras so that they could overthrow the elected Sandinista government. Additionally, the Justice Department exempted the CIA from reporting about their cocaine smuggling, even though federal law required the agency to report any drug trafficking by the Contras. The CIA also oversaw the mining of the harbors of Nicaragua, while U.S. government officials denied the action. Ultimately, the World Court unanimously condemned the mining. In spite of constitutional violations that far exceeded those involved in the Watergate cover-up, only fourteen criminal prosecutions came out of subsequent investigations of the Iran-Contra affair, and after he became president George H. W. Bush pardoned six of those who had been convicted, including former Defense Secretary Casper W. Weinberger and Elliot Abrams, currently Deputy National Security Adviser for Global Democracy Strategy.[18]

In the interim, the International Court of Justice (ICJ) declared this attempt at regime change in Nicaragua illegal by a vote of twelve to three and ordered the United States to pay $17 billion in restitution. The Reagan administration ignored this negative adjudication, marking the first time that a major world power had ignored an ICJ decree. This was to be expected, since the Iran-Contra policy had already violated the charters of both the UN and the Organization of American States, various U.S. domestic laws such as the War Powers Resolution, several congressional appropriations, and the 1982 and 1984 Boland Amendments forbidding assistance to the Contras.[19]

Most importantly, "the true significance of Iran-Contra lay ... in its implications for democracy and constitutional government," which the Democrats in Congress (to say nothing of the Republicans) and investigative reporters essentially swept under the rug because most thought that another impeachment attempt so soon after Watergate would harm the stability of the country's political system. The failure of Congress to seriously investigate and, at the very least, censor President Reagan and Vice President George H. W. Bush over their roles in the Iran-Contra affair opened the door for even the greater violations of the Constitution committed by George W. Bush, because many of the same figures, with tainted reputations from Iran-Contra, "voiced no regret or repentance with regard to the consequences of their deception" and ended up in his administration.[20]

Iran-Contra singularly exemplified the Faustian Cold War assumption that the ends justify the means, especially when implicitly or explicitly endorsed by a popular modern president with enhanced semi-constitutional powers and a staff willing to provided him with "plausible denability." It also demonstrated the degree to which during the Cold War "American foreign policy ... [had] lost its moral balance, supporting thugs, murders and right-wing dictators as aggressive antibodies to the Communist virus." This came about because beginning in the 1950s "Congress in effect permitted the CIA, an agency that serves the executive branch, to make foreign policy on the spot, to function as an 'invisible government,' and to have access to a secret budget over which Congress [had] no real control."[21]

The Reagan (Kirkpatrick) Doctrine

The Cold War policy in Central America (and to a lesser degree in Latin America) was based on a domino theory as incongruous as the one applied to East

Asia during the Vietnam War. According to this hypothesis, the Soviet Union would establish a series of bases beginning with Nicaragua and El Salvador in order to attack America "through the 'soft underbelly' of Central America." The underlying rationale (apart from the domino theory) of the Reagan administration for U.S. support of right-wing governments (e.g., El Salvador, the Philippines, Chile, South Korea, and South Africa) and actions against left-wing ones (e.g., Nicaragua, the People's Republic of China, the USSR, and Cuba) turned out to be a theory developed by the political scientist Jeane Kirkpatrick, who became the U.S. ambassador to the UN in 1981. As a Democrat, Kirkpatrick became so disillusioned with the nomination of George McGovern in 1972 that she helped found the bipartisan Coalition for a Democratic Majority. Ultimately, in 1976 this group morphed into and revitalized the Republican-dominated Committee on the Present Danger (CPD) that had been founded in 1950 as a bipartisan group to promote the anticommunist policies in NSC-68.[22]

In a single article that attracted the attention of President Reagan, Kirkpatrick argued that brutal authoritarian regimes, such as General Anastasio Somoza's in Nicaragua, were preferable to "immutable" communist totalitarian ones because the former practiced some form of capitalism and would consequently respond to suggestions for liberal, democratic reform, while the latter could not be converted to anything resembling the "American way." This meant that throughout the 1980s (and down to the present) the United States has reduced human rights standards for those authoritarian governments friendly toward the United States and openly supported anticommunist "freedom fighters" such as the Contras (whom Reagan compared to the Founding Fathers), Islamic fundamentalists, and a variety of insurgents and terrorists in Angola, Cambodia, and Ethiopia.[23]

The Reagan Doctrine capsulized Kirkpatrick's ideas and just as well could have been named after her. This proclamation asserted that the United States would support "democratic revolutions" in order to spread democracy all over the world through force. It was based on the spurious distinction between authoritarian and totalitarian governments (and on the right of the United States to declare which elections were legitimately democratic and which were not). Thus, like all other Cold War presidential doctrines, this one assumed a life of its own, even though "within a few years of its publication, the Kirkpatrick thesis . . . proved spectacularly wrong" because neither totalitarian nor authoritarian regimes performed according to this rigid neo-con model.[24]

The goal of the United States in almost all of these Cold War interventions was seldom democracy but rather stability. Stable anticommunist dictatorships and military juntas (arbitrarily dubbed authoritarian) trumped democratic and/or socialist regimes (arbitrarily dubbed totalitarian) that might not align themselves with America against the Soviet Union. This was most evident in Central and South America, especially under Eisenhower, Nixon, and Reagan, where the mantra became freedom and the "restoration of democracy." In actuality, American interventions and proxy wars were designed to maintain undemocratic anti-Soviet governments. The loss of life through U.S. covert and overt support of military regimes and the CIA-trained and advised death squads under Reagan in the 1980s was particularly horrendous in Guatemala (100,000 to 150,000), El Salvador (75,000), and Nicaragua (20,000–30,000).[25]

Cold War Independent Internationalism Blowback

From 1945 to 1989 the practice of independent internationalism reached an apex, especially in Central and South American, where the United States continued to enforce the Monroe Doctrine unilaterally and intervene arbitrarily on behalf of noncommunist dictatorial regimes. The United States vigorously extended the Monroe Doctrine after World War II by controlling all foreign military aid and sales to Latin American countries in order to insure its own dominance in the area. This included training Hispanic military officers at the School of the Americas in the United States, equipping their armies, and negotiating regional defense arrangements such as the Rio Pact and the Organization of American States (OAS). Gaddis Smith has come to the conclusion that the Cold War perverted the Monroe Doctrine because of (1) of the ideological nature of that bipolar conflict, (2) the covert and overt U.S. military interference in Central and South America, and (3) the partisan use of the doctrine for domestic political purposes.[26]

It cannot be emphasized enough that when the United States practiced independent internationalism during the Cold War, the scales were usually tipped in favor of unilateral actions prevailing over ostensibly collective actions. This can be seen in the country's relationship with the United Nations. Even before nonaligned nations began to dominate the UN General Assembly in the 1950s, the United States had all but abandoned collective UN actions in favor of the independent economic arrangements coming out of the 1944 Bretton Woods meeting, such as the World Bank, the International Monetary Fund (IMF), and the various rounds of the General Agreement on Tariffs and Trade (GATT). While these institutions were supposed to be subjected to UN oversight and function as multilateral UN agencies, voting rights were weighted according to financial shares held by member states, so they functioned largely at the behest of the United States outside of UN jurisdiction, and fairly successfully, until the excessive expenses of the Cold War made evident by the Vietnam War began to wreak havoc on the guns-and-butter American economy.[27]

With little confidence in the United Nations, American presidents practiced independent internationalism with impunity by engaging in the aforementioned types of unilateral and sometimes pseudo-multilateral activities during the Cold War, largely without congressional approval or consultation. The result was quite a few unintended and undesirable consequences, known in CIA terminology as "blowback." This refers to unanticipated negative results stemming from intelligence and/or military operations that "spill . . . back onto the country initiating the operation." Most simply put, it means that "a nation reaps what it sows." The examples of "blowback" have been legion since 1945, so it is difficult to know where to begin to describe them. Moreover, this involves some counterintuitive analysis, since so much of the secret intelligence activity of the United States remains classified and because globalization has created a worldwide economic blowback that still is not fully understood.[28]

Probably the most stunning example of political blowback to come out of American support for the Taliban in Afghanistan – in addition to the creation of a stateless cadre of wandering *mujahadin* terrorists – was the Talibanization of Pakistan. By 1989 the Taliban had taken over most of Afghanistan in the wake of the Russian pull-out. From 1977 until his assassination in 1988, Zia ul-Haq unsuccessfully tried to make Islamic law the basis of Pakistani justice, but it took almost two decades for Islamization of social discourse and policy in Pakistan to become a reality. By the time government of Nawaz Sharif initiated a bloody clash with Islamist organizations in 1999 to stop this Talibanization, it was too late. His actions simply culminated in his ouster in October through a military coup led by General Pervez Musharraf. Musharraf, instead of continuing Sharif's attempt to contain Islamic right-wing groups in his own country, announced his military support for the complete Taliban takeover of Afghanistan. While U.S. relations with Musharraf became rocky after he developed nuclear power, they have been solidified since September 11 because, once again, Pakistan is acting as a conduit for the American military – this time in its war against Iraq. Unlike the 1980s, however, the Faustian alliance with this undemocratic dictator is public for all to see.[29]

Incremental blowback seems particular evident in U.S. Cold War policy in the Middle East and South Asia. The 1953 CIA conspiracy to overthrow the democratically elected prime minister of Iran, Mohammad, Mossadegh, because he had nationalized the country's oil supply led to the American-backed repressive regime of the shah and ultimately to his control of OPEC and the rise in oil prices. Then there is the long-term, unfortunate result of the 1959 CIA-supported coup in Iraq. This ultimately put the Baath Party, under the ruthless leadership of Saddam Hussein, in control. With massive American military and diplomatic support, Saddam's anticommunism and secularism served American purposes well until the early 1990s.[30]

In the area of international economics, blowback is easier to trace because monetary and financial paper trails are not as easy to classify or hide in a global economy. By conceding to the protective tariffs of countries whose economies it had rebuilt after the Second World War, the United States hollowed out its own key industries. This policy worked as long as the American economy grew. But in the 1970s debt and stagflation set in, and the United States began to reconsider the preferential treatment it had given the exports of some of these nations since 1945 and to change its international economic policies by applying more rigidly the "Washington–Wall Street consensus" through the World Bank and IMF both in Central and South America and in Asia. This created so much economic chaos and misery in certain areas of Latin America that there has been a political backlash against the United States.[31]

Nixon was the first president to try to deal decisively with the drain on the American economy that had built up during the Cold War and that the Vietnam War exacerbated in the form of inflation and ever-increasing threats by foreign countries to convert their dollars to gold. In the course of the 1960s these nations came to possess more dollars than all the gold in Fort Knox because the United States "paid out more dollars for imports, foreign investments, military and economic aid, and travel than it earned from exports and return on foreign investment." The time had come, Nixon decided, to end the postwar Bretton Woods monetary system. That agreement set up fixed exchange rates in 1944 to avoid the protectionism and devaluation of national currencies that were thought to have contributed to the rise of totalitarianism in the 1930s. Because the dollar was substituted for gold in the immediate postwar years, it became the world's reserve currency. By 1971, the American trade surplus had disappeared while its payment deficits had burgeoned, in part because the Vietnam War cost so much. So Nixon unilaterally cancelled the convertibility of the dollar on the international exchange market and placed a surcharge on imports, especially those coming from Japan. He also initiated wage and price controls in order to curb inflation at home.[32]

Although Nixon's New Economic Policy (NEP) proved a short-term domestic success, a number of unintended international economic consequences ensued. While John Ralston Saul exaggerated when he called Nixon's action "perhaps the single most destructive act of the postwar world," floating the dollar did contribute to the growth of finance capitalism – a throwback to the unregulated exploitative capitalism of the nineteenth century. Nixon's policy actions also created three rival economic trading blocks, each with its own separate regional monetary order based on the yen, the mark, and the dollar. The blowback from this contributed to exchange rate instability and currency speculation. It also soon became evident that floating exchange rates did not promote free trade. Instead, such instability led to complaints about unfair trading practices and pressures for more protectionism. Finally, after the United States began to insist that Asian governments conform to the American capitalist model, it contributed to the ultimate collapse of some of some of these "miracle" economies in the 1990s. Many of them had successfully developed managed economies based on conglomerates of industrial combines, private banks, and government savings institution until the United States changed its post–World War II economic policies beginning in the 1970s, creating various forms of financial blowback.[33]

Origins of Neo-Conservatism

The story of the transformation of the modern imperial presidency is not complete without focusing on a relatively small faction within the Republican Party that began a systematic campaign against Nixon's foreign (and domestic) policies. This little-known story begins with a group of Republicans, made up of both civilian and military anticommunist extremists (those Norman Podhoretz referred to as subscribing to "hard anti-Communism"), who had supported Nixon in 1968, mistakenly thinking that he was as conservative as they were. Subsequently, they could not tolerate Nixon's attempt to bring both China and the USSR into the international community in ways that the military containment of both countries since the beginning of the Cold War had not. Nor could they support his policy of Vietnamization designed to turn the war over the South Vietnamese. Most of all, however, they could not tolerate any weaponry accommodation of the USSR, as represented by the Anti-Ballistic Missile (ABM) treaty and the Strategic Arms Limitation (SALT I and II) Agreements.[34]

Détente and rapprochement (and ultimately defeat in Vietnam) prompted these nascent neo-conservative Republicans to organize against Nixon's foreign policy, giving birth to a radical conservatism inside and outside the Nixon administration in the early 1970s. Such men as James Schlesinger, Donald Rumsfeld, Richard (Dick) Cheney, and Admirals Thomas Moorer and Elmo Zumwalt wanted Nixon weakened and ultimately supported his resignation. Watergate thus facilitated their opposition to his major diplomatic initiatives. Beginning in 1976, this nucleus of radical conservatives utilized the Committee on the Present Danger to emerge as a full-blown neo-con movement within the Republican Party by 1980. These neo-cons dominated Reagan's foreign policy in his first term and completely took over George W. Bush's after September 11.[35]

In one sense, these new conservatives were selectively reinventing the wheel that had been created by some traditional intellectuals and academics, many of whom eschewed politics, dating back at least to the 1950s and represented by such publications and individuals as *Commentary*, *Public Interest*, *National Review*, William F. Buckley, Irving Kristol, Podhoretz, Leo Strauss, Russell Kirk, Ludwig von Mises, and Milton Friedman, and later by such Democrats as Senator "Scoop" Jackson and Daniel Patrick Moynihan. It is often forgotten that there was a strong anti-elitist, populist tinge to Republicanism in the United States after World War I – at least in the West and Midwest – under the tutelage of such notables as Robert La Follette, Smith Brookhart, Gerald P. Nye, William Borah, George Norris, Hiram Johnson, and Jeannette Rankin. However, many of these Republican progressives from the 1920s turned into discredited isolationists and anti–New Dealers in the 1930s, leaving the base of Republican conservatism rooted in its elitist, moderately internationalist members located in northeastern and Great Lakes states. But by the late 1960s, a "New Right" began to emerge that no longer shunned the "evils of the majority." Richard Viguerie, Paul Weyrich, and Howard Phillips led this neo-populist group within the Republican Party. They were joined during Nixon's presidency by William (Bill) Kristol, James Woolsey, William Bennett, Elliot Abrams, John Bolton, Richard Perle, and Paul Wolfowitz – all of whom opposed the president's Chinese, Russian, and Vietnamese policies. Slowly during the 1970s neo-conservatives emerged within the GOP who began to combine religious, democratic, capitalist, populist, and American superior values into a winning majority–abandoning many traditional conservative values along the way, such as limited federal government, balanced budgets, and, most importantly, non-interventionism.[36]

Viewed in light of the neo-conservative and religious right takeover of the Republican Party, Watergate and the Nixon presidency have a contemporary importance that has been largely ignored in the transformation of the American presidency and U.S. diplomacy, which seems to have peaked with the George W. Bush administration. This new interpretation also finally confirms the obvious about Richard Nixon's political career: he had never been an arch-conservative on either domestic or foreign policy.[37] Instead of his conservatism being the cause of his downfall, as many have claimed, his more liberal and/or centrist policies so alienated radical conservatives (many of whom urged him to resign) that they contributed to his leaving office and vowed to discredit and reverse both his foreign and domestic policies. In essence, Watergate marked the beginning of the end of Republican centrism and opened the door for radical conservatives to dominate the Republican Party – those whom Claes G. Ryn has referred to as the new Jacobins. By the 1980s, they were most commonly called neo-conservatives. Within ten years they had so damaged the reputation of détente, often with specious intelligence and fear propaganda, that they successfully turned the Soviet Union into the "evil empire."

What is also curious about the new Jacobinism is that, unlike traditional conservatism with its limited, realist view of American foreign policy, it openly advocates a missionary moralistic diplomacy based on the presumed universality of democratic and capitalist values as exemplified by the United States. This is very similar to the American exceptionalism that Woodrow Wilson advocated when promoting self-determination during and after the First World War. These new Jacobins view both capitalism (free markets) and democracy as undisputed progressive forces and, thus, "powerful agent[s] for remaking traditional regimes." According to Ryn, they also "want the United States to take preemptive action to dislodge unfriendly regimes and sanitize entire regions of the world ... even though the country usually has almost nothing to fear militarily from the regimes singled out for special criticism." The fact that the new Jacobinism appeals not only to powerful financial and political interests and intellectuals who like the idea of an "aggressive foreign policy in behalf of democracy ... [but] also to people of more pragmatic but nationalistic outlook who like the idea of their country being able to tell other countries how to behave" gave it considerable credibility after September 11. Above all, its "democratist rhetoric ... puts a nice gloss on the "will to power" or "wish to dominate." It also "puts great emphasis on democracy's superiority and missionary task."[38]

Often today's neo-conservatives use language about American values in such a way as to disguise the fact that they are really "democratic imperialists" who want to bring "freedom to the world at the barrel of a gun." If there ever was a time when U.S. foreign policy might have been based on a type of American exceptionalism that simply meant difference rather than superiority, it died with emergence of these new Jacobins – the neo-conservatives.[39]

"Will to power" and "wish to dominate" are key terms for understanding the perseverance and ultimate success of these modern-day Jacobins in influencing U.S. foreign policy. While they had the will back in the 1960s, they were not organized enough politically to take advantage of the 1964 candidacy of

Barry Goldwater. In any case, they considered him too much of a traditional conservative on most foreign policy issues, except the use of nuclear weapons, and too liberal on some domestic matters such as abortion and homosexuality. Their first opportunity for "real" power and influence within Republican political circles came in 1969 during the congressional fight over the Safeguard ABM program. Conservatives in both parties did not think the administration would support them strongly enough to obtain passage because of Nixon's early negotiations with the Soviets. (In fact, Safeguard represented a downgrading by Nixon of the proposed more comprehensive ABM system that he had inherited from the Johnson administration.) Democratic Senator "Scoop" Jackson called for help to pass Safeguard and initially found it coming from such old Cold Warriors as Paul H. Nitze, author of NSC-68, former Secretary of State Dean Acheson, and University of Chicago math professor and RAND Corporation consultant Albert Wohlstetter. Together they formed the Committee to Maintain a Prudent Defense Policy and raised enough money to allow Wohlstetter to hire graduate students Richard Perle and Paul Wolfowitz. William Casey, future director of the CIA under Reagan, organized a similar group, and the two combined to give the pro-Safeguard charts prepared by Perle and Wolfowitz considerable clout in congressional hearings. Nonetheless, the program passed only after Vice President Spiro Agnew broke a tie vote. Because of this narrow but significant victory, Jackson invited Perle to join his Senate staff. And so began the political rise of radical conservatives in government.[40] In and of itself, however, the battle they successfully fought over the Safeguard ABM program would not have given a sufficient boost to their extreme conservative views without the aid of two obscure Pentagon insiders.

Above All – Avoid "Provocative Weakness"

Unknown to most until recently, two government bureaucrats had been exercising considerable behind-the-scenes influence on a number of Cold War civilian and military policy makers. They were Fritz A. G. Kraemer, Kissinger's first foreign policy mentor beginning in the 1940s when they were in the army and after Kissinger went to Harvard, and Andrew W. Marshall, whom Nixon appointed director of the Pentagon's Office of Net Assessment in 1973 and whom all other presidents reappointed. From 1951 until 1978, Kraemer worked as a senior civilian counselor to defense secretaries and top military commanders such as Rumsfeld, General Creighton Abrams, General Alexander M. Haig, Jr., General Vernon A. Walters, Lt. General Edward Rowny, and Major General Edward G. Lansdale. JFK appointed Kraemer's son Sven to the National Security Council, where he remained until 1976, only to be reappointed by Reagan from 1981 to 1987 as NSA director of arms control – all the while promoting his father's and other neo-conservatives' views. During Bush's first term he became policy adviser to Douglas Jay Feith, undersecretary of defense for policy. Kraemer's and Marshall's protégées and devoted admirers included, among many others, Haig, Cheney, Rumsfeld, Nitze, Perle, and Wolfowitz.[41]

For example, a direct line can be drawn from Kraemer's post–World War II insistence that the United States should never demonstrate "provocative weakness" to Bush's insistence on "complete victory" in Iraq. Likewise, the Bush administration's return to the Strategic Defense Initiative (SDI) missile defense program of the Reagan years and its attempt to restructure the military by downplaying the role of ground troops in favor of a first-strike computerized defence based, if necessary, on low-yield nuclear weapons came straight out of Marshall's ideas going back to the 1950s, when he was at the RAND Corporation. As of 2006, Marshall remains in his Pentagon office – alive and well at the age of eighty-two. Kraemer, ever the *éminence grise*, died in 2003 at the age of ninety-five, much praised by those he had tutored, especially by Kissinger, Haig, Rumsfeld, and Wolfowitz. "There are people who worship death frankly, and not life. People who worship the devil, I believe, and not God. They are an evil that has to be confronted," Wolfowitz unabashedly said at a book party in praise of Kraemer, "[a]nd fortunately, *we do have a president that* [sic] *is prepared to see it the way I think Fritz Kraemer would have seen it, and is prepared to confront it. I believe his spirit still lives.*"[42]

Kraemer saw "provocative weakness" in the Munich deal between Neville Chamberlain and Adolf Hitler, and in the ideas of the "brilliant fools" in the foreign policy establishment who did not understand the "devastating effect of provocative weakness on totalitarian dictatorships like the USSR [and China]," because they took advantage of such weakness. Kraemer also thought that "it was only by the grace of God that we did not lose" the Cold War. He saw institutional weakness at work in the September 11 attacks because the terrorists did not think they had to fear any hard reaction from the United States or its allies after years of "deficient will power." Although long retired from his Pentagon position, Kraemer publicly reminded Rumsfeld on the eve of 2003 invasion of Iraq: "No provocative weakness, Mr. Secretary."[43]

Beginning with their support of the Safeguard ABM program, many radical conservatives inside and outside government had come under the influence of Kraemer or Marshall or both. Many of them purposely began trying to discredit the realism of Nixon's détente policy in 1974 through an obscure group within the Pentagon known as "Team B." It formed in the mid-1970s after Wohlstetter, along with other hard-line conservatives, purposively began to criticize the CIA for underestimating the power of the Soviet Union. The CIA was already susceptible to attack because it had been criticized by Republican and Democratic hard-liners who resented the fact that the CIA had refused to see "light at the end of the tunnel" in its assessments of the Vietnam War, had been misused by Nixon in covert foreign and domestic operations, and had been investigated by by two congressional committees.[44]

In this anti-CIA atmosphere, Wohlstetter's and others' criticism prompted extreme Republican conservatives to search for an appropriate body within the government to look into the agency's estimates about Soviet power and intentions. Specifically, they believed that the standard Cold War fear campaign against Communism needed more convincing figures and projections than the CIA was providing. They chose to infiltrate the President's Foreign Intelligence Advisory Board (PFIAB), which Eisenhower had established back in 1956 as the Board of Consultants on Foreign Intelligence Affairs. Made up of individuals who held no formal government positions, the PFIAB had been revitalized by Kennedy, after the Bay of Pigs, but by 1975 it consisted primarily of such conservatives as John Connally, William Casey, John Foster, Clare Booth Luce and Edward Teller. Initially, "Team B" within the PFIAB was made up of three teams – each of which was to assess one of three separate subject areas: [1] the yearly National Intelligence Estimates (NIEs) in terms of "Soviet low-altitude air defense capabilities, . . . [2]intercontinental ballistic missile (ICBM) accuracy (which became Paul Wolfowitz's specialty at the time), and . . . [3]Soviet strategic policy and objectives." The third "Team B" group and its subject matter came to dominate the other two. In 1975, under the direction of Richard Pipes, a Harvard professor and Soviet specialist, the PFIAB began to criticize what it considered the CIA's underestimation of Soviet military might and expenditures.[45]

At first, Nixon and his CIA director William Colby warded off this "ad hoc 'independent' group of government and non-government analysts" on procedural grounds, saying that a new NIE was already being prepared. They both questioned the raison d'être for anything like "Team B" within in the PFIAB. One top Nixon analyst described it as a "kangaroo court of outside critics all picked from one point of view"; others correctly insisted that "its mission was to hype the Soviet threat." Once George H. W. Bush became head of the CIA under Ford he gave the go-ahead, with the president's approval, for the PFIAB to begin to submit alternative or competitive threat assessments to those of the CIA, apparently not understanding that "Team B" members had a pre-set radical conservative agenda.[46]

Ford did not anticipate what giving free access to intelligence material to a group already critical of the CIA might produce. His approval stemmed from the fact that his presidential bid was in trouble in 1976 because supporters of Reagan's candidacy made the most of Ford's January 1976 statement indicating that he thought it would be "unwise for a President – me or anyone else – to abandon détente. . . . it is in the best interest of world stability, world peace." In March, Ford reversed himself on détente, going so far as to tell his staff that "we are going to forget the use of the word." In support of the president's abandonment of détente, Secretary of Defense Rumsfeld added that "the Soviet Union has been busy . . . expanding their capability to increasingly improve the sophistication of those [nuclear] weapons." Nonetheless, Reagan's handlers continued to criticize Ford's initial support for détente and his subsequent signing of the Helsinki Accords throughout the primaries. Most importantly, a group of Republican hawks (Richard Allen, Max Kamperlman, Nitze, Eugene Rostow, and Admiral Zumwalt) opposed détente and the Helsinki Accords and helped in the revitalization of the Committee on the Present Danger "to alert the public to the 'growing Soviet threat.'" Nitze, Pipes, and William R. Van Cleave from "Team B" sat on its executive committee, and for the next four years the group concentrated on blocking SALT II.[47]

Its first report, issued right after the 1976 election, entitled "Common Sense and the Common Danger," echoed the ideas of "Team B" – not surprisingly, as Nitze, Pipes, and Van Cleave had helped write it. The Committee on the Present Danger recommended "revitalized containment," to be achieved by placing an economic "squeeze" on the Soviet Union through an excessive U.S. military expansion and by announcing the technologically unrealistic Strategic Defense Initiative (SDI) designed to block all incoming Soviet missiles. This report called for campaigns in favor of greater defense spending, including for the SDI, to be fueled by a "disingenuous exaggeration of the extent of Soviet power." Based on a 1976 hypothetical worst-case scenario about future Soviet missile power, they misleadingly projected that the United States would face a "window of vulnerability" in the early 1980s. So they set out to undermine the ABM treaty, as well as both SALT I and SALT II (and the later strategic arms reduction treaties, START I and II) and to advocate increasing U.S. nuclear power until it reached a level that RAND consultant Herman Kahn called "escalation dominance." This complicated concept essentially came down to the idea the United States needed "military superiority [not parity]... to win [the nuclear] game of 'chicken'" against the Soviet Union.[48]

Except for Carter, who abolished the PFIAB during his presidency, all modern presidents have relied upon it. In ways reminiscent of the propaganda about weapons of mass destruction in Iraq before the second Gulf War, from the beginning "Team B" members often attributed to the Soviet Union weapons it did not have, such as a "non-acoustic anti-submarine system." Pipes defended these outlandish conclusions on the grounds that Soviet intent trumped hard evidence about Soviet weapons and, despite his Soviet expertise, even allowed misleading translations of Russian strategic concepts in order to further slant the evidence.

It took sixteen years for the full reports of "Team B" to be declassified through a Freedom of Information Act (FOIA) request. They reveal that for over a quarter of a century "perceptions about U. S. national security were colored by the [neo-con] view that the Soviet Union was on the road to military superiority over the United States" and that the public should be kept in a fearful state about this alleged threat. This was not unlike the manner in which many early Cold Warriors opposed negotiating with the USSR on the fallacious grounds that Stalin intended to mount an ideologically expansionist course right after 1945. The notion quickly prevailed among postwar presidents and policy makers that any negotiations with, or policy of moderation toward, Soviet leaders would be nothing less than a repeat of pre–World War II appeasement at Munich. In the 1980s, the neo-cons successfully promoted "Muniching" as a "master narrative and a political bludgeon" by disseminating mendacious information about Soviet intent, military power, and defense spending. As a result, they succeeded in obtaining a trillion-dollar defense buildup under Reagan as the

United States went from the largest creditor in the world to the largest debtor "in order to pay for arms to counter the threat of a nation that was collapsing."[49]

In seeking to understand the early history of what became the neo-con movement of the 1980s, the extent of the military distrust and dislike of Nixon cannot be underestimated. The same year that the CPD issued its first report, Admiral Elmo Zumwalt publicly made military suspicions and resentment of the Nixon administration abundantly clear in his book, *On Watch: A Memoir*. Zumwalt and many within the American military elite thought that Nixon's foreign policies bordered on the traitorous because they "were inimical to the security of the United States." Zumwalt's rage certainly knew no bound, and he continued his tirade against détente and Kissinger during Ford's short presidency. In fact, during the 1976 primaries the negative comments about Kissinger and détente in the admiral's book became flashpoints for those Republican conservatives supporting Reagan against Ford.[50] More than Ford's pardon of Nixon, military and civilian neo-conservative support of Reagan for president in 1976 contributed to his failure to be elected president.

Reagan and the End of the Cold War

After infiltrating the first term of Reagan's presidency, these same neo-cons went out of their way to credit Reagan with ending the Cold War single-handedly. However, a number of other factors played a role – not the least of which was Nixon's attempt to abandon containment in favor of enticing both China and the Soviet Union to engage in more international cooperation and civil competition (sometimes referred to as "competitive coexistence"). This is probably the greatest myth about the fortieth president's administration. Not only did he personally claim that he had won the Cold War by causing the collapse of the Soviet Union, but George H. W. Bush, who actually presided over the demise of Communism, also "honed [this] legend to perfection." According to this interpretation, Reagan, at the behest of leftover, older conservatives from the Nixon administration – namely, Schlesinger, Rumsfeld, Cheney, and Admirals Zumwalt and Moorer, in addition to Nitze and Pipes and a younger crop of such anti-Soviet zealots as Perle and Wolfowitz – succeeded in having the president label the Soviet Union the "evil empire" and advanced the massive American arms buildup that the Carter administration tentatively had initiated. This time, however, they were backed by favorable Pentagon reports that a nuclear war was "winnable." It was obviously in the best interests of the neo-cons and their adherents to claim that Reagan won the Cold War by himself because he abandoned what they called the "soft-on-Communism" policies of Nixon.[51]

In the end, once Reagan came to a belated personal realization of the horrors of nuclear power in his second term in office, he stopped following the hawkish and hyped advice from the most radical of the neo-cons in his administration and in 1985 began negotiating with Mikhail Gorbachev, who had already unilaterally "decided on military cuts *despite* the Reagan military buildup." These negotiations resulted in the 1987 Intermediate-Range Nuclear Forces (INF) Treaty, freeing the Soviet leader to pursue his *perestroika* (restructuring) and *glasnost* (opening) reforms in earnest.[52] Ironically, these Gorbachev reforms marked the beginning of the end of the Soviet Union because they came too late. By that time the communist system was, in all likelihood, not reformable.

The USSR imploded, not because of Reagan's conflicting "hard" and "soft" approaches, but because of internal structural economic flaws and external events indicating that the country was dissolving from within – flaws that "Team B" reports ignored as it deliberately exaggerated the military superiority and hostile intentions of the Soviet Union. These economic flaws and external events included an increasingly untenable imbalance between spending on guns and butter; a growing high-tech weakness; systematic corruption; generational and intra–Communist Party divisions; the decline in oil prices; devaluation of the dollar; loss of Western loans to Eastern European satellite nations, whose loyalty to communism was already on the wane; a tired ideology worn down by false disciples and a decline in the prestige of Communism in the Third World; the mercurial, and sometimes contradictory, politics of Gorbachev; the Chernobyl accident; and finally, the enlightening and disruptive impact of the economic, scientific, and cultural aspects of the détente set in motion by Nixon and by West German *Ostpolitik* – both of which radical conservatives of the 1970s had vehemently opposed. One other, more intangible cause of the fall of Communism may have been the influence of the visit of Pope John Paul II to Poland in 1979 and his support of the *Solidarnosc* uprising in his homeland.[53] This gave rise to the rumor that the Soviets had helped plan the assassination attempt against Pope John Paul II. What is clear is that the Soviet Union collapsed for myriad reasons, most of which had little to do with neo-con theories or policies, especially Kraemer's advice to American civilian and military leaders about not showing "provocative weakness."

With the Cold War ended, one would have thought the "semi-constitutional" powers of modern presidents might have come under hard congressional scrutiny, not only because of their Faustian implementation but also because they infringed upon the doctrine of separation of powers. After all, Senator Frank Church pointed out as early as 1970 that "as a result of the passing of the war power and much of the purse power out of the hands of Congress, the most important of our constitutional checks and balances have been overturned. For the first time in our history, there has come into view the possibility of our president becoming a Caesar." He also attributed what had gone on from the 1950s into the 1970s "to the fantasy that it lay within our power to control other countries through the covert manipulation of their affairs. It formed part of a greater illusion that entrapped and enthralled our Presidents – the illusion of American omnipotence."[54]

These statements were made during the Nixon administration, but they exemplify the enhanced powers of the presidency that had come into existence long before Nixon took office and that remained after he resigned. Such accumulation of overwhelming presidential power began with FDR, and this process was simply perfected under subsequent Cold War presidents. There has been no diminution of executive power because of Watergate or the loss of the Vietnam War, as neo-conservatives continue to claim. In summary, there has been no "erosion of the powers and ability of the president of the United States to do his job," as Vice President Dick Cheney and others in the George W. Bush administration have repeatedly insisted.[55] Such statements simply contribute to making the presidency more imperial, imponderable, and beyond the understanding of most Americans.

Diplomatic historians may one day write the history of U.S. foreign policy in the twentieth century by attempting to speculate about how different the American presidency and American values at home and abroad would have been if there had been no Cold War. To undertake this difficult, counterintuitive task it will be necessary for future scholars, pundits, and politicians to view the Cold War as an aberration – one that cost the United States as much as it gained from winning it. In addition to creating a problematic American empire and a national security state heavily in debt, the Cold War created the imperial, imponderable presidency that has undermined the separation of powers envisioned by the Founders. The post–Cold War presidents of the 1990s had a unique opportunity to try to return some of their enhanced semi-constitutional powers to the other branches of government and to rescue American electoral politics from its current money and media domination. They also had the first opportunity to address the more unsavory diplomatic problems created by the long-undeclared war between the United States and the Soviet Union. Both tasks were formidable, and, unfortunately, George H. W. Bush and Bill Clinton accomplished little with respect to either. This left the door open for George W. Bush and his neo-conservatives advisers to mix and match at will the worst domestic politics and foreign policy policies he had inherited.

6

The United States Adrift in the Post–Cold War World

> We must sail sometimes with the wind and sometimes against it – but we must sail, and not drift, nor lie at anchor.
>
> Oliver Wendell Holmes, *The Autocrat of the Breakfast Table* (1858)

Unlike the situation at the end of the Second World War, when the United States found itself a victorious creditor nation with little foreign economic competition, at the end of the Cold War in the late 1980s and early 1990s the country faced serious debt problems at home and abroad. These problems came about in part because of the burden garnered from over forty years of almost single-handedly protecting the "free" world from Communism, and also because of revitalized regional trade and technological competition from Asia and the European Community.[1]

Despite (or because of) these negative economic circumstances, in less than a couple of years after the end of the Cold War a short, "hot" military conflict ensued instead of a "cold" peaceful transition to what George H. W. Bush called a New World Order. This was something that America had theoretically been pursuing since its inception, and particularly since the presidency of Woodrow Wilson, even though the president who led the United States into the First World War did not use the phrase. Bush defined it in his "Toward a New World Order" address to a joint session of Congress on September 9, 1990, when he said: "Today that new world is struggling to be born, a world quite different from the one we've known. A world where the rule of law supplants the rule of the jungle. A world in which nations recognize the shared responsibility for freedom and justice." In this speech and in his State of the Union address on January 1, 1991, he seemed to be advocating a universal morality based on the idea of international law, presumably through the United Nations, but as he pointed out: "Among the nations of the world, only the United States of America has both the moral standing and the means to back it [the New World Order] up." Bush's New World Order also included an enhanced attempt to control the United Nations after the breakup the Soviet Union. Without a strong

Soviet presence on the Security Council, the United States would be more free to shape the world in its image than ever before.[2]

Unfortunately, the phrase "New World Order" brings to mind the pan-German foreign policy of the 1930s about a European New Order, and the Japanese use of the term "New Order" after proclaiming their East Asia Co-Prosperity Sphere in 1938. In both instances the United States had protested the validity of these "new order" proclamations. While Bush revived the term "New World Order," it remained for his successors to implement it. Little wonder that just before the first Gulf War began, *Time Magazine* compared Bush to Wilson. The comparison became all the more germane when, after the quick military victory, like Wilson at Versailles Bush abandoned the idea of defending ethnic and religious rights – in this case, those of the Kurds and Shiites in Iraq. The first Gulf War proved once again that short "wars sow disorders that last 20 times longer than lengthy wars do," and it left Iraq's problems to fester throughout the 1990s. Indeed, Bush's New World Order, while not a new concept in the history of American diplomacy, did contain one very dangerous facet: it showed that the United States could take action in the Middle East (and implicitly elsewhere) without the restraints that existed during the Cold War when there was superpower rivalry.[3]

The First Gulf War

The 1991 Gulf War marked the first major exercise of presidential authority in a post–Cold War world unstructured by the lengthy undeclared conflict between the United States and the Soviet Union. Despite UN approval, some still regard it as "the use of a multilateral instrument to carry out a unilateral war" by the first Bush administration. According to this argument, the United States did not consider ending Iraq's occupation of Kuwait through negotiation or sanctions because it had to assert its worldwide military power immediately in the post–Cold War world. As important as Kuwait's oil was, "the real goal was the reaffirmation of U.S. strategic power...[in the] oil-rich Middle East" to show the world that even with the collapse of the Soviet Union, America would not relinquish its goal of hegemony in the area. Bush simply turned the Carter Doctrine, which had been issued to keep "any outside force" from dominating the Persian Gulf, on its head by asserting the right of the United States to control the region. Without having to fear a Russian veto in the Security Council – because the Soviets needed Western economic aid, and that guaranteed Mikhail Gorbachev's cooperation – Bush obtained UN approval despite years of American hostility toward that organization. To avoid concerns in Congress about waging war before sanctions could be imposed against Saddam Hussein, Bush did not ask that body to approve the Desert Storm operation until he had committed over 500,000 American troops, put together an international coalition, and obtained UN Resolution 678 authorizing the use of force in Iraq.[4]

During this process Bush offered several different reasons for the invasion–none of which was oil. Instead, the list included: deterring an Iraqi attack on

Saudi Arabia; insisting that Saddam was a tyrant like Hitler and had toppled a "legitimate" government that in reality was a quasi-feudal monarchy; protecting Americans taken hostage by Saddam, even though they had been taken only after the U.S. military operation began; and, finally, claiming that Saddam was developing nuclear weapons. Since Saddam had been an American ally in the 1980s, Saddam's real offense was that his invasion of Kuwait upset "the status quo in an area where the United States had vowed repeatedly to go to war, if necessary, to prevent adverse change." Bush's New World Order simply reaffirmed the country's long-standing covert claims to Middle Eastern oil "in case anyone thought that the end of the cold war made them obsolete." In this sense, the first Gulf War "was a grotesquely logical denouement to 45 years of U.S. policy in the Middle East."[5]

The fact that American oil policy changed in the 1990s from accepting dependence on a continuous supply of oil to exerting control over that resource was the most underpublicized reason for both Gulf Wars. This came about in large measure because of increased demands on Middle Eastern oil by others nations, especially China, and the fact that the United States could no longer depend on Saudi Arabia because it appeared to represent a bundle of contradictions: spawning global terrorism and anti-Americanism, all the while buying American arms to protect itself from domestic chaos.[6]

Clinton also exemplified this change in oil diplomacy when in 1994 he laid the plans for helping the British energy giant BP and the American firms Unocal and Conoco to create a $3.6 billion pipeline linking the Caspian Sea oil fields off Baku through Azerbaijan to Tbilisi in Georgia and on to the Mediterranean at Ceyhan, Turkey (known as the BTC pipeline after the cities it passes through). Notably, this route bypasses Russia and Iran (to say nothing of the struggling state of Armenia) and so lessens American dependence on Russian oil and gas production. To protect this line, the United States unofficially established a military base in the former Soviet state of Georgia (which has almost no gas or oil) and spent $64 million to train Georgian forces to protect the pipeline because the area is ethnically volatile. The Clinton administration also backed the vicious Taliban regime in Afghanistan until 1997, despite its human rights violations, largely "because the American oil company Unocal had signed a deal with the Taliban to build a $2 million gas line and a 2.5 billion oil line . . . from Turkmenistan to Pakistan via Afghanistan." All in all, in trying to balance oil interests and relations with Russia, the Taliban, and Central Asia countries, Clinton's policy amounted to a "cluster of confusions" in keeping with the general drift that characterized other aspects of his diplomacy, to be discussed later.[7]

To his credit, the first President Bush, unlike his son, correctly recognized the importance of an exit strategy in a Middle Eastern war. As he noted in his 1998 memoir:

Trying to eliminate Saddam . . . would have incurred incalculable human and political costs. Apprehending him [in 1991] was probably impossible. . . . We would have been forced to occupy Baghdad and, in effect, rule Iraq. There was no viable 'exit strategy' we could see, violating another of our principles. . . . Had we gone the invasion route, [we] could conceivably still be an occupying power in a bitterly hostile land.

Also, unlike his son, before the 2003 Gulf War, President George H. W. Bush put together an international coalition guaranteeing that U.S. allies would ultimately pay 80 percent of the $80 billion that the war cost.[8] In doing so he reaffirmed America's sole superpower domination in the Persian Gulf, without admitting in public that for the first time in the twentieth century the United States could not afford to finance its own participation in a war effort.

The 1991 images conveyed by political cartoons, patriotic military parades, and pundits gave the distinct impression that the country had won a "fun," essentially bloodless war – like a Nintendo game played on a real world stage. Some newspaper columnists referred to the 1991 Middle East conflict as the best "splendid little war" the United States had fought since the Spanish-American War of 1898; others said it was the equivalent of sending an elephant to stomp on a mouse. They were all partially accurate. Saddam Hussein's forces did conduct a basically static defense, and often his troops refused to fight during this unbelievably short (forty-three-day) and intensely technological "hyperwar." Certain stated military objectives were achieved: the Iraqis left Kuwait; Saddam's army was destroyed, although not to the degree that Americans were led to believe; and Iraq's nuclear, chemical, biological, and Scud warfare capabilities were so severely damaged that they were never reconstituted in the 1990s. Most allied political objectives of the first Gulf War were not achieved: Saddam remained in power; the "free" nation of Kuwait remained undemocratic, with its oil wells on fire and incapacitated until well into 1992; and the Middle East was left no more stable than before the war.

Nonetheless, most Americans greeted the achievement of this partial status quo ante as an unconditional international success. Then, in a confounding turn of fate, Bush, who had come out of that war in 1991 with the highest job approval rating (89 percent in February 1991) ever recorded, saw his popularity plummet to 29 percent in July 1992 on his way to losing the election that year to Bill Clinton. What had happened? It was more than "It's the Economy, Stupid." Bush's precipitous rise and fall had something to do with the transformation of the American presidency from its modern to its postmodern phase. He never perfected a political persona to compete with that of Clinton – a prerequisite of the imponderable, imperial presidency. He also got caught in the tricky transition to an amorphous post–Cold War world without the countervailing force of the USSR. Most importantly, Bush was the first American president faced with confronting the Faustian bargains that had helped the country to win the Cold War. Finally, he had to come to grips with the perennial radical Republican neo-conservatives, who had first organized themselves against Nixon's foreign policy, and whom Reagan had temporarily abandoned in his second term. They were especially furious over Bush's decision to stop the first Gulf War after liberating Kuwait instead of going to Bagdad and getting rid of Saddam.

Neo-Cons in the 1990s

The neo-cons responded to this rebuff by producing from the bowels of the Pentagon in March 1992 a new national defense policy document called the Defense Planning Guidance. The work of Paul Wolfowitz when he served under Secretary of Defense Richard Cheney, this position paper contained four major points: (1) increase American defense spending; (2) take preemptive action when the United States perceived a threat in order to deter "potential competitors from even aspiring to a larger regional or global role" (including not simply China and Russia but all "advanced industrial nations"); (3) act unilaterally whenever possible, even when a signatory to treaties, because "all alliances were only temporary"; and (4) prevent any nation from developing weapons of mass destruction and/or threatening U.S. access to vital natural resources. The Defense Planning Guidance completely ignored taking collective action in conjunction with the United Nations. Leaked to the *New York Times*, this so-called Wolfowitz Doctrine argued that the United States had to take advantage of winning the Cold War by preventing the rise of any future rivals and by protecting Persian Gulf oil at all costs. Bush "hastily repudiated... [this] inflammatory document," but nonetheless it laid the foundation for what is now called post–Cold War unilateralism or interventionism based on an even greater aggrandizement of presidential power.[9]

While the first President Bush did not embrace the ideas of the neo-cons as they probably expected he would, he neglected to develop an alternative "vision thing" for post–Cold War diplomacy, except for the vague notion that the United States should become a "kinder, gentler nation" and establish a New World Order. Instead of rethinking why the United States emerged victorious, Bush remained as ethically challenged as his predecessors in the Oval Office, with the possible exception of Carter, but at the same time he did not pursue world domination.[10]

Temporarily out of government when Bush lost his bid for reelection, Wolfowitz became head of the Johns Hopkins School for Advanced International Studies. Most of his ideological Republican colleagues ensconced themselves in think tanks, issuing with his help such diplomatic prescriptions as the 1994 "A Safe and Prosperous America: A U.S. Foreign Policy and Defense Policy Blueprint." Later, during the 1996 presidential campaign, Richard Perle, Douglas J. Feith, David and Meyrav Wurmser, and a half-dozen other neo-cons took it upon themselves to write and/or sign a position paper entitled "A Clean Break: A New Strategy for Securing the Realm." Originally written for the benefit of Benjamin Netanyahu after he became prime minister of Israel, it asserted: (1) that "removing Saddam from power in Iraq" would be in Israel's best interest; and (2) that instead of honoring the Oslo Peace Accords, Israel should militarily reassert its claim to the West Bank and Gaza and consider a preemptive invasion of Lebanon, regardless of whether the threat was genuine, and a strategic initiative along its northern borders by engaging Hizballah [sic],

Syria, and Iran – as long is it could rally American support. While "the price in blood would be high," these neo-cons matter-of-factly averred, "it would be a necessary form of detoxifcation – the only way out of Oslo's web." In summary, this neo-con position paper advised Netanyahu to make a "clean break . . . by reestablishing the principle of preemption, rather than retaliation alone."[11] (The Israeli prime minister in 1996 did not take this advice, but Ehud Olmert seemed to follow it in 2006 after the preemptive example of the Bush administration in Iraq.)

After Clinton's reelection the neo-conservatives from the Bush administration once again operated out of their think tanks, including one they had founded in 1997, the Project for the New American Century (PNAC). In addition to Donald Rumsfeld, Wolfowitz, Feith, Perle, Bill Kristol, and Sven Kraemer, prominent members of PNAC included Dick Cheney, I. Lewis "Scooter" Libby, and Stephen Cambone. At the beginning of 1998, Rumsfeld, Wolfowitz, Feith, Perle, Sven Kraemer, and William Kristol, along with thirty-four neo-con members of the Committee for Peace and Security in the Gulf (CPSG), signed an open letter to Clinton insisting that regime change in Iraq "needs to become the aim of American foreign policy." This meant, they said, the removal of Saddam Hussein. They reiterated this advice in a letter to Republican leaders of the House and Senate later that same year. It is worth noting that among the signatories of both letters were Donald Rumsfeld, Elliott Abrams, John Bolton, William J. Bennett, Richard Armitage, and Cheney's protégé Zalmay Khalilzad, who had both Unocal oil and Taliban connections. Ten of the eighteen signing these letters later joined the George W. Bush administration.[12]

In September 2000, PNAC, some of whose prominent members had signed the 1998 letters to Clinton and Republicans in the House and Senate, issued a ninety-page report based on the "clean break" document and the previous 1992 Defense Planning Guidance document. This one was entitled "Rebuilding America's Defenses: Strategy, Forces and Resources for a New Century." It called for $100 billion (or a 24 percent increase) in defense spending; weaponization of the sky while denying to other countries the military use of outer space; development of tactical nuclear weapons to destroy underground bunkers; withdrawal from the 1972 Anti-Ballistic Missile treaty (ABM); a preemptive action against Iraq having nothing to do with Saddam Hussein; the construction of several permanent bases in Iraq to protect oil fields and pipelines; the transfer of Iraq's nationalized oil industry to Western petroleum corporations; and the targeting of weapons against Iran and North Korea. Although the authors of "Rebuilding American's Defenses" ultimately "played a central role in spreading neo-Jacobin ideas outside and inside the U.S. government," they realized that their millennium ideas remained too extreme to become policy *"absent some catastrophic and catalyzing event like a New Pearl Harbor."*[13] From this neo-con point of view, September 11 was heaven-sent because it provided the needed excuse for executing the PNAC blueprint for U.S. world domination. By 2000, for the first time since their angry nascence over Nixon's foreign policy, they had finally found a president in George W. Bush who would not reject them in midstream as Reagan had or disregard them as Bush Sr. and Clinton had.

While neither Bush Sr. nor Clinton followed the extreme advice of these radical conservatives, they indirectly made both presidents less inclined to reassess the independent internationalism or unilateral internationalism based on American exceptionalism that the country had practiced during the Cold War and less inclined to question the Faustian ways in which the country had won that conflict. At the same time, both presidents were encouraged to think about the feasibility of maintaining a global Pax Americana. Both also inherited a set of theoretical post–Cold War problems and questions after the Soviet Union collapsed. At first the ideological mania of the Cold War had prevented them from being widely discussed, let alone resolved, and then post–Cold War triumphalism temporarily made them seem less important. Since September 11 they have all but been lost in the fog of fighting terrorism all over the world. Neither the first Bush nor the Clinton administration came to terms in the 1990s with these three seemingly intractable post–Cold War problems: (1) selective application of humanitarian interventions on behalf of minority rights that don't always produce humanitarian results or place real limits on state sovereignty, (2) functioning versus fictional democracies, and (3) practical international aid for developing nations in a globalized economy.

Humanitarian Limits on Sovereignty

Perhaps the most difficult problem of the 1990s proved to be the basic "contradiction between sovereignty and international human rights." Traditional sovereignty would definitely have been questioned much earlier had it not been for the Cold War. During that conflict the United States allied with foreign leaders wherever it could find them, regardless of what they did within their borders. But since the end of the Cold War, traditional sovereignty has been found wanting in terms of human rights. In other words, human rights enforcement could no longer be considered the exclusive domestic domain of individual nation-states, and it could no longer be assumed that nations established in the 1990s would reflect the best of Western democratic and ethical values. This has given rise to international humanitarian interventions, or what is also called the new military humanism.[14]

Because of the effusion of ethnic, religious, and gender cleansing *within* old and new national boundaries during the first Bush administration, international lawyers scrutinized the meaning of sovereignty as never before. While not all such atrocities occurred in Eastern Europe in the 1990s, the incidents in Bosnia and Kosovo convinced some within Western jurisprudence circles and committees of the UN that traditional national self-determination and its corollary, inviolate sovereignty, needed to be redefined. Increasingly, they debated whether such slaughter within self-determined borders could any longer be honored as the right of nation-states and whether the UN's (and earlier the

League of Nation's) commitment to noninterference in the internal affairs of member states should be reexamined. In 1992, the General Assembly passed a consensus resolution entitled the Declaration on the Rights of Persons Belonging to National or Ethnic, Religious, and Linguistic Minorities. This marked the first time since World War II that the United Nations had made protection of group minority rights and promotion of minority identity a primary issue. However, the declaration was nonbinding, and the relationship between this new definition of sovereignty and nation building remained unaddressed.[15]

In part, ethno-religious conflicts came back to haunt the post–Cold War world because most of them, such as the Armenia genocide, had not been addressed, let alone resolved, in the 1920s and 1930s. Then, their very existence seemed to be denied or minimized by mandatory migration of populations because of the universalization of human rights following World War II. As noted, few significant attempts at binding enforcement of human rights were made during the Cold War. Especially outside Europe, "binding international enforcement [of human rights] remain[ed] the exception rather than the rule."[16] For this reason, the end of the Cold War should not be compared to the end of the Second World War. In many ways the decades of the 1920s and 1930s have more in common with those of the 1980s and 1990s than the 1940s and 1950s because of the unprecedented outbursts of ethnic and religious strife abroad, the return of the religious right in American culture and politics, conservative domestic reform legislation, and destabilizing global economic foreign policies.

This unresolved relationship between state autonomy and human rights forced George H. W. Bush and his secretary of state, James Baker, to reconsider the definition of sovereignty. In 1991, Bush refused to recognize six governments emerging from the former Soviet Union until "[he was] satisfied they have made commitments to responsible security policies and democratic principles." Subsequently, Secretary of State James Baker submitted criteria for obtaining diplomatic recognition that included strong pro-democratic, pro–human rights, and anti–internal violence policies. The European Union accepted these at an extraordinary European Political Council meeting on December 16, 1991, in a joint declaration entitled "Guidelines on the Recognition of New States in Eastern Europe in the Soviet Union."[17] The Clinton administration, despite its intervention into Bosnia and Kosovo, did not see fit to improve theoretically upon these early Republican attempts to redefine sovereignty in the post–Cold War world.

Equally perplexing, the UN and the major post–Cold War Western nations never seriously questioned whether it remained correct to equate the right of people to assert their national self-determination and their right to secede, as Woodrow Wilson had seemed to suggest over eighty years ago. As before, the problem of "who are the people" loomed large, as it had after World War I. So did the apparent mutual exclusiveness of the principle of self-determination and the principle that existing sovereign borders are sacrosanct and should not be altered. Even if this conundrum could be resolved (and it wasn't in the

1990s), then the question remained: "why [was] the principle of the right to secede . . . applied selectively to Slovenia, Croatia, and Bosnia but not to other ethnic groups demanding secession elsewhere in the world?" The question still is unanswered in the first decade of the twenty-first century. According to Raju G. C. Thomas: "Slovenes, Croats, Muslims, and Albanians have all been conceded the right of self-determination but the Serbs of Croatia, Bosnia and Kosovo have been denied that right."[18]

This asymmetrical application can only partially be explained in terms of international law. When Wilson's concept of self-determination was written into the UN Charter it was a euphemism for decolonization, and as such it was never specifically defined. This meant self-determination did not allow for secession as Wilsonianism had implied in the interwar years. In fact, this post–World War II idea of self-determination did not include the idea that all peoples had a right to self-determination, only that all colonies had the right to be independent. The group human rights of minorities within these newly independent colonies (and established nations) was not a concern until toward the end of the Cold War because, as previously noted, the international community chose to reduce the number of ethnic groups facing hostile majorities through massive forced repatriation after World War II. As a result, the right of self-determination has not yet been redefined in the twenty-first century to mean the general right of sescession, that is, "external self-determination," but rather has evolved to include the right of "internal self-determination." Thus, the protection of group rights within a state is still considered a domestic issue under international law as it relates to minorities, meaning they should be accorded economic, social, and cultural development through legislation or a federal option of a certain amount of cultural or political autonomy.[19]

Clearly, the meaning of sovereignty is changing in the post–Cold War world, but this does not by any stretch of the imagination mean that nation-states are going to disappear soon or that their ability to oppress their citizens has dissipated.[20] Nonetheless, sovereignty has never been absolute, and misuse of it is now subject to world scrutiny because of the globalization of mass communications through twenty-four-hour television coverage.

Promoting Democracy

The second major post–Cold War problem facing American presidents was the future of democracy. The United States took advantage of the evolving definition of traditional sovereignty and increased concern about human rights by promoting democracy as never before. The problem was that throughout the Cold War the United States had not understood the difference between "exporting" its model of democracy and "promoting" conditions that foster the foundations of democracy: economic security, independent judicial systems, property law, an educated middle class, civic responsibility, civilian control of the military, and multiparty free expression of opinion with a guaranteed, peaceful succession of power. By the middle of the 1990s, American promotion of the expansion of democracy, however gratifying, had very shallow roots because the United States pursued democracy inconsistently as a idealist global crusade, while it primarily continued to practice a realist foreign policy based on ensuring stability in order to secure its material and strategic interests.[21]

Bill Clinton indiscriminately praised the democratization of the post–Cold War world in hyperbolic rhetoric on his trips to Eastern Europe and Russia in 1994 and to Africa, Latin American, and China in 1998. One would never have known from his remarks that, worldwide, half of the "democratizing" countries he so uncritically praised either conducted questionable elections or remained what has been called "illiberal democracies" – that is, democracies that did not accord the freedom of constitutional liberalism to their people, especially their female citizens.[22]

Newly emerging nations, in particular, are more often than not "hypernationalistic and war-mongering" compared to established autocracies or liberal democracies. Thus, some political scientists have questioned Clinton's unequivocal and Wilsonian-sounding declaration in 1993 that he was pursuing "a strategy of enlargement – enlargement of the world's ... community of market democracies ... [because] democracies rarely wage war on one another ... [and] the movement toward democracy is the best guarantor of human rights." This assertion was highly dubious then (and still is, even though it has been taken up by George W. Bush), in part because newly elected executives often lack control over the military or are, in fact, dependent on the military. Also questionable is the idea that "elections by themselves ... translate into parliamentary rule or civilian control or an independent judiciary or fair taxes or protection for private property and minorities."[23]

For example forty-nine of the new nations that emerged through elections from 1989 to 1996 represented small states and so did not substantially increase the number of "free" people worldwide. Many of them also cannot be called liberal democracies according to Freedom House, a nonpartisan research organization. Of the 117 electoral democracies in the world as of August 2004, 88 could be considered liberal or "free" countries, and 56 percent of the world's population lived in these states. Worldwide, however, a Freedom House study in December 2004 found that 37 percent of all people lived under forty-nine regimes considered "not free," and another 54 countries with 17 percent of the world's population were deemed only "partly free, leaving 44 percent enjoying life in 'free' countries."[24]

Additionally, there is little reason to believe, other than on the grounds of ethnocentrism and American exceptionalism, that democracy as a political base for nation-states is destined to triumph in any enduring sense. The New World Order may, instead, be characterized by numerous failed or disintegrating nation-states that Western countries did not anticipate when they first celebrated the collapse of Communism.[25] In the current globalized economy, oligarchic city-states, regional states within national borders resembling tribal fiefdoms, or nomadic, one-dimensional, anarchistic or religious communities without territory and only erratic political power, rather than democratic nation-states, could become the norm if the New World Order continues to develop along the paradoxical lines of globalism and tribalism. Such a scenario is not promising in terms of democratic practice or theory. It may well be that the common end result of globalism and tribalism will be international fragmentation and anarchy rather than "common will and that conscious and collective human control under the guidance of law [that] we call democracy."[26]

Whither Globalization?

The third unresolved post–Cold War problem facing the United States in the 1990s had to do with the foreign policy implications of the switch from a quantitative trend of economic interdependence to a qualitative change in the international economic system based on the revolution in computer technology, known as globalization. This development has had an impact not only on the traditional sovereignty of individual states and the future of democracy but also on the multinational organizations that were established after the Second World War.[27] For example, many, such as the Marshall Plan, NATO, the General Agreement on Tariffs and Trade (GATT), the International Monetary Fund (IMF), the World Bank, and the Exchange Rate Mechanism of the European Monetary System (which came into existence after the collapse of the Bretton Woods system), were products of the Cold War. All were initially designed to promote integrative functions and produce regional security, regional markets, and some modicum of currency stability. However, the ideological dispute between the United States and the Soviet Union also meant that "wartime multilateral dreams of a united, stable, global economy supervised by international institutions gradually fell by the wayside … [and] national security concerns trumped the open-door vision of an open, nondiscriminatory world."[28]

These same Cold War institutions, however, may not be reliable or adequate ones for structuring collective security and a global market of the future in a world without Soviet Communism. Until the World Trade Organization (WTO) was created in 1995 under GATT, the latter had lowered industrial tariffs and created trade preferences for developing nations, but it had neglected to remove the protectionist agricultural subsidies of the industrialized nations or to create a mechanism for resolving trading disputes among nations. Similar criticisms of the domestic and international impact of GATT have been made of its successor – the WTO. Likewise, before the end of the Cold War it was evident that the IMF had not fulfilled its original mission, which was to provide a collective response to countries in economic trouble by intervening because free markets often disadvantaged developing nations. Instead, it became an enforcer of the "Washington Consensus" and operated at the expense of poorer nations. While financial considerations prevailed under the IMF, trade policy prevailed under the WTO to the detriment of the environment and labor. GATT, the World Bank, and the IMF simply became instruments of the American capitalist market model in the course of the Cold War, and this trend continued after the end of that conflict.[29]

It has been suggested that these deficiencies of globalization, caused by the current multilateral financial institutions, could be overcome if those institutions would focus on aiding low-income emerging democratic nations rather than autocratic regimes, because the former economically outperform the latter. Given the difficulties in evaluating the level of democracy actually practiced by countries in the developing world and in overcoming the entrenched interests governing the World Bank, the IMF, and the WTO, it is not likely that such advice will be, or could be, followed in the near future. Others, such as Joseph Stiglitz, believe that only wholesale reform of existing international institutions and the "creation of new ones like a global reserve system" to make trade fairer and to discourage despotism and corruption is necessary. He thinks only international rather than national democratic control can rescue worldwide economic institutions from special interests. Whether national politicians would allow the creation of institutions beyond domestic politics in order to save globalization is dubious.[30]

Clintonian Diplomacy

After six months in office the Clinton administration had not yet come up with clear foreign policies addressing the three theoretical post–Cold War problems just discussed. At first, Clinton simply followed Bush's foreign policy lead during his first term and could claim only two foreign policy "triumphs" after eighteen months in power, both of which took place in 1993: the ratification of the North American Free Trade Agreement (NAFTA) and the 1993 Arafat-Rabin agreement, although this had been brokered by Norway and, in truth, had more to do with Carter's Camp David diplomacy than any initiative on the part of Clinton or his foreign policy team. This rocky start did not improve until 1995, and even in his second term U.S. diplomacy remained erratic and hard to understand, except for Clinton's New Democratic (i.e., old style conservative) adherence to spreading free market democracy. Otherwise, his foreign policy seemed to consist of "directionless compromises" based on endless, anguished "process[ing] without purpose."[31]

The only consistent diplomatic hallmark of the Clinton presidency can be found in his promotion of "economism" in foreign policy. Comparing the United States to a "big corporation competing in the global marketplace," Clinton and such cabinet members as Secretary of Commerce Ron Brown, Secretary of Labor Robert Reich, Secretary of the Treasury Robert Rubin, Trade Representative Mickey Kantor, and Secretary of State Warren Christopher unapologetically placed economic security at the top of their foreign policy agenda in their pursuit of a particular type of globalization. Economism is associated with managed trade, market access through bilateral and regional agreements, and an obsession with national trade deficits rather than global imbalances. It is sometimes called "Third Way" globalism, market fundamentalism, or corporate libertarianism. Economism often finds itself at odds with the American myth of free trade and the promotion of democracy and human rights and also seemes to contradict some of the tenets of the "Washington Consensus" or neo-liberal economic theories followed during the Cold War.[32]

It was not just "economism" that contained some internal contradictions in terms of traditional American capitalism; so did Clinton's pursuit of a more peaceful and humanitarian world through globalization. When this contradiction became evident in relations with China, Clinton quickly abandoned "making human rights a cornerstone of our foreign policy" by relating it to trade. On May 28, 1993, he granted temporary most-favored-nation status (MFN) to China, saying: "I decided, with the unanimous support of my foreign policy and economic advisors, to extend MFN," Clinton later explained, *"and, for the future to delink our human rights efforts from trade."* Later, the Clinton administration not only granted permanent MFN status for China, but also strongly supported Chinese admission to the WTO after that country perfunctorily promised not to use prison labor in products exported to the U.S., to release political and/or religious prisoners, and not to discriminate against American businesses – once again confirming that Clinton's only diplomatic consistency came in the area of economic foreign policy.[33]

Clintonian diplomacy also left a more unilateral than cooperative legacy than is usually acknowledged. For example, the 1999 "A National Security Strategy for a New Century" (NSS), written after the 1993 attack on the World Trade Center and the 1999 bombings of the U.S. embassies in Kenya and Tanzania, stated that the United States would take unilateral preemptive action against terrorists. So did the earlier 1995 Presidential Decision Directive 39, issued in June 1995. The last Clinton NSS issued in December 2000, "A National Security Strategy for a Global Age," stated: "We will do what we must to defend these [U.S. vital] interests. They may involve the use of military force, including unilateral action, where deemed necessary or appropriate." Moreover, by the end of his presidency Clinton had expressed dissatisfaction with the Kyoto Treaty and the International Criminal Court, and he did not sign the Land-Mines Treaty. Nonetheless, his administration, like the elder Bush's, never completely abandoned the Wilsonian ideal of relying on the United Nations, on a network of alliances and other international organizations, on the promotion of democracy and trade as a way to foster global peace, and on countering individual rogue nations and terrorism in general.[34]

Clinton legitimately claimed success for the 1995 Middle Eastern diplomatic initiative coordinated by State Department official Dennis Ross, and his administration does deserve credit for the October 1998 Wye River Memorandum, which kept the negotiations between Benjamin Netanyahu and Yasser Arafat from completely falling apart. However, within weeks the Israeli cabinet decided against implementing the Wye Memorandum. Then Clinton engaged in an ultimately fruitless quest to bring about an agreement between Ehud Barak and Arafat at Camp David in July 2000. After violence broke out once again when Ariel Sharon visited the Temple Mount complex in September 2000, Clinton made a final proposal to both Barak and Arafat at the very end of his second term. Israel responded with lengthy reservations and continued to increase the number of settlements in the occupied territories. Arafat rejected this proposal outright because no Palestinian leader would have survived accepting its terms, which, among other things, would have released Israel from complying with UN resolutions calling for its withdrawal from land occupied in 1967. The talks between Israelis and Palestinians at Taba in January 2001 also failed, but did lay the groundwork for the unofficial 2003 Geneva Initiative.[35] In the end, Clinton's various efforts to broker peace between the Palestine Authority and Israel proved too little, too late and left the impression that Arafat alone, rather than the Israeli leadership, was responsible for his failed Middle Eastern policy.

In addition to these matters, Clinton faced two immediate and concrete foreign policy problems: (1) how to deal with the Cold War legacy of the proliferation of nuclear weapons and conventional arms races, and (2) what to do about ethnic cleansing in the former Yugoslavia. Initially, Clinton took no significant action on either of these issues.

Nuclear and Conventional Weapons

With respect to the problem of weapons proliferation Clinton faced the conundrum that despite the end of the Cold War, the U.S. economy remained on a wartime footing, and there was little talk of demobilizing as there had been after the First and Second World Wars. In this sense, he did not deviate from the first post–Cold War National Security Strategy Report (NSS) issued by the Bush administration in March 1990, which talked about "threats to our interests" that required the country to strengthen its "defense industrial base" by investing "in new facilities and equipment as well as in research and development," including high-tech counterinsurgency and low-intensity conflict resolution weapons and tactics. Following this line of reasoning, both the Bush and Clinton administrations urged the Soviet Union to demilitarize, and Clinton set an example by reducing the troop force by 300,000. In 1992, the United States had also stopped making and testing nuclear arms, settling for an arsenal of 10,000 warheads – each with a nuclear-core life span of a half-century. In 1996, the United States became the first country to sign the Comprehensive Nuclear Test Ban Treaty (CTBT), but in 1999 Congress refused to ratify this treaty, which Clinton blamed on the development of nuclear weapons by both India and Pakistan and growing isolationism among Republicans. His memoirs do not indicate that he expended any great effort on behalf of this treaty, perhaps because of his preoccupation with personal, political, and legal problems.[36]

Since Clinton's record on nuclear proliferation left much to be desired, critics naturally turned to conventional weapons and asked: If the United States did not "promote a world substantially less armed and substantially less economically and psychologically dependent on the global arms trade," who would? Ultimately, Clinton turned the United States into the largest arms dealer in the post–Cold War world after his administration spent eight years talking about nonproliferation of both conventional and nuclear weapons. This trend continued unabated under George W. Bush until, by 2005, the United States accounted for 47 percent of all arms sales in the world.[37]

At first, in keeping with the policy set in motion by Nixon twenty years earlier, Clinton simply accepted his predecessor's decision to sell seventy-two F-15 aircraft to Saudi Arabia, ensuring another round in the Middle East arms race. While the administration supported what it called "counterproliferation," it did little except to obfuscate the problem with rhetoric. In fact, his first secretary of defense, Les Aspin, spoke about preemptive military action and promoted U.S. theater missile defenses (TMDs) by substituting a ground-based missile defense system for Reagan's space-based one at little or no savings to the American people. Instead of Star Wars or the Strategic Defense Initiative (SDI), the Clinton administration adopted the Ballistic Missile Defense Organization (BMDO).[38]

This antimissile defense system violated the 1972 Anti-Ballistic Missile (ABM) treaty and represented a devious kind of unilateralism. Despite Russian and allied opposition, on Clinton's watch both parties in Congress endorsed some version of a nuclear defense system, also in violation of the ABM treaty. While Republicans said that the treaty should just be chucked, the Clinton administration came up with an even more ingenious and Faustian way to violate the ABM treaty. Rather than forthrightly withdrawing from the treaty, Clinton's advisers told him to go ahead with his limited missile defense system and simply "let the next administration decide whether to abrogate the Antiballistic Missile Treaty." That way, he could avoid the charge that "breaking the treaty [was] his lasting legacy in arms control."[39]

Finally, it should be remembered that Clinton intervened in more countries than any president since Woodrow Wilson. He engaged in a series of overt, but largely unilateral and fitful, military actions in Somalia (initiated under Bush and continued by the UN), Bosnia, Haiti, Iraq, Sudan, Afghanistan, and finally, Kosovo. All of these unilateral actions were undertaken in the name of U.S. economic or national security and sometimes on behalf of free market democracy (self-determination) or peacekeeping (now called nation building), but seldom in the name of fighting terrorism. This pattern of intervention did nothing to take the United States from its traditional practice of independent internationalism even though he compiled with the War Power Resolution twice as many times as his five predecessors. Thus, Clinton did not contribute in any way to the systematic overhaul of U.S. foreign policy so needed because the Cold War had ended.[40]

Ethnic Cleansing

With respect to the second immediate post–Cold War diplomatic problem – ethnic cleansing in Eastern Europe – the Clinton administration inherited from its predecessor a most complex and murky situation in the former Yugoslavia. After all, even Woodrow Wilson, who wanted to save the world for democracy, had warned back in 1919: "If you want to put out a fire in the Balkans, if you want to stamp out the smoldering flames in some part of Central Europe, you don't send to the United States for troops."[41]

Once war broke out in Croatia in 1991, Western leaders in general did not comprehend the real causes any more than they had in the interwar years. On the one hand, they thought that civil war was inevitable in the Balkans, especially in Bosnia, because of its history of ethnic and religious conflict whenever the area was not ruled by imperial or communist dictatorships. On the other, they viewed the conflict in Yugoslavia as typical Greater Serbian territorial ambitions based on *revanche*. In either case, Western leaders regarded the implosion of Yugoslavia as an anachronism in the post–Cold War world – a world they triumphally envisioned as one based on prosperity and peace. Out of their own nationalist ethnocentrism, they objectified the nationalism of the Balkans as "other" and barbaric. Most simply stated, with the fall of Communism, Yugoslavia lost its strategic importance as an economic and potential military deterrent to the Soviet Union. As a result of all of the above, the West failed to take action.[42]

In his first months in office Clinton conceded to the fait accompli created by the Serbian (and then Croatian) ethnic cleansing policy when he announced an ineffectual food drop and no-fly zone and allowed the Serbian siege of Sarajevo and other cities to continue. A year later, the U.S. Senate voted by a close margin to force the president to end the embargo of weapons for the Bosnian Muslims, but in the interim American leadership on this question was notable by its absence and resulted in 100,000 more deaths between 1993 and 1995, for a total of 250,000 in four years of slaughter.[43] While some Americans argued that Bosnia-Herzegovina was Europe's problem, once it became clear that neither the EC nor the UN would act, it became incumbent upon the United States to do so, for the following reasons.

First, faster intervention would have saved more lives and been cheaper in the long run rather than waiting for full-scale ethnic wars to develop, as later demonstrated in Rwanda. Second, clearly the humanitarian principles at stake in the area were those for which so much had been sacrificed during World War II. It made a mockery of the Holocaust for the United States to turn a blind eye to what was happening simply because no easy victory could be ensured. Third, American inaction simply confirmed the worst critique of the U.S. during the Cold War, namely, that the country was capable of military action only when Communism or essential resources such as oil were at stake. Fourth, inaction in Bosnia-Herzegovina divided Western nations as the Soviet Union never had. Their disagreement over military action in Eastern Europe between 1992 and 1995 set the stage for a much more bitter disagreement over the 2003 invasion of Iraq and general confusion about when cooperative humanitarian action should take place. Finally, the integrity and credibility of NATO had reached a new low by 1995, and so the Clinton administration came to the conclusion that intervening in Bosnia-Herzegovina could revitalize it.[44] Sadly, NATO intervention in 1995 did not prevent the ethnic partition of Bosnia-Herzegovina as it came to be embodied in the Dayton Accords.

The Dayton meeting in November 1995 demonstrated once again that Western leaders had made a mistake with respect to the question of self-determination and minority rights. This time the mistake stemmed from talking in generalities about guaranteeing minority rights but in practice focusing almost exclusively on the Kosovo Albanians. This set the stage for the later armed intervention against what remained of the Federal Republic of Yugoslavia under Milosevic. In Dayton other minority problems, such as the Serbs in Croatia, were largely ignored and not represented. For this reason, the Dayton Accords are an oxymoron. They did not create common central institutions with Muslim, Serb, or Croat support, thus precluding a unified Bosnian state. There was no agreement for the return of refugees so that millions might finally assume their former lives. Finally, the apartheid arrangement among the Bosnian-Croatian Federation, the Croatian community of Herceg-Bosna, and the Republika Srpska, each backed by armies and other paramilitary groups, foreclosed the possibility of the creation of a nonethnic Bosnian citizenry.[45]

Intervention in Haiti but not Rwanda

Unlike his economic foreign policy, Clinton's political foreign policy wavered between action and inaction and also between multilateralism and unilateralism. For example, he did not welcome Haitian immigrants, reversing a campaign promise, but later used military force in 1994 to restore Jean-Bertrand Aristide to power and then did not provide the promised aid after withdrawing U.S. troops. Haiti's history since declaring its independence from the French in 1804 (which the United States did not recognize until 1862) is a nightmare of multiple constitutions, coups, revolts, revolutions, assassinations, dictators, and self-perpetuating poverty, often aided and abetted by sporadic U.S. military interventions, indifference, and economic interference. The only relatively honest election in the country's history occurred in December 1990, bringing the former Catholic priest Jean-Bertrand Aristide to the presidency. Even before Aristide – a Salesian priest and the product of liberation theology and the poor – could be inaugurated, a failed military coup took place. Once in office, his disappointedly violent administration only lasted until September 1991, when Lt. General Raoul Cédras replaced him and established a ruling military junta. While it is widely believed in Haiti that the United States was involved in the coup, there is no concrete proof of this, although the American Embassy was probably aware that a coup would take place. George H. W. Bush followed the lead of the Organization of American States by freezing Haiti's assets in the United States and ordering a trade embargo in October. At the same time, he refused to accept Haitians trying to escape to the United States by boat. Instead, he declined to screen them for refugee status, as required by both a 1981 bilateral interdiction agreement with Haiti and the 1951 UN Convention Relating to the Status of Refugees, ordering them returned to Haiti.[46] Enter Bill Clinton.

Despite his criticism during the 1992 campaign of Bush's treatment of Haitians attempting to escape Haiti for political reasons, after winning the presidency Clinton followed his predecessor's refugee policy. Procrastinating as usual, Clinton did not order a general review of Haitian policy until March

1994, and on May 2 he announced that he could no longer rule out the use of U.S. force. At the same time he reinstated screening procedures for Haitian refugees, and the UN Security Council passed a comprehensive set of sanctions and embargos against Haiti and the junta. As Haitian refugees flooded into U.S. territorial waters, the military cabal became more defiant throughout the summer of 1994. This led the United Nations in July to approve an invasion of Haiti by a Multinational Force (MNF) led by the United States. In September, former President Jimmy Carter and members of the Clinton State Department, National Security Council, and Pentagon were in Port-au-Prince negotiating with Cédras and the junta. The resulting accord called for Aristide's return on October 15, with Cédras to receive a generous $1 million in U.S. payments and services upon his departure. Hearing this, Clinton cancelled the military operation, ostensibly because Carter and other American negotiators were still in Haiti. Belatedly, on September 19, American troops landed in a "permissive atmosphere," finding themselves greeted on the beach by members of the press who dubbed the action an "intervasion."[47]

Throughout this process Clinton predicted that democracy and prosperity would soon flower under Operation Restore Democracy. The failure of the previous American occupation of Haiti initiated by Woodrow Wilson in 1915, which lasted until 1934, to deliver on the same idealistic promises should have tempered Clinton's rhetoric and hopes. In March 1995, the UN Mission in Haiti (UNMIH) took over for the MNF with a contingent of 2,400 U.S. troops out of 6,000, but the situation continued to deteriorate through the end of 1997, when these UN peacekeepers were replaced by the UN Civilian Police Mission in Haiti (MIPONUH). All vestiges of the UN mission ended in February 2001. In their memoirs, both President Clinton and his secretary of state, Madeleine Albright, ignored the fact that, as of the end of 2003, conditions in Haiti were worse than they had been before U.S. intervention in 1994.[48]

Just as they had in Haiti, aides to Clinton promised to develop a new African policy, but none emerged. This proved especially true with regard to the Cold War legacy in Angola, where, as noted previously, UNITA, long backed by the United States, refused to accept the outcome of the democratic election of José Eduardo dos Santos. As of May 1993, American civil rights leaders pressured the Clinton administration into recognizing dos Santos in order to help end a civil war that had raged there since 1975, killing a half-million people. Otherwise, the United States ignored the fighting that continued throughout the 1990s. The Clinton administration's other African policies consisted of refusing suggestions to meet with President Ibrahim Babangida of Nigeria as a show of support for that country's multiparty elections held in June 1993 and declining to develop a strategy forcing one-time American ally Mobutu Sese Seko, who had driven Zaire into bankruptcy, to step down.[49]

Probably the most ethically suspect inaction of the Clinton administration in Africa occurred when it did not attempt to prevent the genocide that took place in Rwanda in 1994. Despite the president's highly publicized "apology" to a tightly guarded group of Rwandan officials at the Kigali Airport in 1998, it has now been documented beyond any doubt that he and his top advisers "knew enough about the genocide early on to save lives, but passed up countless opportunities to intervene." While the slaughter of 800,000 Tutsis took place in a three-month period in 1994, the Clinton administration refused to use the term genocide, blocked UN action, and never even held a "principals' meeting" of cabinet officers to discuss the massacre. Most senior officials denied knowing about the extent of the killings.[50]

Typically, Clinton apparently convinced himself that if he had known more he would have taken action, but the facts contained in recently declassified documents belie his stance and that of then UN Ambassador Albright. Sadly, the post–Cold War lesson of Rwanda is that top U.S. policy makers "will suffer no sanction if they do nothing to curb atrocities. The national interest remains narrowly constructed to exclude stopping genocide." Not surprisingly, the United States remains the only major government that has not conducted an official inquiry into its role during the Rwandan crisis.[51]

NATO Expansion and Intervention in Kosovo

The Clinton administration's singular unilateral action occurred when it insisted on expanding NATO over considerable opposition from prominent members of the foreign policy establishment. This included the dean of U.S. Cold War diplomacy, George Kennan, the former senator Sam Nunn, and a two-to-one majority of those on the prestigious Foreign Affairs Council, to say nothing of Russian President Yeltsin, who viewed such expansion not only as hostile to Russia but also as a renewal of the Cold War. These critics argued that NATO was no longer needed because the United States had no significant enemy after the end of the Cold War and only American arms makers stood to profit from it. Clearly, NATO's credibility was at stake, and expansion looked like one way to salvage it. Clinton has never offered any plausible explanation for NATO expansion or identified who within his administration first introduced him to and convinced him of the idea, although it appears to have been Tony Lake. His Strategic Concept approved in 1999 for a "new NATO," based on enlargement and out-of-area interventions beyond the borders of member states, seemed to be "treating NATO as an icon that must be preserved" rather than considering other alternatives, such as encouraging a practical build-up of the military and civil-society building skills of the Organization for Security and Cooperation in Europe (OSCE). Instead, in the 1990s the first Bush and Clinton administrations both "maneuvered to keep the OSCE in the background and to discourage it from challenging NATO's primacy in European defense structures."[52]

Although it took from 1993 until 1998 to obtain official Senate approval for the enlargement of NATO, Clinton and his advisers moved ahead with expansion in the interim through the Partnership for Peace (PFP). This document invited the emerging democracies of Eastern Europe and Russia to participate in NATO military exercises, and Clinton eventually convinced NATO foreign ministers to issue invitations to potential new members – Poland,

Hungary, and the Czech Republic – all before he had obtained Senate consent.[53] That the economies of these three countries would have benefitted more from membership in the European Union rather than in NATO, which required them to go further into debt to meet increased military expenditures against a phantom enemy, was simply not explained to the American people or seriously discussed as an option inside the White House. Increasingly, an expanded NATO appears to be simply an existential instrument for symbolizing American hegemony throughout Central and Eastern Europe.

The first use of this expanded NATO occurred when the United States determined that NATO should invade Kosovo in March 1999 with "only the most superficial understanding of the origins of the Kosovo crisis, the complexity of the dispute, and the nature of Serbian nationalism." Secretary of State Albright personified this historical short-sightedness so much that this NATO intervention has been called "Madeleine's War." Albright thought of herself as a "child of Munich" and dogmatically viewed Milosevic as the personification of Hitler, a dictator who should not be appeased. Many questions have been raised about the grossly exaggerated claims the Clinton administration gave as the reasons for invading. The Clinton administration never acknowledged that in 1998 the Kosovo Liberation Army (KLA) had been listed as a terrorist organization because it had received funds from Osama bin Laden. It also never made public that the KLA had deliberately provoked the Serbs to attack in order to force NATO action so that the Albanians could obtain independence. Instead, before the beginning of the seventy-eight-day bombing of Yugoslavia, the Clinton administration misleadingly asserted that a "humanitarian emergency" had been created by the displacement of 250,000 Albanians, and that the Serbs had slaughtered tens of thousands of Kosovars whose bodies were in "mass graves."[54]

The most severe critics have concluded that rather than being a "humanitarian intervention," the Kosovo invasion represented a crime against humanity because of the use of 25,000 cluster bombs and missiles and depleted uranium, which resulted in the killing of an estimated 1,800 civilians of all nationalities. More devastating, perhaps, is the charge that this war "broke a fundamental legal barrier," thus setting the precedent for George W. Bush's invasion of both Afghanistan and Iraq without specific UN approval. In fact, when longtime neo-con Richard Perle "thanked God for the death of the UN," he cited the war in Kosovo as being responsible for the United Nations' demise.[55]

Amnesty International made the nonhumanitarian aspects of the NATO bombing of Kosovo a separate section of its year 2000 annual report, and the media were faulted for not reporting NATO forces' violations of humanitarian international law. Amnesty International found, for example, that instead of the 100,000 dead claimed before the invasion, the Serbs had killed fewer than 2,000 Kosovars, and the report documented that NATO had killed 500 civilians and that the Serbian police, aided by paramilitary units of the Yugoslav army, had forced the expulsion of 850,000 Albanians. Random violent excesses by the Kosovo Liberation Army (KLA) against Serbs followed, resulting in the exodus of 230,000. This displacement of both Albanians and Serbs occurred *after* NATO intervened, primarily because of the inadequate number of ground troops and the fact that peacekeeping simply does not work where there is no effective government. The Amnesty International report concluded that "NATO forces may have violated international humanitarian law." The International Criminal Tribunal for the Former Yugoslavia (ICTY) and Human Rights Watch suggested the same thing in 2000.[56] Needless to say, the American peace movement was confounded by the public relations blitz on the part of the Clinton administration claiming that Kosovo was a successful humanitarian effort.

Nonetheless, after UN officials began administering the region in 1999, vengeful Albanians drove another 100,000 Serbs out of Kosovo. In March 2004, an anti-Serbian attack by the KLA killed 19 and wounded 900. As a result, the Serbs refused to participate in the October parliamentary elections, setting back the peace and reconciliation process there. As of 2003–04, both Bill Clinton and Madeleine Albright continued to claim Kosovo a success and to affirm Kosovo as a model for air campaigns unsupported by ground forces.[57] In truth, another apartheid situation has been created because almost no Serbs now live in major cities, and most are in rural enclaves. Even phone calls between those in Albanian and Serbian areas of Kosovo are international, although the individuals may only live blocks away from one another. Since Clinton's NATO-led intervention into Kosovo, the country has become a geopolitical no-man's-land, the lawbreaking capitol of Europe, where a sex and drug trade and organized crime flourish. The chances of Serbia-(and Russia)-approving independence remain slim.[58] Nonetheless, in May 2007 the UN Security Council began to consider endorsing internationally supervised independence for Kosovo.

Clinton and Terrorism

In retrospect, the most contested aspect of Clinton's foreign policy remains his responses in the 1990s to various terrorists attacks against the United States – most specifically, the way he dealt with the threat represented by al Qaeda and Osama bin Laden. After September 11, Republican critics were quick to blame the Democrats for leaving the country in a vulnerable position vis-á-vis terrorists. Specifically, they took up the charge that Sudanese officials had offered to turn bin Laden over to either the Saudis or the United States and that Clinton had rejected other overtures from the Omar Hassan Ahmed al-Bashir regime because his administration had declared Sudan a state sponsor of terrorism and closed the CIA station in Khartoum in 1995.[59]

Indeed, even by the president's own account, his administration's record on terrorism leaves much to be desired. The forty-second president devoted scarcely 50 pages out of almost 1,000 in his memoir to the subject of terrorism and terrorists, and he did not systematically discuss any of the major terrorist acts his administration confronted. From the investigation and prosecution of the 1993 World Trade Center attacks, to the bombing of suspected terrorist sites in Iraq, Sudan, and Afghanistan, to the 2000 attack on the USS *Cole*, the Clinton administration's responses remained uncoordinated and sometimes unethical. Moreover, Clinton did not mention in his memoirs anything about the likely torturing in the Philippines of Abdul Hakim Murad, one of the witnesses who later testified against those responsible for the bombing of the World Trade Center. According to the *Wall Street Journal*, the Clinton administration also allowed a limited number of suspected terrorists captured in the Balkans to be flown to Egypt, whose interrogation methods could not be conducted in the United States.[60]

Unlike his diplomacy of delay and vacillation before his reelection in 1996, during his second term Clinton acted quickly, but with no prolonged efforts, to the terrorist attacks that occurred during his administration. Cruise missile attacks, while dramatic and seemingly decisive, are no substitute for sustained and coherent endeavors. It remains to be seen whether future declassification of documents will reveal more schematic logic and effective actions behind Clinton's diplomacy with respect to the threat of terrorism. Whether anything the Clinton administration did would have prevented the attacks on September 11 is unlikely, but its vacillating approach certainly encouraged the neoconservatives, who came back into power with George W. Bush, to claim that the Democrats had been remiss in confronting terrorism in the 1990s.

Nonetheless, the Clinton administration did turn over to the incoming Bush administration a thirty-page document written by Clinton's national security adviser, Samuel (Sandy) R. Berger, detailing the terrorist threat to the United States, which Condoleezza Rice apparently disregarded. Later, in October 2003, Berger stole five copies (and destroyed three) of a highly classified document indicating how the Clinton administration had assessed in 1999 the threat of terrorists attacks. Only fifteen people saw this document, which contained twenty-nine recommendations. It is not clear whether this is the document Berger claims to have given to Rice. What is clear is that she ignored an elaborate thirteen-page memorandum dated January 25, 2001 (with attachments dating from 1998 and 2000) she received from Richard A. Clarke, then her top counterterrorism adviser, urgently recommending that there be a "Principals level review" of the global network of al Qaeda. Clinton also has claimed that he warned Bush as he left office in 2001 that the country's "biggest security problem was Osama bin Laden.."[61]

The decade of the 1990s ended with American foreign policy drifting aimlessly on a sea in whose depths lurked both the Kirkpatrick and Wolfowitz Doctrines, waiting to surface when conditions were right so that the neo-cons could abandon even paying lip service to independent internationalism in favor of unbridled unilateralism and the pursuit of U.S. hegemony.

7

Flaunting Faustian Foreign Policy

> The management of foreign relations appears to be the most susceptible of abuse, of all the trusts committed to a Government, because they can be concealed or disclosed, or disclosed in such parts & at such times as will best suit particular views and because the body of the people are less capable of judging & are more under the influence of prejudices, on that branch of their affairs, than of any other. Perhaps it is a universal truth that the loss of liberty at home is to be charged to provisions against danger, real or pretended, from abroad.
>
> James Madison, letter to Thomas Jefferson, 1798

George Walker Bush, after a very shaky start during his initial eight months in office, accompanied by declining polls and a declining economy, seemed on his way to greatness as the first president of the twenty-first century for combatting the terrorism that resulted in attacks upon the twin Trade Center towers and the Pentagon. These remarkably successful suicide missions shocked and united the country as had no event since Pearl Harbor back in 1941–not even the assassination of John F. Kennedy. But presidential greatness is a tricky concept. It often exists more in the eye of the beholder than in reality.

For example, FDR's New Deal did not end the Great Depression in the 1930s; only war production during World War II restored the country's economy. However, his dramatic actions in that time of economic hardship and as a wartime leader were perceived as successes that led to his being elected to an unprecedented four terms. Perhaps it is unfair to compare other presidents to Franklin Roosevelt because he occupied the Oval Office longer than anyone else. But his positive reputation in the minds of most Americans at the time and among most historians since demonstrates that perceived, rather than actual, achievements determine whether presidential influence prevails or fails in any given crisis. Such success is not necessarily based on truth or facts, but often on public relations and virtual reality.

Historians have long argued over whether crises change or radically alter the policies of presidents. Most agree that Pearl Harbor unleashed FDR's latent internationalism, and so his wartime efforts did not represent a dramatic about-face on foreign policy, as did his New Deal programs for handling the Great Depression. There is little indication that September 11 changed the basic domestic policies that George W. Bush had campaigned on in 2000, except that, like Roosevelt, he initially said he favored balanced budgets and less government spending. And like Roosevelt, by the end of his first term he had created the largest federal deficit in history.

Bush's Domestic Policy

Once in the White House, Bush advocated the same domestic programs that he had as a presidential candidate. So he indicated that he would enforce national testing standards, which came to be known as "No Child Left Behind"; allow "faith-based" groups to compete for government social service grants; reform Medicare and subsidize prescription drugs for poor seniors through private companies rather than allow the government to negotiate with pharmaceutical companies for lower prices; let younger workers invest part of their Social Security taxes in personal retirement funds; institute a package of tax cuts (primarily for the rich), including a reduction in income tax rates and elimination of the estate tax; and promote free trade agreements. By the end of his first term Bush had succeeded in getting Congress to approve all of these campaign pledges in some form, with the exception of privatizing Social Security, and he had begun to make significant domestic and foreign faith-based appointments to posts where "right moral attitude was more important than competence" in law enforcement, education, medicine, and science.[1]

The only new aspects of his domestic agenda emerged after September 11, and they consisted of policies with the potential for violating the civil liberties of not only legal and illegal aliens but also American citizens. It began with the Patriot Act and then expanded through a spate of executive orders authorizing warrantless domestic wiretaps and other surveillance programs, military courts without the right of habeas corpus, mass arrests of suspected immigrants without specific charges, unaccountable CIA prisons and secret renditions, and restricted access to government documents, especially the papers of former presidents. As these mostly secret actions were slowly revealed, Bush seemed to be indicating to Americans that he would take care of the terrorists and make decisions to keep the country safe "without involving the courts, Congress or the press."[2]

There is something implicitly hypocritical, paternalistic, and antidemocratic about this approach to governing. Even though Americans were willing to sacrifice for the war on terrorism immediately after September 11, Bush did not ask them to give up anything (with the possible exception of civil liberties). Instead, he told them to go out and shop. Nor were they urged to change any other private behavioral patterns, as was so common during World War II (and to a lesser degree during World War I), when rationing, conservation, a draft, increased taxes, and a lower standard of living became part and parcel of patriotism.

No effective worldwide war has been fought by any country without asking its citizens to forfeit something to the war effort – until Bush initiated a global war against terrorism. The question is why? Why have consumerism and acceptance of lack of government transparency as traditional civil rights are trampled become the major contributions Americans can make to the Iraqi war effort? Normality (or "normalcy," to use President Harding's malapropism) in this war on terrorism has come to mean "home-front business as usual." Isn't shopping exactly what American were doing with abandon before September 11? In fact, according to Lizabeth Cohen, ever since "buying everything in sight became the new patriotism" in the 1950s, consumerism has been at the heart of American national pride. Bush did not invent this type of commercial patriotism, he simply gave it a gigantic boost, especially after he began to talk about an "ownership" society, which appeared to be a euphemism for more conspicuous consumption and privatization of retirement savings and health insurance.[3] Equating consummerism with patriotism in the United States is not a new phenomenon, but when combined with diminished civil liberties at home while espousing freedom, liberty, and democracy abroad it raises serious questions about the message Bush is sending to friends and enemies alike.

Economic Foreign Policy, Indebtedness, and Military Spending

When it came to economic foreign policy, Bush's National Security Presidential Directive (NSPD-1) initially reaffirmed Bill Clinton's support for "economism," even succeeding where his predecessor had failed to obtain "fast track" authority for bilateral trade agreements, now called trade promotion authority. Before September 11, the concept of free markets associated with globalization "fac[ed] a public relations crisis," but soon it was "rebranded, like shopping and baseball, as a patriotic duty." In the long run, however, where the Clinton administration had placed economic issues at the center of foreign policy, Bush's "reversed that trend with its dominant focus being on security issues."[4] Under both administrations, globalization remained based on excessive American consumption and borrowing, regardless of evidence that when it harms smaller, weaker economies, globalization can breed terrorism.

Bush came to office with a projected budget surplus of $5.6 trillion over ten years and turned it into an estimated $2.6 trillion debt over that same decade. This has been called "one of the largest fiscal dislocations in modern American history," largely due to the 2001 tax cuts and projected costs of an unlimited war on terrorism, including homeland security. In addition, the "current account deficit" – made up primarily of the export-import trade imbalance of the United States, plus interest payments on debts, and the earnings of U.S. corporations abroad – also rose to an all-time high, approximately 7 percent of the GDP. In 2005, the current account deficit reached $700 billion, requiring $2 billion a day in new foreign financing. In that same year, the central banks of China and Japan financed 80 percent of the U.S. foreign deficit, and Russia, newly rich from the high price of oil, also began to buy Treasury bonds. While economists do not agree that this "dysfunctional dependence" on foreign banks constitutes an "imminent crisis," they do agree that some adjustment must take place in the form of greater sales of American goods to Asia and an increase in the national savings rate. Yet to eliminate the trade deficit, the value of the dollar would have to fall 30 percent, and in 2006 the United States recorded the first national negative savings rate since the Great Depression. As of the beginning of 2006, the total debt of the United States stood at $8.2 trillion, requiring Congress to increase the debt limit to $9 trillion, the fourth time since Bush took office that this ceiling had been raised.[5]

Notwithstanding this underlying debt problem, the sheer size of the $3-trillion-dollar American economy allowed Congress to rationalize the supplementary emergency funds Bush repeatedly requested for the wars in Afghanistan and Iraq between 2001 and 2007, even though these amounts were above and beyond the budgeted amount for defense. This gave the United States a military budget greater than those of the next sixteen nations in the world combined, or half of the entire world's military spending. As of 2005, the second Gulf war had cost the country around $200 billion. It had approached a half-trillion dollars by the fall of 2006, or $10 billion a month since 2003. Bush's 2008 budget estimated that the wars in Iraq and Afghanistan would still cost another quarter-trillion dollars.[6]

Despite its unprecedented military predominance, the economic power of the United States, so necessary for sustaining its defense system, is more fragile than usually admitted for reasons other than the fact that it is currently the world's largest debtor. America's percentage of the world's manufacturing, its share of the world's income, and its portion of the world's stock of foreign direct investment have all fallen since 1950. American economic growth depends on "systematic and massive expansion of consumer borrowing and government borrowing... [which] is funded by soaking up more than 70 percent of the world's savings."[7]

This shift since World War II to consumption rather than production has produced a financial services economy. Kevin Phillips has called it "financialization," meaning the "process whereby financial services, broadly construed, take over the dominant economic, cultural, and political role in a national economy." He thinks it has approached funding levels "that would have left the 1920s scheme meister Charles Ponzi in awe." This imbalance and the financial shenanigans accompanying corporate mergers, hedge funds, and private equity deals can be maintained only as long as the U.S. dollar remains the leading currency for international payments and Americans keep buying on credit. So far, this fragile financial structure has worked because nations exporting to American consumers do not want the dollar to decline, and American diplomatic influence and military force in oil-rich countries ensure that the bulk of the world's oil trade continues to be carried out in U.S. dollars. Additionally, the United States currently controls most of the world's trade routes. If, however, international investors and central banks were to begin to question the level of U.S. indebtedness and start to move their investments elsewhere, the value of the dollar would decline, domestic interest rates would rise, and consumer spending would decline, causing a global economic turndown.[8] It should also be noted that the United States is running out of domestic import facilities to meet the insatiable consumption needs of Americans that undergird the entire global economy.

"Historically," according to Phillips, "top world economic powers have found 'financialization' a sign of late-stage debilitation, marked by excessive debt, great disparity between rich and poor, and unfolding economic decline." Benjamin Friedman has pointed out an often-overlooked aspect of economic turndowns: with the exception of the Great Depression, they are not good for democracy or civil rights: "American history included several episodes in which stagnating or declining incomes over an extended period have undermined the nation's tolerance and threatened citizens' freedoms."[9] While all aspects of this worst-case scenario are not likely to occur at once anytime soon, they should not be dismissed out of hand.

Because American economic power and military might by the middle of the twenty-first century almost defy imagination, the federal budget deficit and personal debt problem have not been given the attention they deserve. In particular, the degree to which China is financing the American trade imbalance and profligate spending habits is problematic. Among other things, it means that the United States is less likely to oppose Chinese human rights and intellectual property violations because of trade and debt considerations.

Bush Circumvents Clinton's Political Foreign Policy

Unlike Franklin Roosevelt, Bush had no internationalist streak in his background waiting to be unleashed by September 11. Having traveled only to Mexico before becoming president, as a candidate in 2000 he argued for retreating from world affairs and the humanitarian interventions of the Clinton administration, avoiding nation building, modernizing the armed forces, and building a missile defense system reminiscent of Ronald Reagan's Strategic Defense Initiative (SDI), dubbed Son of Star Wars. During the 2000 campaign Bush advocated what at best could be called an inchoate isolationist diplomacy undergirded by a largely unarticulated belief in American exceptionalism. Nevertheless, doctrinaire unilateralism and moralistic arrogance lurked beneath the surface of his words, even though during his first eight months in office Bush's diplomatic agenda remained almost exactly what it had been during the campaign. Then, after September 11, under the influence of neo-conservative advisers, Bush launched two wars to bring freedom and democracy to an area of the world where it has never existed, began expensive programs to pacify and rebuild both Afghanistan and Iraq, and initiated an open-ended global war on terrorism.

Scholars and journalists have detailed the Bush administration's unilateral positions both before and after September 11 on the following: rejection of the Kyoto Protocol on global warming; reinstatement of the U.S. "global gag rule" restricting discussion of abortion by humanitarian organizations; disruption of international population conferences on children, health, and development over the issues of prostitution, condom use, and abortion; continued resistance to the twenty-six-year-old UN Convention on the Elimination of All Forms of Discrimination Against Women (CEDAW); refusal to consider the UN Convention on Cultural Rights because it would harm U.S. trade negotiations; resistance to arms control (anti-proliferation) agreements, which ultimately led to the abandonment of the ABM Treaty; refusal to resubmit the Comprehensive (Nuclear) Test Ban Treaty (CTBT) for ratification; opposition to Chemical and Biological Weapons Conventions and the International Criminal Court (ICC); support for a missile defense à la Reagan; and rejection of the Treaty on (banning) Land Mines (which Clinton had initiated and then failed to support). These examples of self-righteous unilateralism amounted to a concerted effort to overturn a half-century of traditional Cold War foreign policy based on containment and deterrence. After September 11, the Bush administration justified all of these actions in the name of a virtuous global war on terrorism, exaggerating what constituted threats to the national security of the most powerful nation in the world.[10]

Several examples stand out. George W. Bush wasted no time abrogating the ABM Treaty, which Bill Clinton had left in a state of hypocritical limbo, as previously noted. However, even Clinton had the decency to hide behind a subterfuge in order to help a struggling Russia save face despite the fact that the United States wanted to initiate a limited missile defense system. Not Bush. He initially informed Vladimir V. Putin that he did not want a replacement for the original ABM Treaty. Instead, the president said he favored a vague verbal agreement, implicitly indicating that his administration opposed any more bilateral or multilateral treaties. Then Bush summarily notified Russia on June 15, 2002, that the United States had abandoned the ABM Treaty. Putin predictably responded curtly that Russia would no longer be bound by the 1993 Start II accord outlawing multiple-warhead missiles (MIRVs). In the interim, Bush signed a problematic treaty with Russia in May calling for cuts in nuclear warheads. This new nuclear reduction treaty does not require the destruction of warheads, allowing both sides to stockpile such weapons for future deployment. Moreover, reductions are not required before 2012, the year the treaty expires, and both countries can terminate with just three months' notice.[11]

Bush also muddied Bill Clinton's already murky Haitian foreign policy. By January 2004, when Haiti celebrated the bicentenary of its independence, there were demonstrations against Jean-Bertrand Aristide's disappointingly repressive policies since Clinton had restored him to power in 1994. A few months later, on February 29, 2004, George W. Bush sent U.S. Marines to fly Aristide out of Haiti into exile, despite the president's protests and charges of kidnaping. Some thought that, as with the invasion of Iraq, Bush Jr. was completing (or duplicating) what his father had started in 1991 when a rumored American-supported military coup had ousted Aristide. Predictably, Haiti devolved into chaos again. Aristide was not the first Haitian leader to be kidnaped by the

United States. Back in 1915, Woodrow Wilson ordered U.S. Marines to remove Dr. Rosalvo Bobo. This time there were U.S./UN troops in the country, and they installed Gérard Latortue, a former UN bureaucrat and TV talk show host, as prime minister.[12]

By the end of 2004 conditions had worsened because Aristide's Lavalas Family Party and assorted gangs began rioting and disrupting aid and normal services, especially after the new government exonerated and let back into the country Louis-Jodel Chamblain, a notorious political gangster and leader of a death squad in the 1990s. Chamblain had supported both of Aristide's ousters. More UN troops were sent in, and during 2005 they shot and killed rioting Haitians in Cité Soleil, one of the poorest neighborhoods of Port-au-Prince and a hotbed of support for Aristide. That same year the Latortue government arrested the leader of Lavalas, Father Gérard Jean-Juste. U.S. and international aid was promised, but little was delivered before the 2006 presidential election that initially produced more confusion. René Préval, a former president and ally of Aristide and leader of the Lespwa Party, had to challenge the original vote count, which placed him below the 50 percent necessary for victory. Once again, the United States and the international community promised to finance Haiti out of poverty, crime, and general chaos. *Lancet*, the British medical journal, reported that 8,000 people were murdered and 35,000 women and girls raped during the U.S.-backed post-coup regime that followed Bush's ouster of Aristide in 2004.[13]

North Korea

Another policy inherited from the Clinton administration arose out of meetings between the presidents of North and South Korea in the early 1990s. To show his support for President Kim Dae Jung's "sunshine" policy of reaching out to the North, the United States under Clinton decided to lift the trade ban on the communist half of the peninsula. Then former president Jimmy Carter visited Pyongyang and persuaded North Korea to freeze its nuclear activities and to enter into talks with Washington. In 1994 this led to a document called the Agreed Framework, whereby North Korea promised to shut down its nuclear reactor at Yongbyon in return for two light-water nuclear reactors to replace the plutonium ones and the promise from Washington to provide 500,000 tons of heavy fuel annually until these new reactors could produce electricity. In a very short time, based on information provided by Pakistan, it appeared that Pyongyang had violated the Agreed Framework with missile tests and may even have been trying to develop uranium-enrichment facilities needed for nuclear weapons. The United States, for its part, after the 1994 Republican takeover of Congress, appeared to delay the construction of the light-water reactors. Clinton maintained in his memoir that by 1999 he had all but sewn up a new deal with North Korea to end its missile program and to modify its nuclear development and that all Bush had to do was go there and sign on the dotted line.[14]

Instead, the Bush administration immediately reversed Clinton's policy, such as it was, by cutting off natural gas shipments, thus voiding what was left of the 1994 agreement. The president also rationalized a missile defense system aimed at North Korea by declaring that country part of the "axis of evil," along with Iraq and Iran, in his State of Union Address in January 2002. (In May, Undersecretary of State John Bolton expanded the axis of evil to include Cuba, Syria, and Libya.) It was difficult to determine the truthfulness of the administration's assertion that North Korea actually had enough plutonium or enriched uranium to produce nonconventional bombs, since the IAEA inspectors had been kicked out by North Korea in retaliation for Bush's tough policy. Saying that he "loathed" Kim Jong-il and referring to him as a "pygmy," Bush refused to talk one-on-one with Pyongyang, insisting instead that six-country negotiations be set up to include China, Japan, Russia, South Korea, and the United States. North Korea reciprocated by asking the United States to sign a nonaggression pact promising "no hostile intent," that is, not to attack.[15]

In November 2002 the North Korean leader Kim Jong il sent a personal secret message to Bush stating: "If the United States recognizes our sovereignty and assures nonaggression, it is our view that we should be able to find a way to resolve the nuclear issue in compliance with the demands of a new century. . . . If the United States makes a bold decision, we will respond accordingly." The two men who delivered the message to the White House revealed on June 22, 2005, that those close to the president "spurned engagement with North Korea" in the fall of 2002 because they were too "deep in secret planning and a campaign of public persuasion for the invasion of Iraq." Privately, some officials within the administration blamed National Security Adviser Condoleezza Rice for failing to fashion a coherent approach to the problem of North Korea's (and Iran's) nuclear program.[16]

The United States hoped that China would bring pressure to bear on Kim by threatening to agree to UN sanctions that the United States favored, but China did not show any interest in this tactic. Instead, Pyongyang boycotted the six-nation talks in 2004. Early in 2005 the United States toned down its language, and in June North Korea agreed to return to the multilateral negotiations. It even indicated it would rejoin the Nuclear Nonproliferation Treaty (NPT) and allow the return of international nuclear inspectors. In September, the six-nation talks produced a vague joint statement of "principles" that did not improve the situation. Soon relations between Washington and Seoul deteriorated again; South Korea did not support either sanctions or any other tougher measures against the North because its current president, Roh Moo Hyun, continued to pursue his predecessor's "sunshine" policy of unification – regardless of whether Pyongyang developed nuclear weapons.[17]

The situation deteriorated further in 2006 after North Korea fired at least six missiles in June, including a long-range Taepodong-2, despite repeated warnings from the international community, including South Korea. The UN imposed sanctions, but North Korea insisted that these produced the deadlock of the multilateral talks about its nuclear program. Additionally, it threatened to conduct a nuclear test to "'bolster' its self-defense in the face of US military hostility." It carried out its threat on October 9, 2006, and the UN imposed more sanctions. In November 2006, the mercurial Kim Jong-il decided to participate again in the six-nation talks, and hawks in the Bush administration credited increased UN sanctions and the U.S. threat of a naval blockade following the October nuclear test. After the U.S. representatives met one-on-one with North Korea in Berlin, a six-party agreement was announced on February 13, 2007. In return for food and heavy fuel oil from the United States; release of funds frozen in a Macau bank, and being taken off Washington's list of state sponsors of terrorism, North Korea agreed to a "temporary" cessation of its nuclear program. Critics such as the neo-conservatives John Bolton and Elliot Abrams immediately denounced this deal as rewarding bad behavior on the part of a devious leader. The *Wall Street Journal* called it "faith-based nonproliferation" for which the Bush administration did not deserve praise because it was only marginally better than the 1994 Clinton administration agreement and would cost the United States considerably more. Supporters said it might encourage Iran to strike a similarly rewarding deal with the United States – if Kim compiled with the terms in the designated 60 days.[18] Most importantly, the agreement may have signaled a more moderate, realist approach to diplomacy by Bush in an attempt to shore up his presidential legacy in the last two years of his administration While North Korea did not meet the sixty-day deadline, in June 2007 it finally received $25 million previously blocked by the United States and allowed UN inspectors and U.S. envoy Christopher Hill to visit Pyongyang to begin the shutdown of its nuclear program.

Bush and Nuclear Power

Perhaps the most disturbing aspect of the Bush administration's nuclear policy has been its refusal to denounce first-strike use and its tenacious pursuit of the creation and testing of new tactical nuclear weapons. In January 2001, before Bush took the oath of office, one conservative think tank, the National Institute for Public Policy, recommended that he "treat tactical nuclear weapons as an essential part of the U.S. arsenal." From the beginning of the Bush administration, Secretary of Defense Donald Rumsfeld refused in public to exclude the use of such weapons in the fight against terrorists (and so did President Bush on November 6, 2001). In September 2002, a leaked classified version of a White House document called "The National Security Strategy of the United States of America" (NSS) reserved "the right [of the United States] to respond [to threats]with overwhelming force, *including potentially nuclear weapons.*" However, when the White House released this document to the public, it sanitized the last phrase to read: "including through resort to all of our options." This marked a dangerous tactical departure from previous administrations – at least since Truman, although Carter's Presidential Directive 59 issued in July 1980 had recognized newly developed accurate nuclear targeting and so embraced "limited" nuclear war options.[19]

By the end of 2004, the White House had made considerable progress toward the development of tactical nuclear weapons with a new nuclear project known officially as the Robust Earth Penetrator, or more commonly as "bunker busters" or small-yield "mini-nukes." This three-year project began carrying out research to see if a casing could be developed for an existing nuclear warhead to penetrate deep into the earth before exploding. To no avail, critics claimed that such underground facilities can be sealed off using smart, conventional precision-guided weapons.[20] Congress deleted money for this project in 2004 on the grounds that creating a new nuclear weapon would encourage other nations to do likewise and because research had found there was no casing that could withstand a nuclear warhead blast underground without producing radioactive fallout in the atmosphere. Undeterred, Secretary Rumsfeld told the Energy Department in 2005 to include funding for an earth-penetrating nuclear weapon, and it was embodied in the Bush administration's budgets for 2006 and 2007.[21]

Finally, unilateral and deceptively Faustian policies under Bush contributed to the failure of the five-year review of the 1970 Nuclear Nonproliferation Treaty (NPT) held at the UN in May 2005 when the administration insisted that the conference concentrate primarily on the emerging nuclear problems posed by Iran and North Korea. Previously, the Bush administration had announced that it had no intention of joining the Comprehensive Nuclear Test Ban Treaty (CTBT) or signing a verifiable accord ending the production of new fissile material intended for nuclear weapons.[22]

In April 2006, when Bush "refused to rule out nuclear strikes if diplomacy failed to curb [Iran's] atomic ambitions," Washington became awash in rumors that his administration was preparing to take out Iran's nuclear facilities with tactical nuclear bunker busters before it developed "the bomb." It was reported that Bush believed that he must do "what no Democrat or Republican, if elected in the future, would have the courage to do . . . [and] that saving Iran [by bombing its nuclear sites] is going to be his legacy." The president emphatically denied this as "wild speculation," despite the fact that the United States began to deploy additional aircraft carrier groups in the Persian Gulf from which Iran could be bombed, along with minesweepers to protect against any attempt by Iran to blockade the Strait of Hormuz. Bush insisted that he was simply applying his "doctrine of prevention" to Iran, which meant diplomacy. His critics responded that this sounded too much like Iraq redux; that is, too similar to what he said before attacking Iraq. They also suspected that his extreme conservative advisers thought that "attacking Iran . . . is the only way . . . they can rescue their goal of U.S. (and Israeli) hegemony in the Middle East." In fact, some powerful neo-conservatives complained at the end of 2006, just as they had before the war with Iraq, that American intelligence agencies had not adequately documented the threat posed by Iran and advocated military action. They also welcomed the idea that Israel might take on the task of striking Iran. In January 2007, the London *Sunday Times* reported that American and Israeli officials had met to consider military action and that Israeli air force squadrons were training to use low-yield nuclear weapons against Iran's uranium enrichment facilities.[23]

Bush compounded his already seriously flawed nuclear foreign policy by announcing to the world in February 2006 that he had signed a secretly negotiated nuclear treaty with India. This defied the fact that for thirty years the world community had forbidden providing nuclear technology to countries, such as India, that did not sign the Nuclear Nonproliferation Treaty (NPT). Congress dutifully approved American shipments of civilian nuclear reactors and fuel to India even though there is nothing to prevent India from developing nuclear weapons (because only fourteen of its "civilian" nuclear plants will be subject to inspection, leaving eight uninspected ones to produce bomb fuel). Yet the administration continued to demand that Iran and North Korea give up their capacity to make enriched uranium needed for nuclear weapons. The fact that India is one of the fastest-growing consumer markets raises the question of whether commercial calculations and the possibility of large arms contracts played a greater role in creating this new "strategic relationship" than national or international security considerations. Regardless of the reasons for this treaty with India, there is little doubt that it could stimulate a regional race to produce or obtain more weapons-grade nuclear fuel as a defense against American attempts at regime change. Moreover, if this fuel fell into the hands of terrorists or "rogue" governments, it would make the world more rather than less dangerous.[24]

Struggle over Oil Diplomacy

Oil policy proved less susceptible to the unilateral ideas of Bush's neoconservative advisers because, by the time of the second Gulf War, major U.S. petroleum companies had changed the position they had taken under Nixon in the early 1970s. During the last decade of the twentieth century they began allying themselves with the Oil Producing Export Countries (OPEC). In the 1990s, these oil companies had come to the obvious realization that they and their stockholders benefited from the high oil prices dictated by the OPEC cartel. Petroleum executives also knew that since Carter issued his doctrine on January 23, 1980, the American government would not fail to protect their interests (and those of OPEC) in that area of the world, especially as global supplies of oil grew more scarce.[25]

While Donald Rumsfeld and other government officials vociferously denied that the invasion of Iraq had anything to do with oil, a little over a year after Saddam Hussein switched to pricing Iraqi oil in euros late in 2000, Bush gave his "axis of evil" speech and his administration began to spread what amounted to disinformation about other dangers that Iraq posed to the United States. The fear was that other OPEC nations might follow Saddam's move to euros despite a secret agreement between the United States and Saudi Arabia struck in the 1970s that guaranteed all OPEC sales would be conducted in dollars. This "oil-linked value of the dollar" had to be protected in order for the United States to cover its huge trading deficits.[26]

With these concerns in mind, two opposing Iraqi oil scenarios emerged before the invasion: one within the State Department, backed by the oil industry and ultimately by the James Baker Institute in Texas; the other within the Pentagon, supported by neo-cons like Paul Wolfowitz, then deputy secretary of defense, and Douglas Jay Feith, then undersecretary of defense for policy. The first called for retaining state control of Iraqi oil after a quick overthrow of Saddam Hussein and his replacement by a pro-American strongman. The second, also drafted before the second Gulf War, argued that the conflict should be used to smash OPEC's hold on Middle Eastern oil prices. Ariel Cohen of the American Heritage Institute had convinced some neo-conservatives within the Pentagon of this idea, and Ahmed Chalabi, a major source for the neo-cons' exaggerated argument about the existence of weapons of mass destruction, approved the idea of a sell-off of Iraqi oil in order to increase output, to undermine the OPEC cartel, and to continue to ensure that oil would be priced in dollars. Wolfowitz and others even predicted that privatized Iraqi oil would pay for that nation's postwar reconstruction. There is a lot of money there, Wolfowitz arrogantly asserted, "and to assume that we're going to pay for it [the war] is just wrong."[27]

In December 2003, the State Department issued a report entitled "Options for Developing a Long Term Sustainable Iraqi Oil Industry." It argued, as it had earlier, against the privatization of that country's oil fields. Subsequently, privatization did not occur because the State Department and the National Security Council (NSC) – backed by American oil companies, Saudi Arabia, Russia, and especially Vice President Dick Cheney – prevented this from taking place. Additionally, a study by the Baker Institute endorsed "a state-controlled company, which would be very OPEC-friendly and would establish profit-sharing agreements with international oil companies." This position prevailed in part because of the internal quagmire created by inadequate Pentagon planning for rebuilding Iraq, even though the neo-con L. Paul Bremer III, when he oversaw Iraq as proconsul or "ambassador" there, passionately supported privatization.[28]

On a March 2005 BBC program, former Shell CEO Philip Carroll, whom Bush had appointed to study what should be done with Iraqi oil fields after the fall of Saddam, when asked whether the neo-con oil agenda in Iraq agreed with that of the American oil industry, said: "They're absolutely poles apart. Many neo-conservatives are people who do have certain ideological beliefs about markets, about democracy, about this, that and the other. International oil companies without exception, are very pragmatic, commercial organizations. They don't have a theology. They don't have a doctrine. They are going to do what is in the best interests of their shareholders." In particular, the oil industry feared privatization of Middle Eastern oil fields because of the example set after the break-up of the Soviet Union. Big American oil companies had not benefited when these valuable holdings went to nationalistic cronies of former Soviet political leaders, and they suspected that Chalabi's cronies would do the same thing in Iraq.[29] In this case, the practical self-interest of major American oil companies prevailed over the privatization ideas of Republican ideologues. Both plans, however, called for a lifting of UN production limits on Iraqi oil that had been imposed after the first Gulf War and for pricing to remain in dollars.

To temporarily quench America's thirst for secure foreign energy supplies, the Bush administration entered into deals with corrupt and unstable oil-rich regimes in Kazakhstan and Angola and has done little to advocate the spread of democracy or the elimination of poverty and corruption in other oil-rich petro-states. Then, without ever addressing environmental problems posed by the BTC oil pipeline (begun under Clinton), Washington also committed another $100 million to train and equip the Caspian Guard, a network of special forces and police, to protect this pipeline that links Caspian Sea oil to the Mediterranean through Azerbaijan, Georgia, and Turkey (all countries criticized for human rights abuses). The BTC pipeline officially opened in May 2005.[30]

The Bush Doctrine

For all its rhetorical and actual extremism, the Bush administration's unilateralism did not represent a new approach to, or revolution in, American foreign policy as some have claimed. Preemptive or preventive strikes and regime changes are not new elements of U.S. foreign policy. Beginning with secret CIA interference in the 1948 elections in Italy to prevent a communist victory, any summary review of U.S. foreign policy during and after the Cold War reveals an impressive assortment of covert and overt preemptive and/or preventive actions. Between 1945 and 1999, the United States unilaterally attempted to overthrow forty foreign governments; and it intervened at least thirty times to squelch nationalist movements organized against tyrannical rule. Many of these interventions created lingering civil conflicts that the United States treated with "malign neglect" when it emerged from the Cold War as the world's only superpower.[31]

Unilateralism, of course, has always been a consistent part of the country's practice of independent internationalism since the 1920s. As previously noted, this has meant that U. S. diplomacy during the Cold War was usually more unilateral than multilateral. The Bush Doctrine is also not new because Republican neo-conservatives had been openly advocating a unilateralist diplomacy since their 1992 position paper "Defense Planning Guidance" and the 2000 report of the Project for the New America Century (PNAC), "Rebuilding American's Defenses: Strategy, Forces and Resources for a New Century." The 2002 NSS minced no words in claiming that

given the goals of rogue states and terrorists, the United States can no longer rely solely on a reactive posture as we have in the past. The inability to deter a potential attacker, the immediacy of today's threats, and the magnitude of potential harm that could be caused by our adversaries' choice of weapons, do not permit that option. We cannot let our enemies strike first.[32]

Although this strategy document mentions more peaceful and traditional aims of U. S. foreign policy, such as "political and economic freedom; peaceful relations with other states, and respect for human dignity," through the promotion of freedom and democracy, it leaves little doubt that the United States would rely on unilateral force because it drew largely from the militant Pax Americana ideas in the 2000 PNAC report, which disdained cooperation with the UN and with other nations. Bush's 2002 NSS was not as much a product of September 11 as it was a product of previous wish lists of the neo-conservatives, who had realized for some time that only a "new Pearl Harbor" would allow them to realize their diplomatic dreams. Bush's NSS simply shortened and sanitized the earlier PNAC report to make it palatable for public distribution and remained much more militantly assertive and unilateral in tone than Clinton's 1999 NSS. It also downplayed all international alliances and "formal agreements and procedures in favor of loosely organized coalitions (easily dominated by one nation)."[33]

So what is new about the Bush Doctrine? Its blatant arrogance and self-righteous indifference to international law cloaked in evangelical religiosity certainly "repudiates the core idea of the United Nations Charter (reinforced by the decisions of the World Court in the Hague). These prohibit any use of international force that is not undertaken in self-defense after the occurrence of an armed attack across an international boundary or pursuant to a decision by the UN Security Council." This doctrine also marks a dramatic shift away from those times during the Cold War when containment and deterrence sporadically prevailed and thus calls into question U.S. reliance on the UN and other multinational coalitions, including even NATO and the Organization of American States. Such a unilateral and idealist approach stems from the neo-conservatives' long-standing exaggeration about the threats facing the United States and their determination to eliminate them through the "overweening use of American power," their assertion of the "superiority of American values," and the insistence that their brand of morality is universal. All of these views are perfectly in keeping with the influential Pentagon bureaucrat Fritz A. G. Kraemer's insistence since the 1950s that the United States should never demonstrate "provocative weakness."[34] They also represented well-publicized views of the reincarnated Committee on the Present Danger (CPD) that in 2004 equated the Soviet threat with the threat from terrorism and called for "total victory."

The Department of Justice drafted a fifteen-page secret memorandum just two weeks after September 11 that ensured implementation of the Bush Doctrine. Entitled "The President's Constitutional Authority to Conduct Military Operations against Terrorists and Nations Supporting Terrorism," this legal opinion went beyond the authority Congress granted to the president on September 14, 2001, and said the president should use "his best judgement" in using military force, but that his "decisions are for him alone and are unreviewable." The Bush Doctrine and the secret memoranda supporting it represent the culmination of the unilateralism that radical conservatives had been advocating since the Nixon administration. Moreover, it has made traditional European allies of the United States view the country as a threat to global stability and lowered the reputation of America throughout the world, especially in Islamic countries after the invasion of Iraq and the exposure of U.S. mistreatment of prisoners.[35]

In summary, the Bush Doctrine is new only to the degree that it symbolizes a pathological imbalance between the presumed universality of American ideals and the country's actual national security interests that dwarfs previous such periodic imbalances that took place during the Cold War. When ideology, especially in times of perceived crisis, outweighs genuine safety concerns, power tends to be disdainfully undisciplined and applied unilaterally. As in the past, contemporary unilateralism is rooted in American exceptionalism. Usually this type of extreme diplomacy prevails only until more pragmatic policies reassert themselves through domestic political processes. It remains to be seen whether the irrational exuberance of neo-con politics and diplomacy in Bush's first term will be replaced by more moderation in the second half of his second term, especially in light of the Republican loss to the Democrats in the 2006 midterm elections. It has always been up to the America's democratic system to correct previous imbalances in U.S. foreign policy caused by exceptionalism and unilateralism. This has never been more true or more in doubt.

Preemptive versus Preventive Wars

Compounding the obvious defects and dangers of the Bush Doctrine is that "preemption" is actually a misnomer. Preemptive wars are those "initiated on the basis of incontrovertible evidence that an enemy attack is imminent." Instead, the war against Iraq was a *preventive* one, meaning "an exercise in 'anticipatory self-defense.'" According to the Carnegie Endowment, "preemption has *always* been a legitimate strategy to head off an imminent military attack, so long as the anticipation of such an attack is based on sound intelligence." Rather than exercising this right under international law, the Bush administration deliberately set "a loose standard for preventive war under the cloak of legitimate pre-emption." The difference between preemption and prevention is simply a matter of timing: the former means taking action because the enemy is about to strike; the latter means taking action to prevent a potential threat from materializing. Not only is it next to impossible to predict accurately a "grave and growing" threat, as in Iraq (or Iran), because intelligence is always less than perfect, but both concepts also encourage enemies of the United States to acquire nuclear weapons and to use WMDs if faced with the threat of a possible American attack.[36]

Even the publication of a secret Downing Street memorandum in May 2005 did not become a "smoking gun" and produce an official investigation into whether the administration had cooked the books on pre-war intelligence in order to conduct its preventive war disguised as a preemptive one. The minutes from a meeting of Tony Blair and his senior advisers on July 23, 2002, painted a picture of the Bush administration already committed to war against Iraq, and indicated that "the intelligence and facts were being fixed around that policy." In March 2006, the *New York Times* published a new confidential memo summarizing another meeting between Bush and Blair on January 31, 2003, in which they agreed "that no unconventional weapons had been found in Iraq," and so Bush suggested provoking Saddam by "flying U2 reconnaissance aircraft with fighter cover over Iraq, painted in UN colors." At this same meeting, Bush also arbitrarily came up with March 10 as the official date "when the bombing would begin." Other leaked British documents also indicated the United States had not given much thought to postwar reconstruction and that it was prepared to manipulate a UN resolution to make the war appear legal under international law.[37] To say the least, these memoranda make the second Gulf War appear not only premeditated, but also prefabricated as well as preventive in nature.

Earlier in the same year that the first Downing Street memoranda surfaced, the Pentagon codified unilateral, preemptive strike attacks in a March 2005 "National Defense Strategy" document. Calling the policy "active deterrence," neo-con Feith explained that the United States did not need "non-American participation or approval" before taking unilateral, preemptive military action. The document also unequivocally stated that "our strength as a nation-state will continue to be challenged by those who employ a strategy of the weak using international fora, judicial processes, and terrorism." This remark seemed aimed as much at the EU's tendency to insist on UN approval of military interventions as it was at terrorist organizations.[38]

Mentored by none other than the neo-con Richard Perle, it was Feith, after all, who set up a special intelligence unit called the Counter Terrorism Evaluation Group in the Pentagon shortly after September 11, which claimed that the CIA had missed crucial links between Iraq and al Qaeda and which relied on Chalabi's phony information about Hussein's stockpiles of WMDs. He also oversaw the Office of Special Plans (OSP), which framed policy in the months before the invasion of Iraq and was in charge of the disastrous lack of planning for the postwar occupation and reconstruction of Iraq. In February 2007, the inspector general of the Department of Defense concluded his investigation into the OSP by saying that its assessments "evolved from policy to intelligence . . . [and] were inappropriate because a policy office was producing intelligence products and was not clearly conveying to senior decision-makers the variance with the consensus of the Intelligence Community." From retirement, Feith vociferously denied that the OSP had produced its own intelligence when it criticized CIA findings. But the inspector general's findings were eerily reminiscent of the way in which, under control of neo-conservatives, the President's Foreign Intelligence Advisory Board (PFIAB) had begun to submit alternative or competitive threat assessments that exaggerated the Soviet threat to the United States in the 1970s and 1980s.[39]

Unitary Executive Theory and Signing Statements

In 2005, it was revealed that Bush had signed an executive order early in 2002 authorizing the National Security Agency (NSA) to conduct warrantless domestic wiretaps on U.S. citizens in violation of the 1978 Foreign Intelligence Surveillance Act (FISA), which requires approval by a special court. In response to criticism that this violated not only the 1978 legislation but also the privacy and civil liberties of Americans, Bush's aides, especially Vice President Dick Cheney and others such as John Yoo, former deputy assistant attorney general, determinedly defended the practice by citing executive power under Article II of the Constitution, the president's inherent powers as commander-in-chief, and the September 14, 2001, resolution passed by Congress authorizing the president to "use all necessary and appropriate force against those nations, organizations, or persons he determines planned, authorized, committed, or aided the terrorist attacks." Bush, for his part, arrogantly (and perhaps naively) admitted that he had broken the law by ignoring the FISA court. He defended intercepting the communications of Americans as "a vital tool in our war against terrorists."⁴⁰

In August 2006, a federal court ruling held the NSA's wiretapping of international calls of some Americans illegal–the first negative judicial assessment of the administration's formerly secret surveillance program. Bush responded by asking for legislation to give him "additional authority" to continue with warrantless eavesdropping. Using the 2006 anniversary of September 11, he insisted that the lame duck session of Congress pass the Terrorist Surveillance Act, and in August 2007 Democrats allowed the Protect America Act to pass even though it further gutted the FISA and expanded Bush's domestic and foreign spying powers.⁴¹

While other presidents have implicitly claimed limitless power for themselves in time of war, none were engaged in a self-proclaimed, endless preemptive war. Whether Bush understands the sophisticated constitutional theory of unlimited presidential power known as the "unitary executive theory" is arguable, but his closest neo-con advisers do, and so do Supreme Court Justices John Roberts, Samuel Alito, Clarence Thomas, and Antonio Scalia. They are all members of the Federalist Society, which has fostered this idea since the 1970s. Supporters of this theory, known as "unitarians," also maintain that the White House can remove officials of independent regulatory agencies if they disobey the president, thus giving him political control of such bodies.⁴²

Bush has routinely cited his authority to "supervise the unitary branch [of government]" in order to disregard sections of legislation he deemed objectionable by issuing signing statements. These are legal, technical documents quietly filed in federal records, usually without much fanfare. As of May 2006, Bush had issued signing statements for over 750 pieces of legislation – 1 in 10 of all passed by Congress during his administration. If these claims survive judicial and congressional review, they will constitute "the most aggressive formulation of presidential power in our history," fortifying the list of "semi-constitutional" powers presidents already possessed coming out of the Cold War, and the unitary executive theory. For example, Bush has attached signing statements to legislation ranging from nanotechnology guidelines, to the warrantless NSA domestic surveillance program, to the reauthorized Patriot Act, to the postal reform law, to 2006 spending bills, and to Senator John McCain's anti-torture Detainee Amendment.[43]

Because of Bush's extensive use of signing statements based on the unitary executive theory, the American Bar Association (ABA) issued an eleven-page report in July 2006 criticizing the practice and documenting the history of past presidents' use of this method to void sections of laws passed by Congress. Historically, such statements have served a "largely innocuous and ceremonial function." Not until Reagan did they become quantitatively and qualitatively weapons designed to influence the way courts might interpret legislation, to preserve a wide variety of presidential prerogatives, and to violate the rule of law. The *New York Times* pointed out that Bush had not employed any vetoes as of the summer of 2006 because he simply could "declare his intention not to enforce anything he dislikes" with signing statements.[44]

Rights of Detainees and Enemy Combatants

One of the most controversial applications of this theory of unchecked presidential power undergirding the Bush Doctrine occurred with respect to the legal rights of detainees charged with terrorist offensives and held at Guantánamo Bay Naval Station in Cuba. Right after September 11, the president issued a still-classified directive defining the guidelines for CIA detention and interrogation of terror suspects. Less than a year later, the Justice Department specified specific interrogation methods that the agency could use against al Qaeda leaders. In June 2004, the Supreme Court ruled against the Bush administration's position that the federal courts had no jurisdiction over enemy combatants held at that American base. This decision rejected the idea that the president could suspend habeas corpus by claiming such prisoners were beyond the reach of the law. This decision prompted a suit on behalf of Salim Ahmed Hamdan, a former driver for Osama bin Laden, who was about to be tried before a special military tribunal at Guantánamo. After conflicting lower court decisions, in November 2005 the Supreme Court agreed to hear an appeal in the case of *Hamdan v. Rumsfeld*. In December 2005, in an attempt to prevent the justices from reaching a decision in this case, the White House pushed through Congress a special amendment to the Detainee Treatment Act (DTA) that stripped the federal courts of jurisdiction over cases brought by detainees at Gauntánamo.[45]

At stake was whether Bush's secret military order of November 13, 2001, establishing military commissions had proper authorization and whether the DTA removed the federal courts' jurisdiction to hear habeas corpus petitions from Guantánamo detainees. The question is: Did the president and Congress have the right to suspend the writ of habeas corpus when such suspensions are limited by the Constitution to "cases of rebellion or invasion"? On June 29, 2006, in a 5–3 decision the Supreme Court ruled in *Hamdan v. Rumsfeld* that the tribunals violated military law and the Geneva Conventions, specifically Article 3. The majority also said that the DTA did not apply to the other 150 pending cases.[46]

This victory proved short-lived. In the *Hamdan* decision, the Supreme Court left open the door for legislation to legalize the Bush administration's insistence that its detainee policy need not comply with domestic or international law. Using strong-arm tactics just before the 2006 midterm election, the president and his advisers convinced Republicans (and a few Democrats) in Congress to pass the Military Commissions Act (MCA). This September 2006 legislation "gave the president more power over terrorism suspects than he had before the [June] Supreme Court decision. . . . [It] does not just allow the president to determine the meaning and application of the Geneva Conventions, its also strips the courts of jurisdiction to hear challenges to his interpretation." In essence, this is "enabling act" legislation that preserves the appearance of law while empowering the commander-in-chief to do as he pleases. It also broadens the definition of "illegal or unlawful enemy combatant" to subject legal residents of the United States (although not American citizens) as well as foreign citizens in their own countries "to summary arrest and indefinite detention with no hope of appeal."[47]

Most controversially, the MCA denies detainees in U.S. military prisons the right of habeas corpus, that is, the right to challenge their imprisonment. Except for verdicts by military tribunals, there is to be no judicial review of this system. Coerced and secret evidence will be allowed, and coercion is defined so that it "exempts anything done before the passage of the 2005 Detainee Treatment Act, and anything else Mr. Bush chooses." This means that the president and all those who may have committed crimes in carrying out his antiterrorism policies are given a blanket waiver from prosecution because "one of the biggest concerns of the administration is the possibility of evidence emerging that could lead to charges of war crimes against high-ranking officials." Such blanket immunity has further damaged the U.S. reputation abroad as a nation adhering to the rule of law and put at risk any American soldier captured in battle. Finally, the MCA defines what constitutes torture so narrowly that it eliminates even the idea of rape as torture, although it has been declared a crime against humanity by the international community.[48]

Immediately after Bush signed this legislation, the Justice Department informed federal courts that they no longer had the authority to hear the pending Guantánamo lawsuits. In short, the Military Commissions Act "chip[ed] away at the foundations of the judicial system in ways that all Americans should find threatening." A group of legal scholars ultimately concluded in a letter to all members of Congress that they could not "in good conscience stand by while a bill that erodes protections against abuse is enacted."[49] Needless to say, this draconian legislation will be challenged in the courts, but the first such case decided by a lower court in February 2007 upheld the MCA.

"We Do Not Torture"

Long before the passage of the 2006 Military Commissions Act, the same executive branch's unilateral and unethical mentality that produced it had prevailed in memoranda coming out of the Justice Department's Office of Legal Counsel (OLC) and in the Pentagon's authorization of the use of torture against suspected terrorists. Probably more than any other Faustian action taken by the Bush administration in its war on terror this emulated the worst of tactics of the enemy. Once again, the neo-con Feith played a significant role in approving and implementing torture methods through the Office of Special Planning. The Judge Advocates Generals (JAG) Corps claimed Feith's office had bypassed them, relying instead on such civilian political lawyers and ideologues as William J. Haynes II, the Pentagon's general counsel, during the drafting and discussions of whether "stress and duress" techniques, sleep deprivation, and other methods violated the Geneva Conventions. Although Feith's role became public when he denied on ABC News there was any disagreement with JAG officers, negative public scrutiny fell not on him and his OSP, but on the Justice Department and counsel to the president Alberto Gonzales (before he became attorney general) because of two 2002 memoranda leaked in 2004. One written in January by Gonzales and another by then assistant attorney general Jay Bybee in August 2002 said, among others things, that the war on terrorism "renders obsolete [the] Geneva's [Conventions] strict limitation on questioning of enemy prisoners and renders quaint some of its provisions," and so narrowly defined what constituted illegal torture that methods short of death could be used to protect the United States. This document, widely known as the Torture Memo, went on to say that laws prohibiting torture do "not apply to the President's detention and interrogation of enemy combatants because he is Commander-in-Chief," and administration lawyers concurred that the Constitution empowered the president to fight wars as he saw fit.[50]

Even before these statements were drafted, two lawyers in the Office of Legal Counsel, John Yoo and Robert J. Delahunty, had advised the president in a January 9, 2002, memorandum that prisoner-of-war status under the Geneva Conventions did not apply to captured Taliban or al Qaeda fighters and that "customary law of armed conflict in no way binds, as a legal matter, the President or the U.S. Armed Forces concerning the detention or trial of members of al Qaeda and the Taliban." In essence, this memorandum and a series of related ones said that the United States would continue to hold other individuals and nations accountable for formal and customary international laws even though it was not bound by them because they did not have any status in American federal law. Based on such double standard advice and despite State Department opposition, Bush issued a secret order on February 7, 2002, agreeing with Justice Department and Pentagon lawyers that an American president can ignore both U.S. law and international treaties in the treatment of so-called detainees or enemy noncombatants. More appallingly, in March 2005 it was revealed that the Bush administration had approved a secret program right after September 11 allowing the CIA to transfer suspected terrorists ("ghost prisoners") for imprisonment and interrogation in "black hole" prisons in such countries as Egypt, Syria, Saudi Arabia, Jordan, and Pakistan, all noted for torturing their prisoners. This illegal kidnapping process is officially called "extraordinary rendition" and is known colloquially as "torture outsourcing." Individual cases do not have to be approved by the White House or the State or Justice Department, as previous administrations had required.[51]

All of these convoluted legal arguments and unethical rationalizations paved the way for Secretary of Defense Donald Rumsfeld and his undersecretary for intelligence, Stephen Cambone (a position that had never existed before), who had cut his teeth under Feith's tutelage in the OSP, to expand a secret program that "encouraged physical coercion and sexual humiliation of Iraqi prisoners to obtain intelligence about the growing insurgency in Iraq" at the Gauntánamo Bay Naval Base and the Abu Ghraib prison in Iraq. Rumsfeld specifically approved severe interrogation methods in a November 27, 2002, memorandum. Then, without explanation, he rescinded them on January 15, 2003, and appointed a Pentagon panel ("working group") to recommend more appropriate methods. Jane Mayer disclosed in a *New Yorker* article at the beginning of 2006 that Rumsfeld acted because of one man's efforts to curb the officially sanctioned torture and cruel abuse of detainees – Alberto J. Mora, general counsel of the U.S. Navy. Mora thought he had finally convinced his boss, William Haynes, a protégé of Vice President Cheney's chief of staff, David Addington, and through him Rumsfeld that there needed to be new interrogation guidelines. Within a week of the recision, Haynes had trumped Mora by going around the "working group" and obtaining an expansive OLC opinion written by Yoo, who, along with Delahunty, had supported at the beginning of 2002 the legality of the harshest military interrogations discussed earlier. Colin Powell's former chief of staff Lawrence Wilkerson also involved Vice President Cheney in this unorthodox policy-making process, saying that he "want[ed] to do away with all restrictions" on treatment of detainees..[52]

Despite all of the above and the revelation at the end of 2005 that the CIA had purportedly operated secret prisons ("black holes") in connection with torture practices legitimated by the Bush administration, both President Bush and Condoleezza Rice repeatedly denied that the United States engaged in torture. How could they do this in good conscience? Was it just a word game they were playing for national and international audiences? Could they have been convinced by Justice Department and White House lawyers that no laws were transgressed when, according to Mora,

by sanctioning cruelty as policy the government in essence is endorsing torture and alter[ing] the fundamental relationship of man to government. It destroys the whole notion of individual rights. The Constitution recognizes that man has an inherent right ... to personal dignity, including the right to be free of cruelty. It applies to all human beings ... even those designated as "unlawful enemy combatants." If you make this exception, the whole Constitution crumbles. It is a transformative issue.[53]

Or is it simply that Bush and Rice believe that torture is necessary to win the war on terrorism? If so, this is the ultimate example of the United States adopting the tactics of the enemy – a Faustian practice that began during the Cold War.

Neo-Cons Promoted and Reappointed

Except for Feith, who resigned in the summer of 2005 after it became clear that he had run a rogue operation out of his Office of Special Plans, all Bush's top lieutenants either retained their positions in his second term or were bumped up to bigger and better positions. For example, the president appointed Wolfowitz head of the World Bank. John D. Negroponte had been accused of misleading Congress about human rights violations as U.S. ambassador to Honduras and of running political cover for CIA-sponsored Honduran death squads fighting with the Nicaraguan Contras against the Sandinistas during and after the Iran-Contra affair. Nonetheless, in Bush's second term Negroponte became the first director of national intelligence (DNI), charged with coordinating the fight against terrorism, and in January 2007 the president made him the number two man at the State Department. Elliot Abrams, convicted for giving false testimony and illicit fund raising connected to Iran-Contra activity but pardoned by George H. W. Bush, went from special assistant to the president and senior director on the NSC for Near East and North African affairs to deputy national security adviser for global democracy strategy. Not stopping there, the president nominated Undersecretary of State John Bolton as the U.S. representative to the United Nations. This was the same Bolton who had previously said "there is no such thing as the United Nations," who had written in the *Wall Street Journal* that the United States need not be bound by international treaties, and who, as undersecretary of state, had thwarted the First Annual Review Conference of the Biological Weapons Convention in early 2005 by undermining the agreed protocol with last-minute new proposals.[54]

Democrats in the Senate prevented Bolton's original nomination from going to the full Senate because they did not receive requested information about Bolton's purported attempts to replace subordinates who did not provide intelligence with which he agreed, and because he made speeches that skewed intelligence information despite orders from his superiors to stop this practice. Not to be deterred in promotion of neo-cons in his second term, on August 1, 2005, Bush made Bolton U.S. permanent representative to the UN through an interim appointment. In his first action as interim UN ambassador, Bolton insisted that the draft of recommended UN reforms be scrapped in favor of a draft that excluded measures and offices that the United States had opposed in other fora.[55]

Bush obstinately renominated Bolton following the Democratic victory in November, but by that time support from Senate Republicans and even the State Department had waned, and at the beginning of December Bolton unexpectedly announced his resignation.[56]

Condoleezza Rice: Neo-Con Come Lately

Of all these reappointments, only Rice's promotion to secretary of state deserves greater explanation because she is usually not referred to as a neo-conservative or listed as a member of conservative organizations or think tanks. Too young to be present at the creation of the neo-con movement during the Nixon presidency, she cast her first presidential vote for Jimmy Carter but in 1980 voted for Reagan because she thought that Carter's response to the Russian invasion of Afghanistan in 1979 was naive and weak. Rice officially became a registered Republican in 1982. After a meteoric career as an academic in the 1980s at Stanford University, she entered government service in 1988 in George H. W. Bush's administration upon the recommendation of foreign policy realist Brent Scowcroft. Rice served for two years on the staff of the National Security Council (NSC) as director of Soviet and East European affairs. While in that position, she later admitted, she "missed completely, really, the [Gorbachev's] revocation of the Brezhnev doctrine" because she was too focused on the troop reductions the Russian leader had also announced in withdrawing from East Germany. Instead, on her hard-line advice, the United States suspended talks with the Soviet Union, ostensibly to consider Gorbachev's intentions. Before this rethinking took place, the Berlin wall fell. As an expert on the USSR's military, she did not foresee (nor did the CIA) the collapse of the Soviet Union. So Rice left the NSC in 1991 with an undistinguished record to become provost of Stanford University, not staying through the final and dramatic devolution of the USSR under the elder Bush.[57]

In the interim she continued a close personal relationship with the Bush family and in 1999 became coordinator of George W. Bush's foreign policy advisory group. From that point forward she became his personal tutor and confidante.[58] Rice became national security adviser in 2001, criticizing the Clinton administration for its "romantic" foreign policy, especially with respect to Russia, North and South Korea, and China. Most pointedly, she emphasized that the Bush administration was not going to treat "Russia as a special case." Instead, Rice championed a "new realism" for the Bush presidency "stressing the importance of bolstering U.S. alliances and of committing U.S. troops overseas only in cases where the vital national interests were threatened." As head of the NSC she boasted that the United States would "not be the world's 911," only to have 9/11 become the universal reference to the attacks on the twin towers and the Pentagon. At the same time she said that she did not intend to be either a policy initiator or implementor and that she wanted the NSC to be leaner and less visible.[59]

Technically speaking, the secretary of state outranks the person who heads the National Security Council, although since the presidency of Richard Nixon the national security adviser has often exercised more influence on foreign policy than the secretary of state. During her tenure at the NSC, this did not prove true of Rice because she was upstaged and outmaneuvered by the competition and by controversy between Secretary of State Colin Powell and Secretary of Defense Donald Rumsfeld, backed by Vice President Cheney. She seemingly ignored her own job description, which stated that the head of the NSC has to be a "decision maker who is supposed to coordinate the views of the various agencies and present them as a coherent picture to the president of the United States." Instead, she spent much of her time "being the president's 'body man,' at his side every minute, whispering in his ear . . . [and] tutoring him on areas he does not understand or is not up to speed on."[60]

Even before the Senate Foreign Relations Committee grilled her in January 2005 about her qualifications to be secretary of state, the 9/11 Commission held hearings at which Rice denied the importance of six memoranda written by Richard A. Clarke, head of the NSC's Counterterrorism Security Group, in the spring and summer of 2001. Rice also neglected to tell the 9/11 Commission about an urgent briefing she and other top administration officials received from CIA Director George J. Tenet on July 10, 2001. He told them that intelligence pointed to an impending al Qaeda attack (something he had earlier indicated to Congress). She apparently took no significant action on this information.[61]

At that same 9/11 Commission hearing on April 8, 2004, Rice was forced to admit that she could not remember telling the president about the existence of al Qaeda cells in the United States prior to August 6, 2001. Even more incredibly she said that she had not taken seriously the August 6 President Daily Briefing (PDB) entitled "Bin Laden Determined to Attack inside the United States." She defended her inaction when learning about Arabs enrolled in U.S. flight schools by claiming (inaccurately) that no one could have anticipated flying planes into skyscrapers and added somewhat pathetically: "[If] I needed to do anything, I would have been asked to do it. I was not asked to do it."[62]

Equally confounding, in January 2007 she denied ever seeing a 2003 communique from Iran (via the Swiss embassy in Iran) offering a package of concessions to the United States that appeared to be very close to the ones demanded in the second Bush term, namely, Iranian compromises on its nuclear program and its relations with both Hezbollah and Hamas, and support for a Palestinian peace agreement with Israel. It was reported in 2005 that Vice President Cheney (and Carl Rove to whom the message was first delivered) had categorically turned down the offer, much as the 2002 offer from North Korea, discussed earlier, had summarily been turned down by the White House.[63] It is next to impossible to know whether Rice was out of the decision-making loop on these two important matters, whether she was simply outmaneuvered by the powerful male neo-cons surrounding the president in 2002 and 2003, or whether she was providing Bush with "plausible deniability" in case a future agreement was reached with Iran along the same lines that could have been obtained back in 2003.

Confirmed as secretary of state despite this less-than-sterling NSC leadership record, Rice immediately began forcefully reiterating Bush's idealist position about democraticizing the entire Middle East even if it meant creating instability in that region of the world, which she proudly called the "birth pangs" of democracy. This corroborated her belated conversion to neo-con criticism of Cold War policies and extremism in defense of forcing U.S. values on the world.

Transformational Democracy

Because of the important role played by religion in the 2004 election, some began speculating about what they are calling "transformational democracy," "transformational diplomacy," and the "transformational presidency." The president's secular and religious advisers are already calling him a "transformational president," and he used the term in the second debate in 2004. Around the time he delivered his 2006 State of the Union address, White House officials released statements saying that the president believed Americans were living in "transformational times and that with that comes great anxiety "– anxiety that only his administration could quell. In domestic matters, the term refers to an anticipated conservative domination of U.S. politics and "control of all levels of American power [including the Supreme Court] for a generation or more." It even includes transforming portions of the Constitution to conform with the neo-con "unitary executive theory" by undermining the separation of powers through presidential predominance.[64]

This multifaceted transformational process involves the systematic deconstruction of Democratic candidates by turning them into unelectable caricatures of themselves. In foreign affairs, "transformationists," according to Brent Scowcroft, who had been national security adviser under both Ford and Bush Sr., are "the true believers in the George W. Bush administration who argued that after 9/11 the United States could not afford to dicker with the United Nations or foreign appeasers before getting on the with urgent work of democratizing the Middle East – by force if necessary." In this sense, transformational diplomacy is "far more energetic and all-embracing than the limited moralistic agenda embodied in Reagan's Evil Empire."[65]

Perhaps the best description of both domestic and foreign transformationalism came from an aide to Bush who dismissed what he called "reality-based" views of the world. He said:

That's not the way the world really works anymore. We're an empire now, and when we act, we create our own reality. And while you're studying that reality judiciously, as you will – we'll act again, creating other new realities, which you will study too, and that's how things will sort out. We're history's actors . . . and you, all of you, will be left to study what we do.[66]

This is a faith-based or messianic or mystical rather than an empirical or reality-based view of the world that fits perfectly with Bush's view that God is guiding his policies at home and abroad and is perfectly in keeping with view of America as exceptional and virtuous, dating back to the Puritans. As Press Secretary Tony Snow said without hesitation on December 6, 2006, when questioned about the disconnect reflected in Bush's insistence that conditions in Iraq were better than those described by the Iraq Study Group: "The president believes in the transformational power of liberty."

In such a transformational system there would be less debate, with largely ceremonial, money- and media-driven public relations elections. After September 11, and particularly in the 2004 presidential campaign, there was an absence of media questioning of Republican foreign policy claims and of bogus advertisements against Democrats because of fears among mainstream journalists that criticizing the Bush administration would mean loss of access to sources.

Particularly disturbing was the revelation at the end of 2005 that both the *Washington Post* and the *New York Times* had withheld stories about the secret CIA prisons and NSA domestic surveillance for over a year when publication of either before the 2004 elections might have affected the outcome.[67]

Whether transformationalism will prevail is unclear, but there is no doubt that it is being openly talked about by some neo-conservatives and evangelical supporters of President Bush in highly coded language, contributing a new dimension to the imponderable presidency. If it does succeed, it may well mark a crippling blow to the American political system of checks and balances and civil rights and to cooperative internationalism – a transformational blow made possible when the neo-conservatives around Bush took full advantage of the 9/11 tragedy to promote their own domestic and foreign policy agendas. On their advice his legacy will rest.

Epilogue

The Legacy of George W. Bush

> There is no such thing as legacies. At least, there is a legacy, but I will never see it.
>
> George W. Bush to Catholic leaders at the White House,
> January 31, 2001

Despite his reelection in 2004, the Republican loss of Congress in 2006 raised many questions about Bush's likely historical legacy, largely because of the disintegrating situation in Iraq. Presidential legacies are often recounted in terms of the age-old debate about whether the person or the spirit of the times creates history. Most Americans naturally tend, in highly selective ways, to remember the few presidents who survived serious crises – that is, those who conquered the problems they encountered during their administrations. Seldom remembered are the many more who failed their challenges. It is still not clear which camp Bush will ultimately fall into – that elite group of presidents who, like Abraham Lincoln and Franklin Roosevelt, were able to tame and guide the crises of their administrations by successfully exercising prudent presidential influence and leadership with a vision for a better world, or those who did not and so fell into the dustbin of history.

This is why it might be useful to look at the legacies of presidents other than such giants as Lincoln and FDR when trying to place in historical context President Bush's exercise of presidential influence in time of crisis. Second-term presidents, for example, often make mistakes out of hubris or find that policies from their first terms come back to haunt them. There is also a group of "accidental presidents" with whom Bush might be compared. An accidental president is one who was not elected to office initially or who came in after a contested election in which he did not win an Electoral College majority. Such elections are usually decided by Congress – as in 1800, in 1824, and in 1876, when Thomas Jefferson, John Quincy Adams, and Rutherford B. Hayes became accidental presidents by acts of Congress. The United States has had only one other formally contested presidential election and that occurred in 2000, when the Supreme Court determined that George W. Bush had won over Al Gore. All the other accidental presidents have come into office because of assassinations or natural deaths, and in one case a resignation. So there was John Tyler after President Harrison died (1841), Millard Fillmore after President Taylor died (1850), Andrew Johnson after the assassination of President Lincoln (1865), Chester Alan Arthur after the assassination of President Garfield (1881), Theodore Roosevelt after the assassination of President McKinley (1901), Calvin Coolidge after the death of President Harding (1923), Harry Truman after the death of Franklin Roosevelt (1945), Lyndon B. Johnson after the assassination of President Kennedy (1963), and Gerald Ford after the resignation of President Nixon (1974). By this accounting, we have had nine accidental presidents, over half in the twentieth century. I would include Jimmy Carter, making ten, because he would not have been the logical Democratic candidate in 1976 had it not been for Watergate. In effect, when Nixon resigned in disgrace, he in essence created two accidental presidents – Ford and Carter. And George W. Bush makes eleven.

In light of the 2001 terrorist attacks, it is interesting to review the roles of the twentieth-century accidental presidents in terms of how they reacted to perceived or real crises. Of the seven accidental presidents (if Carter is included), only three – TR, Coolidge, and Ford – really did not face any major domestic or foreign crises. Of the other four, Truman, LBJ, and Carter did, and now Bush does. Conventional wisdom has it that Truman rose to the occasion and survived his various crises, although some his foreign policy decisions have been questioned in retrospect. LBJ did not survive his, which was, of course, Vietnam, and in addition that war destroyed much of his liberal domestic agenda. Carter failed to resolve his – the Iranian hostage crisis. So of the four accidental presidents since the Second World War, two failed to deal successfully with the foreign policy crises they faced. Only Truman is credited with diplomatic achievements, even though he left office with low public opinion ratings. The verdict is not yet in on Bush, but his aides have been quick to compare him to Truman.

Bush's Domestic Legacy

Additionally, no president, accidental or not, can be solely a foreign policy or a domestic president if he is concerned about creating a lasting legacy. Presidents have to be both. In the course of his first term Bush achieved certain domestic legislative successes on education, prescription drugs, and reduction of taxes that helped to balance a reputation that had been based primarily on his unilateral foreign policy following September 11. However, less than a year into his second term, for all of the president's talk about making the country more secure, his emphasis on terrorism abroad seemed to have made him and his administration peculiarly insensitive or inattentive to domestic problems such as immigration, the domestic and foreign debt, permanent tax cuts, social security reform, alternative fuels, health insurance, energy policy, insufficient funding for "No Child Left Behind," deficiencies in his prescription drug program, the legal problems of members of his administration, growing income inequality, the increasing unpopularity of his oldest and closest advisers like Vice President Dick Cheney and Secretary of Defense Donald Rumsfeld, and, since the fall of 2005, the surprising ineffectiveness of his much-touted political and public relations strategist Carl Rove.

All of these nagging domestic issues came to a head with Bush's slow and inadequate personal response to Hurricane Katrina at the end of August 2005. This failure of leadership when it came to a major domestic natural disaster and to impoverished black Americans in New Orleans seemed to epitomize neo-con neglect of, and contempt for, use of federal power except to wage war. After September 11, national emergency measures of the Federal Emergency Management Agency (FEMA) were folded into general homeland security defense, where terrorism, rather than natural disasters, became the priority. This resulted in shameful pictures of FEMA's incompetent and dilatory rescue operation along the Gulf Coast and raised the suspicion that the Bush administration was no better equipped to deal with another internal terrorist attack than it had been four years before. These pictures also contributed to a serious questioning of the president's reaction, leadership capabilities, and competence when disasters are not caused by evildoers.[1] At the same time, the public did not seem to appreciate or be aware that by the summer of 2005 Bush had chalked up several controversial domestic achievements in his second term, such as renewal of the Patriot Act, defeat of an attempt by Democrats to initiate an independent investigation of the National Security Agency's (NSA) domestic surveillance program, and, most importantly, the appointment of two conservatives justices to the Supreme Court.

Katrina trumped all of these domestic successes and raised an interesting dilemma facing this particular second-term president. As of the beginning of 2007, Bush had lost control of the situation in Iraq and most other foreign policy issues because of the negative reactions at home and abroad to the war he started in the Middle East. His best chance to leave a positive legacy immediately upon leaving office will rest on his domestic policies, complicated by the Democratic takeover of Congress in 2006. Recognizing this, Bush's seventh State of the Union address in January 2007 stressed a variety of domestic issues. Following it, the president began to tour the country speaking to obtain support for his proposals, but developments in Iraq, Iran, Afghanistan, and North Korea took precedence over most of them, except for immigration and energy policy.

Bush's Foreign Policy Legacy

Compounding the problems that seem inherent in second terms, as an accidental president Bush may find himself lumped with those previous accidental presidents who, especially in the realm of diplomacy, fell victim to bad advice. Specifically, there are disturbing indications that Bush will ultimately relive the predicament of both Presidents Johnson and Carter. He may not have received the best policy advice from some of the neo-cons, who had worked for Ronald Reagan and George H. W. Bush, about waging an all-out war against terrorism – just as LBJ did not always get good advice from Kennedy's former advisers about going for broke in Vietnam. Likewise, Carter's top advisers fostered unnecessarily hostile policies toward the USSR, and did not encourage him to continue with his human rights approach after Iran took American hostages.

With the exception of Colin Powell, who appeared to have become odd man out in opposing the more blatant unilateral actions of Bush's first term by recommending some cooperative actions on the part of the United States, new and old neo-conservatives, famous and infamous from the Cold War period – some dating back to the administration of Richard Nixon – came out of the woodwork to recommend a total war against terrorism. Most simply put: the neo-con "Team B" of the 1970s and 1980s had become "Team A." Surrounded in his first term by such pro-war neo-con advisers as Donald Rumsfeld, Paul Wolfowitz, Douglas J. Feith, John Bolton, and Richard Perle, Bush may end up regretting their advice, as Johnson did that of the leftover hawks from the Kennedy administration. The fact that some of the most prominent among them had resigned or left the administration for other positions by 2007 does not exculpate them from having recommended policies that could negatively affect Bush's legacy.[2]

The continuing influence of neo-conservatives in Bush's second term could be seen immediately after Bush's 2006 State of the Union address, when the Pentagon issued its Quadrennial Defense Review (QDR) entitled "The National Security Strategy March 2006." This policy statement incorporated the long war theory into U.S. strategic planning and built upon the March 2005 "National Defense Strategy" document, discussed previously. It laid out a twenty-year battle plan "against terrorist networks [that] extends far beyond the borders of Afghanistan and Iraq and includes many operations characterized by irregular warfare." Singling out China as having "the greatest potential to compete militarily with the United States," this QDR called for a "new Air Force long-range strike force and the building of undersea warfare capabilities." No longer arguing, as the 2001 QDR had, that the United States had to be capable of military operations in only four areas of the world, namely, Europe, the Middle East, the "Asian littoral," and Northeast Asia, this one stated that the United States needed forces to "operate around the globe, and not only in and from the four [previously outlined] regions." It concluded: "Long-duration, complex operations involving the U.S. military ... will be waged simultaneously in multiple countries around the world, relying on a combination of direct (visible) and indirect (clandestine) approaches." It also ostensibly acknowledged that "to end tyranny we must summon the collective outrage of the free world against the oppression, abuse, and impoverishment that tyrannical regimes inflict on their people and summon their collective action against the dangers tyrants pose to the security of the world."[3]

Despite this call for "collective action," the bulk of this ninety-two-page QDR represented the Bush administration's neo–con plan for expanding American military presence and empire in the twenty-first century, one that deviates little from the Cold War policy of independent internationalism. The difference was that in 2006 the United States faced no formidable nation-state enemy like the Soviet Union to prevent its practice of unilateralism and belief in American exceptionalism from running amok. As the neo-conservatives surrounding Bush defended this national security strategy as part of their plan for an American-dominated New World Order, they insisted that the war on terrorism, beginning with Afghanistan and Iraq and possibly expanding to other undesirable or "axis of evil" nations, would not consist of Faustian bargains with, and more arms sales to, undemocratic regimes and petty dictators. Yet that is exactly what has taken place in U.S. relations with Pakistan's Pervez Musharraf, Sudan's Lt. General Omar Hassan Ahmed al-Bashir, and Uzbekistan's Islam A. Karimov. Additionally, until a June 2007 address in Prague, under neo-con influence Bush had largely ignored such examples of democratic and human rights abuses as China in Tibet and Xinjiang; Russia in Chechnya; Uzbekistan's raids against the city of Andijon in July 2005; and Colombia's paramilitary drug traffickers, who have committed war crimes while receiving more than $3 million in U.S. military aid to destroy crops and fight guerrillas since 2000.[4]

The Bush administration also forged a particularly close relationship with Sudan, reestablishing in 2001 the CIA station in Khartoum that Clinton had closed in 1995 and renewing dealings with Maj. General Salah Abdallah Gosh, head of the country's Mukhabarat, its version of the CIA. Cooperation on counterterrorism has kept the United States from impugning the al-Bashir government's denials that it has committed genocide in Darfur and that Gosh has ordered attacks on civilians – even though Secretary of State Powell publicly accused the Sudanese of carrying out genocide in Darfur back in 2004, a genocide that has spread to Chad. So much for not following the Faustian foreign policies of the Cold War. In February 2006, Bush belatedly recommended sending more international troops into the war-ravaged Darfur region, but did not indicate that U.S. ground troops would be involved in this beefed-up international peacekeeping effort.[5] And in May 2007 the president called for more stringent economic and arms sanctions against Sudan. Nonetheless, with respect to the continuing loss of life in Darfur it is clear that the lesson of Rwanda has not been learned. Once again, U.S. national security interests are shown not to include effective action on behalf of the victims of genocide.

Bush's Rhetorical Legacy

If September 11 unleashed unbridled unilateralism in Bush's foreign policies, his born-again evangelical rhetoric released a flood of speculation about the melding of messianic fundamentalism with secular right-wing politics. Ironically, while neo-conservatives foresee an indefinite period of U.S. hegemonic power, radical Christian fundamentalists and Pentecostal Americans perceive the administration's war on terrorism as facilitating the divine plan for annihilating the Islamic world and hastening the end of human history as we know it in return for a Christian millennium. Thus, the neo-con vision of an American-dominated world is irrelevant to them. Joining this alliance are "right-wing

Catholics over abortion and ... right-wing Jews over the Holy Land," providing Bush's moralistic foreign policy more political force, as demonstrated in the 2004 election, than should have been the case given that he had either lied about or seriously manipulated evidence for going to war. That the truth did not prevail among the most fervently religious who voted for him in 2004 can be explained in part by the fact that they were more interested in the world ending than in the ever-shifting arguments rationalizing the war in Iraq or an American empire. In fact, one study concluded that "cognitive dissonance" seemed to prevail among Bush's most religious supporters after his reasons for going to war were exposed as false.[6]

It has been said that Bush "talks evangelical talk as no other president has, including Jimmy Carter." He began with his Oval Office talk on the night of the attacks by misquoting words of Psalm 23, thereby inadvertently exchanging himself for God.[7] His use of evangelical language when talking about foreign policy affairs continued right after September 11 when he spoke the word "crusade." He quickly dropped the term because it conjured the medieval Christian battles against Arab Muslims.[8]

Then the Pentagon gave the name "Infinite Justice" to the war in Afghanistan. That moniker was also quickly withdrawn "in deference to the sentiments of Muslims" because of "its overtones of Christian fundamentalism." Not surprisingly, the administration resorted to benign euphemisms, calling the war in Afghanistan "Operation Enduring Freedom" and the one in Iraq "Operation Iraqi Freedom." Neither name obviates the fact that both wars are not being fought simply in order to make the world safe for democracy, as President Woodrow Wilson grandiosely said about World War I; they are also being waged "in defense of the United States ... [to] make the world safe for Americans."[9]

Gradually in his first term Bush largely replaced his incessant use of such words as "evil," "evildoers," "evil man," "evil one," "evil deeds," and macho references to "bring 'em on" and smoking terrorists out of their caves with the idea of spreading freedom and liberty in the name of God. He began the transition from images of evil to images of freedom late in September 2001 when he said: "Freedom and justice, justice and cruelty, have always been at war, and we know that God is not neutral between them." By the time of his 2003 State of the Union address Bush was proclaiming: "We do not claim to know all the ways of Providence, yet we can trust in them, placing our confidence in the loving God behind all of life, and all of history." In that same speech the president noted: "As our nation moves troops and builds alliances to make our world safer, we must also remember our calling as a blessed country, to make the world better." Then a little over a year later, on April 13, 2004, at a press conference Americans heard: "So long as I am president, I will press for freedom. ... I have this strong belief, strong belief, that freedom is not this country's gift to the world, freedom is the Almighty's gift to every man and woman in the world." Or as Bush told Bob Woodward: "Freedom is God's gift to everybody in the world. ... And I believe we have a duty to free people.

I would hope we couldn't have to do it militarily, but we have a duty." Later, in the third 2004 presidential debate, he reiterated: "I believe that God wants everybody to be free. That's what I believe. And that's one part of my foreign policy. . . . And so my principles that I make decisions on are a part of me. And religion is a part of me." On a trip abroad on June 2007, Bush continued to proclaim that "freedom is the design of our maker, and . . . the only way to achieve human rights."[10]

Such dogmatic religious references do not make for a rational foreign policy, which, by definition, is supposed to be based on diplomatic compromise and, since 1945, on certain international principles embodied in the Charter of the United Nations. Instead, this kind of moralistic language usually backs a president into a corner, stubbornly obsessing about self-justification and defending abstract principles such as honor, pride, God, and country, rather than trying to find practical solutions to complicated relations with other nations. Past presidents who excessively personalized and moralized foreign policy issues paid a high price for viewing their opponents as evil or irredeemably malevolent or for identifying too closely with a single cause. One has only to think of Woodrow Wilson's refusal to compromise to obtain U.S. entrance into his beloved League of Nations because he viewed Republican Senator Henry Cabot Lodge as his personal bête noir. Lyndon Johnson personalized the war in Vietnam to the degree that he tormented himself and obsessed over each American death, personally choosing bombing targets but never seeing the forest for the trees in terms of whether the war was winnable. Jimmy Carter became so personally identified with American hostages held in Iran that he neglected most domestic issues and turned away from his human rights diplomacy toward a more hard-line policy not only against Iran, but also against the USSR.

"God Made Me Do It"

George W. Bush is certainly not the first American president to moralize about and personalize diplomatic problems. He is also not the first American president to proclaim that the United States is an exceptional "blessed country" and to assume that he is an agent of God when carrying out its foreign policy. His public piety is, however, one of the more blatant examples of a president exhibiting a divinely ordained reaction to national danger or crisis. This conforms with what Bush purportedly told various evangelical leaders, such as Rev. Richard Land of the Southern Baptist Convention, in 1999 and 2000: that "God wants me to be president." On February 15, 1999, for example, Bush told the evangelist James Robison on the latter's TV program that God wanted him to run for president. "I know it won't be easy on me or my family, but God wants me to do it. . . . I feel I am supposed to run for the presidency. I believe my country is going to need me."[11]

The *New York Times* reported that just before Bush delivered his message to a joint session of Congress on September 20, 2001, he met with a group of ministers and told them that he thought that his leadership in this time of crisis was "part of God's plan" for him and the nation, that this was now his life's work. In a private meeting with Amish families on July 9, 2003, according the *Washington Post*, Bush purportedly said, "I trust God speaks through me. Without that, I couldn't do my job." His use of double-coded language to speak to evangelicals about liberty as "the plan of heaven for humanity," asserting that "the Author of freedom is not indifferent to the fate of freedom," has proven most effective from a pragmatic political standpoint. And in January 2005 Bush's second inaugural address sounded more like a sermon than a practical forecast of specific problems facing the country in his second term. Among other things he said: "America's vital interests and our deepest beliefs are now one.... From the day of our founding, we have proclaimed that every man and woman on this earth has rights, and dignity, and matchless value, because they bear the image of the maker of heaven and earth." Repeating the words "liberty" and "freedom" a total of forty-four times, he made it clear that God was the "Author of Liberty."[12]

Given his religious rhetoric, commentators have often noted the moralistic similarities between Bush's and Wilson's public pronouncements. The comparison is accurate but obscures the excessive degree to which Bush does not want to deal with facts that contradict his "gut" views or "instinct," or what he assumes are uncompromisable "God-given values," or his belief that he is on a religious mission fighting a righteous war. For example, just before the invasion of Iraq in March 2003 the president refused to meet with an interdenominational delegation from the National Council of Churches who opposed the war, apparently because they would have presented spiritual views he did not want to hear. Previously the group had been received by heads of state in Great Britain, France, Germany, Russia, and the Vatican. Former GOP insiders such as disillusioned Republican columnist Bruce Bartlett have confirmed Bush's tendency to "dispense with people who confront him with inconvenient facts. He truly believes he's on a mission from God. Absolute faith like that overwhelms a need for analysis. The whole thing about faith is to believe things for which there is no empirical evidence." Barlett then added: "But you can't run the world on faith," and "to trust one man's instinct to be infallible is too much to ask of a democracy," especially if that man more often than not states as fact what is actually in dispute. Accordingly, Bush told Bob Woodward, the insider, neocon reporter for the administration: "I do not need to explain why I say things. That's the interesting part about being the President. Maybe somebody needs to explain to me why they say something, but I don't feel like I owe anybody an explanation."[13]

But there is more to Bush's arrogant religiosity and messianic militarism than simply the fact that he makes decisions based on faith-based gut instincts. He has encouraged inordinately pious support for a militaristic American foreign policy, as reflected in statements by figures ranging from General William G. (Jerry) Boykin ("God put him [Bush] there for such a time as this") to Jerry Falwell ("God is pro-war").[14] There is a disturbing iniquity about believing that wars are the work of God or that God justifies human misery if it is accord with certain rigid religious beliefs. Even more disturbing is the question of what fundamentalists (and the president) will do if God should lose the faith-based war in Iraq.

The world cannot be divided into good and evil by a born-again president and his extreme evangelical followers using apocalyptic language without galvanizing a self-fulfilling biblical prophecy, not only among true believers in the Rapture and dispensationalist dogma, according to teachings of the nineteenth-century British cleric John Darby, but also among those millions of evangelical Christians already inclined to view of U.S. foreign policy as following a biblically determined prophetic plan for the end of the world.[15]

The Rapture

According to Darby (and such contemporary promulgators as televangelists Jerry Falwell, Pat Robertson, Jack Van Impe, and John Hagee, and print popularizers Hal Lindsey, Guy Dury, Tim LaHaye, and Jerry Jenkins),

the present "dispensationalism" will end with the Rapture, when all true believers will join Christ in the air. Next comes a seven-year Tribulation, when a charismatic but satanic figure, the Antichrist [Evil One], will arise in Europe, seize world power, and impose his universal tyranny under the dread sign "666," mentioned in Revelation. After seven years, Christ and the saints will return to vanquish the Antichrist and his armies... near Haifa. From a restored Temple in Jerusalem Christ will then inaugurate a thousand-year reign of peace and justice – the Millennium.[16]

The subtext of this prophetic scenario is that Arab leaders and nations are symbols of the Antichrist and must be destroyed. This is why Franklin Graham (Billy's son) and Falwell took advantage of September 11 to attack publicly "Islam as an evil religion" and why they believe that Saddam Hussein was, if not the Antichrist, the precursor of the Evil One. (It didn't help that Saddam intended to rebuild the city of Babylon on its ancient ruins.) Christian fundamentalists in the United States have become staunch supporters of Israel against the Palestinians, neglecting to point out that the final solution for Jews under Rapture theory is that they must convert to Christianity or burn in hell. Perhaps unknowingly, they are also in alliance with radical Islamists (the *Hojjatieh*) who believe that chaos in the Middle East presages the return of the Twelfth Imam.

So the question remains: if it proves true that the "fantasies of a splendid little war have led to disaster," who is more responsible – neo-con secularists or evangelicals? Regardless of the answer to this question, Kevin Phillips has presciently suggested that "[t]he precedents of past leading world economic powers show that blind faith and religious excesses – the rapture seems to be both – have often contributed to national decline, sometimes even being in its forefront."[17]

Another seldom-discussed aspect of the Rapture is that most of its adherents – because of their belief in prophecy based on a literal interpretation of the Bible and the second coming of Christ – are less concerned than they otherwise might be with a basic set of personal economic conditions ranging from unemployment and credit-card debt to heating bills and the cost of gasoline. Such faith-based nihilism also means that they seem to have little interest in preserving the environment, despite a splinter group of eighty-six evangelical leaders who began urging Bush in 2006 to pay more attention to global warming. On the contrary, environmental destruction (and even the frightening rise in personal and national debt) is fatalistically welcomed by the vast majority of believers in the Rapture as a sign of the anticipated apocalypse. Apparently almost 45 percent of American Christians believe in Armageddon. If such religious views can affect environmental, economic, and social reform policy, can they be held responsible for encouraging Bush to destabilize the entire Middle East based on the literal interpretation of the Bible?[18]

Paths Not Taken toward a More Positive Legacy

There must be more to U.S. foreign policy than a "Grand Strategy" designed to ensure American hegemony in an age of terror. Indeed, "many of its traditional political and military goals [of the United States]...in pursuit of ethical objectives...have disappeared simply because bin Laden arrived on our television screens." Any "Grand Strategy" for the long haul must consist of more than visionary dreams of millennialist goals about imposed democracy and freedom based on American might and exaggerated threat perceptions. As of his address to a military audience at Fort Bragg, North Carolina, on June 28, 2005, there was no indication that Bush had developed any sophisticated "hybrid strategy, a two-level policy" for dealing with the world.[19] Although the speech was nationally televised, he addressed only the already converted in the country with the same simplistic, moralistic notions that he had been repeating since September 11.

Bush simply defied reason when in his Fort Bragg address he linked September 11 five times with the reason for the war in Iraq. It made no sense "to color Iraq with the memory of 9/11" because that country played no role in the attacks. Interestingly, Bush did not mention WMDs at all, preferring to refer to terror and terrorism thirty-four times, to use "freedom" and "free" twenty-three times, and "democracy" or "democratic" eight times. "When the history of this period is written," the president predicted, "the liberation of Afghanistan and the liberation of Iraq will be remembered as the great turning points in the story of freedom." Just as Bush's history of how and why he took the country into the mismanaged preemptive war in Iraq will be debated for some time, so will the outcome of the global war on terrorism.[20]

The real "story of freedom" may ultimately be determined by the paths not taken by the Bush administration. By the time of the Fort Bragg address, the Bush administration had not reassessed its obvious ability to act unilaterally by incorporating a more balanced view of the "relationship between threat perception and the application of power." Such intellectual arrogance on the part of previous administrations during the Cold War has led to abuse of power because when ideology overcomes reality, "risk taking overcomes prudence."[21]

Between September 2001 and June 2005 Bush had many opportunities to make more than empty rhetorical flourishes about the good intentions of U.S. foreign policy. He could have pointed out that a half-century of a national security state has done little to assure American security and has diminished respect for the United States abroad, noting that the same is true of Israel. "He could have said that [years of] support for Israel's occupation of Palestine and for the brutal economic siege of Iraq should [have been] rethought" because both have irreparably damaged the reputation of the United States in the Middle East.[22]

Bush could have told Americans not to consume, but rather to conserve, so that the country would not be dependent on foreign oil. It took him until the beginning of 2006 to admit that Americans are "addicted to oil." It is too much to expect that the president might have added that we are "addicted to war." Accordingly, Walter Hixson has argued that the continuity in America's hegemonic drive for world power has been characterized by "external violence focusing on a never-ending series of enemies [and wars]." He concludes that there is a "remarkable war-like continuity of U.S. foreign policy flowing from a distinctive national culture," primarily based on ideas about the country's exceptionalism – a continuity that has reached its logical extreme in the endless war on terrorism.[23]

Bush also "could have said that there was no need to exacerbate risks at a time of great tension, that there was no need of a rash insistence that our demands 'are not open to negotiation or discussion.'" He need not have threatened to use "every necessary weapon of war which implies use of nuclear weapons," while at the same time authorizing the redesign of a new generation of atomic weapons, in some cases replacing old ones with a new H-bomb nuclear explosives. He could have tried to forge a new international coalition to battle proliferation of nuclear weapons and created a "true alliance of democracies to fight the illiberal currents coming out of the Middle East."[24]

Such an alliance of democracies could also take up the issue of when (and if) future humanitarian interventions should be designed to overturn existing barbarous regimes and to stop genocides before they linger on for years as the one in Darfur has. It is conceivable that the UN is not equipped to deal with such regimes because too many of its members have brutal domestic records. Therefore, an association of liberal democratic countries could take it upon themselves to report to the UN when military intervention for humanitarian reasons is necessary and proportional with a clear plan to ensure that inhumane results do not occur. Inhumane results would include economic sanctions and boycotts that devastate civilian populations, especially when politicians come to power whose policies this elite group of nations do not condone, as has ·been the case with Cuba, Haiti, Iraq, Iran, and the Palestine Authority after the 2006 victory of Hamas. This group could give emerging countries practical advice for peaceful development, including pointing out to them that nation building no longer means that their recently obtained sovereignty is inviolable, as had been the case during the Cold War. Such a group could also help these vulnerable new nations try war criminals before the International Criminal Court or special regional courts when necessary. Above all, it could encourage the UN seriously to take up redefining the meaning of sovereignty to fit post–Cold War conditions.[25]

Finally, September 11, 2001, will mark a positive turning point in U.S. foreign policy only if it finally results in the maturing of America. Mature nations of great power usually act more conservatively than radically. Yet the United States will remain an immature giant until it begins to abandon its belief in the myth of its exceptionalism and perennial good intentions, admits that it has lost its youthful innocence for the last time, and stops practicing independent internationalism by engaging the world cooperatively rather than unilaterally. The United States cannot defeat terrorism unilaterally. Instead of carrying out a cooperative international intelligence effort and coordinating worldwide police operations with democratic allies against stateless terrorists, it has transformed the war on terrorism into actual or threatened unilateral invasions of other states. This might well encourage other nations to claim the right to preemptive wars of choice as their prerogative and to refuse to talk one on one with their enemies until certain preconditions are met, thus relegating international relations to jungle behavior. As of the beginning of 2007, Bush had not publicly indicated that he was willing to fundamentally rethink the policies that had brought about a strategic disaster in Iraq or to make other changes in diplomacy that would place him on a path toward a more positive presidential legacy – although the 2007 agreement with North Korea and face-to-face talks with Syria and Iran held out a ray of hope. By and large, however, Bush and his neo-con advisers have created a cloud of unaccountability in order to keep their foreign policy mistakes from being corrected by themselves or their critics.

Paths Taken toward a Negative Legacy

The faltering occupation of Iraq had already caused the reputation of the United States to plummet among Muslims around the world when Israel decided to invade Lebanon in the summer of 2006, ostensibly over the kidnapping of two Israeli soldiers by Hezbollah. The United States did nothing to stop the destruction in Beruit or of that country's infrastructure or the concurrent attacks on Hamas in Gaza. The latter encouraged Hamas and the Palestine Authority to oppose both al Fatah and Israel's continued occupation of the West Bank. Viewed by many Arabs as a prelude or dry run for an American invasion of Iran, the Israeli military operation in Lebanon did not go as efficiently as planned and left the impression that Hezbollah had won at least a propaganda victory. The damage done by Israel's invasion of Lebanon to the ability of the United States to function as a credible, even-handed negotiator for settling Middle Eastern problems was incalculable. Some Arabs also viewed this attack as an experimental run-up to an Israeli invasion of Iran. If so, it did not bode well.

Most importantly, they thought that Israel served simply as a surrogate of the United States by invading Lebanon, and this further discredited Bush's legacy in that part of the world.[26]

Another negative path taken centers on the Bush's administration refusal to rule out first-strike use of tactical nuclear weapons, discussed previously. For all of its pronouncements about its virtuous intentions, there has been no acknowledgment that the use of weapons of mass destruction is a crime against humanity, whether they are used by the United States or its enemies – even if they are used in retaliation or for what is regarded as a morally justified end. The ethicist Jonathan Glover has suggested that all countries should be forbidden to do evil even when good may come of it. Less categorically, establishment foreign policy experts such as Richard N. Haass and others have urged the United States to declare a "no first use" policy and to promote the elimination of all nuclear weapons. Nor has it seriously promoted international efforts to find practical alternative sources of energy or supported the elimination of nuclear weapons for itself rather than simply for other countries.[27]

Still another policy damaging Bush's legacy is his administration's refusal to address the corruption in Iraq that has taken place under U.S. occupation. It began when L. Paul Bremer III headed the Coalition Provisional Authority (CPA). He gave the Iraqi Ministry of Defense $1.2 billion; $500 to $750 million went into private hands, and only $400 million can be accounted for as being used to build up the country's defenses. This mismanagement of funds has been called the "biggest heist in U.S. history," but neither the American nor the Iraqi government has attempted to investigate the use and misuse of these funds, or the massive amount of Iraqi security forces' weaponry that has gone missing. Probably the worst example of corruption that the Bush administration should have had more direct control over and still did nothing is associated with the $45 billion rebuilding effort in Iraq. Just as in Vietnam, private corporations are "realiz[ing] Haliburton profits by taking advantage of the relative urgency, chaos, and uncertainty of war." One of the worst examples of this corporate incompetence and fraud can be found in the failure of the $220 million portion (originally estimated to cost $75.7 million) of the $2.4 billion no-bid reconstruction contract the Army Corps of Engineers gave to the Haliburton subsidiary KBR (formerly Kellogg Brown & Root) to rebuild the Fatah pipeline after the U.S. Air Force bombed the bridge across the Tigris that had originally carried these oil pipelines. As of 2005, all the money had been spent, despite a geotechnical report back in August 2003 that had indicated the project would fail as designed. In 2006, work to rebuild the Fatah pipeline had to be assigned to two other companies. Given the dominance of big business and oil interests in the Republican Party, the Bush administration did not confront this issue of fraud in reconstruction contracts. However, the Democrats, after winning the 2006 midterm elections, began to curb oil profits and to investigate all such wasteful projects based on the report of a federal oversight agency showing that both "Defense and State department officials condoned or allow repeated work delays, bloated expenses and payments for shoddy work."[28]

The state of democracy in Iraq also remains a blot on Bush's legacy. As Fareed Zakaria and Larry Diamond have pointed out, elections by themselves are no guarantee of a democratic state, especially if the United States simply uses them to garner legitimacy for the war on terrorism and as a subterfuge for controlling the country's oil reserves. Democracy in Iraq will require an end to ethnic and sectarian strife, the rule of law, and a less oil-based economy (as of 2007, no democratic petro-state existed). None of these preconditions for democracy was in place by the time of the first Iraqi election at the beginning of 2005, and the United States not only had to "lock down" the entire country in order to hold the election, but there is also evidence that it tried to manipulate the results of that election. If so, it did not succeed. A plurality of conservative clerical parties won in the 2005 Iraqi parliamentary election – a fact that the Bush administration has turned into a well-kept secret. In June of that year, elections in Iran made hard-line conservative Mahmoud Ahmadinejad the president of Iran, and also produced the victory of Hamas in the Palestine Authority in 2006. When elections do not produce the results wanted by the United States, it often takes punitive action.[29] Additionally, Bush has never expressed interest in any plan for collectively reforming the global order. Clearly, this will not be part of his legacy because of the neo-con path he chose. Likewise, his administration has not supported any significant reevaluation at the UN of the concept of national sovereignty and international responsibility, or of ways to prevent humanitarian interventions from having inhumane results, nor has it come out against the opportunistic granting of sovereignty to nonviable entities. As noted, the administration has not supported most attempts at UN reform, let alone one that would have included a discussion of limiting unilateral military actions on the part of all nation states, including the United States.

Finally, Bush's worst legacy is his record on human and civil rights in general and on torture in particular – a legacy that will be difficult for his successors in the Oval Office, whether Democrat or Republican, to reverse. He has so successfully used the "politics of fear" and government secrecy to distract Americans from the diminution of civil rights at home and human rights abuses abroad that in 2007 Amnesty International USA urged Congress to take the lead in restoring respect for humane standards and practices domestically and in the world. To date, it has not, and neither has the president. This means that the United States and the world may be on the road to producing a "culture of atrocity" if the only response to terrorism is perpetual war. Al Gore has noted that terrorists use fear for political ends by distorting reality and indicating that they are capable of more than they can actually accomplish. He thinks that the Bush administration has emulated their methods in taking the nation to war in Iraq. Amnesty International has pointed out that the United States is not alone in spreading fear in order to wage war and to divert attention from violations of human rights, but as the most powerful nation in world, America's loss of ethical authority as a "beacon of hope and a leader in justice" portends ill for the entire world.[30]

The fact that there is no longer any countervailing force to stop the behemoth the United States has become poses some interesting questions for the Bush Doctrine in particular and for American exceptionalism in general, since the administration has taken it upon itself "to remake everyone else's world" in its own image. How can the United States insist that the world become like itself and still remain exceptional? Since its origins, but especially since 1900, its concept of national greatness included the messianic notion that by example (or force, as it turned out) the United States should undertake an "experiment in self-duplication" for the rest of the world.[31]

This attempt at global cloning was based on the assumption that America's democratic and capitalistic brand of liberty was universally transferable and would benefit people everywhere if they would only emulate the "American way of life – even if that life showed distinct signs of decline by the end of the twentieth century. According to critics at home and abroad, "the increasing unregulated rule of capital [was] detrimental to the moral life and traditional values of the United States" as demonstrated by a growing wage gap between rich and poor, the weakening social cohesion of the middle class, a high rate of crime and incarceration, and fewer people voting because the corporate elites dominated both parties, controlling electoral politics and the economy.[32] An aging and imperfect democracy, forcing its values on the rest of the world while suppressing civil liberties at home, threatens not only global stability but the very concept of an "empire of liberty" that the United States has so carefully cultivated over the last 200 years. To continue to pursue the American myth of exceptionalism through endless unilateral actions requires unbridled hegemonic arrogance on the part of diplomatic decision makers.

Revolts of the Realists and Neo-Conservatives

By 2006, the combination of arrogance and incompetence of the Bush administration not only had produced general dissatisfaction in the country, it had also provoked two internal revolts within the Republican Party. The first was the more moderate, consisting of criticism by foreign policy realists, sometimes called pragmatists. The report of the 2006 bipartisan Iraq Study Group (ISG), chaired by James A. Baker III and Lee H. Hamilton, conveyed a certain amount of intellectual honesty about the deteriorating situation in Iraq. Basically, this report provided Bush "cover," courtesy of his father's "realist" older friends and advisers, with suggestions for a moderate "change of course." But it should be noted that these recommendations would neither end the war nor produce anything like the kind of total victory Bush had been insisting upon. They would, however, allow Bush to show that he was willing to try something different so that in the end he could argue that the United States did not lose the war, the Iraqis did.[33]

The ISG report probably arrived two years too late, since basically it called for the "Iraqization" or "Iraqafication" of this war in a way similar to the "Vietnamization" of that war. In both cases, the object was (is) to co-opt domestic dissatisfaction with the conduct of the war by reducing American casualties and turning more of the fighting over to American-trained native soldiers. Nixon initiated this policy in 1969, but the war continued for another three years with the loss of more than 20,000 U.S. military personnel. At that time antiwar groups correctly predicted that Vietnamization would prolong rather than end the war. The same will likely prove true of Iraqization – if it is implemented.[34]

Of the report's seventy-nine recommendations, the most questionable was number sixty-four, calling on the United States to help the Iraqi government draft a new oil law. A leaked copy of this proposed law emerged in February 2007, with vague language and terms that favored the interests of foreign oil companies, especially American ones. This recommendation contradicts the national ownership approved by the State Department and the James Baker Institute in Texas, discussed earlier, following the invasion of Iraq back in 2003 and casts doubt on the claim that the United States did not invade Iraq for its oil reserves. It provides an opening for the privatization of the country's oil reserves long advocated by the neo-cons, especially by Bremer when he was in charge of the CPA and by Zalmay Khalilzad when he was U.S. ambassador to Iraq. Privatization not only would violate Iraq's sovereignty, it could remove it from OPEC if the central government lost control over its own levels of production to regions negotiating their own technical service contracts under the influence of foreign companies. If approved by the Iraqi Council of Representatives, it could eventually privatize the current nationally run oil reserves if the country ends up with a weak central government. Since the ISG's recommendations were based on the flawed process of consensus, there is no way to know whether Baker disagreed with this recommendation, or whether he had simply changed his mind. Some sections of the ISG report seem to favor the central government retaining control of the oil and gas reserves, while others open the possibility of regions and foreign companies taking control – fostering the breakup of the country into three ethnic areas.[35]

The president initially expressed little interest in the ISG's comprehensive recommendations or in implementing them "in a coordinated fashion." He even implied that at least some of the ideas of the Baker–Hamilton Commission "would lead to defeat." Saying he wanted to wait for other reports from the Pentagon and State Department, Bush took a characteristically defensive position in a press conference on December 13, 2006, repeating: "We can't leave before the job is done." With these words Bush seemed to have fallen into the mind-set of his accidental predecessor LBJ, who also feared that his legacy would be that of a president who lost a war. Nixon complicated and prolonged his ending of the Vietnam War by insisting it had to be a "peace with honor," a goal he never achieved. That God – the author of liberty, freedom, and democracy, according to Bush – would also be losing the war in Iraq is an added incentive for him to continue it until America achieves something he can call victory. Bush has much more at stake over the loss of the war in Iraq than simply his own legacy; it is also God's.

Many moderate Republicans expressed some unhappiness with the Baker–Hamilton commission's work, but the neo-conservatives were most vocal in rejecting the bulk of its recommendations. This neo-con reaction came as no surprise, since many of them had begun in 2006 to criticize Bush's ineffective execution of the war ("a mind-bending level of incompetence") and to call for a greater commitment of American troops and an attack on Iran's nuclear facilities. Prominent neo-cons also opposed the suggestion that the United States renew a sustained commitment to a comprehensive Arab-Israeli peace, which included calling an international conference at which Israel, Syria, and Lebanon would negotiate with each other as they had at the 1991 Madrid Conference. Richard Perle referred to this and other aspects of the report as "absurd," and Kenneth Adelman, who had once predicted the Iraqi war would be a "cakewalk," also expressed strong skepticism and called for sending in 20,000 to 30,000 more U.S. troops.[36]

Evidence that the revolt of the neo-cons was in full swing came in November 2006 when *Vanity Fair* pre-released excerpts from an article not originally scheduled for publication until January 2007 (well after the midterm elections). In it, such neo-conservatives as Eliot Cohen, David Frum, Frank Gaffney, Michael Ledeen, Richard Perle, Kenneth Adelman, and Michael Rubin all criticized Bush's conduct (but not the original purpose) of the war. Earlier in the summer, conservative radio show hosts and newspaper columnists had also expressed doubts about Bush's insistence that progress was being made in Iraq. Even retired generals joined in, focusing their attack on Secretary Rumsfeld. Bob Woodward, ever the front man for the most extreme of the neo-conservatives, expressed their (and presumably his) dissatisfaction with the Bush administration by viciously criticizing Secretary of Defense Rumsfeld in his 2006 book, *State of Denial*. He even half-heartedly attempted to resurrect the influence of Henry Kissinger and his so-called realist diplomacy by indicating that the former secretary of state was meeting with Bush and Cheney, apparently telling them (à la his mentor Fritz Kraemer) that "victory is the only exit strategy" (à la Vietnam).[37]

Not content to publicize their about-face on Bush in *Vanity Fair*, on January 28, 2007, neo-con members of the powerful think tank The Project for the New American Century (PNAC) wrote a letter to Congress calling for an increase in U.S. forces in Iraq, an increase in military personnel in general (which in some versions appears to be a thinly disguised call for renewal of the draft system), and making arguments for taking military action against Iran eerily suggestive of those made before the invasion of Iraq in 2003. By May 2007, the neo-con Perle became particularly outspoken in his criticism of Bush, calling him a "failure." Clearly, these dissatisfied neo-cons still believe in the Kraemer Doctrine, that is, the necessity for the United States not to show "provocative weakness" and not to negotiate with its enemies. On December 15, when the White House staged a pomp-and-circumstance ceremony for Rumsfeld, who had abruptly resigned in November, the former secretary of defense did not indicate that he had rethought anything about his stewardship, despite the secret memorandum he had written just before resigning that seemed to anticipate some of the recommendations of the Iraq Study Group. Instead, he actually paraphrased the *éminence grise* of the neo-cons, Fritz Kraemer, saying: "Today it should be clear that not only is *weakness provocative*, but the perception of weakness on our part can be provocative as well."[38] Like Rumsfeld, most neo-cons were not ready to abandon their idealist dreams of expanding American power and influence in perpetuity, regardless of the cost in lives and U.S. reputation.

This civil war within the Republican Party between the neo-cons and the moderates bodes ill for the GOP's continued reputation as the citadel of national security and patriotism that it has flaunted since September 11. This image brought Bush electoral successes in 2002 and 2004 because few questioned his aggressive neo-con diplomacy, and the neo-cons certainly did not question his or Cheney's or Rumsfeld's ability to wage war. Now Republicans are at each others' throats trying to avoid being held responsible when answering the question: "Who lost Iraq?" At stake is the party's identity, which Republicans will have to resolve before the 2008 presidential election. However, having so successfully not held any government official or agency accountable for domestic and foreign policy mistakes and incompetence, GOP leaders may ironically find themselves falling into an internecine blame game at the expense of party unity.

Ethics and Efficiency

It is imperative that opponents (and even moderate supporters) of the Bush administration demand ethical and efficient (competent) behavior from the president, from his advisers and supporters in Congress, and from the Democrats who took back both houses of Congress in 2006. This would place political focus on evaluating the mistakes and injurious results of the Iraq war as the secular moralists and religious supporters of that conflict have not. A demand for ethical and efficient conduct would also provide a way to explain to average Americans past unethical behavior on the part of the United States (which helped the country win the Cold War) in the hope that such behavior will not continue to be repeated with impunity. Instead of trying to take back morality and religion (and the flag, according to a book by Todd Gitlin), opponents of unilateral preemptive strikes and empty evangelical slogans about good and evil should talk about ethics and efficiency to counter the way in which Bush and his neo-con advisers have used fear tactics to portray their actions as patriotic in order to cover their incompetence. Indeed, they have succeeded in taking the "tapestry of lies" that so often characterized American foreign policy during the Cold War to a new level and in doing so have created the first post-truth presidency.[39]

Opponents of the Bush administration cannot successfully reclaim the language of religion and morality to argue against the immorality of a preemptive war and the militarization of American society to fight terrorism and tyranny all over the world. The neo-cons and evangelicals have a hammerlock on this rhetoric. However, the argument for ethical and efficient (competent) behavior on the part of the United States should stand up well against religion and morality because in many respects it represents a return to diplomacy based on ethical realism, which both Democrats and Republicans once claimed to honor. After all, the Puritans traditionally prided themselves on being ethical and practical before their "errand into the wilderness" turned into a justification for economic expansionism. Security interests must once again begin to "serve the good as far as possible," and American leaders must "observe certain strict limits as to what they are prepared to do on behalf" of the country. There is no other way to restore the credibility and accountability of the United States at home and abroad that has so declined during the Bush presidency.[40]

Katrina, along with decreasing support for the Iraq war, revelations about torture, NSA warrantless wiretaps, and misguided agreements with Dubai over ownership of U.S. ports and with India over nuclear power all coalesced at the beginning of Bush's second term. They were harbingers of the bad luck and/or overreaching and misleading public statements, if not outright lies, that have plagued so many second-term presidents, such as FDR, Eisenhower, LBJ, Nixon, Reagan, and Clinton. The excessive popular support that Bush enjoyed for most of his first term because of a very ambitious open-ended war against terrorism began to diminish in 2004 when it became evident that the major reason given for the war in Iraq – the presence of weapons of mass destruction (WMDs) – did not exist. Lack of proof of the connection between al Qaeda and Saddam Hussein and evidence of torture at Abu Ghraib and Guantánamo also lowered his standing in the polls and raised questions about his credibility (and the country's), but not enough to prevent his reelection in 2004 because he successfully continued to campaign using fear and faith. However, by the time of the 2006 midterm election, facts and demands for accountability began to prevail over the fictions of Republican political slogans.

The 2006 midterm elections held out the hope that the "revolutionary utopianism" of the neo-conservatives and messianic religious right would not continue to dominate U.S. diplomacy. There was a possibility that the current asymmetry of fiction over fact, of ideology and faith-based policies over ethical and practical ones, could be brought under control. This may place too much trust in the Democrats, who have not distinguished themselves very much from Republican positions in Congress since 1994. However, Faustian foreign policy imbalances of the past have been moderated, and this one may have run its course because of two unrelated events: the incompetence demonstrated by the Bush administration during the Katrina crisis and the occupation of Iraq.

Whether public perception of Bush's incompetence and mendacity as a war leader and his failure during a major domestic crisis will also affect the 2008 presidential election remains to be seen. Much depends on his party's ability to regain full support of the evangelical vote despite the fact Bush has not delivered on some their more extreme demands for constitutional amendments banning abortion and gay marriage. Examples of corruption and anti-family values displayed by a few leading Republican politicians and evangelical leaders have also created cracks in the powerful radical right voting block that did not exist in 2000 and 2004. Bush must also win back dissident neo-conservatives. Unfortunately, he cannot satisfy both his secular and religious bases without becoming more extreme in his remaining months in office as a lame duck.

Clearly, it is time for both moderate Democrats and Republicans to claim that ethical behavior (and the request for efficient competency and accountability in diplomatic and domestic matters) is truly patriotic and need not be above the law, as moralistic and incompetent behavior often are. The outcome in Iraq will not be known for years, perhaps decades, but the botched occupation of Iraq seems doomed to go down in history with other bungled or unnecessary military actions based on imperial folly. Initial incompetence is not usually forgotten regardless of the ultimate long-term consequence of a war, especially when it can be blamed on an accidental second-term president.

March of Freedom or Folly?

In the best of all possible worlds, the century that celebrated and promoted Wilson's notion of national self-determination after both world wars through international organizations should have seen the United States enter the twenty-first century with a sustained commitment to a truly global cooperative foreign policy rather than continuing to practice independent internationalism. But that would have required a more candid discussion of the evolution of the purpose and mission of the United States over the last fifty years, especially during the 1990s. The basic unanswered question is whether the myth of exceptionalism from John Winthrop to Woodrow Wilson and now George W. Bush serves the needs of the nation or the world. National myths are necessary for "coherent public action," but only those that "yield acceptable results" continue over time. All myths tend to exceed their original purpose. This may be true of American exceptionalism. Either the United States will succeed in remaking the world in its own image, and thus no longer be exceptional, or its attempts to do so will alienate the rest of the world. In any case, the myth of exceptionalism is no longer serving the best interests of the United States, to say nothing of the world. Mythical or fictional characters who sell their souls to the devil seldom triumph in the long run. Unless the United States, having won the Cold War without its soul intact, can now magnanimously admit that its goals and Faustian tactics in that conflict were not always ethical, it may end up wondering later in this century why it lost the post–Cold War world.

Clearly, since September 11 the United States has stood at a juncture in history, a moment, a watershed, in which its foreign policy could have followed a direction other than the one dictated by extreme Republican ideologues. Instead of taking advantage of the historic crossroads created by September 11 so that the twenty-first century would not repeat the murderous path of the last one, the president and those of his advisers who had not resigned by the end of 2006 seemed determined to "stay the course" on their "march to folly...toward bombastic nationalism, military quagmire and escalating debt, all of which have made its access to the oil controlled by the seething countries of the Middle East ever more precarious."[41]

The Bush administration has not yet absorbed the most important lesson of the second Gulf War, namely, that a war of choice launched under false pretenses based on deliberately distorted intelligence must be examined and investigated again and again because the way a country enters a war usually determines the way it emerges from the conflict. Significant American involvement in Vietnam started with the lie about what happened in the Gulf of Tonkin, and it ended with the deception known as "peace with honor." An equally fraudulent conclusion will no doubt characterize the end of the war in Iraq because there is no "right" solution to the civil war and haven for terrorism that the United States has created there.

In his 2006 State of the Union address and in a half-dozen frantic ones before Christmas 2005, and in an earlier talk on October 6, Bush underscored the importance of the historical moment in which he found himself. He simplistically insisted that the United States now sought "total" and "complete" victory in the war in Iraq, and also "the end of tyranny in our world" because the "future security of America depends on this." Although he had spoken about ending tyranny in his second inaugural address in January 2005, in these talks at the end of that year and at the beginning of 2006 his rhetoric became almost completely devoid of reality. He called criticism "misguided idealism" and charged individual critics with being protectionists or isolationists and implicitly unpatriotic for not joining up "when freedom is on the march." Bush proudly predicted in his sixth State of the Union address that he had started a "long war against a determined enemy, a war that will be fought by presidents of both parties" indefinitely into the future. Until the fall of 2006, Bush used the phrase "stay the course" to convey his determination to win both ideologically and militarily in Iraq. As of January 2007, in his "New Way Forward" address, he made veiled military threats against both Iran and Syria and still insisted that "failure in Iraq would be a 'disaster' for the United States" because it would mean the terrorists "would have a safe haven from which to plan and launch attacks on the American people." Despite the self-evident strategic, humanitarian, and ethical disaster he had created in Iraq, Bush did not waver in his commitment to the "young democracy" in Iraq and to "the advance of freedom [as] the calling of our time."[42]

How a march of freedom could result from practicing torture, massive surveillance at home and abroad, restricting the civil liberties of innocent civilians as well as those designated "enemy combatants," and endless war in the name of peace makes sense only to a president completely beguiled by the neoconservative version of Orwell's Newspeak. Nonetheless, Bush continued at the beginning of 2007 to call upon the world to join the United States in his global war against evil. Ironically, the first major stage of that war received a negative evaluation in the February 2007 National Intelligence Estimate on Iraq. It stated that the "overall security situation [there] will continue to deteriorate" at rates comparable to the latter part of 2006. Faced with this harsh reality, in May Bush began contradicting his earlier defense of the war in Iraq, namely, that the United States was fighting there so that the terrorists would not come here, by saying that the terrorists now being trained in Iraq by al Qaeda (without acknowledging that it had become a breeding ground because of the war) would come here if American soldiers were withdrawn. With the creation of this circular scenario, the president came perilously close to having no clothes. As Bush's standing in the polls plummeted, his advisers insisted that he was simply being Trumanesque.[43] Regardless, the presidency remained as powerful, imponderable, and imperial as ever.

America needs political leaders who, instead of endorsing more unilateral diplomatic actions, can see what a calamity some past foreign policies have been and what unintended negative consequences (blowback) they have produced. The country needs leaders of both parties or from a third party who will try to rectify the worldwide resentment of the United States that the Bush administration has managed to create with its "double standards and double talk . . . crass ignorance and arrogance . . . wrong assumptions and dubious policies." Without reformed or new leadership, the United States seems well on its way to setting in motion, as did the First World War, another bloodthirsty century, thus contributing to one more rupture in the seamless chronological web of humankind. Most of all, "we need people with vision who can imagine what a just world would look like" and not simply talk about waging a war on terrorism to make the world look like America. In summary, the country needs leaders who can see beyond the limits of the myth of American exceptionalism, which projects a perennial view of the country as an innocent victim of evil forces, motivated only by good intentions, commitment to just causes, and general law-abiding uniqueness among nations. This "masquerading as a force for good" must at long last be exposed as it was not during the Cold War.[44] Current and future American leaders must not let the country be dragged into Bush's long war for generations to come. This could amount to a legacy of bloodshed exceeding even that of the twentieth century.

Unless Bush can extract himself from the unethical and increasingly inefficient tentacles of the neo-conservatives, who have not served him well, he will go down in history as a hapless accidental president instead of a lauded transformational one – a man who set in motion an endless war and sectarian violence throughout the Middle East at the beginning of the twenty-first century while claiming to do God's work. Indeed, this would be a "memorable" legacy – far beyond, and in contradiction of, Woodrow Wilson's.

Notes

Introduction: Toward a Faustian Diplomacy

1. Perry Miller, "Errand into the Wilderness," in his *Errand into the Wilderness* (Cambridge, MA: Harvard University Press, 1958), pp. 8–9 (first quotation); Sacvan Bercovitch, *The American Jeremiad* (Madison: University of Wisconsin Press, 1978), p. 7 (second quotation); and Anders Stephanson, *Manifest Destiny: American Expansionism and the Empire of Right* (New York: Hill and Wang, 1995), pp. 10–11, 28–65.

2. Since historical lies are often at the heart of any sense of nationhood, Ernest Renan said that scholarly research often yield results that are at odds with founding myths at the heart of nationalism. See Renan, *Qu'est-ce qu'une nation?* (Paris, 1882), pp. 7–8. All nation-states create less-than-truthful stories about their origins. One of the best (or worst) examples of nationalistic myth making at work in the post–Cold War world was the Serbian one about their defeat in the 1389 battle of Kosovo, which resurfaced in the mid-1980s. Ultimately it led to the NATO intervention in 1999, ostensibly to protect Albanians from Serbian aggression, and the downfall of Slobadan Milosevic's pan-Slavic objectives. See Florian Bieber, "Nationalist Mobilization and Stories of Serb Suffering," *Rethinking History* 6 (Spring 2002): 95–110. For the problem nations have dealing with the trauma of defeat, see Wolfgang Schivelbusch, *The Culture of Defeat: On National Trauma, Mourning and Recovery* (London: Metropolitan Books, 2003) on the South after the Civil War, the French after the Franco-Prussian War, and the Germans after World War I.

3. Walter L. Hixson, *Myth to Power: National Identity and U.S. Foreign Relations* (New Haven, CT: Yale University Press, 2008). Quotations are from a paper he delivered at the Historians against the War conference, Austin, Texas, February 18, 2006. For why belief in national myths is necessary for "coherent public action," while only those that "yield acceptable results" succeed over time, see William H. McNeill, "The Care and Repair of Public Myth," *Foreign Affairs* 61 (Fall 1982): 23–42. This article also notes the important role historians play in perpetuating and/or "supplanting decrepit myths" because of their ability to perceive and generalize about old and new patterns in American history.

4. Winthrop quoted in Edmund S. Morgan, *The Puritan Dilemma: The Story of John Winthrop* (Boston: Little, Brown, 1958), p. 70; Joan Hoff, "The City on the Hill:

America's Role in the World," in *The Humanities and the Art of Public Discussion* (Washington, DC: Federation of State Humanities Councils, 1991), vol. 3, pp. 16–26; Pew Center 2003 poll, <http://www.prorev.com/statculture.htm> "2001 Religious Identification in the United States," <http://www.religioustolerance.org/chr_prac2.htm>; McNeill, "The Care and Repair of Public Myth," p. 39 (quotation); and Richard Falk, "State Terrorism versus Humanitarian Law," in Mark Selden and Alvin Y. So, eds., *War and State Terrorism: The United States, Japan, and the Asia-Pacific in the Long Twentieth Century* (Lanham, MD: Roman and Littlefield, 2004), p. 41.

5. Kevin Phillips, *American Theocracy: The Peril and Politics of Radical Religion, Oil, and Borrowed Money in the 21st Century* (New York: Viking, 2006), pp. 125–31; Bercovitch, *The American Jeremiad*, pp. xi–xiv, 3–30, 93–131, 176; Jack P. Greene, *The Intellectual Construct of America: Exceptionalism and Identity from 1492 to 1800* (Chapel Hill: University of North Carolina Press, 1993), pp. 130–6; and John B. Judis, *The Folly of Empire: What George W. Bush Could Learn from Theodore Roosevelt and Woodrow Wilson* (New York: Scribner, 2004), pp. 13–14.

6. The outbreak of war in Europe in 1914 prompted Wilson to proclaim the country's unique service to the world. In his relatively short annual message to Congress on December 8, 1914, he used the term "self-possession" in reference to the United States no less than three times, and each time he implicitly expressed his belief in American exceptionalism. See Arthur S. Link et al., eds., *The Papers of Woodrow Wilson* (Princeton, NJ: Princeton University Press, 1979) 31: 414–24 [hereinafter Link, PWW], year published and volume]; and Patrick Devlin, *Too Proud to Fight: Woodrow Wilson's Neutrality* (New York: Oxford University Press, 1974), pp. 673–88. Also see Elizabeth Edwards Spalding, "True Believers," *The Wilson Quarterly* 30, no. 2 (Spring 2006): 41 (quotation).

7. Walter LaFeber, "The Bush Doctrine," *Diplomatic History* 26, no. 4 (Fall 2004): 550; Liah Greenfeld, *Nationalism: Five Roads to Modernity* (Cambridge, MA: Harvard University Press, 1992), pp. 407–8, 448; John Higham, "The Future of American History," *Journal of American History* 80 (March 1994): 1292–9; Marcus Raskin, "Bennett's Pledge of Allegiance," *The Nation*, August 5/12, 2002, p. 36; and McNeill, "The Care and Repair of Public Myth," pp. 39–41.

8. "Europeans' Doubt over US Policy Rises," report on a German Marshall Fund survey, *International Herald Tribune*, September 4, 2003.

9. *The Christian Science Monitor* paraphrased in George Packer, "Dreaming of Democracy," *The New York Times Magazine*, March 2, 2003, p. 60; and Minxin Pei and Sara Kasper, "The Inevitable 'Morning After' of Regime Change," *The Christian Science Monitor*, January 15, 2003, p. 9. Packer's paraphrase should have indicated that there was also one multilateral success in Grenada after the 1983 invasion. Also see Todd S. Purdum, "The World: People's Choice; It's Democracy, Like It or Not," WR, March 9, 2003, Tom Zeller, "Building Democracy Is Not a Science," WR, April 27, 2003, and Steven Erlanger, "Why Democracy Defies the Urge to Implant It," WK, February 15, 2004 – all in *New York Times*; Michael and Antonio Negri, *Multitude: War and Democracy in the Age of Empire* (New York: Penguin, 2004), pp. 237 (last two quotations), 392, note 10; and Dankwart A. Rustow, "Democracy: A Global Revolution," *Foreign Affairs* 69, no. 4 (Fall 1990): 75.

10. William A. Lovett, Alfred E. Eckes, Jr., and Richard L Brinkman, *U.S. Trade Policy: History, Theory, and the WTO* (Armonk, NY: M.E. Sharpe, 1999),

pp. 99–100, 148–50; Michael Mann, *Incoherent Empire* (London: Verso, 2003), pp. 57–8; Warren Hoge, "Latin America Losing Hope in Democracy, Report Says," *New York Times*, April 22, 2004, p. A3 (first quotation); José Saramago, "¿Qué es exactamente la democracia?" *Le Monde diplomatique*, no. 44 (August 2004): 4–5; Rupert Cornwell, "How Latin America Turned to the Left," *Independent* (UK), March 1, 2005; and David Bacon, "Central America Up in Arms over CAFTA," April 12, 2005, truthout/Perspective, <http://www.truthout.org/issues_05/article_041305LA.shtml>.

11. Robert F. Samuelson, "The Spirit of Capitalism," *Foreign Affairs* 88, no. 1 (January/ February 2001): 205–11 (quotation at 206); Hernando De Soto, *The Mystery of Capital: Why Capitalism Succeeds in the West and Fails Everywhere Else* (New York: Basic Books, 2000), passim; Noreena Hertz, *The Silent Takeover: Global Capitalism and the Death of Democracy* (New York: The Free Press, 2001), pp. 1–36, passim; Mann, *Incoherent Empire*, pp. 67–70; Hardt and Negri, *Multitude*, pp. 231–7; Niall Ferguson, *Colossus: The Price of America's Empire* (New York: Penguin, 2004), p. 301; and Lawrence E. Harrison and Samuel P. Huntington, eds., *"Culture Matters: How Values Shape Human Progress* (New York: Basic Books, 2000), passim.

12. John Ralston Saul, *Voltaire's Bastards: The Dictatorship of Reason in the West* (New York: The Free Press, 1992), pp. 359–61; Benjamin R. Barber, *Jihad vs. McWorld* (New York: Times Books, 1995), pp. 14–15 (quotation); and Hoff, "The City on the Hill," pp. 16–26.

13. Joan Hoff Wilson, *American Business and Foreign Policy, 1920–1933* (Lexington: University Press of Kentucky, 1971), pp. xiv-xvii, 26, 241; and *Recent Social Trends in the United States*, Report of the President's Research Committee on Social Trends (New York: McGraw-Hill, 1933), vol. 1, p. lxix. Walter Russell Mead has suggested another way to reconceptualize the modus operandi of U.S. foreign policy through the prisms of Harmiltonianism, Jeffersoniasm, Jacksonianism, and Wilsonianism. These categories do not explain the erratic way in which the country practiced multi- or unilateralism in the twentieth century as well as my concept of independent internationalism. See his *Special Providence: American Foreign Policy and How It Changed the World* (New York: A Century Foundation Book, 2001).

14. Frank Ninkovich, *The Wilsonian Century: U.S. Foreign Policy since 1900* (Chicago: University of Chicago Press, 1999), pp. 288–92.

15. Richard Rosecrance, "A New Concert of Powers and U.S. Foreign Policy," in Eugene R. Wittkopf, ed., *The Future of American Foreign Policy*, 2nd ed. (New York, 1994), p. 61; *Dædalus* 124 (Spring 1995): xiv; Susan Strange, "The Defective State," in op. cit., p. 72; Mathew Horsman and Andrew Marshall, *After the Nation-State: Citizens, Tribalism and the New World Disorder* (New York: HarperCollins, 1994), p. 236; Kenichi Ohmae, *End of the Nation State* (New York: HarperCollins, 1996), p. vii, passim; Nicholas Lemann, "The Next World Order," *The New Yorker*, April 1, 2002, pp. 42–8; and Arthur Schlesinger, Jr., "Eyeless in Iraq," *The New York Review of Books*, October 23, 2003, p. 24. One of the few books to relate all the various forms of globalization in the course of the twentieth century to U.S. foreign policy is Alfred E. Eckes, Jr., and Thomas W. Zeiler, *Globalization and the American Century* (New York: Cambridge University Press, 2003). For debates about whether globalism threatens such traditional Enlightenment values as democracy, freedom, and equality, which the United States has asserted are universal principles, see Claes G. Ryn, *America the Virtuous: The Crisis of Democracy and the Quest*

for Empire (New Brunswick, NJ: Transaction, 2003), pp. 15–24; and Hardt and Negri, *Multitude*, pp. 231–46.

16. Ronald Steel, "The Missionary" and "Mr. Fix-It," *New York Review of Books*, October 5, 2000, p. 19 (first and second quotations), and November 20, 2003, p. 26 (third quotation); and Ferguson, *Colossus*, pp. 8, 22–3 (fourth quotation), 24, 301.

17. Ferguson, *Colossus*, p. 63 (first two quotations); and Steel, "The Missionary," p. 35 (last quotation).

18. Falk, "State Terrorism versus Humanitarian Law," p. 42.

19. Edward Pessen, *Losing Our Souls: The American Experience in the Cold War* (Chicago: Ivan R. Dee, 1993; Elephant Paperbacks, 1995 ed.), p. 215.

20. Frederick Calhoun, *Uses of Force and Wilsonian Foreign Policy* (Kent, OH: Kent State University Press, 1993), p. 5. H. W. Brands refers to these two types of Wilsonians as "exemplarists," who wanted the United States to set a nonaggressive, humane, democratic, and prosperous example for the rest of the world, and "vindicators," who favored military action to forcibly bring the world up to American standards. See *What America Owes the World: The Struggle for the Soul of Foreign Policy* (Cambridge: Cambridge University Press, 1998), pp. vii–ix, 317–19.

21. Margaret MacMillan, *Paris 1919: Six Months That Changed the World* (New York: Random House, 2001), p. 14; and Anita Durkin, "Metaphorical War-Mongering, or, The Tales of Two Bushes," paper presented at the Historians against the War conference, February 18, 2006, Austin, Texas. Durkin uses the term "universal morality."

22. Ryn, *America the Virtuous*, pp. 2–3 (quotation); and Falk, "State Terrorism versus Humanitarian Law," pp. 50–2, 60–1, note 22.

23. David Ryan and Victor Pungong, eds., *The United States and Decolonization: Power and Freedom* (London: Macmillan, 2000), especially Michael Hunt's, Walter LaFeber's, and Dennis Merrill's articles; William Blum, *Rogue State: A Guide to the World's Only Superpower* (Monroe, ME: Common Courage Press, 2000), passim; Chalmers Johnson, *Blowback: The Costs and Consequences of American Empire* (New York: Henry Holt, 2000), pp. 3–33, 216–29; Hastedt, *American Foreign Policy*, pp.1–8; Phyllis Bennis, *Calling the Shots: How Washington Dominates Today's UN* (New York: Interlink Publishing Group, 1996), p. 25; Grande, *Our Own Backyard*; Thomas J. McCormick, *America's Half-Century: United States Foreign Policy in the Cold War* (Baltimore: Johns Hopkins University Press, 1989); Thomas G. Paterson, *On Every Front: The Making and Unmaking of the Cold War*, rev. ed. (New York: Norton, 1992); Chomsky, *Humanitarian Intervention*; Michael Parenti, *The Terrorism Trap: September 11 and Beyond* (San Francisco: City Lights Books, 2002), pp. 79–84; Falk, "State Terrorism versus Humanitarian Law," pp. 45 (quotation)–6, 50 (quotation), 56 (quotation)–8, 61, note 28; Bruce Cumings, "American Airpower and Nuclear Strategy in Northeast Asia since 1945," in Mark Selden and Alvin Y. So, eds., *War and State Terrorism: The United States, Japan, and the Asia-Pacific in the Long Twentieth Century* (Lanham, MD: Roman and Littlefield, 2004), pp. 63–4, 77–82; and Mark Selden, "The United States and Japan in Twentieth Century Asian Wars," in op. cit., pp. 30–6.

24. Michael T. Klare, "Oil Moves the War Machine," *The Progressive*, June 2002, pp. 18–19; idem, "Mapping the Oil Motive," March 18, 2005, TomPaine.com; and Falk, "State Terrorism versus Humanitarian Law," p. 51. George H. W. Bush did negotiate the 1991 START treaty with Moscow, which reduced both countries'

nuclear arsenals by 30 percent, and later he proclaimed a unilateral reduction in the number of U.S. missiles, but the United States and other nuclear nations did not consider any comprehensive decrease in their stockpiles. See John Dumbrell, *American Foreign Policy: Carter to Clinton* (New York: St. Martin's Press, 1997), pp. 146–8.

25. David S. Foglesong, *America's Secret War against Bolshevism* (Chapel Hill: University of North Carolina Press, 1995), pp. 1–7 (quotations at 2); Scott Shane and Mark Mazzetti, "Advisers Fault Harsh Methods in Interrogation," *New York Times*, May 30, 2007; Robert S. McNamara and James G. Bright, *Wilson's Ghost: Reducing the Risk of Conflict, Killing, and Catastrophe in the 21st Century* (New York: Public Affairs, 2001), pp. 49–50; Ferguson, *Colossus*, p. 63; and MacMillan, *Paris 1919*, p. 14 (last quotation).

26. Johnson, *Blowback*, passim; Lawrence F. Kaplan, "Regime Change," *The New Republic*, March 3, 2003, pp. 21–2; and Douglas Valentine, "Echoes of Vietnam: Phoenix, Assassination and Blowback in Iraq," April 8, 2004, Counterpunch, <counterpunch.org/valentine04162004.html>. For a general review of U.S. intelligence activities before and after the creation of the CIA, see Rhodri Jeffreys-Jones, *Cloak and Dollar: A History of American Secret Intelligence* (New Haven, CT: Yale University Press, 2002), passim. See Lloyd E. Ambrosius, "Woodrow Wilson and George W. Bush: Historical Comparisons of Ends and Means in Their Foreign Policies," *Diplomatic History* 30, no. 3 (June 2006): 509–43, for a review of the numerous works that have compared Wilson and Bush and praised or criticized the means they chose to achieve their ends.

27. William Pfaff, "The Question of Hegemony," *Foreign Affairs* 80, no. 1 (January/February 2001): 227 (quotation); and Durkin, "Metaphorical War-Mongering, or, The Tales of Two Bushes."

28. Anthony Lewis, "Abroad at Home; The Inescapable World," op-ed, *New York Times*, October 20, 2001, p. A21 (quotation); and Stephen Kinzer, *Overthrow: America's Century of Regime Change from Hawaii to Iraq* (New York: Times Books, 2006), pp. 1–6, passim.

29. Lea Brilmayer, *American Hegemony: Political Morality in a One-Superpower World* (New Haven, CT: Yale University Press, 1994), pp. 11–31, 114–18; Charles P. Kindleberger, "Dominance and Leadership in the International Economy: Exploitation, Public Goods, and Free Rides," *International Studies Quarterly* 25 (1981): 242–53; idem, "Hierarchy versus Inertial Cooperation," *International Studies Quarterly* 40 (1986): 841, passim; and Joseph Gilpin, *War and Change in World Politics* (Cambridge: Cambridge University Press, 1981), pp. 34, 28–30, 144.

30. Ferguson, *Colossus*, pp. 14–17, 280–5, 301.

31. John Bellamy Foster, "Imperial America and War," *Monthly Review*, May 27, 2003.

32. Ian Traynor, "How American Power Girds the Globe with a Ring of Steel," *Guardian* (UK), April 21, 2003; Chalmers Johnson, *Sorrow of Empire: Militarism, Secrecy, and the End of the Republic* (New York: Metropolitan Books, 2004), pp. 4–5, 64, 153–4, 189–90; idem, *Blowback*, pp. 4–5; Michael Howard, "US Military to Build Four Giant New Bases in Iraq," *Guardian* (UK), May 23, 2005; and Kevin B. Zeese, "The Army Is Staying," April 23, 2006, GlobalSecurity.org. According to Michael T. Klare, "forward operating sites . . . will consist of logical facilities (an airstrip or port complex) plus weapons stockpiles" and no large combat units, only military technicians. "Cooperative security locations will be 'bare bones' facilities utilized in times of crisis only; such sites will have no permanent US presence

but will be maintained by military contractors and host-country personnel." See Klare, "Imperial Reach: The Pentagon's New Basing Strategy," *The Nation*, April 25, 2005, pp. 13–18 (quotations at 13).

33. Ferguson, *Colossus*, p. 14. Ferguson maintains there have been a total of seventy empires, with China and the European Union now constituting numbers sixty-nine and seventy, but neither is yet a challenge to the current American empire.

34. Quotation from Higham, "The Future of American History," p. 1304.

35. Pessen, *Losing Our Souls*, p. 15; Woolsey quoted in David E. Sanger, "Viewing the War as a Lesson to the World," *New York Times*, April 6, 2003; and Hixson, quotation from a paper he delivered at the Historians against the War conference, Austin, Texas, February 18, 2006.

36. Schivelbusch, *The Culture of Defeat*; pp. 22–9, 294; and Robert Jay Lifton, "American Apocalypse," *The Nation*, December 22, 2003, pp. 11–17.

37. Ryn, *America the Virtuous*, p. 8 (first quotation), 38 (third quotation); Hardt and Negri, *Multitude*, pp. 235–7; Ferguson, *Colossus*, pp. 301–2 (second quotation); George Orwell, *1984* (New York: Signet Classics, 1961; reprint of the original 1949 Harcourt Brace Jovanovich edition), pp. 17–27, 152–65; and Geoffrey Nunberg, "If It's 'Orwellian,' It's Probably Not," *New York Times*, WK, June 22, 2003.

38. Ryn, *America the Virtuous*, pp. 2–3; Falk, "State Terrorism versus Humanitarian Law," pp. 50–2, 60–1, note 22.

39. Liah Greenfeld, "Is Nationalism Legitimate?" in Jocelyne Couture et al., eds., *Rethinking Nationalism, Canadian Journal of Philosophy*, supplementary volume 22 (Calgary, Canada: University of Calgary Press, 1998), pp. 102–3; and Arthur Schlesinger, Jr., "The Necessary Amorality of Foreign Affairs," *Harper's Magazine*, August 1971, pp. 72–7. It should be pointed out, however, that Schlesinger did not take this amoral stance on foreign affairs until Richard Nixon inherited the Vietnam War from JFK and LBJ – a war that Schlesinger had supported under the two Democratic presidents. In this article, Schlesinger quoted and agreed with Reinhold Niebuhr when the latter wrote, in *Moral Man and Immoral Society*: "unselfishness must remain the criterion of the highest morality." Then he quotes both Hugh Cecil and Alexander Hamilton: " . . . [unselfishness] is inappropriate to the action of a state. No one has the right to be unselfish with other people's interests. . . . The rule of morality . . . is not precisely the same between nations as between individuals. The duty of making its own welfare the guide of its action is much stronger upon the former than upon the latter. Existing millions and for the most part future generations, are concerned in the present measures of a government; while the consequences of the private action of an individual ordinarily terminate with himself, or are circumscribed with a narrow compass." (p. 72) However, Alan Wolfe has pointed out that if a citizenry are ill-informed or misled by politicians, their private moral freedom can embrace immoral state actions. See Wolfe, *Moral Freedom: The Impossible Idea That Defines the Way We Live Now* (New York: Norton, 2001), pp. 160–6.

40. Richard Falk, "The New Bush Doctrine," *The Nation*, July 15, 2002, pp. 10–11 (quotations).

41. John le Carré, *The Spy Who Came In from the Cold* (New York: Coward-McCann, 1963), pp. 23–4, 26.

42. Matthew Rothchild, "Empire's Apologists," *The Progressive*, March 2003, pp. 35–6; and Lewis H. Lapham, "Notebook: 'Light in the Window'," *Harper's Magazine*, March 2003, pp. 7–9 – criticizing Michael Ignatieff's advocating less timidity and

more use of power on the part of the United States if is to be a successful imperial power in "The Burden [of] The American Empire (Get Used to It)," *The New York Times Magazine*, January 5, 2003, pp. 22–7; Niall Ferguson, "2011," *The New York Times Magazine*, December 2, 2001, pp. 74–9; and Max Boot, *The Savage Wars of Peace: Small War and the Rise of American Power* (New York: Basic Books, 2002), pp. xiii–xx, 336–52.

43. Ryn, *America the Virtuous*, pp. 1–3, 10–11; and Jonathan Rauch, "Firebombs over Tokyo," *The Atlantic Monthly*, July/August 2002, p. 22 (quotation).

44. Other presidents such as James Garfield, Lyndon Johnson, and Ronald Reagan were also evangelicals, but only Carter and George W. Bush were born-again evangelicals. "University of Notre Dame Address at Commencement Exercises," *Public Papers of the Presidents of the United States: Jimmy Carter, 1977, Book 1: January 20–June 24, 1977* (Washington, DC: U.S. Government Printing Office, 1977), p. 956; and David F. Schmitz and Vanessa Walker, "Jimmy Carter and Foreign Policy of Human Rights: The Development of a post–Cold War Foreign Policy," *Diplomatic History* 28, no. 1 (January 2003): 113–43 (quotation).

45. Bill Emmott, "Present at the Creation: A Survey of America's World Role," *The Economist*, June 29, 2002, pp. 20–5; Peter J. Spiro, "The New Sovereigns: American Exceptionalism and Its False Prophets," *Foreign Affairs* 79, no. 6 (November/December 2000): 10 (quotation); Fareed Zakaria, "Democracies That Take Liberties," *New York Times*, November 2, 1997; idem, "The Rise of Illiberal Democracy," *Foreign Affairs* 76 (November/December, 1997): 22–43. The four older covenants or conventions that remain unratified by the United States are the Convention to Eliminate Discrimination against Women, the American Convention on Human Rights, the International Covenant on Economic and Social Cultural Rights, and the International Convention on the Elimination of All Forms of Racial Discrimination.

46. Hertz, *The Silent Takeover*, passim.

47. Spiro, "The New Sovereigns," pp. 13–14; TRB [Peter Beinart], "Sovereign Powers," *The New Republic*, March 31, 2003, p. 6; Hardt and Negri, *Multitude*, pp. 231–7; and Joan Hoff, "September 11: Watershed in U.S. Foreign Policy?," *Irish Studies in International Affairs* 13 (2002): 9–21.

Chapter 1: The United States Forms and Refines Its Diplomacy

1. Liah Greenfeld, *Nationalism: Five Roads to Modernity* (Cambridge, MA: Harvard University Press, 1992), pp. 407–16 (quotation); Jack P. Greene, *The Intellectual Construct of America: Exceptionalism and Identity from 1492 to 1800* (Chapel Hill: University of North Carolina Press, 1993), pp. 55–6, 204–6; and Amitai Etzioni, "The Evils of Self-Determination," *Foreign Policy* 89 (Winter 1992–93): 23.

2. David M. Fitzsimons, "Tom Paine's New World Order," *Diplomatic History* 19 (Fall 1995): 569–82.

3. Derek Heater, *National Self-Determination: Woodrow Wilson and His Legacy* (New York: St. Martin's Press, 1994), pp. 1–3; Hilary Charlesworth, Christine Chinkin, and Shelley Wright, "Feminist Approaches to International Law," *American Journal of International Law* 85 (October 1991): 643; and Greenfeld, *Nationalism*, pp. 449–60.

4. Heater, *National Self-Determination*, p. 3 (first quotation); and Greenfeld, *Nationalism*, p. 10 (second quotation).

5. Greenfeld, *Nationalism*, pp. 490–91; idem, "Is Nationalism Legitimate?," in Joce-lyne Couture et al., eds., "Rethinking Nationalism," *Canadian Journal of Philosophy*, supplementary volume 22 (Calgary, Canada: University of Calgary Press, 1998), pp. 101–3, 108; Lea Brilmayer, *American Hegemony: Political Morality in a One-Superpower World* (New Haven, CT: Yale University Press, 1994), pp. 11–31, 114–18; Charles P. Kindleberger, "Dominance and Leadership in the International Economy: Exploitation, Public Goods, and Free Rides," *International Studies Quarterly* 25 (1981): 242–53; idem, "Hierarchy versus Inertial Cooperation," *International Studies Quarterly* 40 (1986): 841, passim; and Joseph Gilpin, *War and Change in World Politics* (Cambridge: Cambridge University Press, 1981), pp. 28–30, 34, 144.

6. Michael Nelson, ed., *Historic Documents on the Presidency: 1776–1989* (Washington, DC: Congressional Quarterly, 1989), pp. 48–52. Adams delivered this Independence Day address to the House of Representatives on July 4, 1821, because of his concern about public pressure on the government to recognize the newly independent countries of South America. He feared that these countries were not viable and, hence, did not want the United States to entangle itself in European affairs over this issue. "Famous Speeches and Documents," uiowa.edu.

7. Fitzsimons, "Tom Paine's New World Order," pp. 571–7. For a more complete treatment of Paine's views and his contribution to Americans' sense of their own superiority and exceptional characteristics that by 1776 had made them a model for not simply Europe but the entire world, see Greene, *The Intellectual Construct of America*, pp. 132–41, 164–7.

8. Anders Stephanson, *Manifest Destiny: American Expansion and the Empire of Right* (New York: Hill and Wang, 1995), p. 59; and Gaddis Smith, *The Last Years of the Monroe Doctrine, 1945–1993* (New York: Hill and Wang, 1994), pp. 22–4. Smith points out that, taken together, the noncolonization and nonexpansion provisions also implicitly contained a "no-transfer" principle because it was feared that weak European powers might begin to transfer their colonies in the New World to strong ones that could threaten the United States. This nontransfer principle was formalized in 1870 with the Fish Corollary. See note 15 to this chapter.

9. Stephanson, *Manifest Destiny*, pp. 59–60; and Walter LaFeber, *The American Age: U.S. Foreign Policy at Home and Abroad*, 2nd ed. (New York: Norton, 1994), vol. 1, pp. 83–8. Adams was particularly perspicacious with respect to Cuba as indicated in his instructions to the U.S. minister to Spain in April 1823: "There are laws of political as well of physical gravitation; and if an apple severed by the tempest from its native tree cannot choose but fall to the ground, Cuba forcibly disjointed from its own unnatural connection with Spain, and incapable of self-support, can gravitate only towards the North American Union, which by the law of nature cannot cast her off from its bosom" (quote from LaFeber at 85).

10. These are the five formal corollaries to the Monroe Doctrine (Polk's attempts in 1845 and 1848 are usually not considered official), the first three of which were issued by secretaries of state: (1) *The Hamilton Fish Corollary (1870)* originated as a memorandum on July 14, 1870, and stated that the Monroe Doctrine prohibited the transfer of any colonial territory in the New World from one European power to another; (2) *The James G. Blaine Corollary (1881)* announced on June 24, 1881, that the Monroe Doctrine implied that no European power could control any future isthmian canal, and President Rutherford B. Hayes concurred; (3) *The Richard Olney Corollary (1895)* told the English government on July 20, 1895, that

the boundary disputes between England and Venezuela had to be settled by arbitration because any direct action against Venezuela by Britain would be in violation of the Monroe Doctrine; (4) *The Roosevelt Corollary (1904)*, issued by President Theodore Roosevelt on December 4, 1904, was meant to forestall any armed intervention by European nations to collect debts by asserting the sole right of the U.S. to intervene in Western Hemisphere; (5) *The Henry Cabot Lodge Corollary (1912)* resulted from a congressional resolution passed on August 2, 1912, that extended the Monroe Doctrine to exclude non-European powers and foreign companies from buying or controlling land in the Western Hemisphere when such land could be used for purely nationalistic purposes.

11. John A. S. Grenville and George Berkeley Young, *Politics, Strategy, and American Diplomacy: Studies in Foreign Policy, 1873–1917* (New Haven, CT: Yale University Press, 1966), p. 303.

12. Greenfeld, *Nationalism*, pp. 6–11, 29–87, 488; idem, "Is Nationalism Legitimate?," pp. 93–9, 103–8; and Michael Hardt and Antonio Negri, *Multitude: War and Democracy in the Age of Empire* (New York: Penguin, 2004), p. 237.

13. Ibid. (quotation at 108).

14. Greenfeld, *Nationalism*, pp. 11–12; 91–395, 476–7; and idem, "Is Nationalism Legitimate," pp. 104–8.

15. Dankwart A. Rustow, "Democracy: A Global Revolution?," *Foreign Affairs* 69, no. 4 (Fall 1990): 74–91; and Minxin Pei and Sara Kasper, "The Inevitable 'Morning After' of Regime Change," *The Christian Science Monitor*, January 15, 2003, p. 9. Also see Niall Ferguson, *Colossus: The Price of American Empire* (New York: Penguin, 2004), pp. 52–60; and Robert L. Hutchings, *American Diplomacy and the End of the Cold War: An Insider's Account of U.S. Policy in Europe, 1989–1992* (Baltimore: Johns Hopkins University Press, 1997), pp. 339–54.

16. Fitzsimons, "Tom Paine's New World Order," pp. 569–82.

17. Heater, *National Self-Determination*, pp. 4–10; and Rustow, "Democracy: A Global Revolution?," pp. 76–7.

18. Paul A. Varg, *United States Foreign Relations, 1820–1860* (East Lansing: Michigan State University Press, 1979), pp. 50–9; and LaFeber, *The American Age*, vol. 2, pp. 82–4.

19. Thomas A. Bailey, *A Diplomatic History of the American People*, 9th ed. (Englewood Cliffs, NJ: Prentice-Hall, 1982), p. 273 (quotation); Stephanson, *Manifest Destiny*, pp. 34–6; and Varg, *U.S. Foreign Relations*, pp. 168–94, 207–8.

20. Steven J. Valone, "Seward and the Reassertion of the Monroe Doctrine," *Diplomatic History* 19 (Fall 1995): 583–99 (quotation); Walter LaFeber, *The American Search for Opportunity, 1865–1913* (Cambridge: Cambridge University Press, 1993), vol. 2 of *The Cambridge History of American Foreign Relations*, pp. 7–20; and Stephanson, *Manifest Destiny*, pp. 58–63.

21. Valone, "Seward and the Reassertion of the Monroe Doctrine," pp. 583–99. The Platt Amendment was attached to a 1901 military appropriations bill and appended to the Cuban constitution. It specifically prohibited Cuba from entering into any treaty with a foreign power that would impair its independence and from contracting any public debt in excess of its capacity to pay. At the same time, the Platt Amendment gave the United States the right to intervene to preserve Cuban independence or to maintain law and order. It also forced Cuba to sell or lease land for American naval and coaling stations. General Wood is quoted in H. Hagedorn, *Leonard Wood*, 2 vols. (New York: Harper, 1931), vol. 1, p. 362.

Also see LaFeber, *The American Search for Opportunity, 1865–1913*, pp. 129–36, 151–2.

22. Peter Kornbluh, ed., *Bay of Pigs Declassified: The Secret CIA Report on the Invasion of Cuba* (New York: The Free Press, 1998); Stephen G. Rabe, *The Most Dangerous Area in the World: John F. Kennedy Confronts Communist Revolution in Latin America* (Chapel Hill: University of North Carolina Press, 1999), passim; idem, "John F. Kennedy and the World," in James N. Giglio and Stephen Rabe, eds., *Debating the Kennedy Presidency* (Lanham, MD: Rowman and Littlefield, 2002), pp. 7 (quotation), 29–45; and "Election-Year Cuba Policy," *New York Times*, WK, June 27, 2004.

23. Alfred E. Eckes, Jr., and Thomas W. Zeiler, *Globalization and the American Century* (New York: Cambridge University Press, 2003), pp. 11, 261–2 (Appendix: Tables A.1, A.2); LaFeber, *The American Search for Opportunity, 1865–1913*, pp. 1–2; and W. W. Rostow, *The Stages of Economic Growth: A Non-Communist Manifesto*, 3rd ed. (New York: Cambridge University Press, 1990; originally published in 1960), pp. 36–40, 61, 214–30. Rostow's views on the efficacy of pouring foreign capital into developing nations to produce a "take-off" period that would lead to middle-class development and democracy were very popular beginning with the Kennedy administration, but have recently been challenged. See David Landes, *The Wealth and Poverty of Nations: Why Some Are So Rich and Some So Poor* (New York: Norton, 1998).

24. Eckes and Zeiler, *Globalization and the American Century*, pp. 6–7; and Barbara Garson, *Money Makes the World Go Round* (New York: Viking, 2001), pp. 321–5.

25. Alfred E. Eckes, "Cowboy Capitalism: Lessons from the Asian Meltdown," *Chronicles*, pp. 26–8; and Joseph E. Stiglitz, *Globalization and Its Discontents* (New York: Norton, 2002), pp. 3–22.

26. Fred I. Greenstein, ed., *Leadership of Modern Presidents* (Cambridge, MA: Harvard University Press, 1988), p. xx (quotation); and LaFeber, *The American Search for Opportunity, 1865–1913*, pp. 1, 134, 235–6. LaFeber argues that presidential power gradually increased in the last quarter of the nineteenth century, creating the foundation for its dramatic explosion in the twentieth century. The driving forces behind this expansion of executive power were the success of U.S. industrialization, which created unprecedented foreign economic opportunities combined with "the era's racism and missionary impulse" (p. 1), which forced, even reluctant presidents and their secretaries of state to take up the cause of expansionism. I believe that this increase in presidential power was more sporadic than systematic until after the First World War.

27. Kathleen Dalton, *Theodore Roosevelt: A Strenuous Life* (New York: Knopf, 2003); and LaFeber, *The American Search for Opportunity, 1865–1913*, pp. 199–200.

28. LaFeber, *The American Search for Opportunity, 1865–1913*, pp. 182–201, 210–27; Howard K. Beale, *Theodore Roosevelt and the Rise of America to World Power* (New York: Collier Books, 1962; reprint of the original 1956 Johns Hopkins University Press edition), pp. 76–84; and Max Boot, *The Savage Wars of Peace: Small Wars and the Rise of American Power* (New York: Basic Books, 2002), pp. 105–40.

29. Eckes and Zeiler, *Globalization and the American Century*, pp. 26–32; Michael H. Hunt, *The Making of a Special Relationship: The United States and China to 1914* (New York: Columbia University Press, 1983), pp. 209–10; and LaFeber, *The American Search for Opportunity, 1865–1913*, pp. 210–35.

30. David S. Foglesong, *America's Secret War against Bolshevism* (Chapel Hill: University of North Carolina Press, 1995), pp. 11–12; Mary A. Renda, *Taking Haiti: Military Occupation and the Culture of U.S. Imperialism, 1915–1940* (Chapel Hill: University of North Carolina Press, 2001), pp. 91–130 (quotation at 94); Hans Schmidt, *The United States Occupation of Haiti, 1915–34* (New Brunswick, NJ: Rutgers University Press, 1971), passim; Philippe R. Girard, *Clinton in Haiti: The 1994 U.S. Intervention in Haiti* (New York: Palgrave Macmillan, 2004), pp. 12–13; Boot, *The Savage Wars of Peace*, pp. 231–52; and Ferguson, *Colossus*, pp. 56–8.

31. Girard, *Clinton in Haiti*, pp. 14–20; Rayford Logan, *Diplomatic Relations with Haiti, 1776–1891* (Chapel Hill: University of North Carolina Press, 1941), pp. 186, 188, 207–9, 213–14, passim; Tim Matthewson, *Proslavery Foreign Policy* (New York: Praeger, 2003), pp. 133, 145; Boot, *The Savage Wars of Peace*, pp. 156–67; and Michael Kamber, "Haiti's Political Vacuum Stokes Flames of Gang Violence," *New York Times*, November 2, 2004.

32. David Healy, *Drive to Hegemony: The United States in the Caribbean, 1898–1917* (Madison: University of Wisconsin Press, 1988), p. 71; LaFeber, *The American Search for Opportunity, 1865–1913*, p. 196; and Renda, *Taking Haiti*, p. 93 (quotation from an October 31, 1913, draft of an address to Congress).

33. Ferguson, *Colossus*, pp. 53 (quotations from first week in office), 54 (last quotation); Renda, *Taking Haiti*, pp. 93, 108–14 (quotation at 113 from an October 31, 1913, draft of an address to Congress); Arthur S. Link, *Woodrow Wilson*, vol. 3: *The Struggle for Neutrality, 1914–1915* (Princeton, NJ: Princeton University Press, 1960), p. 479 [hereinafter cited as Link, *Struggle for Neutrality*]; and Healy, *Drive to Hegemony*, pp. 178–9.

34. Elizabeth Edwards Spalding, "True Believers," *The Wilson Quarterly* 30, no. 2 (Spring 2006): 41 (first quotation); August Heckscher, *Woodrow Wilson* (New York: Charles Scribner's Sons, 1991), pp. 4–12, 24, 26–7, 31, 47 (second quotation); Francis P. Weisenberger, "Middle Western Antecedents of Woodrow Wilson," *Mississippi Valley Historical Review* 23 (December 1936): 375–90; Louis Auchincloss, *Woodrow Wilson* (New York: Lipper/Viking, 2000), pp. 5–18; H. W. Brands, *Woodrow Wilson* (New York: Times Books, 2003), pp. 1–10; and Sigmund Freud and William C. Bullitt, *Thomas Woodrow Wilson: A Psychological Study* (Boston: Houghton Mifflin, 1966), pp. 3–33.

35. Heckscher, *Woodrow Wilson*, p. 47.

36. Ibid., pp. 13–14 (quotation), 16, 25–6, 34, 45–6, 50, 56; Frank N. Magill, *The American Presidents: The Office and the Men*, 3 vols. (Pasadena, CA: Salem Press, 1986), vol. 2, p. 501; Freud and Bullitt, *Thomas Woodrow Wilson*, pp. 3–31; E. A. Weinstein, *Woodrow Wilson: A Medical and Psychological Biography* (Princeton, NJ: Princeton University Press, 1981), pp. 14–19. In response to Freud and Bullitt (and in anticipation of Weinstein's work), it should be noted that the late eminent Wilson scholar Arthur Link at first virulently denied that Wilson was "a weak and sickly" boy, that he exhibited psychosomatic illnesses and neuroses, and that he suffered a series of "breakdowns" in the 1880s. Link did admit that Wilson suffered from arteriosclerosis as early as 1906 and that such major and minor attacks (strokes) "were probably caused by overwork and sheer nervous exhaustion." See Arthur S. Link, "The Case for Woodrow Wilson," *Harper's Magazine*, April 1967, pp. 88, 91. Link finally accepted the work of medical historians suggesting that Wilson may have been neurologically impaired at the Versailles Peace Conference and that in July 1919 he "may have suffered yet another small stroke" that caused

serious changes in the president's personality and in his ability to negotiate and to remember. See Bert E. Park, "Wilson's Neurologic Illness during the Summer of 1919," in Arthur S. Link et al., eds., *The Papers of Woodrow Wilson* (Princeton, NJ: Princeton University Press, 1988), 58: 611–38 and (1990), 62: 628–38 [hereinafter Link, *PWW*, year published and volume].

37. Foglesong, *America's Secret War against Bolshevism*, pp. 30 (quotation)–32 (quotation); Saunders, *In Search of Woodrow Wilson*, p. 25; and Brands, *Woodrow Wilson*, p. 133. Of course, it is well known that Wilson endorsed and viewed in the White House the 1915 racist movie about Reconstruction, '*Birth of a Nation*,' directed by D. W. Griffith.

38. Derek Heater, *National Self-Determination: Woodrow Wilson and His Legacy* (New York: St. Martin's Press, 1994), pp. 24–5.

39. Renda, *Taking Haiti*, pp. 110–11.

40. Renda, *Taking Haiti*, pp. 11–14, 113–15; Girard, *Clinton in Haiti*, p. 18; Schmidt, *The United States Occupation of Haiti, 1915–34*, pp. 48, 111; Ferguson, *Colossus*, pp. 49–52; and Healy, *Drive to Hegemony*, p. 71.

41. Renda, *Taking Haiti*, pp. 93, 99, 100 (all quotations from these pages).

42. Wilson quoted in Arthur S. Link, *Woodrow Wilson and the Progressive Era, 1910–1917* (New York: Harper Torchbooks, 1954), pp. 119, 281; and Ferguson, *Colossus*, pp. 57–60. See text of the June 1, 2002, Bush address to West Point Academy; text of the Bush address to the American Enterprise Institute, February 26, 2003; and text of the November 6, 2003, address on the twentieth anniversary of the National Endowment for Democracy – all in online version of the *New York Times*.

43. Spalding, "True Believers," p. 41 (quotations).

44. Gaddis Smith, *The Last Years of the Monroe Doctrine*, pp. 28–9; Arthur P. Whitaker, *The Western Hemisphere Idea: Its Rise and Decline* (Ithaca, NY: Cornell University Press, 1954), p. 123 (second quotation); and Charles Seymour, *The Intimate Papers of Colonel House: Arranged as a Narrative* (Boston: Houghton Mifflin, 1926), vol. 1, pp. 207–34 (first quotation at 233, third at 221, 224–5).

45. Link, *PWW* (1982), 40: 533–53; Lloyd E. Ambrosius, *Wilsonian Statecraft: Theory and Practice of Liberal Internationalism during World War I* (Wilmington, DE: SR Books, 1991), pp. 38, 55–8, 70–1.

46. Seymour, *The Intimate Papers of Colonel House*, pp. 219, 232–3; Smith, *Last Years of the Monroe Doctrine*, pp. 29 (quotations), 30–1; and Margaret MacMillan, *Paris 1919: Six Months That Changed the World* (New York: Random House, 2001), pp. 95–6. For the roots of the rational realism of TR's foreign policy compared to Wilson's idealism, see Kathleen Dalton, *Theodore Roosevelt: A Strenuous Life* (New York: Knopf, 2003).

47. Derek Heater, *National Self-Determination: Woodrow Wilson and His Legacy* (New York: St. Martin's Press, 1994), p. 25; and Purvis M. Carter, *Congressional and Public Reactions to Wilson's Caribbean Policy, 1913–1917* (New York: Vantage Press, 1977), pp. 118–20, passim.

48. Smith, *Last Years of the Monroe Doctrine*, pp. 8–9, 28–9; Walter LaFeber, "The Evolution of the Monroe Doctrine from Monroe to Reagan," in Lloyd C. Gardner, ed., *Redefining the Past: Essays in Diplomatic History in Honor of William Appleman Williams* (Corvalis: Oregon State University Press, 1986), pp. 121–41; and John P. Vloyantes, "Spheres of Influence: A Framework for Analysis" (Tucson: Institute of Government Research, University of Arizona, 1970, typed manuscript), pp. 15–16.

Chapter 2: The Faustian Impact of World War I on U.S. Diplomacy

1. Arthur S. Link et al., eds., *The Papers of Woodrow Wilson* (Princeton, NJ: Princeton University Press, 1981), 36: 213–14 [hereinafter Link, *PWW*, year published and volume]. Link acknowledges that "this was President Wilson's most important pronouncement on American neutral rights and duties," but then denies that it represented a non-negotiable position that put the United States on a collusion course with Germany.

2. N. Gordon Levin, Jr., *Woodrow Wilson and World Politics: America's Response to War and Revolution* (New York: Oxford University Press, 1968), pp. 247–8 (quoting the December 1918 memorandum); Robert Lansing, *The Peace Negotiations: A Personal Narrative* (Boston: Houghton Mifflin, 1921), pp. 96–7; David Callahan, *Unwinnable Wars: American Power and Ethnic Conflict* (New York: Hill and Wang, 1997), p. 12 (last Lansing quotation).

3. For a list of Wilson's additional thirteen points, see Arthur S. Link, *Wilson the Diplomatist: A Look at His Major Foreign Policies* (Chicago: Quadrangle Books, 1963; reprint of the original 1957 edition), p. 107, note 13.

4. For details about the "magnitude of Polish suffering – only rivaled by Serbia, and far surpassing the better-known distress of Belgium," see M. B. Biskupski, "The Diplomacy of Wartime Relief: The United States and Poland, 1914–1918," *Diplomatic History* 19, no. 3 (Summer 1995): 431–51.

5. Derek Heater, *National Self-Determination: Woodrow Wilson and His Legacy* (New York: St. Martin's Press, 1994), pp. 32–43 (first quotation at 43); Robert M. Saunders, *In Search of Woodrow Wilson: Beliefs and Behavior* (Westport, CT: Greenwood Press, 1998), pp. 130–1 (other Wilson quotations).

6. Heater, *National Self-Determination*, pp. 32–43 (quotations at 36–7); George F. Kennan, *The Decision to Intervene* (New York: Atheneum, 1967); and Matthew Stachiw, *Ukraine and the European Turmoil, 1917–1919* (Toronto: Harmony Printing, 1973), p. 176.

7. Heater, *National Self-Determination*, pp. 89–108 (quotation at 93).

8. N. Gordon Levin, Jr., *Woodrow Wilson and the World Politics: America's Response to War and Revolution* (New York: Oxford University Press, 1968), p. 248 (first quotation); Margaret MacMillan, *Paris 1919: Six Months That Changed the World* (New York: Random House, 2001), pp. 12 (second quotation)–13 (third quotation), 486–7; and A. Sharp, "The Genie That Would Not Go Back into the Bottle: National Self-Determination and the Legacy of the First World War and the Peace Settlement," in S. Dunn and T. G. Fraser, eds., *Europe and Ethnicity: The First World War and Contemporary Ethnic Conflict* (London: Routledge, 1996), pp. 10–29.

9. The phrase "unredeemably stupid fatality" comes from the Hannah Arendt's description of global war in the twentieth century: "Nothing which was being done, no matter how stupid, no matter how many people knew and foretold the consequences, could be undone or prevented. Every event had the finality of a last judgment, a judgment that was passed neither by God nor by the devil, but looked rather like the expression of some unredeemable stupid fatality." (Quoted in Jonathan Schell, "No More unto the Breach," *Harper's Magazine*, March 2003, p. 34.) The second quotation about the First World War being the "greatest error of modern history" comes from Niall Ferguson, *The Pity of War: Explaining World War I* (New York: Basic Books, 1999), p. 462, and the third from the Carnegie Commission on

Preventing Deadly Conflict, *Preventing Deadly Conflict: Final Report with Executive Summary* (Washington, DC: Carnegie Commission, 1997), p. 13.

10. Burns, "Disturbed Spirits: Minority Rights and New World Orders, 1919 and the 1990s," p. 42 (quotation); Amitai Etzioni, "The Evils of Self-Determination," *Foreign Policy* 89 (Winter 1992–93): 21–35; Niall Ferguson, "The Next War of the World," *Foreign Affairs* 85, no. 5 (September/October, 2006): 61–3; and Jonathan Glover, *Humanity: A Moral History of the Twentieth Century* (New Haven: Yale University Press, 1999), pp. 41–2.

11. Walter A. McDougall, "How – and How Not – to End Wars," *Foreign Policy Research WIRE* 8, no. 4 (October 2000), np.

12. Link, *PWW* (1984), 45: 551; Heckscher, *Woodrow Wilson*, pp. 446–8; and Spalding, "True Believers," pp. 41, 48 (quotations).

13. MacMillan, *Paris 1919*, 465; and Ferguson, *The Pity of War*, pp. 439–41.

14. Link, *PWW* (1984), 45: 551; and McDougall, "How – and How Not – to End Wars," np; MacMillan, *Paris 1919*, pp. 193, 466–7.

15. Vahakn N. Dadrian, "Genocide as a Problem of National and International Law: The World War I Armenian Case and Its Contemporary Legal Ramifications," *The Yale Journal of International Law* 14, no. 2 (Summer 1989): 238–52; Christopher J. Walker, ed., *Armenia and Karabagh: The Struggle for Unity* (London: Minority Rights Publications, 1991), pp. 21–5; and Permanent Peoples' Tribunal [hereinafter PPT], *A Crime of Silence: The Armenian Genocide* (London: Zed Books, 1985), pp. 213–14.

16. L. P. Mair, *The Protection of Minorities: The Working and Scope of the Minority Treaties under the League of Nations* (London: Christophers, 1928), p. 217; Walker, *Armenia and Karabagh*, pp. 24–9; and Paul Glastris, "Armenia's History, Turkey's Dilemma," *Washington Post*, March 11, 2001, pp. B1, B4.

17. Link, *PWW* (1984), 45: 417, 419, 459 (note 1), 472; and 56: 127 (quotation).

18. Link, *PWW* (1990), 62: 116, 241, 259–60, 285.

19. Heater, *National Self-Determination*, p. 93; Paul C. Helmreich, *From Paris to Sèvres: The Partition of the Ottoman Empire at the Peace Conference of 1919–1920* (Columbus: Ohio State University Press, 1974), pp. 64–82; Harry N. Howard, *An American Inquiry in the Middle East: The King-Crane Commission* (Beirut: Khayats, 1963), pp. 38–41, 90, (note 1), 91, 133–5; and MacMillan, *Paris 1919*, pp. 233, 406, 422 (quotation), 423.

20. MacMillan, *Paris 1919*, pp. 422–3 (quotation); Howard, *An American Inquiry in the Middle East: The King-Crane Commission*, pp. 178–81, 311–13; and Charles R. Crane and Henry C. King, "Recommendations of the King-Crane Commission," p. 358. Although the report was sent to the State Department, its contents remained unknown to the public until September 1922, when it appeared, with Wilson's permission, as a supplement to *Editor & Publisher*. For details, see Link, *PWW* (1990), 62: 607–8, note 1.

21. John Milton Cooper, Jr., *Breaking the Heart of the World: Woodrow Wilson an the Fight for the League of Nations* (Cambridge: Cambridge University Press, 2001), pp. 341–2 (note 21), 379–80; and Link, *PWW* (1992), 66: 421–8, 444, 489–90.

22. Cooper, *Breaking the Heart of the World*, p. 380, note 7; Link, *PWW* (1992), 66: 421–3, note 2 (quotations at 422 and 444, 490, 517–18); Henry Morgenthau, *Ambassador Morgenthau's Story* (Plandome, NY: New Age Publishers, 1975; reprint of the 1919 Doubleday, Page, and Co. edition), pp. 308, 321–2; and Vigen Guroian, "Politics and Morality of Genocide," in Richard G. Hovannisian, ed.,

The Armenian Genocide: History, Politics, Ethics (New York: St. Martin's Press, 1992), p. 312 (second quotation).

23. Link, *PWW* (1992), 66: 421–3, 427–8, 444, 489, 490, 517; Mair, *Protection of Minorities*, pp. 46–8, 216–18; Cooper, *Breaking the Heart of the World*, pp. 341–3, 379–80; Lawrence Evans, *United States Policy and the Partition of Turkey, 1914–1924* (Baltimore: Johns Hopkins University Press, 1965), pp. 269–91; Heater, *National Self-Determination*, pp. 69–70; and MacMillan, *Paris 1919*, pp. 426–55.

24. Link, *PWW* (1992), 66: 65, 86, 110, 350, 357; and Cooper, *Breaking the Heart of the World*, pp. 2–3, 341–2.

25. Heckscher, *Wilson*, pp. 585, 608–9; PPT, *A Crime of Silence*, pp. 217–18; Mair, *Protection of Minorities*, pp. 46–7, 216–18 (quoting Kemal); Walker, *Armenia and Karabagh*, pp. 32–5; and Evans, *United States Policy and the Partition of Turkey, 1914–1924*, pp. 289–91, 376–417. Wilson expressed his antipathy toward the former Allies to his third secretary of state, Bainbridge Colby, especially toward the British and French, as early as the spring of 1920, when he refused to allow the United States to be represented other than as an observer at the San Remo meeting of Allied premiers in April 1920. See Daniel M. Smith, *Aftermath of War: Bainbridge Colby and Wilsonian Diplomacy* (Philadelphia: American Philosophical Society, 1970), pp. 40–1; Guroian, "Politics and Morality of Genocide," pp. 315, 337 (note 10); MacMillan, *Paris 1919*, p. 453; and Susan Sachs, "Some Hard-Liners in Turkey See Diversity as Divisive," *New York Times*, November 21, 2004.

26. Annette Höss, "The Trail of Perpetrators by the Turkish Military Tribunals," in Hovannisian, ed., *The Armenian Genocide*, pp. 210, 219, Vahakn N. Dadrian; "Ottoman Archives and Denial of the Armenian," in ibid., p. 303; and Susan Sachs, "Some Hard-Liners in Turkey See Diversity as Divisive," *New York Times*, November 21, 2004.

27. Guroian, "Politics and Morality of Genocide," p. 312 (quoting Hitler).

28. David S. Foglesong, *America's Secret War against Bolshevism* (Chapel Hill: University of North Carolina Press, 1995), pp. 24–8, 32–46.

29. Heater, *National Self-Determination*, pp. 82–4; and Lloyd E. Ambrosius, *Woodrow Wilson and the American Diplomatic Tradition: The Treaty Fight in Perspective* (New York: Cambridge University Press, 1987), p. 178 (quotations).

30. Georg Schild, *Between Ideology and Realpolitik: Woodrow Wilson and the Russian Revolution, 1917–21* (Westport, CT: Greenwood Press, 1995), pp. 69–90; Frederick S. Calhoun, *Uses of Force and Wilsonian Foreign Policy* (Kent, OH: Kent State University Press, 1993), pp. 113–23; Lloyd C. Gardner, *Woodrow Wilson and Revolutions, 1913–1921* (Lanham, MD: University Press of America, 1976), pp. 42–6, 124–8; Foglesong, *America's Secret War against Bolshevism*, pp. 189–218; and David Steigerwald, "The Reclamation of Woodrow Wilson?," in Michael J. Hogan, *Paths to Power: The Historiography of American Foreign Relations to 1941* (New York: Cambridge University Press, 2000), pp. 148–73.

31. Norman E. Saul, *War and Revolution: The United States and Russia, 1914–1921* (Lawrence: University Press of Kansas, 2001), p. 169, passim; Joan Hoff Wilson, *Ideology and Economics: U.S. Relations with the Soviet Union, 1918–1933* (Columbia: University of Missouri Press, 1974), p. 16; Saunders, *In Search of Woodrow Wilson*, pp. 130–1.

32. Foglesong, *America's Secret War against Bolshevism*, passim; Steigerwald, "The Reclamation of Woodrow Wilson?," pp. 159–65; Betty Miller Unterberger, *America's Siberian Expedition, 1918–1920* (New York: Greenwood Press, 1969, reprint

of the original 1956 Duke University Press edition), pp. 86–8, 230–8; idem, *The United States, Revolutionary Russia, and the Rise of Czechoslovakia* (Chapel Hill: University of North Carolina Press, 1989), passim; Lloyd C. Gardner, *Safe for Democracy: The Anglo-American Response to Revolution, 1913–1923* (New York: Oxford Univerisity Press, 1984), pp. 125–202; John Bradley, *Allied Intervention in Russia* (London: Wiederfeld & Nicholson, 1968), p. 214; Levin, *Woodrow Wilson and World Politics*, pp. 87–119; Daniel M. Smith, *Aftermath of War: Bainbridge Colby and Wilsonian Diplomacy, 1920–1921* (Philadelphia: American Philosophical Society, 1970), pp. 20–1, 55, 61–70; and Hoff Wilson, *Ideology and Economics*, pp. 14–18.

33. For more details about the "Colby Note," see Hoff Wilson, *Ideology and Economics*, pp. 14–18 (all quotations).

34. Ibid., p. 18 (first quotation); and Saul, *War and Revolution*, p. 307 (second quotation).

35. Jacob Robinson et al., *Were the Minority Treaties a Failure?* (New York: Institute of Jewish Affairs, 1943), pp. 4–41; Fink, "The League of Nations and the Minority Question," p. 204, note 2; and Heater, *National Self-Determination*, pp. 84–9.

36. Heater, *National Self-Determination*, p. 93 (quotation); Chistoph M. Kimmich, *Germany and the League of Nations* (Chicago: University of Chicago Press, 1975), pp. 131–49; and Carole Fink, "The League of Nations and the Minority Question," *World Affairs* 157 (Spring 1995): 197–205.

37. Danilo Türk, "Protection of Minorities in Europe," in *Collected Course of the Academy of European Law*, vol. 3, book 2 (The Netherlands: Kluwer, 1994), pp. 155–60; and Fink, "The League of Nations and the Minority Question," p. 198.

38. Sterling J. Kernek, "Woodrow Wilson and National Self-determination along Italy's Frontier: A Study of the Manipulation of Principles in the Pursuit of Political Interests," *Proceedings of the American Philosophical Society* 126, no. 4 (August 1982): 243–300; and Elizabeth F. Defeis, "Minority Protections and Bilateral Agreements: An Effective Mechanism," *Hastings International and Comparative Law Review* 22, no. 2 (Winter 1999): 291–321.

39. Defeis, "Minority Protections and Bilateral Agreements," pp. 298–301.

40. Türk, "Protection of Minorities in Europe," pp. 161–6, passim; and MacMillan, *Paris 1919*, pp. 486–7.

41. Fogleson, *America's Secret War against Bolshevism*, p. 298 (first set of quotations); and Amos Perlmutter, *Making the World Safe for Democracy: A Century of Wilsonianism and Its Totalitarian Challengers* (Chapel Hill: University of North Carolina Press, 1997), pp. x, 5, 30, 33, 166.

42. Ninkovich, *The Wilsonian Century*, pp. 77–8; Ronald Steel, "Mr. Fix-It," *New York Review of Books*, October 5, 2000, p. 19; and John B. Judis, "Beyond National Interest," *The New Republic*, online edition, June 21, 1999, www.thenewrepublic. com.

43. Thomas Borstelmann, "Jim Crow's Coming Out: Race Relations and American Foreign Policy in the Truman Years," *Presidential Studies Quarterly* 29 (September 1999): 550.

44. Ninkovich, *The Wilsonian Century*, p. 49 (first quotation); Heater, *National Self-Determination*, p. 117. For other criticism of the ambiguousness of Wilson's views on self-determination and European ethnicity, see D. Perman, *The Shaping of the Czechoslovak State* (Leiden: E. J. Brill, 1962), pp. 139 (second quotation), 206;

and John Maynard Keynes, *The Economic Consequences of the Peace* (London: Macmillan, 1919; 1971 edition), p. 27.

45. Alfred E. Eckes, Jr., and Thomas W. Zeiler, *Globalization and the American Century* (New York: Cambridge University Press, 2003), pp. 38 (quotation)–45.

46. Eckes and Zeiler, *Globalization and the American Century*, pp. 53–5; Joan Hoff Wilson, *American Business and Foreign Policy, 1920–1933* (Lexington: The University Press of Kentucky, 1971), p. 22 (quotation); and William O. Walker III, "Crucible for Peace: Herbert Hoover, Modernization, and Economic Growth in Latin America," *Diplomatic History* 30, no. 1 (January 2006): 83–90.

47. Eckes and Zeiler, *Globalization and the American Century*, pp. 53–8 (quotation at 55); and Hoff Wilson, *American Business and Foreign Policy*, pp. xv–xvii, 20–5, 42.

48. Michael H. Hunt, *The Making of a Special Relationship: The United States and China to 1914* (New York: Columbia University Press, 1983), pp. 153–4.

49. Frank Ninkovich, *The United States and Imperialism* (Oxford: Blackwell, 2001), pp. 91–152 and map; Walter LaFeber, *The American Age: U.S. Foreign Policy at Home and Abroad*, 2nd ed. (New York: Norton, 1994), p. 283 (map); idem, *The American Search for Opportunity, 1865–1913* (Cambridge: Cambridge University Press, 1993), pp. xiii, 6–7, 134–6, 235–6; and Stephen Kinzer, "U.S. and Central America: Too Close for Comfort," *New York Times*, WK, July 28, 2002, p. 14 (quotation).

50. John P. Vloyantes, "Spheres of Influence: A Framework for Analysis" (Tucson: Institute of Government Research, University of Arizona, 1970, typed manuscript), pp. 13–14; idem, *Velvet Glove Hegemony* (Kent, OH: Kent State University Press, 1975); and Joseph S. Nye, Jr., *The Paradox of American Power: Why the World's Only Superpower Can't Go It Alone* (New York: Oxford University Press, 2002), pp. 9–12, 176, (notes 29, 31). Nye claims to have coined the term "soft power" in a book published in 1990, but Vloyantes appears to have originated it back in the 1970s.

51. Heater, *National Self-Determination*, pp. 25, 32 (last quotation, Wilson replying to Pope Benedict XV's appeal for peace after the United States entered World War I). Also see Thomas J. Knock, *To End All Wars: Woodrow Wilson and the Quest for a New World Order* (New York: Oxford University Press, 1992), pp. 34–5, 42–3, 56–7, 249–50; Arthur Walworth, *America's Moment, 1918: American Diplomacy at the End of World War I* (New York: Norton, 1977), pp. 172–94; Lloyd E. Ambrosius, "Wilsonian Self-Determination," *Diplomatic History* 16 (Winter 1992): 141–8. For a more positive view of Wilson's definition and practice of self-determination, see Betty Unterberger, "The United States and National Self-Determination: A Wilsonian Perspective," *Presidential Studies Quarterly* 26 (Fall 1996): 926–41.

52. Jason Knirch, *Woodrow Wilson and the Irish Case for Self-Determination, 1914–1920* (Pullman: Washington State University Press, 1986), p. 83 (quotation); and MacMillan, *Paris 1919*, pp. 11–14, 486–7. For other similar statements by Wilson about the right of people to choose their governments, see Niall Ferguson, *The Pity of War: Explaining World War I* (New York: Basic Books, 1998), p. 439; and Thomas J. Knock, *To End All Wars: Woodrow Wilson and the Quest for a New World Order* (New York: Oxford University Press, 1992), pp. 35, 77, 113, 152.

53. Knirch, *Woodrow Wilson and the Irish Case for Self-Determination*, pp. 9, 94, 123, passim.

54. Foglesong, *America's Secret War against Bolshevism*, pp. 31–2 (quotation), 37–8, 41; and Robert M. Saunders, *In Search of Woodrow Wilson: Belief and Behavior* (Westport, CT: Greenwood Press, 1998), pp. 25–6, 441–2, 54–5, 69, 77.

Chapter 3: The Faustian Aspects of Prosperity, Depression, and War

1. Joan Hoff Wilson, *American Business and Foreign Policy, 1920–1933* (Lexington: The University Press of Kentucky, 1971), pp. 123–218, 239.
2. Ibid., pp. 51–9, 227–8, 235–6; and Gaddis Smith, *The Last Years of the Monroe Doctrine, 1945–1993* (New York: Hill and Wang, 1994), pp. 32–3 (quotation).
3. Alfred E. Eckes, Jr., and Thomas W. Zeiler, *Globalization and the American Century* (New York: Cambridge University Press, 2003), pp. 73–4; Melvyn P. Leffler, "1921–1932: Expansionist Impulses and Domestic Constraints," in William H. Becker and Samuel F. Wells, Jr., eds., *Economics and World Power: An Assessment of American Diplomacy since 1789* (New York: Columbia University Press, 1984), pp. 244–6; and Frederick C. Adams, *Economic Diplomacy: The Export-Import Bank and American Foreign Policy* (Columbia: University of Missouri Press, 1976), pp. 1–40.
4. Eckes and Zeiler, *Globalization and the American Century*, pp. 74–5; and Hoff Wilson, *American Business and Foreign Policy*, pp. 11–12, 99, 123–4.
5. Hoff Wilson, *American Business and Foreign Policy*, pp. 101–12 (quotations); William O. Walker III, "Crucible for Peace: Herbert Hoover, Moderization, and Economic Growth in Latin America," *Diplomatic History* 30, no. 1 (January 2006): 98–9; and Adams, *Economic Diplomacy*, pp. 9–10, 31–2, 255.
6. Hoff Wilson, *American Business and Foreign Policy*, pp. 167–8; Eckes and Zeiler, *Globalization and the American Century*, pp. 74–7; Thomas F. O'Brien, *The Revolutionary Mission: American Enterprise in Latin America, 1900–1945* (Cambridge: Cambridge University Press, 1996), pp. 33–6, 51 (note 10), 68–70, 80–1, 163–4, 205–29, 253–4, 283–4, 317–18; Walker, "Crucible for Peace, pp. 91–4; Benjamin H. Williams, *Economic Foreign Policy of the United States* (New York: McGraw-Hill, 1929), pp. 175–216.
7. Hoff Wilson, *American Business and Foreign Policy*, pp. 12, 105–6, 119–22, 170–83.
8. Ibid., pp. 123–56.
9. Howard H. Quint and Robert H. Ferrell, eds., *The Talkative President: The Off-the-Record Press Conferences of Calvin Coolidge* (Amherst: The University of Massachusetts Press, 1964), pp. 175, 178; Adams, *Economic Diplomacy*, pp. 16–20, 47–8; and Niall Ferguson, *The Pity of War: Explaining World War I* (New York: Basic Books, 1999), pp. 395–432, 439 (quotation). The total owed the United States by 1920 included money lent to such European succession states as Austria and Hungary and the $636 million lent to Russia before the Bolshevik Revolution. It did not include the $1.7 million loaned to Europe by Americans through Liberty and Victory Loans bonds. By November 1925, accrued interest had increased Allied indebtedness to $12,088,885,709. See Williams, *Economic Foreign Policy of the United States*, p. 232 (table).
10. Quint and Ferrell, eds., *The Talkative President*, pp. 151–2, 174–6; and Hoff Wilson, *American Business and Foreign Policy*, p. 126.
11. Hoff Wilson, *American Business and Foreign Policy*, pp. 126–7, 134–44; Eckes and Zeiler, *Globalization and the American Century*, pp. 83–4; and Adams, *Economic Diplomacy*, pp. 19–20.

12. Williams, *Economic Foreign Policy of the United States*, pp. 232 (table), 237–8.
13. Dallek, *Franklin D. Roosevelt and American Foreign Policy* (New York: Oxford University Press, 1995), pp. 91–3 (quotation).
14. Eckes and Zeiler, *Globalization and the American Century*, pp. 81–2 (quotations).
15. Smith, *The Last Years of the Monroe Doctrine, 1945–1993*, pp. 33 (first quotation)– 34; and Arthur S. Link et al., eds., *The Papers of Woodrow Wilson* (Princeton, NJ: Princeton University Press, 1992), 66: 183; 67: 385 (quotation to Colby) [hereinafter Link, *PWW*, year published and volume].
16. Hoff Wilson, *American Business and Foreign Policy*, pp. 162–7; idem, *Herbert Hoover: Forgotten Progressive* (Prospect Heights, IL: Waveland Press, 1992; reprint of the original 1975 edition), pp. 199–202; and Walker, "Crucible for Peace," pp. 83–117 (quotations at 87–8, 89–90, and 116).
17. Walker, "Crucible for Peace, pp. 86, 89–90, 97, 107, 110–17; Hoff Wilson, *Herbert Hoover*, pp. 200–2; and idem, *American Business and Foreign Policy*, pp. 175–7.
18. Ibid.
19. Walker, "Crucible for Peace," pp. 105–6; and Hoff Wilson, *American Business and Foreign Policy*, pp. 175–6.
20. David M. Kennedy, *Freedom from Fear: The American People in Depression and War, 1929–1945* (New York: Oxford University Press, 1999), pp. 391–2; Irwin F. Gellman, *Good Neighbor Diplomacy: United States Policies in Latin America* (Baltimore: Johns Hopkins University Press, 1979), passim; and Hoff Wilson, *American Business and Foreign Policy*, p. 169 (quotation).
21. Hoff Wilson, *American Business and Foreign Policy*, p. 169 (first three quotations); Kennedy, *Freedom from Fear*, p. 392 (fourth and fifth quotations); Lloyd C. Gardner, *Economic Aspects of New Deal Diplomacy* (Madison: University of Wisconsin Press, 1964), pp. 47, 61; Bryce Wood, *The Making of the Good Neighbor Policy* (New York: Columbia University Press, 1961), pp. 129–31; Smith, *Last Years of the Monroe Doctrine*, pp. 34–5; Federick W. Marks III, *Wind over Sand: The Diplomacy of Franklin Roosevelt* (Athens: University of Georgia Press, 1988), pp. 217–50; and Frederick B. Pike, *FDR's Good Neighbor Policy: Sixty Years of Generally Gentle Chaos* (Austin: University of Texas Press, 1995), passim.
22. Pike, *FDR's Good Neighbor Policy*, pp. 228–75; and Hoff Wilson, *American Business and Foreign Policy*, pp. 170–1 (quotation).
23. Pike, *FDR's Good Neighbor Policy*, pp. 245–50; Hoff Wilson, *American Business and Foreign Policy*, pp. 170–1; and Smith, *The Last Years of the Monroe Doctrine, 1945–1993*, pp. 32–5.
24. Kennedy, *Freedom from Fear*, pp. 143–4, 154–7, 388; Barry Eichengreen, *Golden Fetters: The Gold Standard and the Great Depression, 1919–1939* (New York: Oxford University Press, 1995), pp. 323–47; Charles P. Kindleberger, *The World in Depression, 1929–39* (Berkeley: University of California Press, 1986), pp. 191–231; Marks, *Wind over Sand*, pp. 21–6; and Dallek, *Roosevelt and American Foreign Policy*, pp. 49–56.
25. Eckes and Zeiler, *Globalization and the American Century*, pp. 82–5.
26. Dallek, *Roosevelt and American Foreign Policy*, pp. 102–6; and Kennedy, *Freedom from Fear*, pp. 394–5.
27. Hoff Wilson, *American Business and Foreign Policy*, pp. 219–21; idem, *Herbert Hoover*, pp. 204–8; and Kennedy, *Freedom from Fear*, pp. 93–4.
28. Hoff Wilson, *American Business and Foreign Policy*, pp. 221–4, 230–2.

29. Marks, *Wind over Sand*, pp. 42, 46; and Irvine H. Anderson, Jr., *The Standard-Vacuum Oil Company and United States East Asian Policy, 1933–1941* (Princeton, NJ: Princeton University Press, 1975), pp. 71–103, 455.

30. Hoff Wilson, *American Business and Foreign Policy*, pp. 209–18; Marks, *Wind over Sand*, pp. 46, 311–12 (note 14); and Hadley Cantril, "Opinion Trends in World War II: Some Guides to Interpretation," *Public Opinion Quarterly* 12 (1948): 36–7.

31. Paul W. Schroeder, *The Axis Alliance and Japanese-American Relations, 1941* (Ithaca, NY: Cornell University Press, 1958), pp. 1–28.

32. Ibid., pp. 19–20, 125.

33. Joan Hoff, "All Presidents Lie about Going to War," *Progressive Review*, June 2003; and Norman Solomon, *War Made Easy: How Presidents and Pundits Keep Spinning Us to Death* (New York: Wiley, 2005), passim.

34. For a list of FDR's misstatements, exaggerations, and lies between 1933 and 1945, see Marks, *Wind over Sand*, pp. 304–5, note 23; and Eric Alterman, *When Presidents Lie: A History of Official Deception and Its Consequences* (New York: Penguin, 2005), pp. 23–46.

35. Cantril, "Opinion Trends in World War II, pp. 36–7.

36. Kennedy, *Freedom from Fear*, pp. 514–15; Anderson, *The Standard-Vacuum Oil Company*, pp. 39–43, 103, 105; Hoff Wilson, *American Business and Foreign Policy*, pp. 200–21; and Adams, *Economic Diplomacy*, pp. 226–49.

37. Howard Jablon, "Cordell Hull, His 'Associates,' and Relations with Japan, 1933–1936," *Mid-America* 56 (July 1974): 160–75 (first quotation at 171); Smith, *The Last Years of the Monroe Doctrine, 1945–1993*, p. 35 (second quotation).

38. Schroeder, *The Axis Alliance and Japanese-American Relations*, p. 170; Anderson, *The Standard-Vacuum Oil Company*, pp. 103, 116–17; Marks, *Wind over Sand*, pp. 42–3; Noam Chomsky, "The Fire This Time," *Ramparts* 5 (April 1967): 48 (first quotation); and Smith, *The Last Years of the Monroe Doctrine, 1945–1993*, p. 35 (second quotation).

39. The inevitability of war with Japan by 1940 is a still the standard interpretation and can be found in Dallek, *Roosevelt and American Foreign Policy*, p. 97. Even though revisionist scholarship has cast serious doubt on this interpretation, the latest example of it can still be found in Kennedy, *Freedom from Fear*, pp. 465–515.

40. Schroeder, *The Axis Alliance and Japanese-American Relations, 1941*, pp. 202–16.

41. Marks, *Wind over Sand*, p. 83; Kennedy, *Freedom from Fear*, pp. 505–6; and Anderson, *The Standard-Vacuum Oil Company*, pp. 123, 191 (quotation).

42. Marks, *Wind over Sand*, pp. 100–1; and Kennedy, *Freedom from Fear*, pp. 510–11.

43. Anderson, *The Standard-Vacuum Oil Company*, pp. 174–91 (quotation).

44. Anderson, *The Standard-Vacuum Oil Company*, pp. 4, 32–8, 79–103. Anderson's book remains the best source for the details about the close cooperation between Stanvac, Shell, and the Anglo-American diplomatic corps and their dominant influence on U.S. Far Eastern policy.

45. Ibid., pp. 168–71 (quotation).

46. Ibid., pp. 168–71, 191; and Schroeder, *The Axis Alliance and Japanese-American Relations, 1941*, pp. 180–2.

47. Anderson, *The Standard-Vacuum Oil Company*, p. 122; Schroeder, *The Axis Alliance and Japanese-American Relations, 1941*, pp. 183–5; Cantril, "Opinion Trends in World War II," pp. 36–7; and Wayne S. Cole, *Roosevelt and the Isolationists, 1932–45* (Lincoln: University of Nebraska Press, 1983), pp. 12–13, 364.

48. Kennedy, *Freedom from Fear*, pp. 506–15; Marks, *Wind over Sand*, pp. 97–119; and Peter Mauch, "Revisiting Nomura's Role in the Japanese-American Negotiations, 1941," *Diplomatic History* 28, no. 3 (June 2004): 353–83.

49. Kennedy, *Freedom from Fear*, pp. 514–15 (quotation); Dallek, *Roosevelt and American Foreign Policy*, p. 305; and Marks, *Wind over Sand*, pp. 108–19.

50. Schroeder, *The Axis Alliance and Japanese-American Relations, 1941*, pp. 85–7; Kennedy, *Freedom from Fear*, pp. 515, 519–20.

51. Richard F. Hill, "Hitler's Misunderstood Declaration of War," *SHAFR Newsletter*, June 2002; and idem, *Hitler Attacks Pearl Harbor: Why the US Declared War on Germany* (Boulder, CO: Lynne Riener, 2003).

52. Kennedy, *Freedom from Fear*, p. 496. Kennedy notes that FDR and Churchill had actually met casually for the first time in July 1919, but neither apparently remembered the encounter (p. 6, note 11).

53. Dallek, *Roosevelt and American Foreign Policy*, pp. 281–4; Cordell Hull, *Memoirs* (New York: Macmillan, 1948), vol. 2, p. 975; and Kennedy, *Freedom from Fear*, p. 496.

54. Kennedy, *Freedom from Fear*, pp. 575, 586–8; and Dallek, *Roosevelt and American Foreign Policy*, pp. 373–6.

55. Kennedy, *Freedom from Fear*, pp. 670–4 (quotation at 673).

56. Kennedy, *Freedom from Fear*, pp. 669–70, 673–4; Lloyd C. Gardner, *Spheres of Influence: The Great Powers Partition Europe, from Munich to Yalta* (Chicago: Ivan R. Dee, 1993), pp. 173–6.

57. Kennedy, *Freedom from Fear*, pp. 674–86; and Gardner, *Spheres of Influence*, pp. 172–6, 184–5.

58. Jacob Heilbrunn, "Once Again, the Big Yalta Lie," *Los Angeles Times*, May 10, 2005. For the complete text of the much-maligned Yalta agreement, see "Protocol of Proceedings of Crimea Conference, March 24, 1945, <http://www.fordham.edu/halsall/mod/1945YALTA.html>.

59. Kennedy, *Freedom from Fear*, pp. 800–7; Dallek, *Roosevelt and American Foreign Policy*, pp. 506–25; and Marks, *Wind over Sand*, pp. 175–6, 189–90.

60. Sheldon L. Richman, "'Ancient History': U.S. Conduct in the Middle East since World War II and the Folly of Intervention," Cato Policy Analysis no. 159, August 16, 1991.

61. Robert Baer, *Sleeping with the Devil: How Washington Sold Our Soul for Saudi Crude* (New York: Three Rivers Press, 2003), pp. 73–84; Dilip Hiro, "Playing the Democracy Card: How America Furthers Its National Interests in the Middle East"(Hull quotation), March 17, 2005, posted on TomDispatch.com.

Chapter 4: Faustian Aspects of U.S. Cold War Foreign Policy

1. For the complete text of Luce's lengthy, celebratory proclamation in *American Century*, see Michael J. Hogan, ed., *The Ambiguous Legacy: U.S. Foreign Relations in the "American Century"* (Cambridge: Cambridge University Press, 1999), pp. 11–29. Also see Blanche Wiesen Cook, "'Turn toward Peace': ER and Foreign Affairs," in Joan Hoff-Wilson and Marjorie Lightman, eds., *Without Precedent: Eleanor Roosevelt* (Bloomington: Indiana University Press, 1984), p. 117; and Alan Brinkley, "For America, It Truly Was a Great War," *New York Times Magazine*, May 7, 1995, p. 57.

2. Cook, "'Turn toward Peace': ER and Foreign Affairs," p. 117.

3. Ibid.
4. Brinkley, "For America, It Truly Was a Great War," p. 57.
5. Gore Vidal, "The Menopause of Empire," *The Progressive*, May 1998, p. 21 (Wallace quotation); John Fousek, *To Lead the Free World: American Nationalism and the Cultural Roots of the Cold War* (Chapel Hill: University of North Carolina Press, 2000), pp. 120–4; Daniel Yergin, *Shattered Peace: The Origins of the Cold War and the National Security State* (Boston, MA: Houghton Mifflin, 1977); Joan Hoff, "The Foreign Policy of Eleanor Roosevelt," in Maurine Beasley and Holly Shulman, eds., *The Eleanor Roosevelt Encyclopedia* (Westport, CT: Greenwood, 2001), pp. 195–8; and Allida M. Black, *Casting Her Own Shadow: Eleanor Roosevelt and the Shaping of Postwar Liberalism* (New York: Columbia University Press, 1997), pp. 4, 78–9, 81, 83–4, 138, 166.
6. Fredrik Logevall, "A Critique of Containment," *Diplomatic History* 28, no. 4 (September 2004): 473–99, especially 476, note 5, and 496–9 (Wallace quotation at 476 and last one at 473); and Arnold A. Offner, *Another Such Victory: President Truman and the Cold War, 1945–1953* (Stanford, CA: Stanford University Press, 2002), pp. 173–8.
7. Daniel Yergin, "Harry Truman – Revived and Revised," *New York Times Magazine*, October 24, 1976, pp. 87–8; and idem, *Shattered Peace* (Boston: Houghton-Mifflin, 1978), passim. For works suggesting that Stalin did not have expansionist intentions and actually indicated a desire to negotiate, see Logevall, "A Critique of Containment," pp. 482–3 (notes 21–2), 484–5 (notes 24–8).
8. Elizabeth Olson, "Enola Gay Exhibit Omits Mention of Hiroshima Bombing," *San Francisco Chronicle*, November 2, 2003, p. A20 (Agnew quotation) from a *New York Times* article.
9. Henry L. Stimson, "The Decision to Use the Atomic Bomb," *Harper's Magazine*, February 1947, p. 102; Harry S. Truman, *Memoirs: 1945: Year of Decisions* (New York: Signet Books, 1965; reprint of the original 1955 edition), vol. 1, p. 460; Barton J. Bernstein, "A Postwar Myth: 500,000 Lives Saved," *Bulletin of Atomic Scientists* 42 (June/July 1986): 38–40; idem, "Understanding the Atomic Bomb and the Japanese Surrender," Paul Boyer, "Exotic Resonances: Hiroshima in American Memory," and J. Samuel Walker, "History, Collective Memory, and the Decision to Use the Bomb," – all three in *Diplomatic History* 19 (Spring 1995): 263–4 and notes 126, 129, 299, 320. The debate over the estimated casualties continues, but I believe that Bernstein has won this numerical battle based on close evaluation of the primary documents available as of 1985; see Bernstein, "Marshall, Leahy, and Casualty Issues – A Reply to Kort's Flawed Critique," *Passport: The Newsletter of the Society for Historians of American Foreign Policy* 35, no. 2 (August 2004): 5–14; and Michael Kort, "Casualty Projections for the Invasion of Japan, Phantom Estimates, and the Math of Barton Bernstein," ibid. 27 (December 2003): 4–11.
10. Paul Boyer, *By the Bomb's Early Light: Thought and Culture at the Dawn of the Atomic Age* (New York: Pantheon, 1985), pp. 7, 22–4; H. W. Brands, *What America Owes the World: The Struggle for the Soul of Foreign Policy* (Cambridge: Cambridge University Press, 1998), pp. 182–208.
11. Leilah Danielson, "Christianity, Dissent, and the Cold War: Reinhold Niebuhr and A. J. Muste," paper delivered at the Society for Historians of American Foreign Relations 2004 conference; A. J. Muste, "The H-Bomb as Deterrent," *Christianity and Crisis*, June 14, 1954; Campbell Craig, *Glimmer of a New Leviathan: Total*

War in the Realism of Niebuhr, Morgenthau, and Waltz (New York: Columbia University Press, 2003), p. 90 (quotation)–92; James G. Hershberg, "A Footnote on Hiroshima and Atomic Morality: Conant, Niebuhr, and an 'Emotional' Clergyman, 1945–46," *SHAFR Newsletter* 33, no. 4 (December 2002): 1–15 (quotation at 1–2). For more details about the differences between Muste and Niebuhr over the atomic bomb and other Cold War issues, see Boyer, *By the Bombs Early Light,* pp. 219–20, passim.

12. Roger Angell, "The Talk of the Town," *The New Yorker,* January 19, 2004, pp. 31–2 (comments on the documentary about McNamara *The Fog of War*); Richard Falk, "State Terrorism versus Humanitarian Law," in Mark Selden and Alvin Y. So, eds., *War and State Terrorism: The United States, Japan, and the Asia-Pacific in the Long Twentieth Century* (Lanham, MD: Rowman and Littlefield, 2004), pp. 50–1; and Fousek, *To Lead the Free World,* pp. 23–5, 197 (note 26).

13. Whether Assistant Secretary of War John J. McCloy actually argued against its use at that meeting remains unclear, as does whether Truman ever considered any alternative course of action, such as telling the Japanese about the atomic bomb's destructive potential and using it to bargain with them about surrender by offering to retain the emperor. There is no corroborating proof for McCloy's retrospective claim in his 1953 book, *The Challenge to American Foreign Policy* (Cambridge, MA: Harvard University Press, 1953), nor is there in the official minutes of this meeting or in the diaries of Admiral William Leahy, Secretary of Navy James Forrestal, Stimson, or even in McCloy's own diaries. See Bernstein, "Understanding the Atomic Bomb and the Japanese Surrender," pp. 233–4, notes 17, 23; and idem, "Seizing the Contested Terrain of Early Nuclear History: Stimson, Conant, and Their Allies Explain the Decision to Use the Atomic Bomb," *Diplomatic History* 17 (Winter 1993): 62 and note 105.

14. Bernstein, "Understanding the Atomic Bomb and the Japanese Surrender," pp. 233–8; and Alonzo Hamby, *Man of the People: A Life of Harry S. Truman* (New York: Oxford University Press, 1995), p. 334.

15. For Truman's own reasons for using the bomb, see *Harry S. Truman, Memoirs: 1945: Year of Decisions* (New York: Signet Books, 1965; reprint of the original 1955 edition), vol. 1, pp. 465–6. Also see Michael Walzer, *Just and Unjust Wars: A Moral Argument with Historical Illustrations,* 3rd ed. (New York: Basic Books, 2000), pp. 264–5; and Richard Falk, "State Terrorism versus Humanitarian Law," pp. 52–3. Falk suggests that had Germany or Japan developed and used the atomic bomb, "such weaponry would have been definitely criminalized, and possibly the world would have been spared the specter of nuclear war."

16. Robert H. Ferrell, *Harry S. Truman: A Life* (Columbia: University of Missouri Press), p. 210; Jonathan Glover, *Humanity: A Moral History of the Twentieth Century* (New Haven, CT: Yale University Press, 1999), p. 1; Walzer, *Just and Unjust Wars,* pp. 263–8; and Bruce Cumings, "American Air Power and Nuclear Strategy in Northeast Asia since 1945," in Selden and So, eds., *War and State Terrorism,* pp. 82–4.

17. Tsuyoshi Hasegawa, *Racing the Enemy: Stalin, Truman, and the Surrender of Japan* (Cambridge, MA: Harvard University Press, 2005). For the ongoing debate over this book, see H-Diplo Roundtable on Hasegawa, January 18 and 31, 2006, h-diplo@MAIL.H-NET.MSU.EDU.

18. One of the few books that attempts a serious reevaluation of Truman's role in helping to precipitate the Cold War is Arnold A. Offner, *Another Such Victory:*

President Truman and the Cold War, 1945–1953 (Stanford, CA: Stanford University Press, 2002).

19. Ibid.; Offner, *Another Such Victory*, pp. 365–7; Ernest R. May, ed., *American Cold War Strategy: Interpreting NSC 68* (Boston: Bedford, 1993), passim; Samuel F. Wells, Jr., "Sounding the Tocsin: NSC 68 and the Soviet Threat," *International Security* 4 (Spring 1980):16–58; and John Lewis Gaddis, *Strategies of Containment: A Critical Appraisal of Postwar American National Security* (New York: Oxford University Press, 1982), pp. 89–126, 374 (negotiating quotation). For the text of NSC 68, see <http://www.mtholyoke.edu/acad/intrel/nsc-68/nsc68-1.htm>.

20. This last point has been documented by Melvyn P. Leffler in his book on national security during the Truman administration. See Leffler, *A Preponderance of Power: National Security, the Truman Administration, and the Cold War* (Stanford, CA: Stanford University Press, 1992); and idem, "The American Conception of National Security and the Beginnings of the Cold War," *American Historical Review* 89 (1984): 346–81.

21. One Truman biographer, Alonzo Hamby, suggests that Truman's lack of confidence, peevishness, and provincialism affected many of his domestic and especially his diplomatic decisions. Another biographer, Robert Ferrell, makes a persuasive case for Truman's early, stoic deliberateness stemming from his experiences as a farmer. When arriving at decisions, Ferrell says, Truman would ponder the problem, but once he made up his mind "the moment of worry had passed." This gave his decisions an offhand quality they may not always have deserved. At the same time, Ferrell does not show much of this deliberation functioning in foreign policy decisions. In fact, Ferrell admits that Truman's ignorance and indifference to (rather than deliberation about) foreign affairs can be traced back as far as World War One. In a word, Truman's worst decision-making characteristics dominated rather than diminished after he became president. And to the degree that they did, Truman did not triumph over his particular intellectual deficiencies and personality flaws while president, as is usually argued by mainstream historians like David McCullough. See Alonzo L. Hamby, "Harry S. Truman: Insecurity and Responsibility," in Fred I. Bernstein, ed., *Leadership in the Modern Presidency* (Cambridge, MA: Harvard University Press, 1988), pp. 41–75; idem, *Man of the People*; Ferrell, *Harry S. Truman*, pp. 54, 56, 198, 203, 208, 214; and David McCullough, *Truman* (New York: Simon and Schuster, 1992).

22. Melvyn P. Leffler, "National Security and US Foreign Policy," in Leffler and David S. Painter, eds., *Origins of the Cold War: An International History* (New York: Routledge, 1994), pp. 15–39 (quotation at 30); and idem, *Preponderance of Power*, pp. 297–310, 496–516, 665–71.

23. Both Acheson and Truman are quoted in Denna Frank Fleming, *The Cold War and Its Origins* (New York: Doubleday, 1961), pp. 435–6.

24. Fleming, *The Cold War and Its Origins*, pp. 465–6; Walter LaFeber, *The American Age: U.S. Foreign Policy at Home and Abroad*, 2nd ed. (New York: Norton, 1994), vol. 2, p. 478.

25. Fleming, *The Cold War and Its Origins*, pp. 465–6; LaFeber, *The American Age*, vol. 2, pp. 476–9 (Fulbright quotation); and Vidal, "The Menopause of Empire," p. 20 (Wallace quotation).

26. Michael J. Hogan, *The Marshall Plan: America, Britain, and the Reconstruction of Western Europe, 1947–1952* (Cambridge: Cambridge University Press, 1987), pp. 1–25 (quotation at 3), 93–6, 427–45; Offner, *Another Such Victory*, pp. 240–4;

Geir Lundestad, "Empire by Invitation? The United States and Western Europe, 1945–52," *SHAFR Newsletter* 15 (September 1954): 1–21; and Melvyn P. Leffler, "National Security and US Foreign Policy," Michael MccGwire, "National Security and Soviet Foreign Policy," Charles S. Maier, "Hegemony and Autonomy within the Western Alliance," and Charles Gati, "Hegemony and Repression in the Eastern Alliance," all in Leffler and Painters, eds., *Origins of the Cold War*, pp. 15, 76, 154–98.

27. Hogan, *The Marshall Plan*, pp. 2 (first quotation), 88–94; Sallie Pisani, *The CIA and the Marshall Plan* (Lawrence: University Press of Kansas, 1991), p. 6 (second quotation), passim; Mario Del Pero, "The United States and 'Psychological Warfare' in Italy, 1948–1955," *Journal of American History* 87, no. 4 (March 2001): 1304–34; John Prados, *Presidents' Secret Wars: CIA and Pentagon Covert Operations from World War II through the Persian Gulf* (Chicago: Ivan R. Dee, 1996; revised and expanded version of 1986 edition), pp. 13–107; Rhodri Jeffreys-Jones, *The CIA and American Democracy* (New Haven, CT: Yale University Press, 1998), pp. 69–85; and idem, *Cloak and Dollar: A History of American Secret Intelligence* (New Haven, CT: Yale University Press, 2002), pp. 154–78.

28. Sonia L. Nelson, "The Impact of U.S. International Economic Plans on Czechoslovakia's Postwar Development, 1943–1948" (Ph.D. dissertation, Northern Illinois University, 1994); and Bradley F. Abrams, *The Struggle for the Soul of the Nation: Czech Culture and the Rise of Communism* (Lanham, MD: Rowman and Littlefield, 2004), pp. 6 (quotation), 104, 255, passim.

29. Offner, *Another Such Victory*, pp. 460–3 (quotation at 461).

30. Hogan, *The Marshall Plan*, pp. 430–45 (last quotation at 445); idem, "American Marshall Planners and the Search for a European Neocapitalism," *American Historical Review* 90 (February 1985): 44–72 (quotations at 45); and Lundestad, "Empire by Invitation? The United States and Western Europe, 1945–52."

31. Danilo Türk, "Minority Protection in Human Rights Conventions," *La Comunità Internazionale*, vol. 4, "Tipologia e Protezione delle Minoranze in Europa" (Trieste, November 3–4, 1990), p. 27.

32. Ibid., pp. 25–7. Türk points out that by 1967 only nine multilateral or bilateral international treaties had been signed since 1945 that specifically protected particular minority groups. Also see Timothy Garton Ash, "Cry, the Dismembered Country," *New York Review of Books*, January 14, 1999, pp. 29–35.

33. Nicholas J. Wheeler, *Saving Strangers: Humanitarian Intervention in International Society* (New York: Oxford University Press, 2002), pp. 1–13 (quotation), p. 15.

34. William Pfaff, "The Question of Hegemony," *Foreign Affairs* 80, no. 1 (2001): 226–7 (quotation); and John B. Judis, "Beyond National Interest," *The New Republic*, online edition, June 21, 1999, www.thenewrepublic.com. See Chapter 6 for a discussion of the evolution of the meaning of self-determination during the Cold War.

35. David Ryan and Victor Pungong, eds, *The United States and Decolonization: Power and Freedom* (London: Macmillan 2000), especially Michael Hunt's, Walter LaFeber's, and Dennis Merrill's articles.

36. Anthony Lake, *The "Tar Baby" Option: American Policy toward Southern Rhodesia* (New York: Columbia University Press, 1976), pp. 123–57; Mohammed A. El-Khawas and Barry Cohen, eds., *The Kissinger Study of Southern Africa* (Westport, CN: Lawrence Hill, 1976), pp. 107–20; Hoff, *Nixon Reconsidered*, pp. 247–8; and Gerald Horne, *From the Barrel of a Gun: The United States and*

the War against Zimbabwe, 1965–1980 (Chapel Hill: The University of North Carolina Press, 2001), pp. 145–57, passim.

37. Daphne Eviatar, "Africa's Oil Tycoons," *The Nation*, April 12, 2004, p. 12; William G. Hyland, *Mortal Rivals: Superpower Relations from Nixon to Reagan* (New York: Random House, 1987), pp. 133–6; John Marcum, *The Angolan Revolution*, vol. 2: *Exile Politics and Guerilla Warfare* (Cambridge, MA: MIT Press, 1978), passim; U.S. Congress, Senate, Fourth Congress, First Session, Subcommittee on African Affairs, "Angola" (Washington, DC: U.S. Government Printing Office, 1976), pp. 172–4; and John Robert Greene, *The Presidency of Gerald Ford* (Lawrence: University of Kansas Press, 1995), pp. 112–14.

38. Seymour Hersh, "Angolan Aid Issue Opens Rift in State Department," *New York Times*, December 14, 1975, p. A1; and Dick Clark, "Frustration," *New York Times*, January 26, 1976; Roger Morris, "The Proxy War in Angola: Pathology of a Blunder," *The New Republic*, January 31, 1976, 19–23; John Stockwell, *In Search of Enemies: A CIA Story* (New York: Norton, 1978), pp. 54–69; Greene, *Presidency of Ford*, pp. 114–16; and "Ford Press Conference, December 23, 1975," *Department of State Bulletin* 74 (January 19, 1976): 71–2.

39. Bill Keller, "After Big Gains, Angolan Rebel Offensive Is Halted," *New York Times*, September 24, 1993; Lynne Duke, "Heavy Fighting in Angola Eclipses Peace Accord," *Washington Post Foreign Service*, October 13, 1998; and Rachael L. Swarns, "Angola's Goal: Stepping Back from the Abyss," *New York Times*, December 24, 2000.

40. Eviatar, "Africa's Oil Tycoons," pp. 11–16 (quotation); Hoff, *Nixon Reconsidered*, pp. 248–9; Jon Jeter, "Angola's Paradox: Awash in Oil, Mired in Poverty; Angola's Oil Wealth Fuels War and Corruption," *Washington Post*, September 18, 2000; Colum Lynch, "Private Firms Aid U.N. on Sanctions," *Washington Post*, April 21, 2001; Henri E. Cauvin, "Rebel Leader May Be Dead, but Angolans Want Proof," *New York Times*, February 24, 2002; and idem, "Near Angolan Rebel's Battleground, Suffering Survives Him," *New York Times*, March 2, 2002. One would never know that dire conditions still exist in Angola from a special advertising supplement published in the *New York Times*, September 26, 2004.

41. Larry Diamond, "Promoting Democracy," in Eugene R. Wittkopf, ed., *Future of American Foreign Policy*, 2nd ed. (New York: St. Martin's Press, 1994), pp. 101–16 (quotations at 102 and 105).

42. Offner, *Another Such Victory*, pp. 138–44; and Sheldon L. Richman, "'Ancient History': U.S. Conduct in the Middle East since World War II and the Folly of Intervention," Cato Policy Analysis no. 159, August 16, 1991.

43. Ibid.; and James A. Bill, *The Eagle and the Lion: The Tragedy of American-Iranian Relations* (New Haven, CT: Yale University Press, 1988), p. 76ff. (quotation at 86).

44. Dilip Hiro, "Playing the Democracy Card: How America Furthers Its National Interests in the Middle East," March 17, 2005, posted on TomDispatch.com.

45. Michael T. Klare, *Blood and Oil: The Dangers and Consequences of America's Growing Dependency on Imported Petroleum* (The American Empire Project) (New York: Metropolitan Books, 2004), passim; and Robert Baer, *Sleeping with the Devil: How Washington Sold Our Soul for Saudi Crude* (New York: Three Rivers Press, 2003), pp. 73–128, 208–12.

46. Joan Hoff, *Nixon Reconsidered* (New York: Basic Books, 1994), pp. 259–66; and Baer, *Sleeping with the Enemy*, p. 209 (quotation). The title of the CRS report was "Oil Fields as Military Objectives: A Feasibility Study."

47. William A. Lovett, Alfred E. Eckes, Jr., and Richard L Brinkman, *U.S. Trade Policy: History, Theory, and the WTO* (Armonk, NY: M. E. Sharpe, 1999), p. 131 (quotation); Melvyn Leffler, *Preponderance of Power: National Security, the Truman Administration, and the Cold War* (Stanford, CA: Stanford University Press, 1992), p. 317 (quotations); Judith Stein, *Running Steel, Running America: Race, Economic Policy, and the Decline of the Liberals* (Chapel Hill: University of North Carolina Press, 1998), p. 4 (Volcker quote), passim; and Anthony P. O'Costa, *The Global Restructuring of the Steel Industry: Industry, Innovations, and Industrial Change* (London: Routledge, 1999), passim. When President George W. Bush reimposed tariffs on imported steel in 2002, he was forced to back down by the World Trade Organization.

48. Paul A. Tiffany, *The Decline of American Steel: How Management, Labor, and Government Went Wrong* (New York: Replica Books, 2001; reprint of the original 1988 edition), p. 77, quoting Eugene Grace of Bethlehem Steel; Stephen D. Krasner, "The Tokyo Round: Particularistic Interests and Prospects for Stability in the Global Trading System," *International Studies Quarterly* 23 (December 1979): 494; and Charles S. Maier, "The Politics of Productivity: Foundations of American International Economic Policy after World War II," *International Organization* 31 (Autumn 1977): 630.

49. Lovett et al., *U.S. Trade Policy*, pp. 111–32; and John M. Culbertson, *The Trade Threat: And U.S. Trade Policy* (Madison, WI: 21st Century Press, 1989), pp. 3–23 (quotation)–40.

50. Lovett et al., *U.S. Trade Policy*, pp. 101–5, 131–2 (quotations)–35; Chalmers Johnson, *Blowback: The Costs and Consequences of American Empire* (New York: Henry Holt, 2000), p. 17; Paul Krugman, "Free Trade and Protectionism," in Wittkopf, ed., *Future of American Foreign Policy*, pp. 341–4 (quotations at 343); idem, ed., *Strategic Trade Policy and the New International Economics* (Cambridge, MA: MIT Press, 1986), passim; and Brown, *Myths of Free Trade*, passim. For a more positive view of GATT, see Patrick Low, *Trading Free: The GATT and US Trade Policy* (New York: The Twentieth Century Fund Press, 1993). It should be noted that Congress from 1947 to 1994 never passed legislation authorizing GATT. Congress always resisted formal membership in GATT, and one president after another treated GATT as a contractual agreement among nations, not a treaty or executive agreement. What passed in 1962 was the Trade Expansion Act, authorizing U.S. participation in another multilateral round (the Kennedy Round). It concluded in 1967, and the concessions were implemented over a five-year period ending in 1972. In short, GATT (or the Kennedy Round) had nothing to do with export expansion.

51. Lovett et al., *U.S. Trade Policy*, pp. 106–20, 131 (quotation); Alfred E. Eckes, Jr., and Thomas W. Zeiler, *Globalization and the American Century* (New York: Cambridge University Press, 2003), pp. 9–10, 36–7; David C. Korten, *When Corporations Rule the World* (West Hartford, CT: Kumarian Press, 1995), pp. 53–68; and Sherrod Brown, *Myths of Free Trade: Why American Trade Policy Has Failed* (New York: New Press, 2004), passim.

Chapter 5: Cold War Transformation of the American Presidency

1. Fred I. Greenstein, ed., *Leadership of Modern Presidents* (Cambridge, MA: Harvard University Press, 1988), pp. xx, 3–4, 347; idem, *The Presidential Difference:*

Leadership Style from FDR to Clinton, with a New Afterword on George W. Bush (Princeton, NJ: Princeton University Press, 2000), pp. 2–4. See Richard Nathan, *The Administrative Presidency* (New York: Wiley, 1983), p. 2, for an explanation of why the open-ended original language of Article II, Section 1 of the U.S. Constitution implicitly gives the president vast powers.

2. Edward Pessen, *Losing Our Souls: The American Experience in the Cold War* (Chicago: Elephant Paperbacks, 1995 edition of the original 1993 Ivan R. Dee edition), pp. 219, 221 (first quotation); Joan Hoff, *Nixon Reconsidered* (New York: Basic Books, 1994), pp. 25–7; Joseph A. Pika and John Anthony Maltese, *The Politics of the Presidency*, 6th ed. (Washington, DC: CQ Press, 2006), pp. 235–9; and John Dumbrell, *The Making of US Foreign Policy* (Manchester, UK: Manchester University Press, 1997), p. 47. See Chapter 7 for a discussion of George W. Bush's use of signing statements.

3. Dumbrell, *The Making of US Foreign Policy* (Manchester, UK: Manchester University Press, 1997), pp. 134–6; and Pika and Maltese, *The Politics of the Presidency*, pp. 235–9.

4. Pika and Maltese, *The Politics of the Presidency*, pp. 238–9; and Walter LaFeber, *America, Russia, and the Cold War, 1945–2002*, 9th ed. (New York: McGraw Hill, 2002), p. 275.

5. Steve Weissman, "Americans: The Missionary Position," July 22, 2004, truthout/ Perspective, <http://www.truthout.org/docs_04/072204A.shtml> (Dooley quotation); and Greenstein, *The Presidential Difference*, p. 3.

6. Adam Young, "War Gave Us Caesar," posted October 4, 2004, Mises.org Articles Archive (Wilson quotation); and Greenstein, ed., *Leadership in the Modern Presidency*, p. 4 (last two quotations).

7. Papers by Joan Hoff, "The Presidency: Imperial or Imperiled," delivered at the Frank Church Conference on Public Affairs, Boise State University, September 28, 2000, and "Personality, Character, and Persona: The Imponderable Presidency," delivered at the conference on The Modern Presidency: FDR to Clinton, University of Illinois, Chicago, October 13, 2000.

8. Richard L. Berke, "What a Mind! In Politics, That's Not What Matters," *New York Times*, June 25, 2000, sec. 4, pp. 1, 3.

9. Martin Hart-Landsberg, *Korea: Division, Reunification, and U.S. Foreign Policy* (New York: Monthly Review Press, 1998), pp. 90–138; Melanie Billings-Yun, *Decision against War: Eisenhower and Dien Bien Phu, 1954* (New York: Columbia University Press, 1988); George Herring, *America's Longest War: The United States and Vietnam, 1950–1975* (New York: McGraw-Hill, 1986), pp. 25–72; Richard H. Immerman, "The United States and the Geneva Conference of 1954," *Diplomatic History* 14 (Winter 1990): 43–66; idem, "Confessions of an Eisenhower Revisionist: An Agonizing Reappraisal," *Diplomatic History* 14 (Summer 1990): 319–42; Robert F. Burk, "Eisenhower Revisionism Revisited: Reflections on the Eisenhower Scholarship," *Historian* 50 (February 1988: 196–209; Nick Cullather, *The CIA's Classified Account of Its Operations in Guatemala, 1952–1954* (Stanford, CA: Stanford University Press, 1999); Stephen G. Rabe, *Eisenhower and Latin America: The Foreign Policy of Anti-Communism* (Chapel Hill: University of North Carolina Press, 1988); John Prados, *Presidents' Secret Wars: CIA and Pentagon Covert Operations from World War II through the Persian Gulf* (Chicago: Elephant Paperback, 1996; rev. ed. of the original 1986 Ivan R. Dee edition), pp. 91–170; Jacob G. Hornberger, "An Anti-Democratic Foreign Policy: Guatemala," February 12,

2005, posted at <futureoffreedomfoundation.com>; Stephen Schlesinger and Stephen Kinzer, *Bitter Fruit: The Story of the American Coup in Guatemala* (Cambridge, MA: Harvard University Press, 2005); and Robert McMahon, "Eisenhower and Third World Nationalism: A Critique of the Revisionists," *Political Science Quarterly* 101 (Fall 1986): 453–73.

10. Alfred McCoy, *A Question of Torture: CIA Interrogation, from the Cold War to the War on Terror* (New York: Henry Holt/Metropolitan, 2006), passim; Prados, *Presidents' Secret Wars*, pp. 171–238; Stephen G. Rabe, *The Most Dangerous Area in the World: John F. Kennedy Confronts Communist Revolution in Latin America* (Chapel Hill: University of North Carolina Press, 1999), passim; idem, "The Caribbean Triangle: Betancourt, Castro, and Trujillo and US Foreign Policy," *Diplomatic History* 20 (Winter 1996): 55–78; idem, "John F. Kennedy and the World," in James N. Giglio and Stephen Rabe, eds., *Debating the Kennedy Presidency* (Lanham, MD: Rowman and Littlefield, 2002), pp. 38–45; Laurence Chany and Peter Kornbluh, eds., *The Cuban Missile Crisis, 1962: A National Security Archive Documents Reader* (New York: The New Press, 1992); Seymour Hersh, *The Dark Side of Camelot* (Boston: Little, Brown, 1997), p. 34; Tony Judt, "On the Brink" (review of books on the Cuban missile crisis), *New York Review of Books*, January 15, 1998, pp. 52–8; Graham Allison, *Essence of Decision Making: Explaining the Cuban Missile Crisis*, 2nd ed. (London: Longman, 1999), passim; Lawrence Freedman, *Kennedy's Wars: Berlin, Cuba, Laos, and Vietnam* (New York: Oxford University Press, 2000), pp. 123–45; David J. Ulbrich, "Research Note: A Program for Covert Action against the Castro Regime, 16 March 1960," *SHAFR Newsletter* 33, no. 3 (September 2002): 1–19; Steve Weissman, "Torture from J.F.K. to Baby Bush," truthout/Perspective, December 31, 2004, <http://www.truthout.org/docs>; and Eric Alterman, *When Presidents Lie: A History of Official Deception and Its Consequences* (New York: Penguin, 2005), pp. 90–159.

11. Max Boot, *The Savage Wars of Peace: Small Wars and the Rise of American Power* (New York: Basic Books, 2002), pp. 180–1; Rabe, "John F. Kennedy and the World," pp. 7 (quotation), 45–54; Piero Gleijeses, *The Dominican Crisis: The 1965 Constitutional Revolt and American Intervention* (Baltimore: Johns Hopkins University Press, 1978); Prados, *Presidents' Secret Wars*, pp. 239–96; Peter Fenton, "Yankee, Go Home and Take Me with You," in H. W. Brands, ed., *The Foreign Policies of Lyndon Johnson: Beyond Vietnam* (College Station: Texas A&M University Press, 1999), pp. 98–144; Weissman, "Torture from J.F.K. to Baby Bush"; and Alterman, *When Presidents Lie*, pp. 160–237.

12. Prados, *Presidents' Secret Wars*, pp. 274–356; Christopher Hitchens, "The Case against Henry Kissinger," Part One, *Harper's Magazine*, February, 2001, p. 33ff.; Peter Kornbluh, *The Pinochet File: A Declassified Dossier on Atrocity and Accountability* (New York: The New Press, 2003); idem, "Letter From Chile," *The Nation*, January 31, 2005, pp. 22–4; Diana Jean Schemo, "Kissinger Cool to Criticizing Juntas in '76," *New York Times*, October 1, 2004, p. A9; Gustavo Gonzales, "Pinochet Once Again in the Hands of the Courts," *New York Times*, August 27, 2004; Associated Press, "Pinochet Indicted on Human Rights Charges," December 13, 2004; Prados, *Presidents' Secret Wars*, pp. 297–325; and Larry Rohter, "The Unkindest Cut for Pinochet: Irrelevance," *New York Times*, WK, December 19, 2004; Peter Kornbluh, "U.S. Leaders Are Using Pinochet's Playbook," *Baltimore Sun*, December 9, 2005; and Amy Goodman, "Ask Kissinger about Pinochet's Regime," *Seattle Post-Intelligence*, December 14, 2006.

13. For a review of the pros and cons of Carter's foreign policy, see David F. Schmitz and Vanessa Walker, "Jimmy Carter and the Foreign Policy of Human Rights: The Development of a Post-Cold War Foreign Policy," *Diplomatic History* 28, no. 1 (January 2004): 113–43; and John Dumbrell, *American Foreign Policy: Carter to Clinton* (New York: St. Martin's Press, 1997), pp. 11–52; and Gaddis Smith, *Morality, Reason and Power: Diplomacy in the Carter Years* (New York: Hill and Wang, 1986).

14. Interview with Brzezinski, *Le Nouvel Observateur*, January 15–21, 1998; Dumbrell, *American Foreign Policy*, pp. 47–50; Christian Ostermann, "New Evidence on the 1979–1989 War in Afghanistan," *SHAFR Newsletter* 33, no. 3 (September 2002): 41–3; and Steve Weissman, "Bush Is No Reagan, But...," June 10, 2004, <http://www.truthout.org/docs_04/article_061004A.shtml>.

15. Ostermann, "New Evidence on the 1979–1989 War in Afghanistan," pp. 41–3; Prados, *Presidents' Secret Wars*, pp. 357–76; Dumbrell, *American Foreign Policy*, pp. 100 (first quotation)–101; Hugh Eakin, "When U.S. Aided Insurgents, Did It Breed Future Terrorists?," *New York Times*, April 10, 2004; Mahmood Mamdani, *Good Muslim, Bad Muslim: America, the Cold War, and the Roots of Terror* (New York: Pantheon, 2004); and "Ghost Wars: How Reagan Armed the Mujahadeen in Afghanistan," *Democracy Now!*, June 10, 2004, <http://www.democracy.org/article.pl?sid=04/06/10/1425222>.

16. Larry P. Goodson, *Afghanistan's Endless War: State Failure, Regional Politics, and the Rise of the Taliban* (Seattle: University of Washington Press, 2001), pp. 144–7, 163–4; Prados, *Presidents' Secret Wars*, pp. 360–7; and Dumbrell, *American Foreign Policy*, pp. 100–1.

17. Sheldon L. Richman, "'Ancient History': U.S. Conduct in the Middle East since World War II and the Folly of Intervention," Cato Policy Analysis no. 159, August 16, 1991; Michael Dobbs, "When an Ally Becomes the Enemy," *Washington Post National Weekly Edition*, January 6–12, 2003; Dana Priest, "Rumsfeld '84 Visit Was to Reassure Iraqis," *Seattle Post*, December 19, 2003; Andrew Buncombe, "Rumsfeld Backed Saddam Even after Chemical Attacks," *The Independent* (UK), December 24, 2003; Alan Friedman, *Spider's Web: The Secret History of How the White House Illegally Armed Iraq* (New York: Bantam, 1993); idem, "The Reagan-Saddam Connection: 'We Create These Monsters and When It's Not Convenient We Cover Them Up,'" and Jeremy Skahill, "The Saddam and Rumsfeld's Closet," interviews aired on *Democracy Now!*, June 9, 2004, <http://www.democracynow.org/article.pl?sid=04/06/09/1445208>.

18. For the latest declassified documents about the Iran-Contra affair on the twentieth anniversary of Reagan's November 25, 1986, admission about the covert arms-for-hostage deals, see <http://ww.nsarchive.org>. Two summaries of the Iran-Contra fiasco can be found in Richard Reeves, *President Reagan: The Triumph of Imagination* (New York: Simon and Schuster, 2005), pp. 246–68, 359, 362–418, 429–31, 462–4; and Alterman, *When Presidents Lie*, pp. 238–93. Also see Robert Parry, *Lost History: Contras, Cocaine, the Press and "Project Truth"* (Arlington, VA: The Media Consortium, 1999), pp. 145–7, 157–8, 178–246; Lawrence Walsh, *Firewall: The Iran-Contra Conspiracy and Cover-up* (New York: Norton, 1998), passim; Prados, *Presidents' Secret Wars*, pp. 375–88, 419–63; idem, *Safe for Democracy: The Secret Wars of the CIA* (New York: Ivan R. Dee, 2006), pp. 572–4, 582–5 (for Robert Gates's questionable role in Iran-Contra); Adam Clymer, "Bush Criticizes Press Treatment of the Pardons," *New York Times*, December 31, 1992. All

told, some 138 officials of the Reagan administration were convicted, indicted, or investigated for misconduct – very few of them related to the Iran-Contra affair.

19. William M. LeoGrande, *Our Own Backyard: The United States in Central America, 1977–1992* (Chapel Hill: University of North Carolina Press, 1998), passim; Michael Taylor, "Iran-Contra Tarnished Credibility," *San Francisco Chronicle*, June 6, 2004; Howard N. Meyer, "Omission from the Late President's Obituary," June 6, 2004, Howard Meyer@aol.com.

20. Dumbrell, *American Foreign Policy*, pp. 37–40, 89–96, 120–5 (first quotation at 24); Roger Peace, "An Ideological Crusade: The Reagan Administration's War against Nicaragua," paper delivered at the Historians Against the War conference, Austin, Texas, February 18, 2006; and Alterman, *When Presidents Lie*, p. 293 (last quotation).

21. Prados, *Presidents' Secret Wars*, pp. 378–85; Parry, *Lost History*, pp. 145–58; Dana H. Allin, *Cold War Illusions: America, Europe and Soviet Power, 1969–1989* (New York: St. Martin's Press, 1994), pp. 75–7 (first quotation at 75); and Pessen, *Losing Our Souls*, pp. 219 (second quotation), 223.

22. James R. Whelan, "Jeane Kirkpatrick: Ideals Come First," *The Saturday Evening Post*, December 1984, p. 54, passim; and Roger Morris, "The Road the U.S. Traveled to Baghdad Was Paved by 'Scoop' Jackson," *Seattle Post-Intelligencer*, April 6, 2003. After its founding in 1950, the CPD went out of existence because its leaders were offered positions in the Eisenhower administration. Its revival in 1976 proved more long-lasting as it lobbied against détente and Salt II. Thirty-three CPD members entered the Reagan administration, and many of them continued in influential positions under both Bush administrations. The third incarnation of the CPD occurred in 2004 to address the war on terrorism.

23. Jeane Kirkpatrick, "Dictatorships and Double Standards," *Commentary* 65 (November 1979); idem, *Dictatorships and Double Standards: Rationalism and Reason in Politics* (New York: Simon and Schuster, 1982), pp. 20–35; Judith Ewell, "Barely in the Inner Circle: Jeane Kirkpatrick," in Edward P. Crapol, ed., *Women and American Foreign Policy: Lobbyists, Critics, and Insiders*, 2nd ed. (Wilmington, DE: Scholarly Resources Books, 1992), pp. 156–63; and H. W. Brands, *What America Owes the World: The Struggle for the Soul of Foreign Policy* (Cambridge: Cambridge University Press, 1998), pp. 274–6.

24. Allin, *Cold War Illusions*, pp. 164 (quotation)–71. The major presidential doctrines are: The *Truman Doctrine (1947)*, proclaimed initially in reference to Greece and Turkey but later applied to other parts of the world, stated that "it must be the policy of the United States to support free peoples who are resisting subjugation by armed minorities or by outside pressures," and that the world had to choose between "two ways of life." The *Eisenhower Doctrine (1957)* gave unilateral notice that the United States would intervene in the Middle East if any government threatened by a communist takeover requested aid. The *Johnson Doctrine (1965)* stated that the president could use military force whenever he thought communism threatened the Western Hemisphere; it was issued when LBJ sent troops into the Dominican Republic. The *Nixon Doctrine (1969)*, originally aimed at "southern tier" Third World countries in East Asia, came to represent the formal institutionalization of the policy of Vietnamization; that is, it noted that while the United States continued to support regional security and national self-sufficiency for nations in the Far East, it would no longer commit American troops to this effort. The *Carter Doctrine (1980)* maintained that any attempt by the Soviet Union "to gain control of the Persian

Gulf will be regarded as an assault on the vital interests of the United States."
The *Reagan (Kirkpatrick) Doctrine (1985)* announced that American foreign policy
would actively promote democracy throughout the world by giving humanitarian
and military aid to "democratic revolutions" against communist regimes wherever
they occurred. The *George W. Bush Doctrine (2003)* asserts the right of the United
States to wage preemptive war – in violation of international law, which prohibits
any use of force that is not undertaken in self-defense – or after the occurrence of
an armed attack across an international boundary, or pursuant to a decision by the
UN Security Council.

25. Tony Smith, "Good, Smart, or Bad Samaritan," p. 41; Allin, *Illusions of the Cold
War*, p. 76 (quotation); Dumbrell, *American Foreign Policy*, pp. 87–96; "Journalist
Allan Nairn: Reagan Was behind 'One of the Most Intensive Campaigns of Mass
Murder in Recent History'," June 8, 2004, transcript, and "Reagan Was the Butcher
of My People: Fr. Miguel D'Escoto Speaks from Nicaragua," aired on *Democracy Now!*, June 8, 2004, <http://www.democracynow.org/article.pl?sid=04/06/08/
1453229 and 1453219>; Allan Nairn, "C.I.A. Death Squads," *The Nation*, April
17, 1995, pp. 511–13; idem, "Reagan Administration's Links to Guatemala's Terrorist Government," *Covert Action Quarterly*, no. 32 (Summer 1989); Robert
Parry, "Reagan and Guatemala's Death Files," May 26, 1999, and idem, "Rating Reagan: A Bogus Legacy," June 7, 2004, <http://consoritumnews.com/1999/
052699al.htmland2004/060704.html>.

26. Leslie Bethell and Ian Roxborough, "The Impact of the Cold War on Latin American," in Leffler and Painter, eds., *Origins of the Cold War*, pp. 293–316; Gaddis
Smith, *The Last Years of the Monroe Doctrine, 1945–1993* (New York: Hill and
Wang, 1994), p. 7; and Stephen Kinzer, "U.S. and Central American: Too Close
for Comfort," *New York Times*, WK, July 28, 2002. Since 1990, peace groups,
notably the School of the Americas Watch, have demanded its closure. In 2004, the
United States government officially refused to disband the SOA, but did rename it
the Western Hemisphere Institute for Security Cooperation (WHINSC). This facil-
ity has trained over 60,000 Central and South American soldiers – many of whom
have returned to their countries to torture and oppress those deemed dissidents. The
ACLU released evidence on May 4, 2006, that the FBI had been monitoring this
peace group, School of the Americas Watch. It was founded by Father Roy Bourgeois in 1990. See "FBI Counterterroism Unit Spies on Peace Group: School of the
Americas Watch," *Democracy Now!*, May 5, 2006, <http://www.democracynow.
org/article.pl?sid=06/05/05/1432207>.

27. David C. Korten, *When Corporations Rule the World* (West Hartford, CT: Kumar-
ian Press, 1995), pp. 17–18, 54, 80, 87–8, 159–60, 173–4; Mathew Horsman and
Andrew Marshall, *After the Nation-State: Citizens, Tribalism and the New World
Disorder* (New York: HarperCollins, 1994), p. 33; and Phyllis Bennis, *Calling the
Shots: How Washington Dominates Today's UN* (New York: Interlink Publishing
Group, 1996), pp. 11–12.

28. Goodson, *Afghanistan's Endless War*, p. 162; and Chalmers Johnson, *Blowback:
The Costs and Consequences of American Empire* (New York: Henry Holt, 2000),
p. 17.

29. Goodson, *Afghanistan's Endless War*, pp. 83–4, 162–3.

30. Robert Parry, "Bush and Democratic Hypocrisy," December 22, 2003, <http://
www.consortiumnews.com/article/122203/html>; and Johnson, *Blowback*, pp. 92,
97.

31. William A. Lovett, Alfred E. Eckes, Jr., and Richard L Brinkman, *U.S. Trade Policy: History, Theory, and the WTO* (Armonk, NY: M. E. Sharpe, 1999), pp. 99–8, 148–50; Michael Mann, *Incoherent Empire* (London: Verso, 2003), pp. 57–8; Warren Hoge, "Latin America Losing Hope in Democracy, Report Says," *New York Times*, April 22, 2004, p. A3 (first quotation); José Saramago, "¿Qué es exactamente la democracia?," *Le Monde diplomatique*, no. 44 (August 2004): 4–5; Rupert Cornwell, "How Latin America Turned to the Left," *Independent* (UK), March 1, 2005; and David Bacon, "Central America Up in Arms over CAFTA," April 12, 2005, truthout/Perspective, <http://www.truthout.org/issues_05/article_041305LA.shtml>.

32. Ibid., pp. 193–215; and Hoff, *Nixon Reconsidered*, pp. 166–73. For the latest documents on Nixon's foreign economic policies, see *Foreign Relations of the United States, 1969–1976*, vol. 3: *Foreign Economic Policy, 1969–1972; International Monetary Policy, 1969–1972* (Washington, DC: U.S. Government Printing Office, 2002), and a review of this volume by Allen J. Matusow, "Richard Nixon and the Failed War against the Trading World," *Diplomatic History* 27, no. 5 (November 2003): 767–72.

33. Johnson, *Blowback*, pp. 95–118, 193–215 (Saul quotation); Hoff, *Nixon Reconsidered*, pp. 140–4; Alfred E. Eckes, Jr., and Thomas W. Zeiler, *Globalization and the American Century* (New York: Cambridge University Press, 2003), pp. 182–3; and Lovett, Eckes, and Brinkman, *U.S. Trade Policy*, pp. 73–6.

34. Brands, *What America Owes the World*, pp. 263–96; Claes G. Ryn, *America the Virtuous: The Crisis of Democracy and the Quest for Empire* (New Brunswick, NJ: Transaction Publishers, 2003), pp. 25–42; and Hoff, *Nixon Reconsidered*, pp. 182–207.

35. Anne Hessing Cahn, "Team B: The Trillion-Dollar Experiment," *Bulletin of the Atomic Scientists* 49, no. 3 (April 1993): 22, 24–7; and Sam Tanenhaus, "The Mind of the Administration," *Boston Globe*, November 11, 2003.

36. Kevin P. Phillips, *Post-Conservative America: People, Politics, and Ideology in a Time of Crisis* (New York: Random House, 1982), pp. 31–52 (quotations at 41 and 43); and Mary C. Brennan, *Turning Right in the Sixties: The Conservative Capture of the GOP* (Chapel Hill: University of North Carolina Press, 1995), pp. 1–81.

37. "The Conservatives," videorecording, Blackwell Corporation, 1987; William A. Rusher, *The Rise of the Right*, (New York: Morrow, 1984); James A. Reichley, *Conservatives in an Age of Change: The Nixon and Ford Administrations* (Washington, DC: Brookings Institution Press, 1981); and Brennan, *Turning Right in the Sixties*, p. 29.

38. Ryn, *America the Virtuous*, pp. 15–17, 24–42, 123–53 (quotations at 16, 25, 35, 37, 41).

39. Parry, "Bush and Democratic Hypocrisy" ("democratic imperialist" quotation); Fredrik Logevall, "A Critique of Containment," *Diplomatic History* 28, no. 4 (September 2004): 498, note 59; Bloom, *The Closing of the American Mind*, p. 330; Francis Fukuyama, "The End of History," *National Interest* 16 (Summer 1989): 3–18; Peace, "An Ideological Crusade"; and Harold Pinter, Nobel Laureate address, "Art, Truth and Politics," December 7, 2005.

40. Cahn, "Team B: The Trillion-Dollar Experiment," pp. 22, 24–7; Tanenhaus, "The Mind of the Administration;" Morris, "The Road the U.S. Traveled to Baghdad Was Paved by 'Scoop' Jackson;" Hoff, *Nixon Reconsidered*, pp. 188–9; and Len

Colodny and Tom Shachtman, *The Long Road to Baghdad: Nixon's Fall and the Rise of the Neocons* (New York: HarperCollins, forthcoming).

41. Nick Thimmesch, "The Iron Mentor of the Pentagon: Why Even Henry Kissinger Needs Dr. Fritz Kraemer," *Washington Post*, March 2, 1975; Michael T. Kaufman, "Fritz Kraemer, 95, Tutor to U.S. Generals and Kissinger, Dies," *New York Times*, November 19, 2003; Andrew Marshall and Sven F. Kraemer, compilation of biographical information posted on SourceWatch.org; and Colodny and Shachtman, *The Long Road to Baghdad*. Even after he left government service under Reagan, Sven Kraemer continued to present specific neo-con positions to the Senate Foreign Relations Committee. For example, see his March 1995 and June 1996 testimony.

42. Ibid.; Victoria Samson, "Congress Rattles Nuclear Saber," *The Progressive Populist*, December 15, 2003, p. 12; Carl Hulse and William J. Broad, "The Great-Grandson of Star Wars, Now Ground Based, Is Back on the Agenda," *New York Times*, June 8, 2004, p. 22; and speech by Deputy U.S. Secretary of Defense Paul Wolfowitz at a book party for Hubertus Hoffman, Army and Navy Club, Washington, D.C., November 15, 2004 (emphasis added).

43. Quotations from Hubertus Hoffmann, *Fritz Kraemer on Excellence* (New York: World Security Network Foundation, 2004). Also see Colodny and Shachtman, *The Long Road to Baghdad*; and Wes Vernon, "U.S. Position on China: 'Provocative Weakness,'" April 28, 2001, <newsmax.com/archives/articles2001/4/27/205658.shtml>.

44. Allin, *Cold War Illusions*, pp. 51–77; "Bush Names Iraq War Architect Paul Wolfowitz to Head World Bank," interview with Jim Lobe, Inter Press Service journalist, aired on *Democracy Now!*, March 17, 2005, <http://www.democracynow.org/article.pl?sid=05/03/17/1442215>; Cahn, "Team B: The Trillion-Dollar Experiment," pp. 24–5; and Hoff, *Nixon Reconsidered*, pp. 157–62, 249–51, 306–15.

45. Cahn, "Team B: The Trillion-Dollar Experiment," pp. 24–6; Tanenhaus, "The Mind of the Administration"; Allin, *Cold War Illusions*, pp. 60–1; Robert Parry, *Secrecy and Privilege: Rise of the Bush Dynasty from Watergate to Iraq* (Arlington, Virginia: The Media Consortium, 2004), pp. 48–55.

46. <http://consoritumnews.com/2004/060704.html>; Morris, "The Road the U.S. Traveled to Baghdad Was Paved by 'Scoop' Jackson"; and Prados, *Presidents' Secret Wars*, pp. 327–9, 371, 375–6, 418.

47. Cahn, "Team B: The Trillion-Dollar Experiment," pp. 24–25(quotation)–26; Craig Shirley, *Reagan's Revolution: The Untold Story of the Campaign That Started It All* (Nashville, TN: Nelson Current, 2005), pp. 43, 45–7; 186, 311, 327, passim; Raymond Garthoff, *Détente and Confrontation: American Soviet Relations from Nixon to Reagan* (Washington, DC: Brookings Institution, 1985), p. 548 (Ford quotes); James C. Roberts, "Engaging Look at Reagan's Pivotal '76 Campaign," posted February 22, 2005, humanevents.com; and Allin, *Cold War Illusions*, p. 61. Also see *The Power of Nightmares*, October 2004, a BBC production about how Rumsfeld, Cheney, and Wolfowitz conspired under Ford to undermine Nixon's détente with the Soviet Union by spreading misinformation in the 1970s and 1980s about Soviet intents and about nonexistent Russian weapons of mass destruction and how they then returned to government to promote the same scam about Saddam Hussein and Iraq before the second Gulf War. This documentary quotes Rumsfeld and Pipes; see transcript of the first half of Episode 1: "Baby It's Cold Outside," pp. 16–20, <http://www.news.bbc.co.uk/1/hi/programmes/3755686.stm>.

48. Cahn, "Team B: The Trillion-Dollar Experiment," pp. 24–6; John Dumbrell, *American Foreign Policy*, pp. 116–17 (all quotations), 142, 146, 149; Brands, *What America Owes the World*, pp. 287–96; Allin, *Cold War Illusions*, pp. 59–77 (chicken quotation at 65); Henry Kissinger, "The Future of NATO," in Kenneth A. Myers, ed., *NATO – The Next Thirty Years: The Changing Political, Economic, and Military Setting* (Boulder, CO: Westview Press, 1980), p. 9; Parry, *Secrecy and Privilege*, pp. 54–5; Robert Gates, *From the Shadows* (New York: Simon and Schuster, 1996), pp. 106–8; and Hoff, *Nixon Reconsidered*, pp. 187–91, 201–3. Kahn came up with an almost unintelligible definition of "escalation dominance" as "the net effect of the competing capabilities on the rung being occupied, the estimate by each side of what would happen if confrontation moved to other rungs, and the means each side has to shift the confrontation to other rungs." His neo-conservative supporters all agreed that the concept represented a needed critique of the "balance of terror" theory at the heart of MAD and of Nixon's acceptance of nuclear parity or sufficiency with the Soviet Union. See Herman Kahn, *On Escalation: Metaphors and Scenarios* (New York: Praeger, 1965), p. 290.
49. Cahn, "Team B: The Trillion-Dollar Experiment," pp. 25–7 (first and last quotations); and Sara Dougherty, "The Munich Analogy and the Persian Gulf War," paper delivered on February 18, 2006, at the Historians against the War conference, Austin, Texas (quotation about "Muniching").
50. Admiral Elmo Zumwalt, *On Watch: A Memoir* (New York: New York Times Book Company, 1979), pp. xii–xiii; Steven F. Hayward: *Age of Reagan: The Fall of the Old Liberal Order* (Roseville, CA: Forum, 2001), p. 434 (quoting Zumwalt criticizing Kissinger); and Roberts, "Engaging Look at Reagan's Pivotal '76 Campaign."
51. H. W. Brands, *What America Owes the World*, pp. 263–305; Allin, *Cold War Illusions*, p. 177 (quotation); Dumbrell, *American Foreign Policy*, pp. 115–20, 149–50; idem, *The Making of US Foreign Policy* (Manchester, UK: Manchester University Press, 1997), pp. 34–42; Morris, "The Road the U.S. Traveled to Baghdad Was Paved by 'Scoop' Jackson"; and Tanenhaus, "The Mind of the Administration."
52. Thomas G. Paterson et al., *American Foreign Relations: A History since 1895*, 4th ed. (Lexington, MA; D. C. Heath, 1995), p. 547 (quotation); John Patrick Diggins, "How Reagan Beat the Neocons," *New York Times*, June 11, 2004; and "The Power of Nightmares," October 2004, BBC production.
53. Mark Kramer, "The Collapse of East European Communism and the Repercussions within the Soviet Union," *Journal of Cold War Studies* (three parts) 5, no. 4 (Fall 2003): 178–256; 6, no. 4 (Fall 2004): 3–64; and 7, no. 1 (Winter 2005): 3–96; and responses to this series of articles posted on listserve@h-net.msu.edu, May 10, 2005, to May 11, 2005, especially those by Tom Nichols; Cahn, "Team B: The Trillion-Dollar Experiment, pp. 26–7 (for details about how "Team B" twisted all the "hard" data about the Soviet Union into worst-case scenarios); Dumbrell, *American Foreign Policy*, pp. 115–20 (quotation at 117); "Epilogue: The End of the Cold War," in Leffler and Painter, eds., *Origins of the Cold War*, pp. 317–22; Allin, *Cold War Illusions*, pp. 171–80; Steve Weissman, "Bush Is No Reagan, But . . . " <http://www.truthout.org/docs_04/printer_061004A.shtml>; and CBC, "Life and Times of Pope John Paul II," Canadian Premier Biography Series, January 7 and 8, 2003, <http://www.cbc/lifeandtimes/pope.html>. For writings supporting the idea that Reagan won the Cold War, see Peter Schweizer, *The Reagan Administration's Secret Strategy That Hastened the Collapse of the Soviet Union* (New York: Atlantic Monthly Press, 1993); idem, ed., *The Fall of the Berlin Wall:*

Reassessing the Causes and Consequences of the End of the Cold War (Stanford, CA: Hoover Institution Press, 2003); and A. R. Dolan, *Undoing the Evil Empire: How Reagan Won the Cold War* (Washington, DC: Washington Institute Press, 1990).

54. Young, "War Gave Us Caesar"; and Prados, *Presidents' Secret Wars*, p. 337 (Church quotation).

55. John Yoo, "How the Presidency Regained Its Balance," op-ed, *New York Times*, September 17, 2006 (quoting and defending all of George W. Bush's unilateral actions as an attempt to "restore" presidential power supposedly lost because of Vietnam and Watergate.

Chapter 6: The United States Adrift in the Post–Cold War World

1. Robert L. Hutchings, *American Diplomacy and the End of the Cold War: An Insider's Account of U.S. Policy in Europe, 1989–1992* (Baltimore: Johns Hopkins University Press, 1997), pp. 339–54; and Randall B. Ripley and James M. Lindsay, eds., *U.S. Foreign Policy after the Cold War* (Pittsburgh: University of Pittsburgh Press, 1997), pp. 3–17, 200–14.

2. Phyllis Bennis, *Calling the Shots: How Washington Dominates Today's UN* (New York: Interlink Publishing Group, 1996), pp. 25–8; and Joseph S. Nye, "What New World Order?," in Eugene R. Wittkopf, ed., *Future of American Foreign Policy*, 2nd ed. (New York: St. Martin's Press, 1994), pp. 50–60.

3. Thomas J. Knock, *To End All Wars: Woodrow Wilson and the Quest for a New World Order* (New York: Oxford University Press, 1992); Lloyd E. Ambrosius, *Wilsonian Statecraft: Theory and Practice of Liberal Internationalism* (Wilmington, DE: SR Books, 1991); Strobe Talbott, "Woodrow Wilson in the Gulf," *Time Magazine*, December 24, 1990, p. 43; Hess, *Presidential Decisions for War*, pp. 213–20; George Will, "Therapeutic Value of War Quick to Fade Away," *Herald Times*, April 7, 1991, p. A12 (quotation); and Sheldon L. Richman, "'Ancient History': U.S. Conduct in the Middle East since World War II and the Folly of Intervention," Cato Policy Analysis no 159, August 16, 1991.

4. Richman, "'Ancient History': U.S. Conduct in the Middle East since World War II and the Folly of Intervention," Phyllis Bennis, *Calling the Shots*, pp. 25 (quoting Middle Eastern scholar Eqbal Ahmad), 26 (second quotation)–27; Jean Edward Smith, *George Bush's War* (New York: Henry Holt, 1992), pp. 169–257; Gary R. Hess, *Presidential Decisions for War: Korea, Vietnam, and the Persian Gulf* (Baltimore: Johns Hopkins University Press), pp. 191–8; and Joseph A. Pika and John Anthony Maltese, *The Politics of the Presidency*, 6th ed. (Washington, DC: CQ Press, 2006), p. 381.

5. Richman, "'Ancient History': U.S. Conduct in the Middle East since World War II and the Folly of Intervention"; Riek Atkinson and Ann Devroy, "Bush: Iraq Won't Decide Time of Ground War," *Washington Post*, February 2, 1991; and Christopher Layne, "Why the Gulf War Was Not in the National Interest," *Atlantic Monthly*, July 1991, pp. 55–81.

6. Robert Baer, *Sleeping with the Devil: How Washington Sold Our Soul for Saudi Crude* (New York: Three Rivers Press, 2003), pp. 151–200; and Michael Scott Doran, "The Saudi Paradox," *Foreign Affairs* 83, no. 1 (January/February 2004): 35–51.

7. Steven Mufson, "Politics of the Pipelines: U.S. Seeks Ways to Route Natural Gas around Russia," *Washington Post*, July 11, 2006; Erin E. Arvedlund, "Pipeline Done, Oil from Azerbaijan Begins Flowing from Turkey," *New York Times*, May 26, 2005; "Pipeline to Promise or Pipeline to Peril? New U.S. Backed Oil Route Starts Moving Crude Oil from Azerbaijan to the West," May 27, 2005, *Democracy Now!* <http://www.democracynow.org/article.pl?sid = 05/05/27/1410246>; Walter LaFeber, "The Bush Doctrine," *Diplomatic History* 26, no. 4 (Fall 2002): 545–6; Noreena Hertz, *The Silent Takeover: Global Capitalism and the Death of Democracy* (New York: The Free Press, 2001), p. 70 (first quotation); and Ahmed Rashid, *Taliban, Militant Islam, Oil, and Fundamentalism in Central Asia* (New Haven, CT: Yale University Press, 2000), pp. 158–82 (second quotation); and Michael T. Klare, "Oil Moves the War Machine," *The Progressive*, June 2002, pp. 18–19.

8. George H. W. Bush, *A World Transformed* (New York: Knopf, 1998), p. 498; and Hess, *Presidential Decisions for War*, pp. 199–220.

9. Patrick E. Tyler, "U.S. Strategy Plan Calls for Insuring No Rivals Develop," *New York Times*, March 8, 1992; Arthur Schlesinger, Jr., "Eyeless in Iraq," *New York Review of Books*, October 23, 2003, p. 24; and Michael Mann, *Incoherent Empire* (London: Verso, 2003), pp. 2–3 (quotations).

10. George H. W. Bush quoted from speech to the National Guard Convention, Salt Lake City, September 15, 1992; John Dumbrell, *The Making of US Foreign Policy* (Manchester, UK: Manchester University Press, 1997), pp. 43–8; Joseph W. Nye, Jr., "What New World Order?," in *The Future of American Foreign Policy*, 2nd ed. (New York: St. Martin's Press, 1994), pp. 50–60; and H. W. Brands, *What America Owes the World: The Struggle for the Soul of Foreign Policy* (Cambridge: Cambridge University Press, 1998), pp. 304–11.

11. Institute for Advanced Strategic and Political Studies, "Study Group on New Israeli Strategy toward 2000" (based on the "clean break" document containing the preemptive strike quotation), <http://www.truthout.org/docs>; Schlesinger, "Eyeless in Iraq," p. 24 (first quotation); and Mann, *Incoherent Empire*, p. 3 (other quotations).

12. Chalmers Johnson, *The Sorrows of Empire: Militarism, Secrecy, and the End of the Republic* (New York: Henry Holt, 2004), pp. 227–9; Phyllis Bennis, "U.N. Ambassador's Oily Past," <http://www.tompaine.com/articles/2007/01/08/un_ambassadors_oily_past.php>; and CNN news announcement, February 20, 1998. CNN described the CPSG as a "bipartisan group whose members are prominent in U.S. international circles," founded in 1990 "to support President George Herbert Walker Bush's policy of expelling Saddam Hussein from Kuwait."

13. For the entire ninety-page 2000 PNAC report, see <http://www.newamerican century.org/RebuildingAmericasDefenses.pdf> (Saddam quotation on p. 26 and Pearl Harbor quotation on p. 63 – emphases added); William Rivers Pitt, February 21 and 27, 2003, articles on PNAC and the George W. Bush administration posted on truthout.com; Mann, *Incoherent Empire*, pp. 2–3; Claes G. Ryn, *America the Virtuous: The Crisis of Democracy and the Quest for Empire* (New Brunswick, NJ: Transaction Publishers, 2003), pp. 29–33 (quotation about spreading neo-Jacobin ideas at 31); and Johnson, *The Sorrows of Empire*, pp. 228–9.

14. Testimony of Ralph Johnson, deputy assistant secretary of state for European and Canadian affairs, October 17, 1991, *Foreign Policy Bulletin* 2 (November/ December 1991): 39, 42 (quotation); George Packer, "Dreaming of Democracy," *New York Times Magazine*, March 2, 2003, p. 60; and Steven Erlanger, "Why

Democracy Defies the Urge to Implant It," *New York Times*, WK, February 15, 2004.

15. Bennis, *Calling the Shots*, pp. 39–40, 246; and Patrick Thornberry, *International Law and the Rights of Minorities* (New York: Oxford University Press, 1991), pp. 16–17, 29–30, 38–40.

16. Douglas Cassel, "A Framework of Norms: International Human-Rights Law and Sovereignty," *Harvard International Review* 22, no. 4 (Winter 2001): 63.

17. John Mattras and Marjorie Lightman, "Clinton's Second Term: Making Women's Rights a Foreign Policy Issue," *Presidential Studies Quarterly* 27 (Winter 1997): 122–6.

18. Michael Mandelbaum and Raju G. C. Thomas, "Sovereignty, Self-Determination, and Secession: Principles and Practice," in Thomas, ed., *The Collapse of Yugoslavia: Histories of Making War and Peace*, pp. 14, 32–4 (quotations).

19. Elizabeth Defeis, "Moldova and Frozen Conflict: International Law Aspects of the Separatist Crisis in Moldova," address to the United Nations Trusteeship Council, November 15, 2006.

20. Cassel, "A Framework of Norms," pp. 46, 63; and Mandelbaum and Thomas, "Sovereignty, Self-Determination, and Succession," p. 52.

21. "War of Intervention: Why and When to Go In," *Economist*, January 6, 2001, pp. 19–20, 24; and Larry Diamond, "Promoting Democracy," in Eugene R. Wittkopf, ed., *Future of American Foreign Policy*, 2nd ed. (New York: St. Martin's Press, 1994), pp. 101–7; and idem, *The Making of US Foreign Policy* (Manchester, UK: Manchester University Press, 1997), p. 45.

22. Fareed Zakaria, "Democracies That Take Liberties," *New York Times*, November 2, 1997; idem, "The Rise of Illiberal Democracy," *Foreign Affairs* 76 (November/December, 1997): 22–43; idem, "Elections Are Not Democracy," *Newsweek*, February 7, 2005, p. 30; and Diamond, "Promoting Democracy," pp. 101–2.

23. Zakaria, "Democracies That Take Liberties," p. 15 (first quotation); William Jefferson Clinton, "Confronting the Challenges of a Broader World," U.S. Department of State, Bureau of Public Affairs, *Dispatch* 4, no. 39 (September 1993): 3; Gary J. Bass, "Are Democracies Really More Peaceful?," *New York Times Magazine*, January 1, 2006, p. 18; Edward D. Mansfield and Jack Snyder, *Electing to Fight: Why Emerging Democracies Go to War* (BCSIA Studies in International Studies) (Cambridge, MA: MIT Press, 2005); John Dumbrell, *American Foreign Policy: Carter to Clinton* (New York: St. Martin's Press, 1997), pp. 189–91; and Steven Erlanger, "Why Democracy Defies the Urge to Implant It," *New York Times*, WK, February 15, 2004, p. 5 (last quotation). For a statistical evaluation of peace literature revealing that there is no significant or inherent relationship between democracy and peace, see Henry S. Farber and Joanne Gowa, "Politics and Peace," *International Security* 20, no. 2 (1995): 123–46.

24. Mathew Horsman and Andrew Marshall, *After the National-State: Citizens, Tribalism and the New World Disorder* (New York: HaperCollins, 1994), pp. x, 260–1; Jean-Marie Guéhenno, *The End of the Nation-State*, trans. Victoria Elliott (Minneapolis: University of Minnesota Press, 1995), p. 43–5; Barber, *Jihad vs. McWorld*, pp. 3–8; Kenichi Ohmae, *End of the Nation-State: The Rise of Regional Economies* (New York: The Free Press, 1995), pp. 5, 79–100, 141–9; "The Unfree World," *The Atlantic Monthly*, March 2004, pp. 52–3; and Roger Cohen, "Change in the Middle East: What's in It for America?," *New York Times*, WK, March 6, 2005, pp. 1, 3 (charts).

25. Guéhenno, *The End of the Nation-State*, pp. 1–3; Antonio Casese, "Self-Determination of Peoples and the Recent Break-Up of the USSR and Yugoslavia," and Rein Mullerson, "Self-Determination of Peoples and the Dissolution of the USSR," both in Ronald St. John MacDonald, ed., *Essays in Honor of Wang Tieya* (Dordrecht: Springer, 1994), pp. 131–44, 567–86; Barber, *Jihad vs. McWorld*, p. 303, note 6.

26. Barber, *Jihad vs. McWorld*, p. 5 (first quotation); Robert Kaplan, "Was Democracy Just a Moment?," *The Atlantic Monthly*, December 1997, pp. 55–6 (second quotation); John Mueller, "Quiet Cataclysm: Some Afterthoughts about World War III," *Diplomatic History* 16 (1992): 66; Gore Vidal, "The Menopause of Empire," *The Progressive*, May 1998, p. 21; and Lafeber, "The Bush Doctrine," p. 543.

27. Oscar Schacter, "The Decline of the Nation-State and Its Implications for International Law," *Columbia Journal of Transitional Law* 36 (1997): 12; *Daedalus* 124 (Spring 1995): xix (quotation), xxiii; Barber, *Jihad vs. McWorld*, pp. 11, 13; Zakaria, "The Rise of Illiberal Democracy," p. 38; Wolfgang H. Reinicke, "Global Public Policy," *Foreign Affairs* 76 (November/December 1997): 127; and O'Meara, et al., *Globalization and the Challenges of a New Century*, pp. 27, 72, 93–7, 118, 184–91.

28. Alfred E. Eckes, Jr., and Thomas W. Zeiler, *Globalization and the American Century* (New York: Cambridge University Press, 2003), pp. 121–30 (quotations at 129–30); and David C. Korten, *When Corporations Rule the World* (West Hartford, CT: Kumarian Press, 1995), pp. 17–18, 54, 80, 87–8, 159–60, 173–4.

29. Eckes and Zeiler, *Globalization and the American Century*, pp. 126–8; Joseph E. Stiglitz, *Globalization and Its Discontents* (New York: Norton, 2002), pp. 12–22, 214–52; Mann, *Incoherent Empire*, pp. 49–76; and Korten, *When Corporations Rule the World*, pp. 54, 160–72.

30. Joseph T. Siegle et al., "Why Democracies Excel," *Foreign Affairs* 83, no. 5 (September/October 2004): 57–71; James Surowicki, "Moreles Mistake," *The New Yorker*, January 23 and 30, 2006, p. 36; Diamond, "Promoting Democracy," pp. 105–7; and Joseph E. Stiglitz, *Making Globalization Work* (New York: Norton, 2006).

31. Sam Smith, *Shadows of Hope: A Freethinker's Guide to Politics in the Time of Clinton* (Bloomington: Indiana University Press. 1994), p. 74 (quotation); Philippe Girard, *Clinton in Haiti: The 1994 U.S. Invasion of Haiti* (New York: Palgrave, 2004), pp. 21–3; and Joseph A. Pika and John Anthony Maltese, *The Politics of the Presidency*, 6th rev. ed. (Washington, DC: CQ Press, 2006), pp. 366–7.

32. Judis, *The Folly of Empire*, pp. 160–2; Dumbrell, *American Foreign Policy*, pp. 181–3 (note 19), 183–4, 189 (quotations); Korten, *When Corporations Rule the World*, pp. 83–6, 116–17, 121–3; and Hertz, *The Silent Takeover*, pp. 70–9, 97–8.

33. Clinton, *My Life*, pp. 597–8 (quotation – emphasis added), 758, 794, 852–3, 922; Sven F. Kraemer presented the neo-con opposition to MFN trade and other relations with China in his June 6, 1996, testimony to the Senate Foreign Relations Committee.

34. For Clinton's 1999 NSS, see <http://www.dtic.mil/doctrine/jel/other_pubs/nssr99>; for Clinton's 2000 NSS, see <http://www.au.af.mil/au/awc/awcgate/nss/nss_decc2000_contents.htm>; Melvyn P. Leffler, "9/11 and American Foreign Policy," p. 404 (quotation)–97, 403–5, and Arnold A. Offner, "Rogue President, Rogue Nation: Bush and U.S. National Security," pp. 434–5 – both in *Diplomatic History* 29, no. 3 (June 2005); Mann, *Incoherent Empire*, p. 7; and Judis, "The Folly of Empire," pp. 156–62.

35. Clinton, *My Life* (New York: Knopf, 2004), pp. 814–20, 828, 831–3, 911–16; Albright, *Madame Secretary: A Memoir* (New York: Miramax Books, 2003), pp. 306–18, 473–98; Lippman, *Albright*, pp. 186–210, 337; Jimmy Carter, *Palestine: Peace Not Apartheid* (New York: Simon and Schuster, 2006), pp. 147–54, 163–8.

36. White House–issued policy paper, "National Security Strategy of the United States," March 1990; Lynda Hurst, "Knocking on the Nuclear Door," *Toronto Star*, February 20, 2005, p. A14; and Bill Clinton, *My Life*, pp. 728, 786, 900, 904.

37. Richard J. Barnet, "Still Putting Arms First: The Cold War Legacy Confronting Clinton, Abroad and at Home," *Harper's Magazine*, February 1993, pp. 59–65 (quotation at 64); Richard F. Grimmett, Congressional Research Service (CRS) annual report, *Conventional Arms Transfers to Developing Nations, 1991–1998* (Washington, DC: Library of Congress, 1999), pp. 16–18, 41–3; idem, "U.S. Is Global Arms Leader Again," August 5, 1999, and "Selected Weapons Deliveries to Developing Nations, 1998–2005," October 1, 2006 – both in Congressional Research Service (CRS) Reports and Issue Briefs (Farmington Hills, MI: Thomson Gale, 2000, 2006); and Frida Berrigan, "U.S. Leads the World in Sale of Military Goods," *Fort Worth Star-Telegram* (Texas), September 12, 2005.

38. Ibid.; keynote address by Frank Wisner, nominee as undersecretary of defense for policy, May 5, 1993, to a conference sponsored by the Atlantic Council of the United States and the EUROGROUP; Mann, *Incoherent Empire*, p. 7; and Dumbrell, *American Foreign Policy*, pp. 191–2.

39. Helen Caldicott, *The New Nuclear Danger: George W. Bush's Military Industrial Complex* (New York: The New Press, 2002), pp. 108–11; William Safire, "Mistake in Moscow," *New York Times*, June 5, 2000, op-ed; Eric Schmitt and Steven Lee Myers, "Clinton Lawyer Gives a Go-Ahead to Missile Shield," *New York Times*, June 15, 2000; idem, "Clinton Seeks to Avoid Acting on Missile Defense System," *New York Times*, June 21, 2000; and "Tortured Ideas on Missile Defense," editorial, *New York Times*, June 19, 2000.

40. Dumbrell, *American Foreign Policy*, pp. 184–9, 194; and Pika and Maltese, *The Politics of the Presidency*, p. 366.

41. John Milton Cooper, Jr., *Breaking the Heart of the World: Woodrow Wilson an the Fight for the League of Nations* (Cambridge: Cambridge University Press, 2001), p. 342. Wilson made this statement rejecting the idea of sending troops to Armenia (or any other far-flung place) in his defense of the League of Nations in Salt Lake City, September 23, 1919.

42. Susan L. Woodward, "International Aspects of the Wars in Former Yugoslavia," in Jasminka Udovicki and James Ridgeway, eds., *Burn This House: The Making and Unmaking of Yugoslavia* (Durham, NC: Duke University Press, 1997), pp. 215–16.

43. Ibid.; and Clinton, *My Life*, pp. 508–13, 581–3, 665–9, 684.

44. William Pfaff, "Bosnia: Another Worthwhile Idea, Likely to Be Ignored," May 22–3, 1993; Anthony Lewis, op-ed, "For America in Europe, the End of an Era," May 25, 1993; and John Thompson, op-ed, "Don't Let the Serbs Destroy the West's Solidarity," May 31, 1993 – all in *International Herald Tribune*; Anthony Lewis, op-ed, "Abroad at Home: Principle of Pose?," *New York Times*, February 21, 1994; and Edward Luttwak, "If Bosnians Were Dolphins," *Commentary*, October 1993, pp. 27–32.

45. Udovički, "Conclusion," in Udovicki and Ridgeway, eds., *Burn This House*, pp. 301–3.

46. Girard, *Clinton in Haiti*, pp. 9–18; and Donald C. F. Daniel and Bradd E. Hayes with Chantal de Jonge Oudraat, *Coercive Inducement and the Containment of International Crises* (Washington, DC: United States Institute of Peace, 1999), pp. 151–2.

47. Madison Smartt Bell, "Mine of Stones: With and without the Spirits along the Cordon de l'Ouest," *Harper's Magazine*, January 2004, pp. 56–66; Girard, *Clinton in Haiti*, pp. 3–6, 37–49; Daniel et al., *Coercive Inducement*, pp. 158–9; and H. W. Brands et al., eds., *The Use of Force after the Cold War* (College Station: Texas A&M University Press, 2000). pp. 38–9 (quotations).

48. Daniel et al., *Coercive Inducement*, pp. 161–7; Girard, *Clinton in Haiti*, pp. 3–8, 14–35, 158–9, 161–7; Albright, *Madam Secretary*, pp. 155–61; Clinton, *My Life*, pp. 648–9. For figures on conditions in Haiti as of 2003, see Tracy Kidder, "The Trials of Haiti," *The Nation*, October 27, 2003, pp. 26–30; John Shattuck, *Freedom on Fire: Human Rights Wars and America's Response* (Cambridge, MA: Harvard University Press, 2003); Lydia Polgreen, "200 Years after Napoleon, Haiti Finds Little to Celebrate," *New York Times*, January 2, 2004; Robert Fatton, Jr., "For Haiti, 200 Years of Mixed Results," *New York Times*, January 4, 2004; AP story, "Haiti Protests Leave at Least Two Dead," *New York Times*, January 8, 2004; and Bell, "Mine of Stones," pp. 56–66.

49. Steven A. Holmes, "Clinton's Policymakers Turn to Africa," *International Herald Tribune*, May 19, 1993.

50. Samantha Power, "Bystanders to Genocide: Why the United States Let the Rwandan Tragedy Happen," *The Atlantic Monthly*, September 2001, pp. 84–108 (quotation at 84).

51. Albright, *Madame Secretary*, pp. 155, 274–5; Dobbs, *Albright*, pp. 377–95; Clinton, *My Life*, pp. 592–3; "Exposed: Washington Ignored U.S. Intel Warning of Genocide in Rwanda," documents declassified at the request of the National Security Archive, aired on *Democracy Now!*, April 1, 2004, <democracynow .org/article.pl?sid=04/04/01/1621238>; John Darnton, "Revisiting Rwanda's Horrors with a Former National Security Adviser," *New York Times*, December 20, 2004, p. E1 (review of the movie *Hotel Rwanda*); Power, "Bystanders to Genocide," pp. 84–108 (quotations at 106); and US Committee for Refugees, "New Report Underscores Need for U.S. Investigation into Passive Response to Rwanda's Genocide of 1994."

52. Albright, *Madame Secretary*, pp. 167–9, 251–64; Clinton, *My Life*, pp. 569, 637, 675, 750, 759; Jonathan G. Clark, "Silver Lining: Renewed Interest in European-Run Security Institutions," and Ted Galen Carpenter, "Kosovo as an Omen: The Perils of the 'New NATO,'" both in Carpenter, ed., *NATO's Empty Victory: A Postmortem on the Balkan War* (Washington, DC: Cato Institute, 2000), pp. 155–69, 171–83 (quotations at 164 and 181).

53. Albright, *Madam Secretary*, pp. 167–9, 251–64; Clinton, *My Life*, p. 785; Clark, "Silver Lining," p. 164; and Brian Mitchell, "NATO at 50: Birthday or Funeral?," *Business Daily*, April 26, 1999.

54. Christopher Layne, "Miscalculations and Blunders Lead to War," and idem, "Collateral Damage in Yugoslavia," both in Carpenter, ed., *NATO's Empty Victory: A Postmortem on the Balkan War*, pp. 11–18 (quotation)–20, 51–8.

55. Layne, "Collateral Damage in Yugoslavia," pp. 54–5; Doug Bandow, "NATO's Hypocritical Humanitarianism," in Carpenter, ed., *NATO's Empty Victory: A Postmortem on the Balkan War*, p. 42; Michael Mandel, *How America Gets*

Away with Murder: Illegal Wars, Collateral Damage and Crimes against Humanity
(Melbourne: Pluto Press, 2004); and Marjorie Cohn, "Getting Away with
Murder," March 21, 2005, <http://www.truthout.org/docs_2005/article_032105B.
shtml>.

56. For "Madeleine's War," see Madeleine Albright, *Madam Secretary,* pp. 410, 421,
    and her defense of NATO intervention in Kosovo, pp. 378–428. For the disturb-
    ing results of U.S. military action in Kosovo, see Christopher Layne and Ben-
    jamin Schwarz, "Was It a Mistake? Were We Suckers for the KLA?," *Washing-
    ton Post,* op-ed, March 26, 2000; William E. Odom, "Intervention for the Long
    Run: Rethinking the Definition of War," *Harvard International Review* 22, no.
    4 (Winter 2001): 52; Amnesty International, *Annual Report 2000,* June 16, 2000,
    <www.amnesty.org/web/ar2000>; Steven Lee Myers, "Kosovo Inquiry Confirms
    US Fears of War Crimes Court," *New York Times,* January 3, 2000, p. A6; Mandel,
    How American Gets Away with Murder; and Cohn, "Getting Away with Murder."
    For deficiencies of investigative reporting in coverage of the war in Kosovo, see
    Audrey Lustgarten and François Debrix, "The Role of the Media in Monitoring
    International Law during Military Interventions: The Case of Kosovo," *Peace and
    Change* 30, no. 3 (July 2005): 359–97; and Norman Solomon, *War Made Easy*
    (New York: Wiley, 2005), pp. 66–71.
57. Albright, *Madam Secretary,* pp. 393–407, 410–28, passim; and Bill Clinton, *My
    Life,* pp. 848–55, 858–60, passim. For figures on conditions in Kosovo as of 2005,
    see Judah, "Impasse in Kosovo," pp. 36–8; Nicholas Wood, "NATO Expanding
    Kosovo Forces to Combat Violence," *New York Times,* March 19, 2004; idem,
    "Serbs Boycott Kosovo Vote, Raising Fear for Future," *New York Times,* October
    25, 2004; "Kosovo's New Chance," editorial, March 9, 2005, "World Briefing,"
    March 16, 2005, and Nicholas Wood, "Kosovo at a Crossroads: U.N. Sees a Deal
    Just Ahead," October 2, 2005"– all in *New York Times.*
58. Robert W. Tucker and David C. Hendrickson, "The Sources of American Legiti-
    macy," *Foreign Affairs* 83, no. 6 (November/December, 2004): 30–1; Tim Judah,
    "Impasse in Kosovo," *The New York Review of Books,* June 10, 2004, pp. 36–
    8; Maj. Gen. Lewis MacKenzie, "We Bombed the Wrong Side," op-ed, *National
    Post* (Canada), April 6, 2004, p. A14; and Martin C. Sletzinger and Nida Gelazis,
    "Kosovo: Mission Not Yet Accomplished," *The Wilson Quarterly* 29, no. 3
    (Autumn 2005): 35–41.
59. Ken Silverstein, "Official Pariah Sudan Valuable to America's War on Terrorism,"
    Los Angeles Times, April 29, 2005.
60. Steve Weissman, "Torture from J. F. K. to Baby Bush," truthout/Perspective, Decem-
    ber 31, 2004, <http://www.truthout.org/docs>; and Michael Foster Rothbart, *A
    Question of Torture: CIA Interrogation from the Cold War to the War on Terror*
    (New York: Metropolitan, 2006); passim.
61. Rothkopf, *Running the World,* p. 404; R. Jeffrey Smith, "Berger Hid Archives
    Papers under a Trailer," December 21, 2006, Larry Margasak, "Report Says
    Berger Hid Archive Documents," December 21, 2006 – both in the *Washington
    Post;* Reuters, "Clinton Says He Warned Bush of bin Laden Threat," October
    16, 2003, <http://www.truthout.org/docs_03article_101703A.shtml>. See Chapter
    7 for Rice's testimony before the 9/11 Commission. Berger pleaded guilty, received
    a criminal sentence, paid a $50,000 fine, and forfeited his security clearance for
    three years.

Chapter 7: Flaunting Faustian Foreign Policy

1. Garry Wills, "A Country Ruled by Faith," *New York Review of Books*, November 16, 2006, pp. 8–12 (quotation at 11); and Rajiv Chandrasekaran, *Imperial Life in the Emerald City: Inside Iraq's Green Zone* (New York: Knopf, 2006), pp. 91, 94.

2. Walter LaFeber, "The Bush Doctrine," *Diplomatic History* 26, no. 4 (Fall 2004): 557; Ted Koppel, "The Long, Cost-Free War," op-ed, *New York Times*, November 6, 2006, p. A21 (quotation); and Paul Kringman, "For God's Sake," op-ed, *New York Times*, April 13, 2007.

3. David M. Kennedy, "What Is Patriotism without Sacrifice?" *New York Times*, WK, February 16, 2003; and Lizabeth Cohen, *A Consumer Republic: The Politics of Mass Consumption in Postwar America* (New York: Knopf, 2003), passim. Cohen also thinks that postwar consumerism was both a triumph for capitalism and the downfall of civil society in the United States as mass consumption replaced social action and the old, civic-minded patriotic citizen was replaced by the new patriot: the citizen purchaser.

4. David Rothkopf, *Running the World: The Inside Story of the National Security Council and the Architects of American Power* (New York: PublicAffairs, 2005), pp. 402–3; *Washington Post*, editorial, April 24, 2001; Laura Flanders, "Warnacular: Post-Blast, Familiar Terms Take on New Meanings," *The Progressive Populist*, October 15, 2001; and Naomi Klein, "Signs of the Times," *The Nation*, October 22, 2001, pp. 15–16 (quotations).

5. Kevin Phillips, *American Theocracy: The Peril and Politics of Radical Religion, Oil, and Borrowed Money in the 21st Century* (New York: Viking, 2006), pp. 265–318; Paul Krugman, "Debt and Denial," *New York Times*, February 13, 2006; Jonathan Rauch, "The New Nixon," and James Fallows, "Countdown to a Meltdown," both in *The Atlantic Monthly*, July/August 2005, pp. 27, 52–3; Peter G. Peterson, "Riding for a Fall," *Foreign Affairs* 88, no. 4 (September/October 2004): 111–25; and "Forum: The Iceberg Cometh: Can a Nation of Spenders Be Saved?" *Harper's Magazine*, June 2005, pp. 39–46.

6. Jonathan Weisman, "War Costs Approach $10 Billion a Month," *San Francisco Chronicle*, April 20, 2006; Linda Bilmes, "The Trillion Dollar War," *New York Times*, August 20, 2005; and Thomas E. Ricks, *Fiasco: The American Military Adventure in Iraq* (New York: Penguin, 2006), pp. 98, 109, 431.

7. Fallows, "Countdown to a Meltdown"; Peterson, "Riding for a Fall," pp. 111–25; and "Forum: The Iceberg Cometh."

8. Ibid.; Phillips, *American Theocracy*, pp. 265–346, 375–82 (definition of "financialization" at 268).

9. Phillips, *American Theocracy*, p. 268; and Benjamin Friedman, "Meltdown: A Case Study," *Atlantic Monthly*, July/August 2005, p. 66–8 (quotation at 66).

10. Stanley Hoffmann, "America Goes Backward," *The New York Review*, June 12, 2003, pp. 74–80; Arnold A. Offner, "Rogue President, Rogue Nation: Bush and U.S. National Security," *Diplomatic History* 29, no. 3 (June 2005): 433–5; Michael Mann, *Incoherent Empire* (London: Verso, 2003), pp. 1–17, 36–7; Ivo H. Daalder and James M. Lindsay, *American Unbound: The Bush Revolution in Foreign Policy* (Washington, DC: Brookings Institution Press, 2003); idem, "Bush's Foreign Policy Revolution," in Fred Greenstein, ed., *The George W. Bush Presidency: An Early Assessment* (Baltimore: Johns Hopkins University Press, 2003), pp. 100–37;

Jennifer Block, "Christian Soldiers on the March: Bush's Handpicked Delegates Disrupt Global Conferences on Women Rights," *The Nation*, February 3, 2003; William Fisher, "Global Gag: USAID Sued for Impeding Foreign Family Planning, AID/HIV Funding with 'Anti-Prostitution Policy,'" Inter Press Service, August 24, 2005; Keith B. Richburg, "After 100 Days, Europe Divided on Bush," *New York Times*, April 29, 2001, Christian Plumb, "U.S. Blasts U.N. Kyoto Pact as 'Strait-jacket,'" Reuters, December 1, 2003; Andrew Buncombe, "How America Plotted to Stop Kyoto Deal," *Independent* (UK), December 8, 2005, Haider Rizvi, "U.S. No Longer Promoting Landmine Abolition," December 28, 2005, and idem," U.S. Opposes Litany of Global Treaties in 2005," December 26, 2005 – both posted on OneWorld.net.

11. "Missing Nuclear Leadership," editorial, May 8, 2005; David E. Sanger, "Nuclear Arms Treaty, May 14, 2002; David E. Sanger and Michael Wines, "Bush and Putin Sign Pact for Steep Nuclear Arms Cuts," May 25, 2002; Michael Wines, "After U.S. Scraps ABM treaty, Russia Rejects Curbs of Start II," June 15, 2002 – all in *New York Times*.

12. Jim Michaels, "Aristide Says U.S. to Blame for Ouster," *USA Today*, March 2, 2004; John Maxwell, "Washington's Tar Baby," *Washington Post*, March 7, 2004; "Aristide Back in Caribbean Heat – Before Arriving in Jamaica, Haitian Details 'Coup' by U.S.," *Washington Post*, March 16, 2004; "Looters Impede Aid to Haiti: U.N. Sending More Troops," *New York Times*, September 28, 2004; "Haiti's Leader Says Aristide Is Behind Violence," *New York Times*, October 18, 2004; and "Haiti Archives," *The Progressive Review* <http://prorev.com/haiti.htm>.

13. "UN Troops Kill Six in Haiti Raid," July 11, 2005; "Father Jean-Juste Arrested in Port-au-Prince, Held Incommunicado," July 25, 2005; and "20 Massacred in Port-au-Prince Soccer Stadium, Jailed Jean-Juste Mulls Presidential Run," August 26, 2005 – all in *Democracy Now!*, http://www.democracynow.org; "Justice Scorned in Haiti," editorial, August 20, 2004; "Looters Impede Aid to Haiti; UN Sending More Troops," September 28, 2004; Michael Kamber, "A Troubled Haiti Struggles to Gain Its Political Balance," January 5, 2005; Ginger Thompson, "Haitians Dance for Joy as Préval Is Declared Winner," February 17, 2006; idem, Préval's Silence Obscures Quiet Bid to Reunite Haiti," February 20, 2006; Marc Lacey, "U.N. Troops Fight Haiti Gangs One Street at a Time," February 10, 2007 – all in *New York Times*; and "Shocking *Lancet* Study," *Democracy Now!*, August 31, 2006, <democracynow.org/article.pl?sid=06/08/31/144231>.

14. Madeleine Albright, *Madam Secretary: A Memoir* (New York: Miramax Books, 2003), pp. 455–69; Bill Clinton, *My Life* (New York: Knopf, 2004), pp. 602–3, 624–5, 828, 856, 935, 938; Mann, *Incoherent Empire*, pp. 198–205; Douglas Frantz, "What Danger Does North Korea Posez," *Los Angeles Times*, December 9, 2003; and Thomas Blood, *Madam Secretary: A Biography of Madeleine Albright* (New York: St Martin's Press, 1997), pp. 107–11.

15. Rothkopf, *Running the World*, pp. 402–4; John Feffer, "Bush Policy Undermines Progress on Korean Peninsula," *Foreign Policy in Focus* 7, no. 2 (March 2002), <http://www.fpif.org/briefs/vol7/v7no2korea_body.html>; and *BBC News*, May 6, 2002, <news.bbc.co.uk/2/hi/americas/1971852.stm>.

16. David E. Sanger, "U.S. Plans to Renew Its Offer of Food Aid to North Korea," *New York Times*, June 23, 2005, p. A3 (quotations); and Glenn Kessler and Thomas E. Ricks, "Rice's NSC Tenure Complicated New Post," *Washington Post*, November 16, 2004.

17. Ibid.; Albright, *Madam Secretary*, pp. 470–2; Glenn Kessler, "What That Accord Really Says," *Washington Post*, September 25, 2005, p. B2; David E. Sanger, "North Korea Returning to Nuclear Talks, U.S. Says," June 7, 2005, David Stout, "Bush and South Korean President Stress Common Goals," June 10, 2005; David E. Sanger, "U.S. and Seoul Try to Ease Rift on Talks With the North," June 11, 2005; AP release, "Bush, S. Korea Try to Bridge Differences," June 11, 2005; David E. Sanger, "U.S. Plans to Renew Its Offer of Food Aid to North Korea"; James Brooke, "Talks Stalled, U.S. Envoy Matches Insults of North Korea," December 15, 2005, and "Diplomacy's Fleeting Moment in Korea," editorial, January 3, 2006 – all in *New York Times*.

18. Robert Parry, "Bush's Tough-Talkin' Korean Bungle," Consortium News, October 10, 2006, <http://www.truthout.org/docs_2006/article_101006C.shtml>; Barbara Demick, "Diverted Attention, Neglect Set the State for Kim's Move," *Los Angeles Times*, October 10, 2006; David E. Sanger, "U.S. to Roll Out Tepid Welcome for President of South Korea," September 14, 2006; Jimmy Carter, "Solving the Korean Stalemate, One Step at a Time," op-ed, October 11, 2006; Warren Hoge, "Security Council Supports Sanctions on North Korea," October 15, 2006; "Testing North Korea," editorial, WK, November 2, 2006; David E. Sanger, "Outside Pressures Broke Korean Deadlock February 13, 2007" – all in *New York Times*; and "Faith-Based Nonproliferation," editorial, *Wall Street Journal*, February 14, 2007.

19. Seymour M. Hersh, "The Iran Plan: Would President Bush Go to War to Stop Tehran from Getting the Bomb?" *The New Yorker*, April 17, 2006, pp. 30–7 (first quotation at 33). Hersh indicates that Stephen Hadley, Stephen Cambone, and Robert Joseph, all of whom became prominent members of the administration, signed this think tank report). Also see Dora Alves, "Not Wandering Off into an International No-Man's Land," *Conflict* 9, no. 4 (1989): 362; Anthony Lewis, op-ed, "Abroad at Home; Mr. Bush's New World," *New York Times*, October 13, 2001; Lynda Hurst, "Knocking on the Nuclear Door," *Toronto Star*, February 20, 2005 (other quotations); and John Dumbrell, *American Foreign Policy: Carter to Clinton* (New York: St. Martin's Press, 1997), p. 49.

20. Sarah Olson, "Bush Pushes Nuclear Weapons Development in US," truthout/ Report, September 1, 2006, <http://www/truthout.org/docs_2006/article_090106J. shtml>; Guy Dinmore, "Bush Promotes 'Nuclear Hawks,'" *The Financial Times* (UK), February 1, 2005; and Richard N. Haass, *The Opportunity: American's Moment to Alter History's Course* (New York: Public Affairs, 2005), pp. 87–8.

21. Hurst, "Knocking on the Nuclear Door;" Walter Pincus, "Rumsfeld Seeks to Revive Burrowing Nuclear Bomb," *Washington Post*, February 1, 2005; and Christopher Smith, "Energy Secretary Pushes to Ramp Up U.S. Ability to Test Nuke Bombs, *Salt Lake Tribune*, February 16, 2005.

22. Julian Borger, "Deadlock Looms over Spread of Nuclear Arms, *Guardian* (UK), May 2, 2005; and "UN Nuclear Review Ending in Failure, Japanese Envoy Says," Bloomberg News.com, May 27, 2005.

23. Saul Hudson, "Bush Won't Exclude Iran Nuke Strike," Reuters, April 18, 2006 (first quotation); Hersh, "The Iran Plan: Would President Bush Go to War to Stop Tehran from Getting the Bomb?," p. 30 (second quotation); idem, "The Next Act: Is a Damaged Administration Less Likely to Attack Iran or More? *The New Yorker*, November 27, 2006, pp. 94–107; Craig Unger, "From the Wonderful Folks Who Brought You Iraq," *Vanity Fair*, March 2007, pp. 292–304 (last quotation at 309);

David Stout, "Bush Calls Reports of Plan to Strike Iran 'Speculation,'" April 10, 2006, and Mark Mazzetti, "Some in G.O.P. Say Iran Threat Is Played Down," August 23, 2006 – both in *New York Times*; Dan Froomkin, "History Repeating Itself," *Washington Post*, August 23, 2006; Uzi Mahnaimi and Sarah Baxter, "Revealed: Israel Plans Nuclear Strike on Iran," *Sunday Times* (London), January 7, 2007; and idem, "Israel Plans for War with Iran and Syria," *The Times* (UK), September 2006.

24. David E. Sanger, "The World: We Are (Aren't) Safer With India in the Nuclear Club," WK, March 5, 2006, Mark Mazzetti, "House Passes Deal with India on Sale of Nuclear Weapons," December 9, 2006, Somini Sengupta, "Interests Drive U.S. to Back a Nuclear India," December 10, 2006 – all in *New York Times*; Research Unit for Political Economy, "Why the United States Promotes India's Great-Power Ambitions," *Aspects of India's Economy*, no. 4 (December 2005); and Dilip Hiro, "A Catch-22 Nuclear World: Nuclear Weapons Programs Are about Regime Survival," June 11, 2007, TomDispatch.com.

25. Michael T. Klare, "Mapping the Oil Motive," March 18, 2005, TomPaine.com; idem, "The Twilight Era of Petroleum," August 5, 2005; TomDispatch.com, and Robert Collier, "Iraq Invasion May Be Remembered as Start of the Age of Oil Scarcity," *San Francisco Chronicle*, March 20, 2005.

26. Phillips, *American Theocracy*, pp. 68–74; and John Chapman, "The Real Reason Bush Went to War," *The Guardian* (UK), July 28, 2004.

27. Greg Palast, "OPEC on the March: Why Iraq Still Sells Its Oil à la Cartel," *Harper's Magazine*, April 2005, pp. 74–7; interview with Palast aired on *Democracy Now!*, March 21, 2005, about the BBC *New Night* report about interview with Phillip Carroll about U.S. oil policy, <http//www.democracynow.org/article.pl?sid=05/03/21/1455245>; David McNeill, "Noam Chomsky, Controlling the Oil in Iraq Puts American in Strong Position to Exert Influence on the World," *The Independent* (UK), January 24, 2005; Paul Krugman, "The Ugly American Bank," op-ed, *New York Times*, March 18, 2005; Ricks, *Fiasco*, p. 98 (Wolfowitz quoted); and Derrick Z. Jackson, op-ed, "Robbery, Not Reconstruction in Iraq," *Boston Globe*, April 18, 2006.

28. Failing to turn Iraqi oil over to American companies, Bremer, as head of the now-defunct Coalition Provisional Authority (CPA), successfully managed to issue one hundred orders designed to privatize all other aspects of the Iraqi economy by giving economic advantage to U.S. and elite foreign interests over those of the Iraqi people. These orders stayed in effect during the provisional government of Prime Minister Ayad Allawi and were incorporated into the interim Iraqi constitution drafted in August. See Antonia Juhasz, "Commentary: The Hand-Over That Wasn't; Illegal Orders Give the U.S. a Lock on Iraq's Economy," *Los Angeles Times*, August 5, 2004. Juhasz argues that Bremer's orders were illegal because they "fundamentally altered Iraq's existing laws." She believes that they violated the American-approved Hague regulations of 1907 and the U.S. Army's Law of Land Warfare – both of which disallow the transformation of an occupied country's laws. For example, Order No. 39 permitted the privatization of around 200 of Iraqi's state-owned enterprises; 100 percent foreign ownership of Iraqi businesses; "national treatment" granting no preferences to local businesses; unrestricted, tax-free status for all profits and other income by foreign companies; and forty-year ownership leases. Also see Antonia Juhasz, "Commentary: A Nice Little War to Fill the Coffers, October 14, 2004, and idem, "Bush's Economic Invasion of Iraq; U.S. Corporations March

into Bagdad, at the Expense of Self-Determination," August 14, 2005 – both in *Los Angeles Times*.

29. Interview with Palast about Carroll aired on *Democracy Now!*; and Erin E. Arvedlund, "Russian Exile from Yukos Assails Putin as a Despot," *New York Times*, March 21, 2005, p. A6.

30. "Rich in Oil, Poor in Everything Else," three op-ed pieces, *New York Times*, December 4, 2003, p. A39; and "Pipeline to Promise of Pipeline to Peril: New U.S. Backed Oil Route Starts Moving Crude Oil from Azerbaijan to the West," aired on *Democracy Now!*, May 27, 2005, <http://www.democracynow.org/article.pl?sid = 05/05/27/1410246>.

31. H. W. Brands, *The Use of Force after the Cold War* (College Station: Texas A&M University Press, 2000), pp. 41–2; Stephen Kinzer, *Overthrow: America's Century of Regime Change from Hawaii to Iraq* (New York: Times Books, 2006), pp. 129–47, 194–259, passim; William Blum, *Rogue State: A Guide to the World's Only Superpower* (Monroe, ME: Common Courage Press, 2000), pp. 125–78; and Gore Vidal, *Perpetual War for Perpetual Peace: How We Got to Be So Hated* (New York: Thunder's Mouth Press, 2002), pp. 22–41 (for listing of U.S. military interventions from 1948 to 1999).

32. For the entire ninety-page 2000 PNAC report, see <http://www.newamerican century.org/RebuildingAmericasDefenses.pdf>; and for the sanitized public version of "The National Security Strategy of the United States of America," September 2002, see <http://www.whitehouse.gov/nsc/nss.html>.

33. Melvyn P. Leffler, "9/11 and American Foreign Policy," and Arnold A. Offner, "Rogue President, Rogue Nation: Bush and U.S. National Security," pp. 434–5 – both in *Diplomatic History* 29, no. 3 (June 2005): 396 (first quotation)–97, 403–5.

34. Richard Falk, "The New Bush Doctrine," *The Nation*, July 15, 2002, pp. 9–11 (first quotation at 9); Gideon Rose, "Get Real," op. ed., *New York Times*, August 18, 2005, p. A25; and Leffler, "9/11 and American Foreign Policy," pp. 395–413 (other quotations at 412). Also see responses to Leffler's assertion that there is more continuity to Bush's foreign policy in contrast to claims that it is revolutionary, pp. 415–44. See Chapter 5 for a discussion of Kraemer's views and the various incarnations of the CPD.

35. Schlesinger, "Eyeless in Iraq, p. 24; Michael Isikoff, "2001 Memo Reveals Push for Broader Presidential Powers," *Newsweek*, December 18, 2004; The Pew Global Attitudes Project, "A Year after Iraq War: Mistrust of America in Europe Ever Higher, Muslim Anger Persists," March 16, 2004, <http://www.peoplepress.org>; and Angus Reid Consultants, "Europeans See U.S. as Threat to Global Security," September 5, 2006, <http://www.angus-reid.com/polls/index.cfm \ fuseaction/ viewItemID/13028>.

36. Chris Mooney, "The Editorial Pages and the Case for War," *Columbia Journalism Review*, March/April, 2004, pp. 28–34 (quotations at 33); Schlesinger, "Eyeless in Iraq," p. 24; Robert Jervis, "Mutual Assured Destruction," *Foreign Policy* 133 (November/December 2002): 40–2; and Haas, *The Opportunity*, pp. 94–8, 187.

37. Mark Danner, "The Secret Way to War," *New York Review of Books*, June 9, 2005, pp. 70–4; Norman Solomon, "From Watergate to Downing Street – Lying for War," Common Dreams News Center, June 6, 2005, <http://www.commondreams.org/ cgi-bin/print.cgi?file=/view05/0606–20.htm>; idem, *War Made Easy: How Presidents and Pundits Keep Spinning Us to Death* (New York: Wiley, 2005); John Daniszewski, "New Memos Detail Early Plans for Invading Iraq," *Los Angeles*

Times, June 15, 2005; "The Downing Street Memo Comes to Washington; Conyers Blasts 'Deafening Sound of Silence'," aired on *Democracy Now!*, June 15, 2005, <http://www.democracynow.org/article.pl?sid=05/06/15/1345223>; and Derrick Z. Jackson, "A Madness for War," *The Boston Globe*, March 29, 2006.

38. John Hendren, "Policy OKs First Strike to Protect US," *Los Angeles Times*, March 19, 2005; and Mark Massetti, "Contentious Defense Official to Depart," *Los Angeles Times*, January 27, 2005.

39. Department of Defense Office of the Inspector General, "Review of Pre-Iraqi War Activities of the Office of the Under Secretary of Defense for Policy," Report No. 07-INTEL-04, February 9, 2007 (quotation from Executive Summary); David S. Cloud and Mark Mazzetti, "Prewar Intelligence Unit at Pentagon Is Critictized," *New York Times*, February 9, 2007; AP, "Ex-Pentagon Official Defends Iraq Stance," *New York Times*, February 11, 2007. See Chapter 5 for details about the PFIAB.

40. James Risen, *State of War: The Secret History of the CIA and the Bush Administration* (New York: The Free Press, 2006), pp. 42–60; idem and Eric Lichtblau, "Bush Lets U.S. Spy on Callers without Courts," December 16, 2005; David E. Sanger, "Bush Says He Ordered Domestic Spying," December 18, 2005, Richard W. Stevenson and Adam Liptak, "Cheney Defends Eavesdropping without Warrants," December 21, 2005; Adam Liptak, "Little Help from Justices on Spy Program," December 23, 2005; "Mr. Cheney's Imperial Presidency," editorial, December 23, 2005, James Bamford, "The Agency That Could Be Big Brother," WK, December 25, 2005; Eric Lichtblau and James Risen, "Justice Deputy Resisted Parts of Spy Program," January 1, 2006; Frank Rich, "The Wiretappers That [sic] Couldn't Shoot Straight," op-ed, WK, January 8, 2006; Eric Lichtblau and Scott Shane, "Basis for Spying in U.S. Is Doubted," January 7, 2006; Bob Herbert, "The Lawbreaker in the Oval Office," op-ed, January 12, 2006; and John Yoo, "How the Presidency Regained Its Balance," op-ed, WK, September 17, 2006 – all in *New York Times*; Noah Feldman, "Who Can Check the President?," *New York Times Magazine*, January 8, 2006, pp. 52–7; Douglas Birch, "NSA Used City Policy as Trackers," *Baltimore Sun*, January 13, 2006; Brian Knowlton, "Specter Expresses Doubts about Surveillance Program," *International Herald Tribune*, January 15, 2006.

41. Adam Liptak and Eric Lichblau, "Judge Finds Wiretap Actions Violate the Law," August 18, 2006; na, "Bipartisanship on Hold," November 10, 2006; James Risen, "The War on Terror under New Scrutiny," December 3, 2006 – all in *New York Times*; Anuska Asthana and Karen DeYoung, "Bush Calls for Greater Wiretap Authority," *Washington Post*, September 8, 2006. Prior to this decision it had been revealed that the Bush administration had been secretly monitoring international bank transactions without court approval. Bush denounced the disclosure as "disgraceful." See Scott Shane, "Behind Bush's Fury, a Vow Made in 2001," *New York Times*, June 29, 2006; and "Is Bush Administration's Bank Spy Program One Part of a Resurgent Total Information Awareness?," *Democracy Now!*, June 27, 2006, <http://www.democracynow.org/article.pl?sid=06/06/27/1433207>.

42. Tim Harper, "Cheney Argues for Nixon-Era Powers," *Toronto Star*, December 21, 2005; Robert Parry, "Alito and the Ken Lay Factor," January 12, 2006, <http://www.consortiumnews.com/article/2006/011106.html>; Jess Bravin, "Judge Alito's View of the Presidency: Expansive Powers," *Wall Street Journal*, January 10, 2006; and "The President and the Courts," editorial, *New York Times*, March 20,

2006. For a discussion of the increased "semi-constitutional" powers of all presidents since the Cold War, including executive agreements, see Chapter 5.

43. Feldman, "Who Can Check the President?," p. 55; James Gordon Meek, "W Pushes Envelope on US Spying," *New York Daily News*, January 4, 2007; Risen, *State of War*, pp. 47–8, 58–9; and Charlie Savage, "Bush Shuns Patriot Act Requirement," *Boston Globe*, March 24, 2006.

44. Charlie Savage, "Bush Challenges Hundreds of Laws," April 30, 2006, and idem, "Panel Chides Bush on Bypassing Laws," July 24, 2006 – both in *Boston Globe*; "Veto? Who Needs a Veto?," editorial, *New York Times*, May 5, 2006, p. A22; and "A White House Power Grab," editorial, *San Francisco Chronicle*, June 12, 2006. For a review of attempts by presidents to implement the unitary executive theory, see "Unitary Executive Theory," <http://en.wikipedia.org>.

45. David Johnson, "C.I.A. Tells of Bush's Directive on the Handling of Detainees," November 15, 2006; AP, "Supreme Court Is Asked to Block Terror Tribunals," August 9, 2005; Linda Greenhouse, "Justices to Rule on a Challenge to U.S. Tribunals," November 8, 2005; idem, "Detainee Case Will Pose Delicate Question for Court," March 17, 2006; idem, "Justices Hint That They'll Rule on Challenge Filed by Detainee," March 29, 2006"; and "The President and the Courts," editorial, March 20, 2006 – all in *New York Times*.

46. Linda Greenhouse, "Guantánamo Case: Military Panels Found to Lack Authority – New Law Possible,"; David E. Sanger and Scott Shane, "Court's Ruling Is Likely to Force Negotiations over Presidential Power," and David G. Savage, "High Court Rejects Bush's Claim That He Alone Sets Detainee Rules," June 30, 2006 – all in *New York Times*.

47. "Stampeding Congress,"editorial, September 15, 2006; "Rushing Off a Cliff," editorial, September 28, 2006 (quotations); and Scott Shane and Adam Liptak, "News Analysis: Shifting Power to a President," September 30, 2006 – all in *New York Times*; James Bovard, "Bush's Torture Ticking Time Bomb," *American Conservative*, December 18, 2006.

48. "Rushing Off a Cliff"(first quotation); and Bob Herbert, "The Kafka Strategy," op-ed, *New York Times*, September 18, 2006, p. A27 (second quotation).

49. "A Dangerous New Order," editorial, *New York Times*, October 19, 2006 (first quotation); and Legal Scholars' Letter to Congress, September 26, 2006.

50. Jim Lobe, "Pentagon's Feith Again at Center of Disaster," Inter Press Service, May 20, 2004; AP release and ABC News, "Bush Claimed Right to Waive Torture Laws," June 23, 2004; Marjorie Cohn, "Redefining Torture," posted January 3, 2005, on truthout/Perspective, <http://truthout.org/docs_05/printer_010305A.shtml>; Feldman, "Who Can Check the President?," p. 55; and Marianne Means,"President Doth Protest Too Much," *Seattle Post-Intelligencer*, June 27, 2004.

51. Michael Isikoff, "Double Standards?," *Newsweek*, May 21, 2004; Douglas Jehl and David Johnston, "C.I.A. Empowered to Send Suspects Abroad to Jails," *New York Times*, March 6, 2005, pp. A1, 11; Edward J. Markey, "US Must Stop 'Outsourcing' Torture," posted March 12, 2005, on commondreams.org; Jane Mayer, "Outsourcing Torture," *The New Yorker*, February 14, 2005; Sidney Blumenthal, "Above the Rule of Law," *Guardian* (UK), August 5, 2005; Dana Priest, "CIA Holds Terror Suspects in Secret Prisons," November 2, 2005; idem, "Covert CIA Program Withstands New Furor," December 30, 2005 – both in *Washington Post*; Douglas Jehl, "Senate Is Set to Require White House to Account for Secret Prisons," *New York Times*, December 15, 2005, p. A19; and "Extraordinary Rendition

Scandal Reaches New Heights: Rice on Offensive in Europe Over Bush Administration's Use of 'Torture Flights,'" _Democracy Now!_ interview with Michael Ratner, president of the Center for Constitutional Rights, December 5, 2005, <http://www.democracynow.org/article.pl?sid=05/12/05/1455239>.

52. AP release, "Rumsfeld Ordered Prisoner Abuse," May 16, 2004; Dana Milbank, "In Cheney's Shadow, Counsel [Addington] Pushes the Conservative Cause," _Washington Post_, October 11, 2004, p. A21; Anne Gearan, "Ex-Powell Aide Criticises Bush on Iraq," AP, November 29, 2005; Julian Borger, "Cheney 'May Be Guilty of War Crime,'" _Guardian_ (UK), November 30, 2005, quoting Wilkerson; Steven R. Weisman, "The Saturday Profile: Ex-Powell Aide Moves from Insider to Apostate," _New York Times_, December 24, 2005; and Jane Mayer, "Annals of the Pentagon: The Memo: How an Internal Effort to Ban the Abuse and Torture of Detainees was Thwarted," _The New Yorker_, February 27, 2006, pp. 32–41.

53. "Secretary Rice's Rendition," editorial, December 7, 2005; Richard Bernstein, "Skepticism Seems to Erode Europeans' Faith in Rice," December 7, 2005; idem, Rice's Visit: Official Praise, Public Doubts," December 11, 2005; Maureen Dowd, "Weaselly Rice Tortures Facts," December 11, 2005 – all in _New York Times_; Savage, "Bush Shuns Patriot Act Requirement;" and Dick Meyer, "Torturing the Truth," CBS News (Bush telling Katie Couric that "we don't torture"), September 8, 2006, <http://truthout.org/docs_2006/article_090906E.shtml>.

54. Gary Cohn and Ginger Thompson, "Unearthed: Fatal Secrets of a Carefully Crafted Deception," _The Baltimore Sun_, June 18, 1995; Scott Shane, "Cables Show Central Negroponte Role in 80's Covert War against Nicaragua," _New York Times_, April 13, 2005; "New Docs Shed Light on Negroponte's Role in Honduras, Iran-Contra Affair," _Democracy Now!_, April 13, 2005, <http://www.democracynow. org/article.pl?sid=005/04/13/1356211>; Mann, _Incoherent Empire_, pp. 4, 37, 177, 201; Marc Ash, "At War," truthout/Perspective, July 2, 2004; Ray McGovern, "Hail, Hail, the Gang's All Here: Negroponte Will Fit Right In," February 19, 2005; and Marjorie Cohn, "Negroponte: Director of Intelligence Manipulation," February 21, 2005 – all in <http://www.truthout.org/docs_2004/2005/ article_070204A and /021905C and 0221005B.shtml>; Trevor Royle, "New Front on the War on Terror," _The Sunday Herald_ (Scotland), February 20, 2005; Robert Scheer, "The Peter Principle and the Neocon Coup," November 16, 2004; and Doyle McManus, "Bush Pulls 'Neo-Cons' Out of the Shadows," January 22, 2005 – both in _Los Angeles Times_.

55. Richard W. Stevenson, "Bush Hints He Will Withhold Other Papers on Bolton," June 1, 2005; Douglas Jehl, "Democrats List More Names in Inquiry on Bolton's Access," June 11, 2005; Sheryl Gay Stolberg, "Democrats Block a Vote on Bolton for the Second Time," June 21, 2005; and Elisabeth Bumiller and Sheryl Gay Stolberg, "President Sends Bolton to U.N.; Bypasses Senate," August 2, 2005 – all in _New York Times_; Julian Borger, "Bolton Throws UN Summit into Chaos," _Guardian_ (UK), August 26, 2005; Ewen MacAskill, "Britain Heads for Clash with US: Disagreement over America's Bid to Derail UN Reform," _The Guardian_ (UK), August 27, 2005; and Phyllis Bennis, "A Declaration of War," August 31, 2005, TomPaine.com.

56. Jonathan Weisman, "GOP Senators' Bid to Confirm Bolton Is Called Off," _Washington Post_, September 8, 2006; Jim Lobe, "Time Runs Out on Bolton Nomination," Inter Press Service News Agency, September 11, 2006, <http://www. ipsnews.net/article.asp?idnews=34685>; and Peter Baker and William Branigin,

"John Bolton Resigns as U.S. Ambassador to U.N.," *Washington Post*, December 4, 2006.

57. David Leigh and Nick Pryer, "Condi Had to Prove to Her Father She Could Be Successful and the Son He Craved," *Mail on Sunday* (London), November 21, 2004, section FB, pp. 32–3; Julia Reed, "The President's Prodigy," *Vogue*, October 2001, pp. 398–403, 448–9; John Prados, "Blindsided or Blind?," *Bulletin of the Atomic Scientists* 60, no. 4 (July/August 2004): 27 (quotation); and Laura Flanders, *Bushwomen: How They Won the White House for Their Man* (New York: Verso, 2004).

58. Mark Z. Barabak, "Not Always Diplomatic in Her First Major Post," *Los Angeles Times*, January 16, 2005; and Ann Reilly Dowd, "What Makes Condi Run?," *AARP*, September/October 2005, pp. 69–74, 141–2.

59. Rothkopf, *Running the World*, pp. 393–5; Condoleezza Rice, "Campaign 2000: Promoting the National Interest," *Foreign Affairs* 79, no. 1 (January/February 2000): 45–62; Reed, "The President's Prodigy," pp. 398–9; Jim Lobe, "Hawks Flying High with Posting of Condoleezza Rice to State Department," *Washington Report of ME Affairs* 24 (January/February 2005): 22 (first quotation); Karen DeYoung and Steven Mufson, "Leaner, Less Visible NSC Taking Shape," February 10, 2001, pp. A1, A6 (second quotation); Steven Mufson and Mike Allen, "'Realism' Cited in a Blunt New Foreign Policy," March 22, 2001 – both in *Washington Post*; and Dowd, "What Makes Condi Run?," (9/11 quotation).

60. Glenn Kessler and Peter Slevin, "Rice Fails to Repair Rifts, Officials Say," *Washington Post*, October 12, 2003; "Why In-Fighting Is Losing Iraq and Could Cost Rumsfeld His Job," *The Glasgow Sunday Herald*, October 12, 2003; Risen, *State of War*, pp. 3, 63–4; Kessler and Ricks, "Rice's NSC Tenure Complicated New Post," p. A7 (first quotation); Mark Danner, op-ed, "A Doctrine Left Behind," *New York Times*, WK, November 21, 2004, p. 13 (second quotation); Rothkopf, *Running the World*, p 404–6 (last quotation at 406); and Fred Kaplan, "Condi Lousy: Why Rice Is a Bad National Security Adviser," *Slate*, April 8, 2004, <http://slate.msn.com/id/200098499> (third quotation).

61. *The 9/11 Commission Report*, pp. 201–3; Philip Shenon, "9/11 Panel Members Weren't Told of Meeting," October 1, 2006; Philip Shenon and Mark Mazetti, "Records Confirm C. I. A. Chief Warned Rice on Al Qaeda," October 3, 2006, p. A18 – both in *New York Times*; Jason Leopold, "Tenet Warned Congress in February 2001 About al-Qaeda," Truthout/Perspective, October 2, 2006, <http://www.truthout.org/docs_2006/article-100206Y.shtml>; and William Rivers Pitt, "Condi Rice, 9/11 and Another Nest of Lies," Truthout/Perspective, October 2, 2006, <http://www.truthout.org/docs_2006/article-100206X.shtml>.

62. *The 9/11 Commission Report*, pp. 199–204, notes 172–85, 263–5; transcript, "Testimony of Condoleezza Rice before 9/11 Commission," April 8, 2004 (quotations); "Text of the President's Daily Brief for Aug. 6, 2001," April 11, 2004; "The Rice Version," editorial, April 9, 2004; Scott Shane, "'01 Memo to Rice Warned of al-Qaeda and Offered Plan," February 12, 2005 – all in *New York Times*; Kessler and Ricks, "Rice's NSC Tenure Complicates New Post"; Kaplan, "Condi Lousy: Why Rice Is a Bad National Security Adviser."

63. Tom Regan, "Washington Snubbed Iran Offer," *BBC Newsnight*, January 18, 2007; Dan Froomkin, "Another Thunderbolt from Wilkerson," *Washington Post*, November 4, 2005; Juan Cole, "Cheney Blew Off Iran in 2003," January 19, 2007, <http://www.juancole.com/index/html>; and Carol Giacomo, "Ex-Aide

Says Rice Misled Congress on Iran," Reuters, February 15, 2007, <http://www.informationclearinghouse,info/article17072.htm>.

64. "Bush Looks to State Address to Reclaim Lost Capital," *The [Australian] Age*, January 20, 2006, World section, p. 8 (quotation about transformational times); David J. Rothkopf, *Running the World*, pp. 396–8; Robert Parry, "Bush's 'Transformational' Democracy," September 22, 2004, <http://www.consortiumnews.com/2004/092204.html> (second quotation); idem, "Bush: Beyond Reason," October 19, 2004, <http://www.consortiumnews.com/article/2004/101904.html>.

65. Ibid.; Dowd, "What Makes Condi Run?" (evil empire quotation); and Suskind, "Without a Doubt," p. 51.

66. Suskind, "Without a Doubt," p. 51.

67. Byron Calame, "Beyond the Eavesdropping Story, a Loud Silence," op-ed, *New York Times*, January 1, 2006.

Epilogue: The Legacy of George W. Bush

1. *New York Times*, editorial, November 5, 2001, p. A16; Paul Krugman, "Killed by Contempt," and Bob Herbert, "A Failure of Leadership," September 5, 2005; idem, "A President Who Can Do No Right, January 26, 2006"; John Tierney, "Magic Market Strategy," and Nicholas D. Kristof, "The Larger Shame," September 6, 2005 – all op-ed pieces in the *New York Times*.

2. For a discussion of the origins of "Team B," see Chapter 5, this volume; Anne Hessing Cahn, "Team B: The Trillion-Dollar Experiment," *Bulletin of the Atomic Scientists* 49, no. 3 (April 1993): 22, 24–7; and Seymour M. Hersh, "The Iraq Hawks," *The New Yorker*, December 24 and 31, 2001, pp. 58–63.

3. Ann Scott Tyson, "Ability to Wage 'Long War' Is Key to Pentagon Plan," *Washington Post*, February 4, 2006; and David S. Cloud, "Pentagon Publishes New Long-Range Paper Setting Goals," *New York Times*, February 4, 2006.

4. Juan Forero, "New Colombia Grants Concessions to Paramilitaries," June 23, 2005; Sheryl Gay Stolberg, "Chastising Putin, Bush Says Russia Derails Reform," June 6, 2007 – both in *New York Times*; Abid Aslam, "US Selling More Weapons to Undemocratic Regimes That Support 'War on Terror,'" May 25, 2005, posted on OneWorld.net, <http://www.democracynow.org/print.pl?sid=05/05/03/1357228>.

5. Raffi Khatchadourian, op-ed, "Blowback in Africa," *New York Times*, April 28, 2006; Ken Silverstein, "Official Pariah Sudan Valuable to America's War on Terrorism," *Los Angeles Times*, April 29, 2005; "Bush Administration Allied with Sudan Despite Role in Darfur Genocide," interview with Ken Silverstein, *Democracy Now!*, May 3, 2005, <http://www.democracynow.org/article.pl?sid=05/05/03/1357228>; Jim Vande Hei and Colum Lynch, "Bush Calls for More Muscle in Darfur," *Washington Post*, February 18, 2006, p. A1; and "Spreading Genocide to Chad," editorial, *New York Times*, March 20, 2006.

6. Arthur Schlesinger, Jr., "Eyeless in Iraq," *The New York Review of Books*, October 23, 2003, p. 26 (quotation); Comment, "Bush's Messiah Complex," *The Progressive*, February, 2003, pp. 8–10; Richard Brookhiser, "The Mind of George W. Bush," *The Atlantic Monthly*, April 2003, p. 63; Joe Klein, "The Blinding Glare of His Certainty," *Time Magazine*, February 24, 2003, p. 19; and *To the Point*, hosted by Warren Olney, March 5, 2002, discussion of the role that religion plays in U.S. foreign policy under Bush, moretothepoint.com, Public Radio International

(PRI); Jeffrey Sharlet, "Jesus plus Nothing: Undercover among America's Secret Theocrats," *Harper's Magazine*, March 2003, pp. 53–64; Gary Wills, "With God on His Side," *New York Review of Books*, March 30, 2003, pp. 26–9; and Phillips, *American Theocracy*, pp. ix, 261.

7. The often-quoted section of Psalm 23 reads in part: "Even though I walk through the valley of the shadow of death/I shall fear no evil for you are with me." Bush said: "Even though I walk through the valley of the shadow of death / *Fear no evil for you are with me.*" I want to thank Anita Durkin for pointing out this misquote in "Metaphorical War-Mongering, or, The Tales of Two Bushes," paper delivered at the Historians against the War conference, Austin, Texas, February 18, 2006.

8. Wills, "A Country Ruled by Faith," *New York Review of Books*, November 16, 2006, p. 8 (quotation); Andrew Sullivan, "This Is a Religious War?," *New York Times Magazine*, October 7, 2001, p. 45l; and Mark Lilla, "Extremism's Theological Roots," op-ed, *New York Times*, WK, October 7, 2001.

9. Rahul Mahajan and Robert Jensen, "America's Unlimited War," *The Progressive Populist*, October 15, 2001, p. 16 (quotations); and *The New Republic*, editorial, "Our Reasons," November 5, 2001, p. 11.

10. Marjorie Cohn, "The Least of These," truthout/Perspective, October 16, 2004, <http://truthout.org/docs_04/article_101604A.shtml>; "Mr. Bush's Press Conference," *New York Times*, editorial April 14, 2004; Bob Woodward, *Plan of Attack* (New York: Simon and Schuster, 2004), pp. 88–9; Robert Parry, "Bush: Beyond Reason," October 19, 2004, <http://www.consortiumnees.com/article/2004/101904.html>; and Stolberg, "Chastising Putin."

11. Frank Rich, "Now on DVD: The Passion of the Bush," *New York Times*, October 3, 2004, (Bush to Land); Stephen Mansfield, *The Faith of George W. Bush* (Peabody, MA: Charisma House, 2004), pp. 110–11 (Bush to Robison); and Wills, "A Country Ruled by Faith," pp. 8–10.

12. Wills, "With God on His Side," pp. 26, 28; Joe Klein, "The Blinding Glare of His Certainty," *Time Magazine*, February 24, 2003, p. 19; Steel, "The Missionary," p. 26; Schlesinger, "Eyeless in Iraq," p. 26; Juan Stam, "Bush's Religious Language," *The Nation*, December 22, 2003, p. 27; "Inaugural Address by George W. Bush," *New York Times*, January 20, 2005; *The Lancaster* (PA) *New Era*, July 10, 2004. The White House denied that Bush told the Amish that God spoke through him. Also see David D. Kirkpatrick, "Speaking in the Tongue of Evangelicals," *New York Times*, WR, October 17, 2004. Relying on the work of Professor Bruce Lincoln at the University of Chicago Divinity School, Kirkpatrick points out that some of Bush's "double-coded signals" are reflected in such simple words or phrases as "wonder-working power," "hills to climb," "valley below," and "plan of heaven for humanity."

13. Ron Lloyd E. Ambrosius, "Woodrow Wilson and George W. Bush: Historical Comparisons of Ends and Means in Their Foreign Policies," *Diplomatic History* 30, no. 3 (June 2006): 509–43; Ron Suskind, "Without a Doubt," *New York Times Magazine*, October 17, 2004, pp. 46-7 (Bartlett quotations); William Boyd Grove, "Republican Presidential Campaign Blasphemous," *West Virginia Gazette*, October 8, 2004, <http://www.wvgazette.com/section/200410071>; and Comment, "Bush's Messiah Complex," *The Progressive*, February 2003, pp. 8–10 (Woodward quotation).

14. Wills, "A Country Ruled by Faith," pp. 10–11 (quotations); Sam Harris, "The Case against Faith," *Newsweek*, November 13, 2006, pp. 42–3; and David Kuo, "Putting

Faith before Politics," op-ed, *New York Times*, November 16, 2006, 5; and idem, *Tempting Faith: An Inside Story of Political Seduction* (New York: The Free Press, 2006), passim.

15. Harris, "The Case against Faith." It is estimated that almost half of all Americans believe that the universe was created 6,000 years ago and that Jesus will return to earth in the next 50 years, ending the world as we know it.

16. Paul S. Boyer, "John Darby Meets Saddam Hussein: Foreign Policy and Bible Prophecy," *The Chronicle of Higher Education*, February 14, 1003, pp. B9–B11 (quotation at B10); and Phillips, *American Theocracy*, pp. 252–62.

17. Boyer, "John Darby Meets Saddam Hussein"; Paul Krugman, "The War President," *New York Times*, June 24, 2005 (first quotation); and Phillips, *American Theocracy*, p. 219.

18. Phillips, *American Theocracy*, pp. 63–4, 253–4; and Laurie Goodstein, "Evangelical Leaders Join Global Warming Initiative," *New York Times*, February 8, 2006 (citing how many more evangelical leaders oppose taking up global warming as an issue).

19. Paul Kennedy, "Maintaining American Power: From Injury to Recovery," in Talbott and Chanda, eds., *The Age of Terror*, p. 61; and Benjamin Schwarz and Christopher Layne, "A New Grand Strategy," *The Atlantic Monthly*, January 2002, pp. 36–42.

20. "Transcript of President Bush's Speech," June 28, 2005; and "President's Bush's Speech about Iraq," editorial, June 29, 2005 (quotation) – both in *New York Times*.

21. Melvyn P. Leffler, "9/11 and American Foreign Policy," *Diplomatic History* 29, no. 3 (June 2005): 395–413; Arnold A. Offner, "Rogue President, Rogue Nation: Bush and U.S. National Security," *Diplomatic History* 29. no. 3 (June 2005): 435.

22. Edward Said, "Is Israel More Secure Now"? *CounterPunch*, January 4, 2002, counterpunch.org/saidsecure; Benjamin Schwarz, "Comment: Will Israel Live to 100?" *The Atlantic Monthly*, May 2005, pp. 29–32; Rahul Mahajan and Robert Jensen, "American's Unlimited War," *The Progressive Populist*, October 15, 2001, p. 16 (quotation); and Celestine Bohlen, "Thinkers Face the Limits of a Just War," *New York Times*, September 22, 2001.

23. Walter L. Hixson, *Myth to Power: Identity and U.S. Foreign Relations* (New Havan, CT: Yale University Press, 2008). Quotations are from a paper he delivered at the Historians against the War conference, Austin, Texas, February 18, 2006.

24. Mahajan and Jensen, "American's Unlimited War" (quotations); William J. Broad, "U.S. Redesigning Atomic Weapons," *New York Times*, February 7, 2005; Ian Hoffman, "Lab Officials Excited by New H-Bomb Project, *The Oakland Tribune*, February 7, 2006; and Richard N. Hass, *The Opportunity: America's Moment to Alter History's Course* (New York: PublicAffairs, 2005), pp. 42–50.

25. UN Report of the High-Level Panel on Threats, Challenges and Change, *A More Secure World: Our Shared Responsibility* (New York: United Nations, 2004); and Haas, *The Opportunity*, pp. 35–50. See Chapter 5 for a discussion of the need for redefining sovereignty in the post–Cold War world.

26. "American Israel Public Affairs Committee (AIPAC) v. Norman Finkelstein," *Democracy Now!*, June 29, 2006, <http://www.democracynow.org/article.pl?=06/06/29/1420258>; Chris Hedges, "Mutually Assured Destruction in the Middle East," July 14, 2006, posted on <http://www.truthdig.com/report/item/200060714>; "Hezbollah, the United States and the Context behind Israel's Offensive on Lebanon," *Democracy Now!*, July 17, 2006, <http://www.democracynow.org/article.pl?sid=06/07/17/1423257>; Robin Wright, "Returning to Old

Approach, U.S. Faces Risky Path Ahead," *Washington Post*, July 20, 2006 and Human Rights Watch, "Israel/Lebanon: End Indiscriminate Strikes on Civilians," <http://www.org/english.docs.2006/08/02lebano13902_txt.htm>.

27. Jonathan Glover, *Humanity: A Moral History of the Twentieth Century* (New Haven, CT: Yale University Press, 1999), p. 1; Haass, *The Opportunity*, pp. 88–9; George P. Shultz, William J. Perry, Henry A. Kissinger, and Sam Nunn, "A World Free of Nuclear Weapons," *Wall Street Journal*, January 4, 2007; and Stanley Hoffman, "America Goes Backward," *New York Review of Books*, June 12, 2003, pp. 79–80.

28. CBS, *Sixty Minutes*, June 17, 2007 (corruption under the CPA); James M. Carter, " 'A National Symphony of Theft, Corruption and Bribery': Anatomy of State Building from Iraq to Vietnam" (first quotation), paper delivered at the Historians against the War Conference, Austin, Texas, February 18, 2006; Robert F. Worth and James Glanz, "Oil Graft Fuels the Insurgency, Iraq and U.S. Say," February 5, 2006, James Glanz, "Reubuilding of Iraqi Oil Pipeline as Disaster Waiting to Happen," April 25, 2006; James Glanz and David Rohde, "U.S. Agency Find New Waste and Fraud in Iraqi Rebuilding Projects," February 1, 2007; and AP, "Auditors: Billions Squandered in Iraq," February 16, 2007 (second quotation) – all in *New York Times*.

29. *New York Times*, December 4, 2003 (three op-ed pieces); Fareed Zakaria, "Elections Are Not Democracy," *Newsweek*, February 7, 2005; Larry Diamond, "Promoting Democracy," in Eugene R. Wittkopf, ed., *Future of American Foreign Policy*, 2nd ed. (New York: St. Martin's Press, 1994), pp. 101–16; Larry Diamond, *Squandered Victory: The American Occupation and Bungled Efforts to Bring Democracy to Iraq* (New York: Times Books, 2005), passim; Seymour M. Hersh, "Get Out the Vote: Did Washington Try to Manipulate Iraq's Election?," *The New Yorker*; July 25, 2005; and Robert Scheer, "Iraq's Fig Leaf Constitution," *Los Angeles Times*, August 30, 2005.

30. Hoffmann, "America Goes Backward;" Eli Dlifton, "Amnesty Report Decries 'Politics of Fear,'" May 23, 2007, <commondreams.org/archive/2007/05/23/1406>; Nora Boustany, "Nationals Use Fear to Distract from Rights Abuses, Group Says," *Washington Post Foreign Service*, May 24, 2007; Al Gore, *The Assault on Reason* (New York: Penguin Press, 2007); and Chris Hedges, "A Culture of Atrocity," June 18, 2007, TruthDig.com (quotation).

31. David Reynolds, "Beyond Bipolarity in Space and Time," *Diplomatic History* 16 (Spring 1992): 231–3; Ghassan Salamé, *Quand l-Amérique refait le monde* (Paris: Fayard, 2005), pp. 519–47 (first quotation); and John M Carroll and George C. Herring, eds., *Modern American Diplomacy*, revised and enlarged edition (Wilmington, DE: Scholarly Resource Books, 1996), p. 10 (quotation).

32. Walter LaFeber, "The Bush Doctrine," *Diplomatic History* 26, no. 4 (Fall 2004): 553; Michael Hardt and Antonio Negri, *Multitude: War and Democracy in the Age of Empire* (New York: Penguin, 2004), pp. 235–6; and Noreena Hertz, *The Silent Takeover: Global Capitalism and the Death of Democracy* (New York: The Free Press, 2001), pp. 9–10, 106–8, 214 (note 16).

33. *The Iraq Study Group Report: The Way Forward – A New Approach* (New York: Vintage Books, 2006), p. xviii, passim.

34. Ibid.; and Joan Hoff, *Nixon Reconsidered* (New York: Basic Books, 1994), pp. 163–4, 212–13, 281–2.

35. *The Iraq Study Group Report*, pp. 61, 65–6, 84–6; and Antonia Juhasz and Raed Jarrar, "Oil Grab in Iraq," February 22, 2007, Foreign Policy in Focus (FPIF),

<http://www.fpif.org/fpiftxt/4020>. See Chapter 7 for the debate between the neo-cons and the State Department over privatization of Iraq's oil fields.

36. John M. Broder and Robin Toner, "Report on Iraq Exposes a Divide within the G.O.P.," *New York Times*, December 10, 2006; and Patrick J. Buchanan, "Coming GOP War over the War!," December 12, 2006, buchanan.org/blog. Adelman now says his "cakewalk" remark applied only to the initial invasion and ousting of Saddam.

37. Ibid., Peter Baker, "Pundits Renounce the President: Among Conservatives Voices, Discord," *Washington Post*, August 20, 2006; David Rose, "Neo Culpa," *Vanity Fair*, November 3, 2006 vanityfair.com/politics/features/2006/12/neocons200612; "Time for Rumsfeld to Go," editorial, ArmyTimes.com, November 4, 2006; Bob Woodward, *State of Denial* (New York: Simon and Schuster, 2006), pp. 406–10, 427; Helen Thomas, "Kissinger in White House Brings Deja," October 4, 2006, hthomas@hearstdc.com; Michael Wolff, "Survivor: The White House Edi-tion," *Vanity Fair*, December 2006; Lt. General Greg Newbold (ret.), "Why I Think Rumsfeld Must Go," *Time Magazine*, April 9, 2006, <http://www/time.com/magazine/printout/0,8816,1181587,00.html>; Thom Shanker, "Third Retired General Wants Rumsfeld Out," *New York Times*, April 10, 2006; and Fred Kaplan, "The Revolt Against rumsfeld," *Washington Post*, April 12, 2006, <http://www/slate.com/id/2139777/>. Those neo-cons quoted in the November *Vanity Fair* article responded by denouncing the early release of their critical remarks; see The Corner, A National Review Online Symposium, "*Vanity Fair* Unfair," <http://article.nationalreview.com>.

38. William Rivers Pitt, "The Story of the Ghost," January 31, 2005, <http://www.truthout.org/docs_2005/article_013105W.shtml>; Nicholas Wapshott, "Perle Turns on Bush in Harsh Terms," *New York Sun*, May 15, 2007; Michael R. Gordon and David S. Cloud, "The Struggle for Iraq; Rumsfeld Memo Proposed 'Major Adjustment' in Iraq," *New York Times*, December 3, 2006.

39. Todd Gitlin, *The Intellectuals and the Flag* (New York: Columbia University Press, 2005); Harold Pinter, Nobel Laureate address, "Art, Truth and Politics," December 7, 2005 (tapestry of lies quote); and Eric Alterman, *When Presidents Lie: A History of Official Deception and Its Consequences* (New York: Penguin, 2005), pp. 294–314.

40. Anders Stephanson, *Manifest Destiny: American Expansionism and the Empire of Right* (New York: Hill and Wang, 1995), pp. 11–12; and Anatol Lieven and John Hulsman, *Ethical Realism: A Vision for America's Role in the World* (New York: Pantheon, 2006).

41. Michael Goldberg, "Decline and Fall," March 16, 2006 (review of Kevin Phillips's book *American Theocracy*), posted on salon.com.

42. "President Bush's Major Speech: Doing the 9/11 Time Warp," editorial, October 7, 2005; transcript of the 2006 State of the Union address, January 31, 2006 (emphasis added); Jim Rutenberg and David S. Cloud, "Bush Abandons Phrase 'Stay the Course' on Iraq," October 24, 2006; "The Real Disaster," editorial, January 1, 2007; transcript of "New Way Forward" speech, January 10, 2007 – all in *New York Times*; Robert Parry, "Bush's Latest Iraq War Lies," October 16, 2005 (about Bush's October 6 address), <http://www.consortiumnews.com/2005/101505>; and Jim VandeHei, "Bush Says U.S. Troops Will Stay in Iraq Past '08," *Washington Post*, March 22, 2006. In March 2006, Madeleine Albright said that Bush's call to "end

tyranny" was a "fantasy." See "Good versus Evil Isn't a Strategy," op-ed., *Los Angeles Times*, March 24, 2006.

43. National Intelligence Estimate, "Prospects for Iraq's Stability: A Challenging Road Ahead," February 2, 2007, <http://www.npr.org/documents/2007/feb/20070202_nie.pdf>; Sheryl Gay Stolberg, "Bush Says Iraq Pullout Would Leave U.S. at Risk," *New York Times*, May 24, 2007 (quotations); Michael Abramowitz, "Bush Blames Iraq Violence on Al-Qaeda," *Washington Post*, May 24, 2007; Garrison Keillor, "What to Do When the Emperor Has No Clothes," *Chicago Tribune*, March 1, 2006.

44. Hoffmann, "America Goes Backward," p. 80 (first quotation); Mahajan and Jensen, "American's Unlimited War," p. 16 (quotation about vision); and Pinter, Nobel Laureate address, "Art, Truth and Politics," December 7, 2005 (masquerading quote).

Bibliography

Books

Abrams, Bradley F. *The Struggle for the Soul of the Nation: Czech Culture and the Rise of Communism*. Lanham, Maryland: Rowman and Littlefield, 2004.

Academy of European Law. *Collected Course of the Academy of European Law*. Volume 3, Book 2. The Netherlands: Kluwer, 1994.

Adams, Frederick C. *Economic Diplomacy: The Export-Import Bank and American Foreign Policy*. Columbia: University of Missouri Press, 1976.

Albright, Madeleine. *Madame Secretary: A Memoir*. New York: Miramax Books, 2003.

Alexander, Edward. *Crime of Vengeance: An Armenian Struggle for Justice*. New York: The Free Press, 1991.

Allin, Dana H. *Cold War Illusions: America, Europe and Soviet Power, 1969–1989*. New York: St. Martin's Press, 1994.

Allison, Graham. *Essence of Decision Making: Explaining the Cuban Missile Crisis*, 2nd ed. London: Longman, 1999.

Alterman, Eric. *When Presidents Lie: A History of Official Deception and Its Consequences*. New York: Penguin, 2005.

Ambrosius, Lloyd E. *Woodrow Wilson and the American Diplomatic Tradition: The Treaty Fight in Perspective*. New York: Cambridge University Press, 1987.

Ambrosius, Lloyd E. *Wilsonian Statecraft: Theory and Practice of Liberal Internationalism during World War I*. Wilmington, Delaware: Scholarly Resources Books, 1991.

Anderson, Irvine H., Jr. *The Standard-Vacuum Oil Company and United States East Asian Policy, 1933–1941*. Princeton, New Jersey: Princeton University Press, 1975.

Auchincloss, Louis. *Woodrow Wilson*. New York: Lipper/Viking, 2000.

Bacevich, Andrew J. *The New American Militarism: How Americans Are Seduced by War*. New York: Oxford University Press, 2005.

Baer, Robert. *Sleeping with the Devil: How Washington Sold Our Soul for Saudi Crude*. New York: Three Rivers Press, 2003.

Bailey, Thomas A. *A Diplomatic History of the American People*, 9th ed. Englewood Cliffs, New Jersey: Prentice Hall, 1982.

Bamford, James. *A Pretext for War: 9/11, Iraq, and the Abuse of America's Intelligence Agencies*. New York: Anchor Books, 2005.

Barber, Benjamin R. *Jihad vs. McWorld*. New York: Times Books, 1995.

Barber, James David. *Presidential Character*. Englewood Cliffs, New Jersey: Prentice Hall, 1972.

Bass, Gary. *Stay the Hand of Vengeance: The Politics of War Crimes Tribunals*. Princeton, New Jersey: Princeton University Press, 2000.

Beale, Howard K. *Theodore Roosevelt and the Rise of America to World Power*. New York: Collier Books, 1962; reprint of the original Johns Hopkins University Press edition published in 1956.

Beasley, Maurine, and Shulman, Holly, eds. *The Eleanor Roosevelt Encyclopedia*. Westport, Connecticut: Greenwood, 2001.

Becker, William H., and Wells, Samuel F., Jr., eds. *Economics and World Power: An Assessment of American Diplomacy since 1789*. New York: Columbia University Press, 1984.

Bennis, Phyllis. *Calling the Shots: How Washington Dominates Today's UN*. New York: Interlink Publishing Group, 1996.

Bercovitch, Sacvan. *The American Jeremiad*. Madison: University of Wisconsin Press, 1978.

Bernstein, Fred I. *Man of the People: A Life of Harry S. Truman*. New York: Oxford University Press, 1995.

Bernstein, Fred I., ed. *Leadership in the Modern Presidency*. Cambridge, Massachusetts: Harvard University Press, 1988.

Bill, James A. *The Eagle and the Lion: The Tragedy of American-Iranian Relations*. New Haven, Connecticut: Yale University Press, 1988.

Billings-Yun, Melanie. *Decision against War: Eisenhower and Dien Bien Phu, 1954*. New York: Columbia University Press, 1988.

Black, Allida M. *Casting Her Own Shadow: Eleanor Roosevelt and the Shaping of Postwar Liberalism*. New York: Columbia University Press, 1997.

Blackman, Ann. *Seasons of Her Life: A Biography of Madeleine Korbel Albright*. New York: Scribner, 2002.

Blood, Thomas. *Madam Secretary: A Biography of Madeleine Albright*. New York: St. Martin's Press, 1997.

Blum, William. *Rogue State: A Guide to the World's Only Superpower*. Monroe, Maine: Common Courage Press, 2000.

Boot, Max. *The Savage Wars of Peace: Small War and the Rise of American Power*. New York: Basic Books, 2002.

Boyer, Paul. *By the Bomb's Early Light: Thought and Culture at the Dawn of the Atomic Age*. New York: Pantheon, 1986.

Bradley, John. *Allied Intervention in Russia*. London: Wiederfeld and Nicholson, 1968.

Brands, H. W. *What America Owes the World: The Struggle for the Soul of Foreign Policy*. Cambridge: Cambridge University Press, 1998.

Brands, H. W., ed. *The Foreign Policies of Lyndon Johnson: Beyond Vietnam*. College Station: Texas A&M University Press, 1999.

Brands, H. W. *Woodrow Wilson*. New York: Times Books, 2003.

Breitman, Richard, et al. *U.S. Intelligence and the Nazis*. New York: Cambridge University Press, 2005.

Brennan, Mary C. *Turning Right in the Sixties: The Conservative Capture of the GOP*. Chapel Hill: University of North Carolina Press, 1995.

Brilmayer, Lea. *American Hegemony: Political Morality in a One-Superpower World*. New Haven, Connecticut: Yale University Press, 1994.

Brown, Sherrod. *Myths of Free Trade: Why American Trade Policy Has Failed.* New York: The New Press, 2004.

Bush, George H. W. *A World Transformed.* New York: Knopf, 1998.

Caldicott, Helen. *The New Nuclear Danger: George W. Bush's Military Industrial Complex.* New York: The New Press, 2002.

Calhoun, Frederick. *Uses of Force and Wilsonian Foreign Policy.* Kent, Ohio: Kent State University Press, 1993.

Callahan, David. *Unwinnable Wars: American Power and Ethnic Conflict.* New York: Hill and Wang, 1997.

Campbell, Charles S., Jr. *Special Business Interests and the Open Door Policy.* New Haven, Connecticut: Yale University Press, 1951.

Carnegie Commission on Preventing Deadly Conflict. *Preventing Deadly Conflict: Final Report with Executive Summary.* Washington, D.C.: Carnegie Commission, 1997.

Carpenter, Ted Galen, ed. *NATO's Empty Victory: A Postmortem on the Balkan War.* Washington, D.C.: Cato Institute, 2000.

Carré, John le. *The Spy Who Came In from the Cold.* New York: Coward-McCann, 1963.

Carroll, John M., and Herring, George C., eds. *Modern American Diplomacy: Revised and Enlarged Edition.* Wilmington, Delaware: Scholarly Resource Books, 1996.

Carter, Jimmy. *Palestine: Peace Not Apartheid.* New York: Simon and Schuster, 2006.

Carter, Purvis M. *Congressional and Public Reactions to Wilson's Caribbean Policy, 1913–1917.* New York: Vantage Press, 1977.

Chandrasekaran, Rajiv. *Imperial Life in the Emerald City: Inside Iraq's Green Zone.* New York: Knopf, 2006.

Chany, Laurence, and Kornbluh, Peter, eds. *The Cuban Missile Crisis, 1962: A National Security Archive Documents Reader.* New York: The New Press, 1992.

Clark, Ramsey. *The Fire This Time: US War Crimes in the Gulf.* New York: Thunder Mouth Press, 1992.

Clinton, Bill. *My Life.* New York: Knopf, 2004.

Cockburn, Andrew, and Cockburn, Patrick. *Saddam Hussein: An American Obsession.* London: Verso Books, 2002.

Cohen, Lizabeth. *A Consumer Republic: The Politics of Mass Consumption in Postwar America.* New York: Knopf, 2003.

Cole, Wayne S. *Roosevelt and the Isolationists, 1932–1945.* Lincoln: University of Nebraska Press, 1983.

Coleman, Peter. *The Liberal Conspiracy: The Congress for Cultural Freedom and the Struggle for the Mind of Postwar Europe.* New York: The Free Press, 1989.

Colodny, Len, and Gettlin, Robert. *Silent Coup: The Removal of a President.* New York: St. Martin's Press, 1991.

Colodny, Len, and Shachtman, Tom . *The Long Road to Baghdad: Nixon's Fall and the Rise of the Neocons.* New York: HarperCollins, forthcoming.

Combs, Jerald A. *American Diplomatic History: Two Centuries of Changing Interpretations.* Berkeley: University of California Press, 1983.

Cook, Blanche Wiesen. *Eleanor Roosevelt.* New York: Penguin, 1999.

Cooper, John Milton, Jr. *Breaking the Heart of the World: Woodrow Wilson and the Fight for the League of Nations.* Cambridge: Cambridge University Press, 2001.

Couture, Jocelyne, et al., eds. *Rethinking Nationalism. Canadian Journal of Philosophy,* supplementary volume 22. Calgary: University of Calgary Press, 1998.

Cox, Michael, et al., eds. *The Interregnum: Controversies in World Politics, 1989–1999.* Cambridge: Cambridge University Press, 1999.

Craig, Campbell. *Glimmer of a New Leviathan: Total War in the Realism of Niebuhr, Morgenthau, and Waltz.* New York: Columbia University Press, 2003.

Crapol, Edward P., ed. *Women and American Foreign Policy: Lobbyists, Critics, and Insiders,* 2nd ed., Wilmington, Delaware: Scholarly Resources Books, 1992.

Culbertson, John M. *The Trade Threat: And U.S. Trade Policy.* Madison, WI: 21st Century Press, 1989.

Cullather, Nick. *The CIA's Classified Account of Its Operations in Guatemala, 1952–1954.* Stanford, California: Stanford University Press, 1999.

Daalder, Ovo H., and Lindsay, James M. *America Unbound: The Bush Revolution in Foreign Policy.* Washington, D.C.: Brookings Institution Press, 2003.

Dallek, Robert. *Franklin D. Roosevelt and American Foreign Policy, 1932–1945.* New York: Oxford University Press, 1995; reprint of the original 1979 edition with a new Afterword.

Dalton, Kathleen. *Theodore Roosevelt: A Strenuous Life.* New York: Knopf, 2003.

Daniel, Donald C. F., Hayes, Bradd E., and Jonge Oudraat, Chantal de. *Coercive Inducement and the Containment of International Crises.* Washington, D.C.: United States Institute of Peace, 1999.

DeSoto, Hernando. *The Mystery of Capital: Why Capitalism Succeeds in the West and Fails Everywhere Else.* New York: Basic Books, 2000.

Devlin, Patrick. *Too Proud to Fight: Woodrow Wilson's Neutrality.* New York: Oxford University Press, 1974.

Diamond, Larry. *Squandered Victory: The American Occupation and Bungled Efforts to Bring Democracy to Iraq.* New York: Times Books, 2005.

Dolan, A. R. *Undoing the Evil Empire: How Reagan Won the Cold War.* Washington, D.C.: Washington Institute Press, 1990.

Drutt, Helen. *Broaching It Diplomatically: A Tribute to Madeleine K. Albright* (museum catalogue, 1998).

Dumbrell, John. *American Foreign Policy: Carter to Clinton.* New York: St. Martin's Press, 1997.

Dumbrell, John. *The Making of US Foreign Policy,* 2nd ed. Manchester, United Kingdom: Manchester University Press, 1997.

Dunn, S., and Fraser, T. G., eds. *Europe and Ethnicity: The First World War and Contemporary Ethnic Conflict.* London: Routledge, 1996.

Eckes, Alfred E., Jr, and Zeiler, Thomas W. *Globalization and the American Century.* New York: Cambridge University Press, 2003.

Eichebreen, Barry. *Golden Fetters: The Gold Standard and the Great Depression, 1919–1939.* New York: Oxford University Press, 1995.

Esthus, Raymond A. *Theodore Roosevelt and Japan.* Seattle: University of Washington Press, 1966.

Evans, Lawrence. *United States Policy and the Partition of Turkey, 1914–1924.* Baltimore: Johns Hopkins University Press, 1965.

Ferguson, Niall. *The Pity of War: Explaining World War I.* New York: Basic Books, 1998.

Ferguson, Niall. *Colossus: The Price of America's Empire.* New York: Penguin, 2004.

Ferguson, Niall. *The War of the World: Twentieth-Century Conflict and the Descent of the West.* New York: Penguin, 2006.

Ferrell, Robert H. *Harry S. Truman: A Life*. Columbia: University of Missouri Press, 2002.

Flanders, Laura. *Bushwomen: How They Won the White House for Their Man*. New York: Verso, 2004.

Fleming, Denna Frank. *The Cold War and Its Origins*. New York: Doubleday, 1961.

Fogelson, David S. *America's Secret War against Bolshevism*. Chapel Hill: University of North Carolina Press, 1995.

Fousek, John. *To Lead the Free World: American Nationalism and the Cultural Roots of the Cold War*. Chapel Hill: University of North Carolina Press, 2000.

Freedman, Lawrence. *Kennedy's Wars: Berlin, Cuba, Laos, and Vietnam*. New York: Oxford University Press, 2000.

Freidman, Alan. *Spider's Web: The Secret History of How the White House Illegally Armed Iraq*. New York: Bantam Books, 1993.

Freud, Sigmund, and Bullitt, William C. *Thomas Woodrow Wilson: A Psychological Study*. Boston: Houghton Mifflin, 1966.

Gaddis, John Lewis. *Strategies of Containment: A Critical Appraisal of Postwar American National Security*. New York: Oxford University Press, 1982.

Gaddis, John Lewis. *The Long Peace: Inquiries into the History of the Cold War*. New York: Oxford University Press, 1987.

Gardner, Lloyd C. *Economic Aspects of New Deal Diplomacy*. Madison: University of Wisconsin Press, 1964.

Gardner, Lloyd C. *Woodrow Wilson and Revolutions, 1913–1921*. Lanham, Maryland: University Press of America, 1976.

Gardner, Lloyd C. *A Covenant with Power: America and World Order from Wilson to Reagan*. New York: Oxford University Press, 1984.

Gardner, Lloyd C. *Safe for Democracy: The Anglo-American Response to Revolution, 1913–1923*. New York: Oxford University Press, 1984.

Gardner, Lloyd C., ed. *Redefining the Past: Essays in Diplomatic History in Honor of William Appleman Williams*. Corvallis: Oregon: Oregon State University Press, 1986.

Garson, Barbara. *Money Makes the World Go Round*. New York: Viking Press, 2001.

Garthoff, Raymond. *Détente and Confrontation: American-Soviet Relations from Nixon to Reagan*. Washington, D.C.: Brookings Institution, 1985.

Gates, Robert. *From the Shadows*. New York: Simon and Schuster, 1996.

Gellman, Irwin F. *Good Neighbor Diplomacy: United States Policies in Latin America*. Baltimore: Johns Hopkins University Press, 1979.

Gilpin, Joseph. *War and Change in World Politics*. Cambridge: Cambridge University Press, 1981.

Girard, Phippe R. *Clinton in Haiti: The 1994 Intervention in Haiti*. New York: Palgrave Macmillan, 2004.

Gitlin, Todd. *The Intellectuals and the Flag*. New York: Columbia University Press, 2005.

Gleijeses, Piero. *The Dominican Crisis: The 1965 Constitutional Revolt and American Intervention*. Baltimore: Johns Hopkins University Press, 1978.

Glover, Jonathan. *Humanity: A Moral History of the Twentieth Century*. New Haven, Connecticut: Yale University Press, 1999.

Goodson, Larry P. *Afghanistan's Endless War: State Failure, Regional Politics, and the Rise of the Taliban*. Seattle: University of Washington Press, 2001.

Gore, Al. *The Assault on Reason*. New York: Penguin, 2007.

Graebner, Norman A. *Ideas and Diplomacy: Readings in the Intellectual Tradition of American Foreign Policy.* New York: Oxford University Press, 1964.

Greene, Jack P. *The Intellectual Construct of America: Exceptionalism and Identity from 1492 to 1800.* Chapel Hill: University of North Carolina Press, 1993.

Greene, John Robert. *The Presidency of Gerald Ford.* Lawrence: University of Kansas Press, 1995.

Greene, John Robert. *The Presidency of George Bush.* Lawrence: University of Kansas Press, 1999.

Greenfeld, Liah. *Nationalism: Five Roads to Modernity.* Cambridge, Massachusetts: Harvard University Press, 1992.

Greenstein, Fred I. *The Presidential Difference: Leadership Style from FDR to Clinton, with a New Afterword on George W. Bush.* Princeton, New Jersey: Princeton University Press, 2000.

Greenstein, Fred I., ed. *Leadership of Modern Presidents.* Cambridge, Massachusetts: Harvard University Press, 1988.

Greenstein, Fred I., ed. *The George W. Bush Presidency: An Early Assessment.* Baltimore: Johns Hopkins University Press, 2003.

Grémion, Pierre. *Intelligence de L'Anticommunisme: Le Congress pour la Liberté de la Culture de Paris: 1950–1975.* Paris: Fayard, 1997.

Grenville, John A. S., and Young, George Berkeley. *Politics, Strategy, and American Diplomacy; Studies in Foreign Policy, 1873–1917.* New Haven, Connecticut: Yale University, 1966.

Grose, Peter. *Operation Rollback: America's Secret War behind the Iron Curtain.* New York: Houghton Mifflin, 2000.

Guéhenno, Jean-Marie. *The End of the Nation-State.* Minneapolis: University of Minnesota Press, 1995.

Haass, Richard N. *The Opportunity: American's Moment to Alter History's Course.* New York: PublicAffairs, 2005.

Hagedorn, H. *Leonard Wood.* 2 vols. New York: Harper Publishers, 1931.

Hardt, Michael, and Negri, Antonio. *Multitude: War and Democracy in the Age of Empire.* New York: Penguin, 2004.

Harrison, Lawrence E., and Huntington, Samuel P., eds. *Culture Matters: How Values Shape Human Progress.* New York: Basic Books, 2000.

Hart-Landsberg, Martin. *Korea: Division, Reunification, and U.S. Foreign Policy.* New York: Monthly Review Press, 1998.

Hasegawa, Tsuyoshi. *Racing the Enemy: Stalin, Truman, and the Surrender of Japan.* Cambridge, Massachusetts: Harvard University Press, 2005.

Hayward, Steven F. *Age of Reagan: The Fall of the Old Liberal Order.* Roseville, California: Forum, 2001.

Healy, David. *Drive to Hegemony: The United States in the Caribbean, 1898–1917.* Madison: University of Wisconsin Press, 1988.

Heater, Derek. *National Self-Determination: Woodrow Wilson and His Legacy.* New York: St. Martin's Press, 1994.

Heckscher, August. *Woodrow Wilson.* New York: Charles Scribner's Sons, 1991.

Heclo, Hugh. *Studying the Presidency: A Report to the Ford Foundation.* New York: Ford Foundation, 1977.

Helmreich, Paul C. *From Paris to Sévres: The Partition of the Ottoman Empire at the Peace Conference of 1919–1920.* Columbus: Ohio State University Press, 1974.

Herring, George. *America's Longest War: The United States and Vietnam, 1950–1975*. New York: McGraw-Hill, 1985.

Hersh, Seymour. *The Dark Side of Camelot*. Boston: Little, Brown, 1997.

Hertz, Noreena. *The Silent Takeover: Global Capitalism and the Death of Democracy*. New York: The Free Press, 2001.

Hess, Gary R. *Presidential Decisions for War: Korea, Vietnam, and the Persian Gulf*. Baltimore: Johns Hopkins University Press, 2001.

Hill, Richard F. *Hitler Attacks Pearl Harbor: Why the US Declared War on Germany*. Boulder, CO: Lynne Riener, 2002.

Hixson, Walter L. *Myth to Power: National, Identity and U.S. Foreign Relations*. New Haven, Connecticut: Yale University Press, 2008.

Hobsbawm, Eric. *The Age of Extremes: A History of the World, 1914–1991*. New York: Vintage Books, 1996.

Hochschild, Adam. *King Leopold's Ghost: A Story of Greed, Terror, and Heroism in Colonial Africa*. New York: Houghton Mifflin, 1998.

Hoff, Joan. *Nixon Reconsidered*. New York: Basic Books, 1994.

Hoffman, Fritz Hubertus. *Kraemer on Excellence*. New York: World Security Network Foundation, 2004.

Hoff-Wilson, Joan. *American Business and Foreign Policy, 1920–1933*. Lexington: University Press of Kentucky, 1971.

Hoff-Wilson, Joan. *Ideology and Economics: U.S. Relations with the Soviet Union, 1918–1933*. Columbia: University of Missouri Press, 1974.

Hoff-Wilson, Joan. *Herbert Hoover: Forgotten Progressive*. Prospect Heights, Illinois: Waveland Press, 1992; reprint of the original 1975 edition.

Hoff-Wilson, Joan, and Lightman, Marjorie, eds. *Without Precedent: Eleanor Roosevelt*. Bloomington: Indiana University Press, 1984.

Hogan, Michael J. *The Marshall Plan: America, Britain, and the Reconstruction of Western Europe, 1947–1952*. Cambridge: Cambridge University Press, 1987.

Hogan, Michael J. *Paths to Power: The Historiography of American Foreign Relations to 1941*. New York: Cambridge University Press, 2000.

Hogan, Michael J., ed. *The Ambiguous Legacy: U.S. Foreign Relations in the "American Century."* Cambridge: Cambridge University Press, 1999.

Holbo, Paul S., ed. *The Eisenhower Era*. Hinsdale, Illinois: The Dryden Press, 1974.

Holmes, Kim R., ed. *A Safe and Prosperous America: A U.S. Foreign and Defense Policy Blueprint*. Washington, D.C.: The Heritage Foundation, June 1994.

Horne, Gerald. *From the Barrel of a Gun: The United States and the War against Zimbabwe, 1965–1980*. Chapel Hill: University of North Carolina Press, 2001.

Horsman, Matthew, and Marshall, Andrew. *After the Nation-State: Citizens, Tribalism and the New World Disorder*. New York: HarperCollins, 1994.

Hovannisian, Richard G., ed. *The Armenian Genocide: History, Politics, Ethics*. New York: St. Martin's Press, 1992.

Howard, Harry N. *An American Inquiry in the Middle East: The King-Crane Commission*. Beirut: Khayats, 1963.

Hull, Cordell. *Memoirs 2 vols*. New York: Macmillan, 1948.

Hunt, Michael H. *The Making of a Special Relationship: The United States and China to 1914*. New York: Columbia University Press, 1983.

Hunt, Michael H. *Ideology and U.S. Foreign Policy*. New Haven, Connecticut: Yale University Press, 1987.

Hutchings, Robert L. *American Diplomacy and the End of the Cold War: An Insider's Account of U.S. Policy in Europe, 1989–1992*. Baltimore: Johns Hopkins University Press, 1997.

Hyland, William G. *Mortal Rivals: Superpower Relations from Nixon to Reagan*. New York: Random House, 1987.

Ignatieff, Michael. *The Warrior's Honor: Ethnic War and the Modern Conscience*. New York: Henry Holt, 1997.

Jeffreys-Jones, Rhodri. *The CIA and American Democracy*. New Haven, Connecticut: Yale University Press, 1998.

Jeffreys-Jones, Rhodri. *Cloak and Dollar: A History of American Secret Intelligence*. New Haven, Connecticut: Yale University Press, 2002.

Johnson, Chalmers. *Blowback: The Costs and Consequences of American Empire*. New York: Henry Holt, 2000.

Johnson, Chalmers. *Sorrow of Empire: Militarism, Secrecy, and the End of the Republic*. New York: Metropolitan Books, 2004.

Johnson, Paul. *Modern Times: The World from the Twenties to the Eighties*. New York: Harper and Row, 1983.

Judis, John B. *The Folly of Empire: What George W. Bush Could Learn from Theodore Roosevelt and Woodrow Wilson*. New York: Scribner, 2004.

Kahn, Herman. *On Escalation: Metaphors and Scenarios*. New York: Praeger, 1965.

Kammen, Michael. *In the Past Lane: Historical Perspectives on American Culture*. New York: Oxford University Press, 1997.

Kegley, Charles W., Jr., ed. *The Long Postwar Peace*. New York: HarperCollins, 1991.

Kelly, Daniel. *James Burnham and the Struggle for the World: A Life*. Wilmington, DE: ISI Books, 2002.

Kennan, George F. *The Decision to Intervene*. New York: Atheneum Press, 1967.

Kennedy, David M. *Freedom from Fear: The American People in Depression and War, 1929–1945*. New York: Oxford University Press, 1999.

Keynes, John Maynard. *The Economic Consequences of Peace*. London: Macmillan, 1919; 1971 edition.

Kimmich, Christoph M. *Germany and the League of Nations*. Chicago: University of Chicago Press, 1975.

Kindleberger, Charles P. *The World in Depression, 1929–1939*. Berkeley: University of California Press, 1986.

Kinzer, Stephen. *Overthrow: America's Century of Regime Change from Hawaii to Iraq*. New York: Times Books, 2006.

Kirkpatrick, Jeane. *Dictatorships and Double Standards: Rationalism and Reason in Politics*. New York: Simon and Schuster, 1982.

Klare, Michael T. *Blood and Oil: The Dangers and Consequences of America's Growing Dependency on Imported Petroleum* (The American Empire Project). New York: Metropolitan Books, 2004.

Knirch, Jason. *Woodrow Wilson and the Irish Case for Self-Determination, 1914–1920*. Pullman: Washington State University Press, 1986.

Knock, Thomas J. *To End All Wars: Woodrow Wilson and the Quest for a New World Order*. New York: Oxford University Press, 1992.

Kornbluh, Peter. *The Pinochet File: A Declassified Dossier on Atrocity and Accountability*. New York: The New Press, 2003.

Korten, David C. *When Corporations Rule the World*. West Hartford, Connecticut: Kumarian Press, 1995.

Krugman, Paul, ed. *Strategic Trade Policy and the New International Economics*. Cambridge, Massachusetts: MIT Press, 1986.

Kunz, Diane. *Butter and Guns: America's Cold War Economic Diplomacy*. New York: The Free Press, 1997.

LaFeber, Walter. *The New Empire: An Interpretation of American Expansion, 1860–1898*. Ithaca, New York: Cornell University Press, 1963.

LaFeber, Walter. *The American Search for Opportunity, 1865–1913*. Cambridge: Cambridge University Press, 1993.

LaFeber, Walter. *The American Age: U.S. Foreign Policy at Home and Abroad*, 2nd ed. New York: Norton, 1994.

LaFeber, Walter. *America, Russia, and the Cold War, 1945–2002*, 9th ed. New York: McGraw Hill, 2002.

Lake, Anthony. *The "Tar Baby" Option: American Policy toward Southern Rhodesia*. New York: Columbia University Press, 1976.

Landes, David. *The Wealth and Poverty of Nations: Why Some Are So Rich and Some So Poor*. New York: Norton, 1998.

Lansing, Robert. *The Peace Negotiations: A Personal Narrative*. Boston: Houghton Mifflin, 1921.

Lee, Martin. *The Beast Reawakens*. Boston: Little, Brown, 2000.

Leech, Margaret. *In the Days of McKinley*. New York: Greenwood Press, 1975.

Leffler, Melvyn P. *A Preponderance of Power: National Security, the Truman Administration, and the Cold War*. Stanford, California: Stanford University Press, 1992.

Leffler, Melvyn P., and Painter, David S., eds. *Origins of the Cold War: An International History*. New York: Routledge, 1994.

LeoGrande, William M. *Our Own Backyard: The United States in Central America, 1977–1992*. Chapel Hill: University of North Carolina Press, 1998.

Levin, N. Gordon, Jr. *Woodrow Wilson and World Politics: America's Response to War and Revolution*. New York: Oxford University Press, 1968.

Lieven, Anatol, and Hulsman, John. *Ethical Realism: A Vision for America's Role in the World*. New York: Pantheon, 2006.

Lifton, Robert Jay, and Mitchell, Greg. *Hiroshima in America: Fifty Years of Denial*. New York: Putnam Press, 1995.

Linenthan, Edward T., and Englehardt, Tome, eds. *History Wars: The Enola Gay and Other Battles for the American Past*. New York: Metropolitan Press, 1996.

Link, Arthur S. *Woodrow Wilson and the Progressive Era, 1910–1917*. New York: Harper Torchbooks, 1954.

Link, Arthur S. *Wilson the Diplomatist: A Look at His Major Foreign Policies*. Chicago: Quadrangle Books, 1963; reprint of the original 1957 edition.

Link, Arthur S., et al, eds. *The Papers of Woodrow Wilson*. Princeton, New Jersey: Princeton University Press, 1966–94.

Lippman, Thomas W. *Madeleine Albright and the New American Diplomacy*. Boulder, Colorado: Westview Press, 2000.

Logan, Rayford. *Diplomatic Relations with Haiti*. Chapel Hill: University of North Carolina Press, 1941.

Lovett, William A., Eckes, Alfred E., Jr., and Brinkman, Richard L., eds. *U.S. Trade Policy: History, Theory, and the WTO*. Armonk, New York: M. E. Sharpe, 1999.

Low, Patrick. *Trading Free: The GATT and US Trade Policy*. New York: The Twentieth Century Fund Press, 1993.

Lucas, Scott. *Freedom's War: The American Crusade against the Soviet Union*. New York: New York University Press, 1999.

MacDonald, Ronald St. John, ed. *Essays in Honor of Wang Tieya*. Dordrecht: Springer, 1994.

MacMillan, Margaret. *Paris 1919: Six Months That Changed the World*. New York: Random House, 2001.

Magill, Frank N. *The American Presidents: The Office and the Men*. 3 vols. Pasadena, California: Salem Press, 1986.

Mahle, Melissa Boyle. *Denial and Deception: An Insider's View of the CIA from Iran-Contra to 9/11*. New York: Thunder's Mouth, 2005.

Mair, L. P. *The Protection of Minorities: The Working and Scope of the Minority Treaties under the League of Nations*. London: Christophers, 1928.

Mandel, Michael. *How America Gets Away with Murder: Illegal Wars, Collateral Damage and Crimes against Humanity*. London: Pluto Press, 2004.

Mann, Michael. *Incoherent Empire*. London: Verso, 2003.

Mansfield, Edward D., and Snyder, Jack, eds. *Electing to Fight: Why Emerging Democracies Go to War* (BCSIA Studies in International Studies). Boston: MIT Press, 2005.

Mansfield, Stephen. *The Faith of George W. Bush* (Peabody, Massachusetts: Charisma House, 2004).

Marcum, John. *The Angolan Revolution*, vol. 2: *Exile Politics and Guerilla Warfare*. Cambridge, Massachusetts: MIT Press, 1978.

Marks, Federick W., III. *Wind over Sand: The Diplomacy of Franklin Roosevelt*. Athens: University of Georgia Press, 1988.

Matthewson, Tim. *Proslavery Foreign Policy*. New York: Praeger, 2003.

May, Ernest R., ed. *Knowing One's Enemies: Intelligence Assessment before the Two World Wars*. Princeton, New Jersey: Princeton University Press, 1984.

May, Ernest R., ed. *American Cold War Strategy: Interpreting NSC 68*. Boston: Bedford, 1993.

McCormick, Thomas J. *America's Half-Century: United States Foreign Policy in the Cold War*. Baltimore: Johns Hopkins University Press, 1989.

McCoy, Alfred. *A Question of Torture: CIA Interrogation from the Cold War to the War on Terror*. New York: Henry Holt/Metropolitan, 2006.

McCoy, John Jay. *The Challenge to American Foreign Policy*. Cambridge, Massachusetts: Harvard University Press, 1953.

McCullough, David. *Truman*. New York: Simon and Schuster, 1992.

McNamara, Robert S., and Bright, James G. *Wilson's Ghost: Reducing the Risk of Conflict, Killing, and Catastrophe in the 21st Century*. New York: PublicAffairs, 2001.

Mead, Walter Russell. *Special Providence: American Foreign Policy and How It Changed the World*. New York: A Century Foundation Book, 2001.

Merry, Robert W. *Sands of Empire: Missionary Zeal, American Foreign Policy, and the Hazards of Global Ambition*. New York: Simon and Schuster, 2005.

Miller, Donald E., and Miller, Lorna Touryan. *Armenia: Portraits of Survival and Hope*. Berkeley: University of California Press, 2003.

Miller, Perry. "Errand into the Wilderness." In his *Errand into the Wilderness*. Cambridge, Massachusetts: Harvard University Press, 1958.

Minear, Richard H. *Victors' Justice: The Tokyo War Crimes Tribunal*. Princeton, New Jersey: Princeton University Press, 1971.

Minow, Martha. *Between Vengeance and Forgiveness: Facing History after Genocide and Mass Violence*. New York: Beacon Press, 1999.

Mitrovich, Gregory. *Undermining the Kremlin: America's Secret Strategy to Subvert the Soviet Bloc 1947–1956*. Ithaca, New York: Cornell University Press, 2000.

Molho, Anthony, and Wood, Gordon S., eds. *Imagined Histories: American Historians Interpret the Past*. Princeton, New Jersey: Princeton University Press, 1998.

Moran, Lindsay. *Blowing My Cover: My Life as a CIA Spy*. New York: Putnam, 2004.

Morgan, Edmund S. *The Puritan Dilemma: The Story of John Winthrop*. Boston: Little, Brown, 1958.

Morgenthau, Henry. *Ambassador Morgenthau's Story*. Plandome, New York: New Age Publishers, 1975; reprint of the 1919 Doubleday, Page, and Co. edition.

Myers, Kenneth A. *NATO – The Next Thirty Years: The Changing Political, Economic, and Military Setting*. Boulder, Colorado: Westview Press, 1980.

Nathan, Richard. *The Administrative Presidency*. New York: Wiley, 1983.

Nelson, Michael, ed. *Historic Documents on the Presidency: 1776–1989*. Washington D.C.: Congressional Quarterly, 1989.

Ninkovich, Frank. *The Wilsonian Century: U.S. Foreign Policy since 1900*. Chicago: University of Chicago Press, 1999.

Ninkovich, Frank. *The United States and Imperialism*. Oxford: Blackwell, 2001.

Nye, Joseph S., Jr. *The Paradox of American Power: Why the World's Only Superpower Can't Go It Alone*. New York: Oxford University Press, 2002.

O'Brien, Thomas F. *The Revolutionary Mission: American Enterprise in Latin America, 1900–1945*. Cambridge: Cambridge University Press, 1996.

Offner, Arnold A. *Another Such Victory: President Truman and the Cold War, 1945–1953*. Stanford, California: Stanford University Press, 2002.

Ohmae, Kenichi. *The Mind of the Strategist: The Art of Japanese Business*. New York: McGraw-Hill, 1982.

Ohmae, Kenichi. *End of the Nation State: The Rise of Regional Economies*. New York: The Free Press, 1995.

O'Meara, Patrick, et al. *Globalization and the Challenges of a New Century*. Bloomington: Indiana University Press, 2000.

Parenti, Michael. *The Terrorism Trap: September 11 and Beyond*. San Francisco: City Lights Books, 2002.

Parry, Robert. *Lost History: Contras, Cocaine, the Press, and "Project Truth."* Arlington, Virginia: The Media Consortium, 1999.

Parry, Robert. *Secrecy and Privilege: Rise of the Bush Dynasty from Watergate to Iraq*. Arlington, Virginia: The Media Consortium. 2004.

Paterson, Thomas G. *On Every Front: The Making and Unmaking of the Cold War*, rev. ed. New York: Norton, 1992.

Paterson, Thomas G., et al. *American Foreign Relations: A History since 1895*, 4th ed. Lexington, Massachusetts: D.C. Heath, 1995.

Pauwels, Jacques. *The Myth of the Good War: The USA in World War II*. Toronto: Lorimer, 2002.

Perlmutter, Amos. *Making the World Safe for Democracy: A Century of Wilsonianism and Its Totalitarian Challengers*. Chapel Hill: University of North Carolina Press, 1997.

Perman, Dagmar. *The Shaping of the Czechoslovak State*. Leiden: E. J. Brill, 1962.

Permanent Peoples' Tribunal (PPT). *A Crime of Silence: The Armenian Genocide*. London: Zed Books, 1985.

Pessen, Edward. *Losing Our Souls: The American Experience in the Cold War*. Chicago: Ivan R. Dee, 1993; Elephant Paperbacks, 1995 ed.

Pfiffner, James P. *The Character Factor: How We Judge America's Presidents*. College Station: Texas A&M University Press, 2004.

Phillips, Kevin. *Post-Conservative America: People, Politics, and Ideology in a Time of Crisis*. New York: Random House, 1982.

Phillips, Kevin. *American Theocracy: The Peril and Politics of Radical Religion, Oil, and Borrowed Money in the 21st Century*. New York: Viking, 2006.

Pika, Joseph A., and Maltese, John Anthony. *The Politics of the Presidency*, 6th ed. Washington, D.C.: CQ Press, 2006.

Pike, Fredrick B. *FDR's Good Neighbor Policy: Sixty Years of Gentle Chaos*. Austin: University of Texas Press, 1995.

Pisani, Sallie. *The CIA and the Marshall Plan*. Lawrence: University Press of Kansas, 1991.

Prados, John. *Presidents' Secret Wars: CIA and Pentagon Covert Operations from World War II through the Persian Gulf*. Chicago: Elephant Paperback, 1996; rev. ed. of the original 1986 Ivan R. Dee edition.

Prados, John. *Safe for Democracy: The Secret Wars of the CIA*. Chicago: Ivan R. Dee, 2006.

Priest, Dana. *The Mission: Waging War and Keeping Peace with America's Military*. New York: Norton, 2004.

Quint, Howard H., and Ferrell, Robert H., eds. *The Talkative President: The Off-the-Record Press Conferences of Calvin Coolidge*. Amherst, Massachusetts: University of Massachusetts Press, 1964.

Rabe, Stephen G. *Eisenhower and Latin America: The Foreign Policy of Anti-Communism*. Chapel Hill: University of North Carolina Press, 1988.

Rabe, Stephen G. *The Most Dangerous Area in the World: John F. Kennedy Confronts Community Revolution in Latin America*. Chapel Hill: University of North Carolina Press, 1999.

Rashid, Ahmed. *Taliban, Militant Islam, Oil, and Fundamentalism in Central Asia*. New Haven, Connecticut: Yale University Press, 2000.

Reeves, Richard. *President Reagan: The Triumph of Imagination*. New York: Simon and Schuster, 2005.

Reichley, James A. *Conservatives in an Age of Change: The Nixon and Ford Administrations*. Washington D.C.: Brookings Institution Press, 1981.

Renan, Ernest. *Qu'est-ce qu'une nation?* Paris, 1882.

Renda, Mary A. *Taking Haiti: Military Occupation and the Culture of U.S. Imperialism, 1915–1940*. Chapel Hill: University of North Carolina Press, 2001.

Renshon, Stanley. *Psychological Need and Political Behavior (A Theory of Personality and Politicians)*. New York: The Free Press, 1974.

Renshon, Stanley. *The Psychological Assessment of Presidential Candidates*. New York: Routledge, 1998; rev. ed. of the original 1996 New York University Press edition.

Ricks, Thomas E. *Fiasco: The American Military Adventure in Iraq*. New York: Penguin, 2006.

Ripley, Randall B., and Lindsay, James M., eds. *U.S. Foreign Policy after the Cold War*. Pittsburgh: University of Pittsburgh Press, 1997.

Risen, James. *State of War: The Secret History of the CIA and the Bush Administration*. New York: The Free Press, 2006.

Robinson, Jacob, et al. *Were the Minority Treaties a Failure?* New York: Institute of Jewish Affairs, 1943.

Rosenman, Samuel, ed. *The Public Papers of Franklin D. Roosevelt.* New York: Random House, 1938.

Rostow, Walter. *The Stages of Economic Growth: A Non-Communist Manifesto.* New York: Cambridge University Press, 1960.

Rothbart, Michael Foster. *A Question of Torture: CIA Interrogation from the Cold War to the War on Terror.* New York: Metropolitan, 2006.

Rothkopf, David J. *Running the World: The Inside Story of the National Security Council and the Architects of American Power.* New York: PublicAffairs, 2005.

Rubenzer, Steven J., and Faschingbauer, Thomas R. *Personality, Character, and Leadership in the White House: Psychologists Assess the Presidents.* Dulles, Virginia: Brassey's, 2005.

Rusher, William A. *The Rise of the Right.* New York: Morrow, 1984.

Ryan, David, and Pungong, Victor, eds. *The United States and Decolonization: Power and Freedom.* London: Macmillan, 2000.

Ryn, Claes G. *America the Virtuous: The Crisis of Democracy and the Quest for Empire.* New Brunswick, New Jersey: Transaction, 2003.

Salamé, Ghassan. *Quand l-Amérique refait le monde.* Paris: Fayard, 2005.

Saul, John Ralston. *Voltaire's Bastards: The Dictatorship of Reason in the West.* New York: The Free Press, 1992.

Saul, Norman E. *War and Revolution: The United States and Russia, 1914–1921.* Lawrence: University Press of Kansas, 2001.

Saunders, Frances Stonor. *The Cultural Cold War: The CIA and the World of Arts and Letters.* New York: The New Press, 2000.

Saunders, Robert M. *In Search of Woodrow Wilson: Belief and Behavior,* Westport Connecticut: Greenwood Press, 1998.

Schild, Georg. *Between Ideology and Realpolitik: Woodrow Wilson and the Russian Revolution, 1917–1921.* Westport, Connecticut: Greenwood Press, 1995.

Schivelbusch, Wolfgang. *The Culture of Defeat: On National Trauma, Mourning and Recovery.* New York: Metropolitian, 2003.

Schlesinger, Arthur Meir, Jr. *The Imperial Presidency.* Boston: Houghton Mifflin, 1973.

Schlesinger, Stephen, and Kinzer, Stephen. *Bitter Fruit: The Story of the American Coup in Guatemala.* Cambridge, Massachusetts: Harvard University Press, 1999.

Schmidt, Hans. *The United States Occupation of Haiti, 1915–1934.* New Brunswick, New Jersey: Rutgers University Press, 1971.

Schroeder, Paul W. *The Axis Alliance and Japanese-American Relations, 1941.* Ithaca, New York: Cornell University Press, 1958.

Schweizer, Peter. *The Reagan Administration's Secret Strategy That Hastened the Collapse of the Soviet Union.* New York: Atlantic Monthly Press, 1993.

Schweizer, Peter, ed. *The Fall of the Berlin Wall: Reassessing the Causes and Consequences of the End of the Cold War.* Stanford, California: Hoover Institution Press, 2003.

Scott-Smith, Giles. *The Politics of Apolitical Culture: The Congress for Cultural Freedom, the CIA, and Postwar American Hegemony.* London: Routledge, 2002.

Seldon, Mark, and So, Alvin Y., eds. *War and State Terrorism: The United States, Japan, and the Asia-Pacific in the Long Twentieth Century.* Lanham, Maryland: Roman and Littlefield, 2004.

Seymour, Charles. *The Intimate Papers of Colonel House: Arranged as a Narrative*. Boston: Houghton Mifflin, 1926.

Shafer, Byron E., ed. *Is American Different? A New Look at American Exceptionalism*. New York: Oxford University Press, 1991.

Shattuck, John. *Freedom on Fire: Human Rights Wars and America's Response*. Cambridge, Massachusetts: Harvard University Press, 2003.

Sheer, Christopher, Scheer, Robert, and Chaudhry, Lakshmi. *The Five Biggest Lies Bush Told Us about Iraq*. New York: Seven Stories Press, 2003.

Shirley, Craig. *Reagan's Revolution: The Untold Story of the Campaign That Started It All*. Nashville, Tennessee: Nelson Current, 2005.

Sivard, Ruth Leger. *World Military and Social Expenditures*. Washington, D.C.: World Priorities, Inc., 1996.

Smith, Daniel. *Aftermath of War: Bainbridge Colby and Wilsonian Diplomacy*. Philadelphia: American Philosophical Society, 1970.

Smith, Gaddis. *Morality, Reason and Power: American Diplomacy in the Carter Years*. New York: Farrar, Straus and Giroux, 1986.

Smith, Gaddis. *The Last Years of the Monroe Doctrine, 1945–1993*. New York: Hill and Wang, 1994.

Smith, Jean Edward. *George Bush's War*. New York: Henry Holt, 1992.

Smith, Paula Bailey. *New European Orders, 1919 and 1991*. Washington, D.C.: Woodrow Wilson Center Press, 1996.

Smith, Sam. *Shadows of Hope: A Freethinker's Guide to Politics in the Time of Clinton*. Bloomington: Indiana University Press, 1994.

Smith, Tony. *America's Mission: The United States and the Worldwide Struggle for Democracy in the Twentieth Century*. Princeton, New Jersey: Princeton University Press, 1994.

Solomon, Norman. *War Made Easy: How Presidents and Pundits Keep Spinning Us to Death*. New York: Wiley, 2005.

Stachiw, Matthew. *Ukraine and the European Turmoil, 1917–1919*. Toronto: Harmony, 1973.

Stein, Judith. *Running Steel, Running America: Race, Economic Policy, and the Decline of the Liberals*. Chapel Hill: University of North Carolina Press, 1998.

Steinson, Barbara. *American Women's Activism in World War I*. New York: Garland Press, 1982.

Stephanson, Anders. *Manifest Destiny: American Expansion and the Empire of Right*. New York: Hill and Wang, 1995.

Sternhell, Wayne Zeev. *The Founding of Israel: Nationalism, Socialism, and the Making of the Jewish State*. Princeton, New Jersey: Princeton University Press, 1998.

Stiglitz, Joseph E. *Globalization and Its Discontents*. New York: Norton, 2002.

Stockwell, John. *In Search of Enemies: A CIA Story*. New York: Norton, 1978.

Talbott, Strobe, and Chanda, Nayan, eds. *The Age of Terror: America and the World after September 11*. New York: Basic Books, 2001.

The 9/11 Commission Report: Final Report of the National Commission on Terrorist Attacks upon the United States. New York: Norton, 2004.

The Iraq Study Group Report: The Way Forward, A New Approach. New York: Vintage Books, 2006.

Tiffany, Paul A. *The Decline of American Steel: How Management, Labor, and Government Went Wrong*. New York: Replica Books, 2001; reprint of the original 1988 edition.

Thomas, Raju G. C., ed. *Yugoslavia Unraveled: Sovereignty, Self-Determination, Intervention.* Lanham, Maryland: Lexington Books, 2003.

Thornberry, Patrick. *International Law and the Rights of Minorities.* New York: Oxford University Press, 1991.

Toland, John. *Infamy: Pearl Harbor and Its Aftermath.* Garden City, New Jersey: Doubleday, 1982.

Truman, Harry S. *Memoirs: 1945: Year of Decisions.* New York: Signet Books, 1965; reprint of the original 1955 edition.

Udovički, Jasminka, and Ridgeway, James., eds. *Burn This House: The Making and Unmaking of Yugoslavia.* Durham, North Carolina: Duke University Press, 1997.

UN Report of the High-Level Panel on Threats, Challenges and Change. *A More Secure World: Our Shared Responsibility.* New York: United Nations, 2004.

Unterberger, Betty Miller. *America's Siberian Expedition, 1918–1920.* New York: Greenwood Press, 1969; reprint of the original 1956 Duke University Press edition.

Unterberger, Betty Miller. *The United States, Revolutionary Russia, and the Rise of Czechoslovakia.* Chapel Hill: University of North Carolina Press, 1989.

U.S. Congress, Senate, Fourth Congress, First Session, Subcommittee on African Affairs. "Angola." Washington, D.C.: U.S. Government Printing Office, 1976.

U.S. Government. *Public Papers of the Presidents of the United States: Jimmy Carter, 1977, Book 1: January 20–July 24, 1977.* Washington, D.C.: U.S. Government Printing Office, 1977.

U.S. Government. *International Monetary Policy, 1969–1972.* Washington, D.C.: U.S. Government Printing Office, 2002.

Varg, Paul A. *United States Foreign Relations, 1820–1860.* East Lansing: Michigan State University Press, 1979.

Vidal, Gore. *Perpetual War for Perpetual Peace: How We Got to Be So Hated.* New York: Thunder's Mouth Press, 2002.

Vloyantes, John P. "Spheres of Influence: A Framework for Analysis." Unpublished manuscript, Institute of Government Research, University of Arizona, 1970.

Vloyantes, John P. *Velvet Glove Hegemony.* Kent, Ohio: Kent State University Press, 1975.

Waal, Thomas de. *Black Garden: Armenia and Azerbaijan through Peace and War.* New York: New York University Press, 2003.

Walker, Christopher J, ed. *Armenia and Karabagh: The Struggle for Unity.* London: Minority Rights Publications, 1991.

Walsh, Lawrence. *Firewall: The Iran-Contra Conspiracy and Cover-up.* New York: Norton, 1998.

Walworth, Arthur. *America's Moment, 1918: American Diplomacy at the End of World War I.* New York: Norton, 1977.

Walzer, Michael. *Just and Unjust Wars: A Moral Argument with Historical Illustrations,* 3rd ed. New York: Basic Books, 2000.

Weinstein, E. A. *Woodrow Wilson: A Medical and Psychological Biography.* Princeton, New Jersey: Princeton University Press, 1981.

Wheeler, Nicholas J. *Saving Strangers: Humanitarian Intervention in International Society.* New York: Oxford University Press, 2002.

Whitaker, Arthur P. *The Western Hemisphere Idea: Its Rise and Decline.* Ithaca, New York: Cornell University Press, 1954.

White, Christine. *British and American Commercial Relations with Soviet Russia.* Chapel Hill: University of North Carolina Press, 1992.

Wicker, Tom. *George Herbert Walker Bush.* New York: Penguin, 2004.

Williams, Benjamin. *Economic Foreign Policy of the United States.* New York: McGraw-Hill, 1929.

Williams, William Appleman. *Contours of American History.* New York: Norton, 1989.

Wilson, Robert. *Character above All: Ten Presidents from FDR to Bush.* New York: Simon and Schuster, 1995.

Wittkopf, Eugene R. *The Future of American Foreign Policy,* 2nd ed. New York: St. Martin's Press, 1994.

Wittkopf, Eugene R. *The Making of US Foreign Policy.* Manchester, United Kingdom: Manchester University Press, 1997.

Wohlstetter, Roberta. *Pearl Harbor: Warning and Decision.* Stanford, California: Stanford University Press, 1962.

Wolfe, Alan. *Moral Freedom: The Impossible Idea That Defines the Way We Live Now.* New York: Norton, 2001.

Wolin, Sheldon S. *The Presence of the Past: Essays on the State and the Constitution.* Baltimore: Johns Hopkins University Press, 1989.

Wood, Bryce. *The Making of the Good Neighbor Policy.* New York: Columbia University Press, 1961.

Woodward, Bob. *Bush at War.* New York: Simon and Schuster, 2002.

Woodward, Bob. *State of Denial.* New York: Simon and Schuster, 2006.

Wyman, David S. *The Abandonment of the Jews: America and the Holocaust 1941–1945.* New York: The New Press, 1998.

Yergin, Daniel. *Shattered Peace: The Origins of the Cold War and the National Security State.* Boston: Houghton-Mifflin, 1978.

Zeiler, Thomas W. *Globalization and the American Century.* New York: Cambridge University Press, 2003.

Zinn, Howard. *Declarations of Independence: Cross-examining American Ideology.* New York: HarperCollins, 1990.

Zumwalt, Admiral Elmo. *On Watch: A Memoir.* New York: New York Times Book Company, 1976.

Articles

Alterman, Eric. "Can We Talk?" *The Nation* (April 21, 2003).

Alves, Dora. "Not Wandering Off into an International No-Man's Land." *Conflict* 9 (1989).

Ambrosius, Lloyd E. "Wilsonian Self-Determination." *Diplomatic History* 16 (Winter 1992).

Ambrosius, Lloyd E. "Woodrow Wilson and George W. Bush: Historican Comparisons of Ends and Means in Their Foreign Policies." *Diplomatic History* 30 (June 2006).

Angell, Roger. "The Talk of the Town." *The New Yorker* (January 19, 2004).

Ash, Marc. "At War." *truthout/Perspective* (July 2, 2004).

Ash, Timothy Garton. "Cry, the Dismembered Country." *New York Review of Books* (January 14, 1999).

Bannister, Judith. "Five Decades of Missing Females in China." *Proceedings of the American Philosophical Society* 140 (1996).

Barnet, Richard J. "Still Putting Arms First: The Cold War Legacy Confronting Clinton, Abroad and at Home." *Harper's Magazine* (February 1993).

Bass, Gary J. "Are Democracies Really More Peaceful?" *New York Times Magazine* (January 1, 2006).

Beinart, Peter. "Sovereign Powers." *The New Republic* (March 31, 2003).

Beinart, Peter. "The Rehabilitation of the Cold-War Liberal." *The New York Times Magazine* (April 30, 2006).

Bell, Madison Smartt. "Mine of Stones: With and without the Spirits along the Cordon de l'Ouest." *Harper's Magazine* (January 2004).

Bernstein, Barton J. "Ideology and the Cold War." *Studies on the Left* 3, no. 1 (1962).

Bernstein, Barton J. "Progressive Republican Senators and American Imperialism, 1898–1916: A Reappraisal." *Mid-America* 50 (July 1968).

Bernstein, Barton J. "A Postwar Myth: 500,000 Lives Saved." *Bulletin of the Atomic Scientists* 42 (June/July 1986).

Bernstein, Barton J. "Seizing the Contested Terrain of Early Nuclear History: Stimson, Conant, and Their Allies Explain the Decision to Use the Atomic Bomb." *Diplomatic History* 17 (Winter 1993).

Bernstein, Barton J. "Understanding the Atomic Bomb and the Japanese Surrender: Missed Opportunities, Little-Known Near Disasters, and Modern Memory." *Diplomatic History* 19 (Spring 1995).

Bernstein, Barton J. "Marshall, Leahy, and Casualty Issues – A Reply to Kort's Flawed Critique." *Passport: The Newsletter of the Society for Historians of American Foreign Policy* 35 (August 2004).

Bieber, Florian. "Nationalist Mobilization and Stories of Serb Suffering." *Rethinking History* 6 (Spring 2002).

Biskupski, M. B. "The Diplomacy of Wartime Relief: The United States and Poland, 1914–1918." *Diplomatic History* 19 (Summer 1995).

Block, Jennifer. "Christian Soldiers on the March: Bush's Handpicked Delegates Disrupt Global Conferences on Women's Rights." *The Nation* (February 3, 2003).

Blumenthal, Sidney. "Bush's Dirty War." *The Progressive Populist* (September 1, 2005).

Borstelmann, Thomas. "Jim Crow's Coming Out: Race Relations and American Foreign Policy in the Truman Years." *Presidential Studies Quarterly* 29 (September 1999).

Boyer, Paul. "Exotic Resonances: Hiroshima in American Memory." *Diplomatic History* 19 (Spring 1995).

Boyer, Paul. "John Darby Meets Saddam Hussein: Foreign Policy and Bible Prophecy." *The Chronicle of Higher Education* (February 14, 2003).

Brinkley, Alan. "For America, It Truly Was a Great War." *New York Times Magazine* (May 7, 1995).

Brinkley, Douglas. "Democratic Enlargement: The Clinton Doctrine." *Foreign Policy* 106 (Spring 1997).

Brookhiser, Richard. "The Mind of George W. Bush." *The Atlantic Monthly* (April 2003).

Brzezinski interview. *Le Novel Observateur* (January 15–21, 1998).

Burk, Robert F. "Eisenhower Revisionism Revisited: Reflections on the Eisenhower Scholarship." *Historian* 50 (February 1988).

Cahn, Anne Hessing. "Team B: The Trillion-Dollar Experiment." *Bulletin of the Atomic Scientists* 49 (April 1993).

Cantril, Hadley. "Opinion Trends in World War II: Some Guides to Interpretation." *Public Opinion Quarterly* 12 (1948).

Cassel, Douglas. "A Framework of Norms: International Human-Rights Law and Sovereignty." *Harvard International Review* 22, no. 4 (Winter 2001).

Castañeda, Jorge G. "Latin America's Left Turn." *Foreign Affairs* (May/June 2006).

Charlesworth, Hilary, Chinkin, Christine, and Wright, Shelley. "Feminist Approaches to International Law." *American Journal of International Law* 85 (October 1991).

Chomsky, Noam. "The Fire THIS Time." *Ramparts* 5 (September 1967).

Chomsky, Noam. "Humanitarian Intervention." *Boston Review* (December 1993–January 1994).

Clinton, William Jefferson. "Confronting the Challenges of a Broader World." U.S. Department of State, Bureau of Public Affairs. *Dispatch* 4 (September 1993).

Cohn, Marjorie. "The Torturer-in-Chief." *truthout/Perspective* (June 18, 2004).

Comment. "Bush's Messiah Complex." *The Progressive* (February 2003).

Dadrian, Vahakn N. "Genocide as a Problem of National and International Law: The World War I Armenian Case and Its Contemporary Legal Ramifications." *The Yale Journal of International Law* 14 (Summer 1989).

Danielson, Leilah. "Christianity, Dissent, and the Cold War: Reinhold Niebuhr and A. J. Muste." Paper delivered at the Society for Historians of American Foreign Relations 2004 conference.

Danner, Mark. "The Secret Way to War." *New York Review of Books* (June 9, 2005).

Defeis, Elizabeth F. "Minority Protections and Bilateral Agreements: An Effective Mechanism." *Hastings International and Comparative Law Review* 22 (Winter 1999).

Deng, Francis M., and Morrison, J. Stephen. "U.S. Policy to End Sudan's War: Report of the Center for Strategic and International Studies (CSIS) Task Force on U.S.-Sudan Policy" (February 2001).

Dickey, Christopher. "Death-Squad Democracy." *Newsweek* (January 11, 2005).

Didion, Joan. "Fixed Opinions, or The Hinge of History." *New York Review of Books* (January 16, 2003).

Doran, Michael Scott. "The Saudi Paradox." *Foreign Affairs* 83 (January/February 2004).

Dougherty, Sara. "The Munich Analogy and the Persian Gulf War." Paper delivered at the Historians against the War conference, Austin, Texas (February 18, 2006).

Dowd, Ann Reilly. "What Makes Condi Run." *AARP* (September/October 2005).

Dowden, Mark. "The Desert One Debacle." *The Atlantic Monthly* (May 2006).

Durkin, Anita. "Metaphorical War Mongering, or, The Tales of Two Bushes." Paper presented at the Historians against the War conference, Austin, Texas (February 18, 2006).

Eckes, Alfred E. "Cowboy Capitalism: Lessons from the Asian Meltdown." *Chronicles* (July 1998).

Emmott, Bill. "Present at the Creation: A Survey of America's World Role." *The Economist* (June 29, 2002).

Etzioni, Amitai. "The Evils of Self-Determination." *Foreign Policy* 89 (Winter 1992–93).

Eviatar, Daphne. "Africa's Oil Tycoons." *The Nation* (April 12, 2004).

Falk, Richard. "The New Bush Doctrine." *The Nation* (July 15, 2002).

Falk, Richard. "State Terror versus Humanitarian Law." In Seldon, Mark, and So, Alvin Y., eds., *War and State Terrorism: The United States, Japan, and the Asia-Pacific in the Long Twentieth Century*. Lanham, Maryland: Roman and Littlefield, 2004.

Fallows, James. "Countdown to a Meltdown." *The Atlantic Monthly* (July/August 2005).

Farber, Henry S., and Gowa, Joanne . "Politics and Peace." *International Security* 20 (1995).

Feldman, Noah. "Who Can Check the President?" *New York Times Magazine* (January 8, 2006).

Ferguson, Niall. "2011." *The New York Times Magazine* (December 2, 2001).

Ferguson, Niall. "The Next War of the World." *Foreign Affairs* 85 (September/October 2006).

Fink, Carole. "The League of Nations and the Minority Question." *World Affairs* 157 (Spring 1995).

Fishman, Ted C. "Making a Killing: The Myth of Capital's Good Intentions." *Harper's Magazine* (August 2002).

Fitzsimmons, David M. "Tom Paine's New World Order." *Diplomatic History* 19 (Fall 1995).

Flanders, Laura. "Warnacular: Post-Blast, Familiar Terms Take on New Meanings." *The Progressive Populist* (October 15, 2001).

"Ford Press Conference: December 23, 1975." *Department of State Bulletin* 74 (January 19, 1976).

"Forum: The Iceberg Cometh: Can a Nation of Spenders Be Saved?" *Harper's Magazine* (June 2005).

Foster, John Bellamy. "Imperial America and War." *Monthly Review* (May 27, 2003).

Fox, Robin. "Human Nature and Human Rights." *Harper's Magazine* (April 2001).

Frankel, Max. "The War and the Law." *New York Times Magazine* (May 7, 1995).

Friedman, Benjamin. "Meltdown: A Case Study." *The Atlantic Monthly* (July/August 2005).

Fukuyama, Francis. "The End of History." *National Interest* 16 (Summer 1989).

Gaddis, John Lewis. "The Cold War, the Long Peace, and the Future." *Diplomatic History* 16 (Spring 1992).

Gati, Charles. "From Sarajevo to Sarajevo." *Foreign Affairs* 71 (Fall 1992).

Green, Philip. "'Anti-Semitism,' Israel and the Left." *The Nation* (May 5, 2003).

Grob-Fitzgiboon, Benjamin. "What Is Terrorism? Redefining a Phenomenon in Time of War." *Peace and Change* 30 (April 2005).

Hersh, Seymour M. "The Iraq Hawks." *The New Yorker* (December 24 and 31, 2001).

Hersh, Seymour M. "Moving Targets." *The New Yorker* (December 8, 2003).

Hersh, Seymour M. "The Gray Zone: How a Secret Pentagon Program Came to Abu Gharib." *The New Yorker* (May 24, 2004).

Hersh, Seymour M. "Get Out the Vote: Did Washington Try to Manipulate Iraq's Election?" *The New Yorker* (July 25, 2005).

Hersh, Seymour M. "The Iran Plan: Would President Bush Go to War to Stop Tehran from Getting the Bomb?" *The New Yorker* (April 17, 2006).

Hershberg, James G. "A Footnote on Hiroshima and Atomic Morality: Conant, Niebuhr, and an 'Emotional' Clergyman, 1945–46." *SHAFR Newsletter* 33 (December 2002).

Higham, John. "The Future of American History." *Journal of American History* 80 (March 1994).

Hill, Richard F. "Hitler's Misunderstood Declaration of War." *SHAFR Newsletter* 33 (June 2002).

Hirsh, Michael, and Barry, John . "The Salvador Option." *Newsweek* (January 9, 2005).

Hitchens, Christopher. "The Case against Henry Kissinger, Part One." *Harper's Magazine* (February 2001).

Hoff, Joan. "The American Century: From Sarajevo to Sarajevo." *Diplomatic History* 23 (Spring 1999).

Hoff, Joan. "How the United States Sold Its Soul to Win the Cold War (and Now Cannot Develop a Coherent Post-Cold War Foreign Policy)." *International Journal* (Summer 2001).

Hoff, Joan. "The Nixon Story You Never Heard." *The Progressive Review* (January 2002).

Hoff, Joan. "September 11: Watershed in U.S. Foreign Policy?" *Irish Studies in International Affairs* 13 (2002).

Hoff, Joan. "All Presidents Lie about Going to War." *Progressive Review* (June 2003).

Hoffman, Stanley. "America Goes Backward." *The New York Review* (June 12, 2003).

Hogan, Michael J. "American Marshall Planners and the Search for a European Neo-capitalism." *American Historical Review* 90 (February 1985).

Home, Sharon K. "Female Infanticide in China: The Human Rights Specter and towards An(other) Vision." *Columbia Human Rights Law Review* 23 (1992).

Hurst, Lynda. "Knocking on the Nuclear Door." *The Nation* (March 31, 2003).

Ignatieff, Michael. "The Politics of Self-Destruction." *New York Review of Books* (November 2, 1995).

Ignatieff, Michael. "When a Bridge Is Not a Bridge." *New York Times Magazine* (October 27, 2002).

Ignatieff, Michael. "The Burden [of] The American Empire (Get Used to It)." *The New York Times Magazine* (January 5, 2003).

Immerman, Richard H. "Confessions of an Eisenhower Revisionist: An Agonizing Reappraisal." *Diplomatic History* 14 (Summer 1990).

Immerman, Richard H. "The United States and the Geneva Conference of 1954." *Diplomatic History* 14 (Winter 1990).

Isikoff, Michael. "Double Standards?" *Newsweek* (May 21, 2004).

Isikoff, Michael. "2001 Memo Reveals Push for Broader Presidential Powers." *Newsweek* (December 18, 2004).

Jablon, Howard. "Cordell Hull, His 'Associates,' and Relations with Japan, 1933–1936." *Mid-America* 56 (July 1974).

Jervis, Robert. "Mutual Assured Destruction." *Foreign Policy* 133 (November/December 2002).

Joynt, Jen, and Poe, Marshall. "The Unfree World." *The Atlantic Monthly* (March 2004).

Judah, Tim. "Impasse in Kosovo." *The New York Review of Books* (June 10, 2004).

Judis, John B. "Beyond National Interest." *The New Republic* (June 21, 1999 [online edition]).

Judt, Tony. "On the Brink" (review of books on the Cuban missile crisis). *New York Review of Books* (January 15, 1998).

Kammen, Michael. "The Problem of American Exceptionalism: A Reconsideration." *American Quarterly* 45 (March 1993).

Kaplan, Lawrence F. "Regime Change." *The New Republic* (March 3, 2003).

Kaplan, Robert. "Was Democracy Just a Moment?" *The Atlantic Monthly* (December 1997).

Kaplan, Robert. "Supremacy by Stealth: Ten Rules for Managing the World." *The Atlantic Monthly* (July/August 2003).

Kernek, Sterling J. "Woodrow Wilson and National Self-Determination along Italy's Frontier: A Study of the Manipulation of Principles in the Pursuit of Political Interests." *Proceedings of the American Philosophical Society* 126 (August 1982).

Kidder, Tracy. "The Trials of Haiti." *The Nation* (October 27, 2003).

Kimball, Jeffrey. "The Influence of Ideology on Interpretive Disagreement: A Report on a Survey of Diplomatic, Military and Peace Historians on the Causes of 20th Century U.S. Wars." *The History Teacher* 17 (May 1984).

Kindleberger, Charles P. "Dominance and Leadership in the International Economy: Exploitation, Public Goods, and Free Rides." *International Studies Quarterly* 25 (1981).

Kindleberger, Charles P. "Hierarchy versus Inertial Cooperation." *International Studies Quarterly* 40 (1986).

Kirkpatrick, Jeane. "Dictatorships and Double Standards." *Commentary* 65 (November 1979).

Klare, Michael T. "Oil Moves the War Machine." *The Progressive* (June 2002).

Klare, Michael T. "Imperial Reach: The Pentagon's New Basing Strategy." *The Nation* (April 25, 2005).

Klein, Joe. "The Blinding Glare of His Certainty." *Time Magazine* (February 24, 2003).

Klein, Naomi. "Signs of the Times." *The Nation* (October 22, 2001).

Klug, Brian. "The Myth of the New Anti-Semitism." *The Nation* (February 2, 2004).

Kornbluh, Peter. "Letter from Chile." *The Nation* (January 31, 2005).

Kort, Michael. "Casualty Projections for the Invasion of Japan, Phantom Estimates, and the Math of Baron Berstein." *Passport: The Newsletter of the Society for Historians of American Foreign Policy* 27 (December 2003).

Kramer, Mark. "The Collapse of East European Communism and the Repercussions within the Soviet Union." *Journal of Cold War Studies* (three parts) 5 (Fall 2003).

Krasner, Stephen D. "The Tokyo Round: Particularist Interests and Prospects for Stability in the Global Trading System." *International Studies Quarterly* 23 (December 1979).

Kristol, William, and Kagan, Robert. "Toward a Neo-Reaganite Foreign Policy." *Foreign Affairs* (July/August 1996).

Krugman, Paul. "The Death of Horatio Alger." *The Nation* (January 5, 2004).

Lapham, Lewis H. "Drums along the Potomac: New War, Old Music." *Harper's Magazine* (November 2001).

Lapham, Lewis H. "Notebook: Mythography." *Harper's Magazine* (February 2002).

Lapham, Lewis H. "Notebook: 'Light in the Window'." *Harper's Magazine* (March 2003).

Layne, Christopher. "Why the Gulf War Was Not in the National Interest." *Atlantic Monthly* (July 1991).

Leffler, Melvyn P. "The American Conception of National Security and the Beginnings of the Cold War." *American Historical Review* 89 (1984).

Leffler, Melvyn P. "9/11 and American Foreign Policy." *Diplomatic History* 29 (June 2005).

Lemann, Nicholas. "The Next World Order." *The New Yorker* (April 1, 2002).

Lifton, Robert Jay. "American Apocalypse." *The Nation* (December 22, 2003).

Link, Arthur. "The Case for Woodrow Wilson." *Harper's Magazine* (April 1967).

Lobe, Jim. "Hawks Flying High with Posting of Condoleezza Rice to State Department." *Washington Report of ME Affairs* 24 (January/February 2005).

Logevall, Fredrik. "A Critique of Containment." *Diplomatic History* 28 (September 2004).

Lundestad, Geir. "Empire by Invitation? The United States and Western Europe, 1945–52." *SHAFR Newsletter* 15 (September 1954).

Lustgarten, Audrey, and Debrix, François. "The Role of the Media in Monitoring International Law during Military Interventions: The Case of Kosovo." *Peace and Change* 30 (July 2005).

Luttwaak, Edward. "If Bosnians Were Dolphins." *Commentary* (October 1993).

Mahajan, Rahul, and Jensen, Robert. "American's Unlimited War." *The Progressive Populist* (October 15, 2001).

Maier, Charles S. "The Politics of Productivity: Foundations of American International Economic Policy after World War II." *International Organization* 31 (Autumn 1977).

Maier, Charles. "Consigning the Twentieth Century to History: Alternative Narratives for the Modern Era." *American Historical Review* 104 (June 2000).

Mattras, John, and Lightman, Marjorie. "Clinton's Second Term: Making Women's Rights a Foreign Policy Issue." *Presidential Studies Quarterly* 27 (Winter 1997).

Matusow, Allen J. "Richard Nixon and the Failed War against the Trading World." *Diplomatic History* 27 (November 2003).

Mauch, Peter. "Revisiting Nomura's Role in the Japanese-American Negotiations, 1941." *Diplomatic History* 28 (June 2004).

Mayer, Jane. "Outsourcing Torture." *The New Yorker* (February 14, 2005).

Mayer, Jane. "Annals of the Pentagon: The Memo: How an Internal Effort to Ban the Abuse and Torture of Detainees Was Thwarted." *The New Yorker* (February 27, 2006).

McDougall, Walter A. "How – and How Not – to End Wars." *Foreign Policy Research WIRE* 8 (October 2000).

McMahon, Robert. "Eisenhower and Third World Nationalism: A Critique of the Revisionists." *Political Science Quarterly* 101 (Fall 1986).

McNeill, William H. "The Care and Repair of Public Myth." *Foreign Affairs* (Fall 1982).

Medoff, Rafael. "Why the Allies Refused to Bomb Auschwitz: A Reply to William J. vanden Heuvel." *Passport: The Newsletter of the Society for Historians of American Foreign Relations* 34 (August 2003).

Minear, Richard H. "Atomic Holocaust, Nazi Holocaust." *Diplomatic History* 19 (Spring 1995).

Mitchell, Brian. "NATO at 50: Birthday or Funeral? *Business Daily* 16, no. 11 (April 26, 1999).

Mooney, Chris. "The Editorial Pages and the Case for War." *Columbia Journalism Review* (March/April 2004).

Morris, Roger. "The Proxy War in Angola: Pathology of a Blunder." *The New Republic* (January 31, 1976).

Moyers, Bill. "Welcome to Doomsday." *New York Review of Books* (March 24, 2005).

Mueller, John. "Quiet Cataclysm: Some Afterthoughts about World War III." *Diplomatic History* 16 (1992).

Muste, A. J. "The H-Bomb as Deterrent." *Christianity and Crisis* (June 14, 1954).

Nairn, Allan. "C.I.A. Death Squads." *The Nation* (April 17, 1985).

Nairn, Allan. "Reagan Administration's Links to Guatemala's Terrorist Government." *Covert Action Quarterly* (Summer 1989).

Nichols, John. "Where Are the Doves in Congress?" *The Progressive* (October 1999).

O'Costa, Anthony P. "The Global Restructuring of the Steel Industry." *Routledge Studies in International Business and World Economics* 13 (1999).

Odom, William E. "Intervention for the Long Run: Rethinking the Definition of War." *Harvard International Review* 22 (Winter 2001).

Offner, Arnold A. "Rogue President, Rogue Nation: Bush and U.S. National Security." *Diplomatic History* 29 (June 2005).

O'Leary, Wayne. "Flawed Foreign Policy and Its Consequences." *The Progressive Populist* (October 15, 2001).

O'Rourke, P. J. "The Art of Policy." *The Atlantic Monthly* (January/February 2005).

Ostermann, Christian. "New Evidence on the 1979–1989 War in Afghanistan." *SHAFR Newsletter* 33 (September 2002).

"Our Reasons." Editorial. *The New Republic* (November 5, 2001).

Packer, George. "Dreaming of Democracy." *The New York Times Magazine* (March 2, 2003).

Palast, Greg. "OPEC on the March: Why Iraq Still Sells Its Oil a la Cartel." *Harper's Magazine* (April 2005).

Peace, Roger. "An Ideological Crusade: The Reagan Administration's War against Nicaragua." Paper delivered at the Historians against the War conference, Austin, Texas (February 18, 2006).

Pei, Minxin, and Kasper, Sara. "The Inevitable 'Morning After' of Regime Change." *The Christian Science Monitor* (January 15, 2003).

Pero, Mario Del. "The United States and 'Psychological Warfare' in Italy, 1948–55." *Journal of American History* 87 (March 2001).

Peterson, Peter G. "Riding for a Fall." *Foreign Affairs* (September/October 2004).

Pfaff, William. "The Question of Hegemony." *Foreign Affairs* 80 (January/February 2001).

Power, Samantha. "Bystanders to Genocide: Why the United States Let the Rwandan Tragedy Happen." *The Atlantic Monthly* (September 2001).

Prados, John. "Blindsided or Blind." *Bulletin of the Atomic Scientists* 60 (July/August 2004).

Rabe, Stephen G. "The Caribbean Triangle: Betancourt, Castro, and Trujillo and US Foreign Policy." *Diplomatic History* 20 (Winter 1996).

Raskin, Marcus. "Bennett's Pledge of Allegiance." *The Nation* (August 5/12, 2002).

Raunch, Jonathan. "Firebombs over Tokyo." *The Atlantic Monthly* (July/August 2002).

Raunch, Jonathan. "The New Nixon." *The Atlantic Monthly* (July/August 2005).

Reed, Julia. "The President's Prodigy." *Vogue* (October 2001).

Reinicke, Wolfgang H. "Global Public Policy." *Foreign Affairs* 76 (November/December 1997).

Research Unit for Political Economy. "Why the United States Promotes India's Great-Power Ambitions." *Aspects of India's Economy* 4 (December 2005).

Reynolds, David. "Beyond Bipolarity in Space and Time." *Diplomatic History* 16 (Spring 1992).

Richman, Sheldon L. "'Ancient History': U.S. Conduct in the Middle East since World War II and the Folly of Intervention." Cato Policy Analysis, no. 159 (August 16, 1991).

Rieff, David. "Goodbye, New World Order." *Mother Jones* (July/August 2003).

Rogin, Michael P. "When the CIA Was the NEA." *The Nation* (June 12, 2000).

Rosenbaum, Ron. "Degrees of Evil." *The Atlantic Monthly* (February 2002).

Rothschild, Matthew. "Empire's Apologists" and "Revealing Rhetoric." *The Progressive* (March 2003).

Rustow, Dankwart A. "Democracy: A Global Revolution?" *Foreign Affairs* 69 (Fall 1990).

Samson, Victoria. "Congress Rattles Nuclear Saber." *The Progressive Populist* (December 15, 2003).

Samuelson, Robert F. "The Spirit of Capitalism." *Foreign Affairs* 88 (January/February 2001).

Sanders, Alain L. "Broaching the Subject Diplomatically." *Time Magazine* (March 24, 1997).

Saramago, José. "¿Qué es exactamente la democracia?" *Le Monde diplomatique* 44 (August 2004).

Schacter, Oscar. "The Decline of the Nation-State and Its Implications for International Law." *Columbia Journal of Transitional Law* 36 (1997).

Schell, Jonathan. "No More into the Breach." *Harper's Magazine* (March 2003).

Schell, Jonathan. "The New American Order." *The Nation* (July 7, 2003).

Schlesinger, Arthur, Jr. "The Necessary Amorality of Foreign Affairs." *Harper's Magazine* (August 1971).

Schlesinger, Arthur, Jr. "Eyeless in Iraq." *The New York Review of Books* (October 23, 2003).

Schmitz, David F., and Walker, Vanessa. "Jimmy Carter and Foreign Policy of Human Rights: The Development of a Post-Cold War Foreign Policy." *Diplomatic History* 28 (January 2003).

Schwarz, Benjamin. "Comment: Will Israel Live to 100?" *The Atlantic Monthly* (May 2005).

Schwarz, Benjamin, and Layne, Christopher. "A New Grand Strategy." *The Atlantic Monthly* (January 2002).

Sen, Amartya. "More than 100 Million Women Are Missing." *New York Review of Books* (December 20, 1990).

Sen, Amartya. "The Many Faces of Gender Inequality." *The New Republic* (September 17, 2001).

Sharlet, Jeffrey. "Jesus plus Nothing: Undercover among America's Secret Theocrats." *Harper's Magazine* (March 2003).

Siegle, Joseph T., et al. "Why Democracies Excel." *Foreign Affairs* 83 (2004).

Sletzinger, Martin C., and Gelazis, Nida. "Kosovo: Mission Not Yet Accomplished." *The Wilson Quarterly* (Autumn 2005).

Spalding, Elizabeth Edwards. "True Believers." *The Wilson Quarterly* (Spring 2006).

Spiro, Peter J. "The New Sovereigns: American Exceptionalism and Its False Prophets." *Foreign Affairs* 79 (November/December 2000).

Stam, Juan. "Bush's Religious Language." *The Nation* (December 22, 2003).

"Statement on Enola Gay Exhibit." *Radical Historian Newsletter* 88 (December 2003).

Steel, Ronald. "The Missionary" and "Mr. Fix-It." *New York Review of Books* (October 5, 2000).

Stimson, Henry L. "The Decision to Use the Atomic Bomb." *Harper's Magazine* (February 1947).

Sullivan, Andrew. "This Is a Religious War." *New York Times Magazine* (October 7, 2001).

Summers, John. "What Happened to Sex Scandals: Politics and Peccadilloes, Jefferson to Kennedy." *Journal of American History* 87 (December 2000).

Surowiecki, James. "Morale's Mistake." *The New Yorker* (January 23/30, 2006).

Suskind, Ron. "Without a Doubt." *The New York Times Magazine* (October 17, 2004).

Talbot, Strobe. "America Abroad: Woodrow Wilson in the Gulf." *Time Magazine* (January 21, 1991).

Tamamoto, Masuru. "Reflections on Japan's Postwar State." *Daedalus* 124 (Spring 1995).

Testimony of Ralph Johnson, Deputy Assistant Secretary of State for European and Canadian Affairs, October 17, 1991. *Foreign Policy Bulletin* 2 (November/December 1991).

"The Torture Administration." Articles appearing in *The Nation* (December 26, 2005).

Tucker, Robert W., and Hendrickson, David C. "The Sources of American Legitimacy." *Foreign Affairs* (November/December 2004).

Türk, Danilo. "Minority Protection in Human Rights Conventions." In *La Comunitá Internazionale*, vol. 4, "Tipologia e Protezione delle Minoranze in Europa." Trieste, November 3–4, 1990.

Türk, Danilo. "Protection of Minorities in Europe." In *Collected Course of the Academy of European Law*, vol. 3, book 2. The Netherlands: Kluwer, 1994.

Tyrell, Ian. "American Exceptionalism in an Age of International History." *American Historical Review* 96 (October 1991).

Ulbrich, David J. "Research Note: 'A Program for Covert Action against the Castro Regime, 16 March 1960'." *SHAFR Newsletter* 33 (September 2002).

Unger, Craig. "From the Wonderful Folks Who Brought You Iraq." *Vanity Fair* (March 2007).

Unterberger, Betty. "The United States and National Self-Determination: A Wilsonian Perspective." *Presidential Studies Quarterly* 26 (Fall 1996).

Valone, Steven J. "Seward and the Reassertion of the Monroe Doctrine." *Diplomatic History* 19 (Fall 1995).

Vidal, Gore. "The Menopause of Empire." *The Progressive* (May 1998).

Walker, J. Samuel. "History, Collective Memory, and the Decision to Use the Bomb." *Diplomatic History* 19 (Spring 1995).

Walker, J. Samuel. "Recent Literature on Truman's Atomic Bomb Decision: A Search for Middle Ground." *Diplomatic History* 29 (April 2005).

Walker, William O. III. "Crucible for Peace: Herbert Hoover, Modernization, and Economic Growth in Latin America." *Diplomatic History* 30, no. 1 (January 2006).

"War of Intervention: Why and When to Go In." *The Economist* (January 6, 2001).

Weisenberger, Francis P. "Middle Western Antecedents of Woodrow Wilson." *Mississippi Valley Historical Review* 23 (December 1936).

Weissman, Steve. "Torture from J.F.K. to Baby Bush." *truthout/Perspective* (December 31, 2004).

Wells, Samuel F., Jr. "Sounding the Tocsin: NSC 68 and the Soviet Threat." *International Security* 4 (Spring 1980).

Whelan, James R. "Jeane Kirkpatrick: Ideals Come First." *The Saturday Evening Post* (December 1984).

White House–issued Policy Paper. "National Security Strategy of the United States" (March 1990).

Whitelaw, Kevin. "An Eye Blind to Murder." *U.S. News and World Report* (April 12, 2004).

Wills, Gary. "With God on His Side." *New York Review of Books*. (March 30, 2003).

Wills, Gary, "A Country Ruled by Faith." *New York Review of Books* (November 16, 2006).

Wohlstetter, Roberta. "Cuba and Pearl Harbor: Hindsight and Foresight." *Foreign Affairs* 43 (July 1965).

Wypijewski, JoAnn. "Whose Steel?" *The Nation* (July 15, 2002).

Yergin, Daniel. "Harry Truman – Revived and Revised." *New York Times Magazine* (October 24, 1976).

Zakaria, Fareed. "The Rise of Illiberal Democracy." *Foreign Affairs* 76 (November/December 1997).

Zakaria, Fareed. "Elections Are Not Democracy." *Newsweek* (February 7, 2005).

Zimmerman, Warren. "The Choice in the Balkans." *New York Review of Books* (September 21, 1995).

Index